Yesterday's News
The British Cinema Newsreel Reader

Edited by Luke McKernan

Research by Jeff Hulbert and Johan Oomen

es Film & Video Council

British Universities Film & Video Council
77 Wells Street, London W1T 3QJ
Tel: 020 7393 1500 Fax: 020 7393 1555
E-mail: ask@bufvc.ac.uk   www.bufvc.ac.uk

ISBN 0 901 299 73 1

The opinions expressed in this book are those of the individual authors and do not necessarily represent views or policy of the British Universities Film & Video Council.

A catalogue record for this book is available from the British Library.

Cover pictures
Front: *British Movietone News* cameraman Norman Fisher (left) and sound recordist Martin Gray in France, January 1940. (BUFVC)
Back: Norman Fisher filming Welsh Guards in France, Christmas 1939. (BUFVC)

Typesetting and layout by Gem Graphics, Trenance, Nr. Newquay, Cornwall TR8 4BY.
Printed in Great Britain by Print Solutions Partnership, 88 Sandy Lane South, South Wallington, Surrey SM6 9RQ

Contents

CONTENTS

Foreword

The British Universities Film & Video Council (BUFVC) built much of its early reputation upon the support and interest of a group of young scholars who started the process to reassess the value and importance of British cinema newsreels. These included Paul Smith, Nicholas Pronay, Anthony Aldgate, Arthur Marwick and many other historians who, during the 1960s, started to engage further with newsfilm as a source for study in social and political history. Thorold Dickinson, Head of the Slade Film School, started the work to collate information on newsreels which the BUFVC would later would use to provide support for scholars.

The BUFVC continues to build its work 'on giant's shoulders'. During the last four decades, we have been privileged to employ talented individuals who have helped to build the essential newsfilm research tools for others to use. Elizabeth Oliver, James Ballantyne, Nicholas Hiley, Sara White, Martyn Glanville, Ruth Sanders, and, currently, Luke McKernan, Linda Kaye, Sarah Easen, Luís Carrasqueiro and Jeff Hulbert are key players.

During the last few years the expression of their achievements has been astonishing. The British Universities Newsreel Database, with its 160,000 records, was released online in March 2000. Now 80,000 script documents and items of ephemera are being filed alongside data for completion in 2003 plus a biographical database and structured oral history recordings and transcripts.

This is an integrated long-term investment that builds an accessible resource for students, researchers and their tutors to explore. Now we expect to see significant quantities of newsfilm released online for study — the next decade is likely to bring even more significant developments than the last four.

This book radically brings together contemporaneous and recent writing on newsreels in a chronological setting. It is a form of scholarly glue which neatly packages essays and articles from diverse sources. Built firmly on the past work of the BUFVC, the construction of the Reader has entirely been the inspiration of Luke McKernan. We are indebted to him for his skill, tenacity and hard work in bringing the work to print. It further extends the platform of context for students in the future — I commend it to you.

Murray Weston
Director
British Universities Film & Video Council
August 2002

Acknowledgements

Grateful acknowledgment must first go to James Ballantyne, former Head of Information at the British Universities Film & Video Council (BUFVC), who researched and collated documents on British newsreels, which he abstracted in the BUFVC's three-volume series, *Researcher's Guide to British Newsreels* (1983, 1988, 1993). His researches formed the basis of this Reader, and his further advice has been gratefully received.

Particular thanks are due to Jeff Hulbert and Johan Oomen, who researched and prepared many of the documents reproduced here, and whose collaborative assistance has been invaluable. Thanks also to colleagues at the BUFVC, Sergio Angelini, Luís Carrasqueiro, Sarah Easen, Linda Kaye, Virginia Ryan, Murray Weston, and especially to BUFVC Publications and Communications Officer Hetty Malcolm-Smith for all that she has done to guide this work into publication. Thanks go out also to all those who assisted in bringing this work together, particularly Jenny Hammerton of British Pathe, Nicholas Hiley, David Sharp of the British Film Institute, and Dorothy Sheridan of the Mass-Observation Archive, University of Sussex.

This Reader comprises texts from the present and the past, and thanks go to those authors who gave permission for works to be reproduced here: Anthony Aldgate, Hannah Caven, Penelope Houston, Philip Norman, Nicholas Pronay; and to those who contributed new essays: Sarah Easen, Jenny Hammerton, Jeff Hulbert and James Taylor.

We acknowledge permission to reproduce the articles in this Reader from the following authors and publishers (original publication details are given after each article in the Reader):

Philip Norman, for Philip Norman, 'The Newsreel Boys'.

Screen International, for Lester Ruah, 'A Criticism of the News-film', Alec Baird *et al*, 'The News-Film: A Symposium', and Arthur Pereira, '"Chez Pathé": The Story of a "Gazette" in the Making'.

Orion Publishing Group, for 'Running the Topical Films'.

The Historical Journal of Film, Radio and Television, Carfax Publishing, Taylor & Francis Group, for Luke McKernan, '"The Supreme Moment of the War": General Allenby's Entry into Jerusalem', and the extract from Hannah Caven, 'Horror in Our Time: Images of the concentration camps in the British media, 1945'.

The Broadcasting Entertainment Cinematograph & Theatre Union for J. Neill-Brown, 'The Industry's Front Page News', Charles Martin, 'Newsreeler at Dunkirk', and Jock C. Gemmell *et al*, 'D-Day as the Newsreel Boys Saw It'.

David Higham Associates and The Spectator (1828) Ltd, for Graham Greene, 'The Cinema. News reels. At various cinemas'.

Independent Labour Productions, Keir Hardie House, 49 Top Moor Side, Leeds LS11 9LW, for Benn, 'Why not a Socialist Newsreel?'

Anthony Lejeune, for C.A. Lejeune, 'The News-Theatre'.

Michael R.B. Williams, for Robert Herring, 'The News-reel'.

The Historical Association, Dr Anthony Aldgate and Professor Nicholas Pronay, for Anthony Aldgate, 'Newsreel Scripts: A Case-Study', Nicholas Pronay, 'British Newsreels in the 1930s: 1. Audience and Producers', and Nicholas Pronay, 'British Newsreels in the 1930s: 2. Their Policies and Impact'.

Peters Fraser & Dunlop, for Cecil Day-Lewis, 'Newsreel'.

British Movietonews and Jim Sanger, for Gerald Sanger, 'We Lived in the Presence of History: The Story of British Movietone News'.

The Mass-Observation Archive, University of Sussex, and Curtis Brown Group Ltd on behalf of the Estate of Dame Laura Knight © Dame Laura Knight, for Mass-Observation File Reports 16, 22 and 314.

The Spectator (1828) Ltd, for Edgar Anstey, 'The Newsreels'.

Alan Martin, for Charles Martin, 'Newsreeler at Dunkirk'.

Tom Priestley, for J.B. Priestley, 'If I Owned Newsreels – What a Row There Would Be!'

BBC Worldwide for P.H. Dorté, 'The B.B.C. Television Newsreel'.

Mavis Noble for the extract from Ronnie Noble, *Shoot First! Assignments of a Newsreel Cameraman*.

Tribune Publications Ltd, for 'Beware of the Newsreels'.

The Financial Times, for G.T. Cummins, 'Cinema Newsreel and the Impact of Television'.

Sight and Sound and Penelope Houston, for Penelope Houston, 'The Nature of the Evidence'.

Every effort has been made to trace copyright owners, but for some of the older articles in this Reader we have not been successful. The BUFVC apologises to any copyright owners whose work is reproduced here without permission, and undertakes to rectify any such omissions in future editions.

INTRODUCTION
British Newsreels: Past and Present

Luke McKernan

This is a collection of articles on British newsreels, written both from the time when they were being shown in cinemas, and from more recent times when they have become the subject of academic study.

The texts have been selected from a wide range of sources: film trade-papers, memoirs, parliamentary debates, newspaper articles, publicity brochures, film reviews and academic essays. Together they serve as a history of the British newsreels, how they were produced and how they were received. The process of newsreel production was not simply a case of editorial decisions and cameramen's experiences, but of the influences and pressures caused by exhibitors, critics, government, censorship, finance, peer rivalries, and the need to keep people entertained in the cinemas.

The texts have been arranged chronologically by event; hence an account by cameraman Richard Butler of his recent experiences filming the Spanish Civil War in 1938 may be found next door to a scholarly analysis of the newsreel commentary scripts for that war written by Anthony Aldgate in 1976. Not every article deals with a specific event as such, but texts such as Benn's call for a Socialist newsreel in 1929, Arthur Pereira's description of Pathe in the 1920s, or J. Neill-Brown's account of newsreel theatres in 1939, are relevant to a particular point in time. Some of the texts take a more general overview, such as Jeff Hulbert on the Newsreel Association, but essentially the treatment is linear, aiming to give a useful history of the newsreels as well as offering some of the key texts generated by that history. A number of the articles have indeed been established as key texts for the study of newsreels, such as those by Philip Norman, Nicholas Pronay, the Mass-Observation reports on the reception of newsreels by a wartime audience, and the parliamentary debate 'Censorship and the Restriction of Liberty'. Other texts have been selected for their proven value to historians, while some it has been a pleasure to bring out of obscurity in the hope that they will be of future value to newsreel research.

We have enjoyed just over a century of actuality recorded in moving images on film, and just over ninety years of those moments of actuality being gathered together into a coherent package, regularly exhibited before an audience. Following Philip Norman's celebration of the newsreel life, the main Reader opens with a report on the first British newsreel, *Pathe's Animated Gazette*, in 1910; and closes with Penelope Houston's consideration of the value of the newsreels as factual evidence, written as the newsreels themselves were fading away yet finding a new life as the stuff of television historical documentaries. The earliest years of the newsreels saw writers such as F.A. Talbot fascinated with the possibilities of this new cinematic medium, while the anonymous author of 'Running the Topical Films' shows the newsreels encountering their first major hurdle, the government restrictions and censorship brought on by the First World War. As Luke McKernan's essay demonstrates, the government would soon find the newsreels to be a powerful medium for war-time propaganda, delivering memorable, influential images to a mass audience.

This Reader is as much about the newsreels today as yesterday. There are examples, from Aldgate and Pronay, of the critical writing that was generated by the first wave of interest in the newsreels from historians in the 1970s. But new and imaginative research continues today, illustrated by the work of Hulbert, Hannah Caven writing on the news media's responses towards the concentration camps, Jenny Hammerton's defence of the popular cinemagazines, James Taylor's painstaking recreation of the reporting of the R101 airship disaster, and Sarah Easen on the neglected role of women in newsreels. Hopefully the selection of texts will make it clear how very contemporary the newsreels still are, in the issues they raise of news management, censorship, competition, and the conflicts faced by news that has to entertain.

The Reader presents the arguments for and against the newsreels that raged throughout their existence, as the debate generated by Lester Ruah's article from as early as 1914 demonstrates. Their defenders were typically the editors and producers, men like Movietone's Gerald Sanger and Pathe's Clement Cave, though the latter sought to put more politics into his newsreel than cinema exhibitors were prepared to tolerate. Their critics were often the intelligentsia, those such as Cecil Day-Lewis, Graham Greene and Robert Herring, wishing that the newsreels could become more engaged with the news itself, more like the radical American news magazine *The March of Time*, and less in thrall to popular taste. Others found the newsreels to be not just trivial, but insidious, actively pursuing a Right-wing agenda, as Brian Crosthwaite, J.B. Priestley and an anonymous *Tribune* contributor protest. Yet other critics, Edgar Anstey and Caroline Lejeune among them, championed the newsreels for their boldness, creativity, and for that very sense of the popular that caused others to look down their noses. The newsreels were exceptionally acute in their sense of their audience's concerns and awareness of the news. Coming as they did after newspapers and radio had already established certain stories as 'news', the newsreels brought to the cinema audiences a shared under-standing of what was current, of what people really wanted to see.

The people whom everyone admired, and whose lively character and knockabout adventures has always been central to the newsreels' particular appeal, were the cameramen. Countless articles appeared in newspapers and film-trade journals of their brave exploits, such as Charles Martin scooping the world with his Dunkirk film, Jock Gemmell and colleagues recalling their experiences filming D-Day, and Enne Fisher's tall tales of newsreel piracy. Robert Humfrey's career guide promotes the cameramen's life as being ideal for the robust type of youth, and Philip Norman's humorous yet subtly wistful celebration of the lost world of 'the newsreel boys' best sums up this classic image of the newsreels. But behind the jocularity and the drinking there were eyes sensitive to life's hard realities: Cherry Kearton's humane observations of war-torn Belgium, Paul Wyand faced with ultimate inhumantity in Belsen, and Ronnie Noble questioning the ability of his camera to record the truth in Korea.

Noble was filming for the BBC's *Television Newsreel*, a hybrid form of newsreel and television news. The newsreels sensed the growing threat of television news throughout the 1940s and 50s, and despite the bullish claims for the medium by Paramount's Tommy Cummins and the anonymous author of 'The Truth About Newsreels', a news medium that was shown twice a week in cinemas was bound to lose out to a medium which, by the mid-1950s, offered a daily news service. Philip Dorté's account of the rise of *Television Newsreel* is filled with the confidence of one who knows he has chosen the winning side. The newsreels began to close soon afterwards: *Universal News* in 1956, *British Paramount News* in 1957, *Gaumont-British News* in 1959. *Pathe News* carried on until 1970, and *British Movietone News* anachronistically hung on in the cinemas until 1979, into the age of JAWS and STAR WARS, with news on video and electronic news-gathering just around the corner.

The Reader concludes with appendices giving a chronological listing of British newsreels and cinemagazines, details of current newsreel collections, and an account of the BUFVC's British Universities Newsreel Database (BUND). This offers online a huge range of primary and secondary sources, from records of newsreel releases, to digitised production documents, to critical and historical texts. In 2001 the BUFVC published the memoirs of newsreel cameraman John Turner, and with the publication of this Reader it hopes to have made available a further reference tool that not only makes a wide selection of key texts available in one place, but serves as an entertaining and rewarding history of an entertaining and rewarding medium.

NOTE ON THE TEXT

The texts reproduced in this volume have been kept as close to the originals as possible, in layout, titling, punctuation, annotation and citation. Where there are end notes, these are the notes that accompanied the original text, and no further annotations have been added by the editor. Historical errors or unclear references have been therefore left to stand as they are. Each text is put in context by a short editorial paragraph. The bibliographical citation is given at the end of each text.

Some harmonisation of the texts has been undertaken, however. Typographical errors or spelling mistakes have been corrected. Quotations are generally indented. All newsreels or cinemagazines, where their name is given in full, are given in italics (e.g. *British Movietone News*). However, short titles, which sometimes refer to the newsreel and sometimes to the company producing it, are not italicised (e.g. Movietone). All film titles and titles of individual news items are given in capitals (e.g. GENERAL ALLENBY'S ENTRY INTO JERUSALEM). The company Pathe, and the various newsreels and cinemagazines using the Pathe name, do not have an acute accent over the 'e', as this was the practice most commonly followed by the newsreel. References to the original French company and its founder Charles Pathé, however, retain the acute accent.

The Newsreel Boys

Philip Norman

Journalist and biographer Philip Norman, grandson of Pathe newsreel cameraman Frank Bassill, wrote this classic account of the newsreels and the men who filmed them, in 1971, when the newsreels were all but gone from British cinema screens. It celebrates the rough-and-tumble image of the newsreel cameraman, and a way of reporting news that was 'blind and deaf to the real issues of life', but which conveyed a greater sense of excitement than its successor, television. Norman provides a testament to a lost way of life: newsfilm as cinema enter-tainment, and conjures up much of the rumbustious atmosphere that made the newsreels what they were.

There is a British Movietone newsreel item of 1935 in which a Colorado dust storm blinds and evicts a wretched family of sharecroppers from whatever dugout they had managed to make habitable – they are just scarecrows, gale-fluttered, trying to start a Model T truck. The tears that come into your eyes are not only in sympathy with the howling white sand, but to Movietone's commentator it is a matter for jollity. '… *Pop the pig in the wagon and off we go. Oops! Where's Grandma?'* The Depression occurs in a miscellany of Parisian corsages, pole-squatters and unsuccessful South Coast bird-men.

Even in the Thirties the newsreels found all foreigners, excluding their Royal Families, comical; and that included Hitler ('Germany's popular Chancellor') and his soldiers dressed up like hock bottles who were preparing to annexe the whole world. Nazis were novelty items for the end of the reel. What the Empire waited to see – what people went into cinemas from Morpeth to Mandalay for, irrespective of the big picture – was the Grand National. It was in the reporting of what funda-mentally was not news at all, but different kinds of national celebration, that five newsreel companies between the wars achieved a level of head-cracking competition to match the robber barons.

They got locked in the maddest fights over cricket: one newsreel would buy the rights to film a Test exclusively, and all the others would go to acrobatic lengths to 'pinch' the event. Newspapers used to publish photographs not of high moments in the play but of the numbers of light aircraft and autogyros circling above, stealing pictures; with Jack Cotter of Movietone always taking most chances in his Puss Moth GAB SO.

The 1934 rights at the Oval were shared by Movietone and Gaumont-British. This was unusual: Movietone were habitual pinchers but the Gaumont editor Castleton Knight was the most artful of them all at it, surpassing even Tommy Cummins of Paramount News, who was the interloper on this occasion. Paramount began by pinching shots from a tower outside the ground. To this the defending newsreels replied with a large, gas-filled balloon which they flew in front of the intruders' camera. Then Paramount built the tower higher and the balloon was raised and raised. A Paramount man got into the stands and began to snipe at it with a rifle; before innocent blood was spilled, however, another Paramount man succeeded in cutting the cable. The balloon shot up and off and the crowd forgot Bradman and gasped.

It was a world – an Empire – in which there was still freedom to rampage home with the pictures. Movietone ran three-ton REO Speedwagon Junior vans, emblazoned like paladins' shields, that could do 80 mph: in any case, police speed-traps of the Thirties were just one constable with a signalling hankie and another with a stopwatch. After the Derby the newsreels used to hire TT motorcyclists to bring the film-cans from Epsom to Wardour Street for processing, with a bounty of £1 for every minute they could cut off half-an-hour by flying round Trafalgar Square on the pavement.

Altogether it was a beautiful life – uncensored. For its editors and cameramen a particular type were attracted: fun-filled, large-overcoated and bibulous men with loud voices and connections as close to Gatti's Music Hall as to any technical union. In the service of the five newsreel emblems – Pathe's cockerel, Movietone's scroll, Gaumont's town crier, Universal's globe and Paramount's 'Eyes and Ears of the World' – they did the most splendid, appalling things. They charmed, bullied, shoved with the shoulder, monopolised buffet-cars on the trains to ship-launches, drew expenses on a monumental scale and antagonised Churchill and the Prince of Wales. At a certain Grand National, one company hired toughs to throw potatoes at another, studded with razor blades. A smoke bomb was dropped on the course during the race and the favourite, Golden Miller, fell. They were the last buccaneers. The fact that for two generations they were also mainly responsible for the continuing British belief that civilisation halted at Southampton docks – as late as 1950 Pathe called Italian footballers 'acrobats from Spaghetti-land' – doesn't diminish the heart and life and lungs they put into photojournalism by their games: TV news is tapioca by comparison.

News is an older commodity than feature-film; in fact the original features were often little more than pathetic confections of real events like famous prizefights, with tubby men in moustachios trying to act the great pugilists. Directly the motion-picture camera was invented it was out on the pavement recording things such as the trotting blur of horse omnibuses and bowlers in the Strand before 1900; that is still in the Pathe library. It was the Frenchman Charles Pathé who in 1907 first had the idea of training news around a stem. He showed his 'newsreel' in London three years later – a sculling contest, a strike of Camden factory-girls, and Queen Alexandra leaving to visit Italy; the Royal Family's boas and trim beards were seldom neglected by any reel from that day forward.

Most of the pioneer companies were French, as befitted the great source of cinema-invention: Pathé Frères' *Animated Gazette*, their great rival Leon Gaumont's *Actualité* newsreel and another that quickly disappeared, Éclair. There was also the Warwick Trading Company, of which no film record survives; but those days, newsreels were arriving and collapsing in some numbers; there was a small Wardour Street pawnshop that held completed first editions in pledge against money to do the second. Some cinema-owners made their own newsreels and some – like Harry Abbott, later of Movietone – did soft-shoe dance routines during the intervals. One of these impresarios in Liverpool was able to show a film of Edward VIIs funeral only seconds after the cortege had arrived at Westminster Abbey. Few people noticed that the late King was riding behind his own coffin looking fat and well – the sequence was of Victoria's funeral.

How did you join a newsreel? Like all the film industry's recruiting then and now, it was just a lottery. Adolph Simon went to Pathe in London having been a boy in Charles Pathé's French labs. Eddie Edmonds left a firm of Bishopsgate candlemakers to get a job with *Gaumont Actualité*, wearing another lodger's coat that his landlady purloined for him; he fell in the mud on the way home. My grandfather Frank Augustus Bassill joined Pathe after working as a projectionist in the Empire cinema, Leicester Square; part of his duties being to run down and stand the screen up again after courting couples, writhing under the Podium, knocked it over.

Pathe's Animated Gazette, with their beautifully-inscribed titles, had advanced sufficiently to be putting out a daily edition before the First World War; a special hot item that could be spliced into the weekly reel. They and Gaumont had also raised enough speed to be able to accompany George V to France in 1914 and to show the film in the West End and even in Maida Vale by eight o'clock the same night. But with mobilisation, very few of the cameramen became war correspondents to record the Tommies vanishing into the Hun-smoke in helmet and bayonet shapes; all that was left to a handful of men like Frank Bassill, for most of his contemporaries simply enlisted. Adolph Simon went back to France and became an observer from a fearful kind of rather typically French man-carrying kite.

Mercifully transferred to normal balloons, he was in the Somme in 1916 when he happened to run into Jack Cotter, Movietone's air-ace of the Thirties. Simon's section handed over a sausage-shaped balloon to Cotter's, who promptly let it blow away. But Simon himself had one of the busiest times in the clouds. The Germans used to deal with enemy balloons by means of a naval gun brought into position on a miniature railway. Usually when the observer saw the puffs of engine smoke he could get himself lowered before the gun fired, but Simon was almost gassed as he stepped out of the basket on the ground; the whole balloon settled over his head. Twice after that he was machine-gunned by German Fokker aircraft and forced to parachute. On the second occasion the German pilot somersaulted past him, having himself been shot down, exploding like a Catherine wheel from the bullets ignited in his bandolier.

Real trials of strength between companies began in the Twenties: the silent Pathe and Gaumont reels with their special women's editions, and *Empire Screen News* and *British Screen News* and *Topical Budget*, which was successful but virtually collapsed after a bad fire that also damaged their neighbours', Pathe's, office facade.

What killed most of the weaklings was the beginning of sound in 1929 and the arrival from America of the flashy Fox-Movietone operation; yet, for a time, most of the cameramen would have preferred the talkies to blow over. Their silent cameras, like the Bell and Howell Eyemo, were heavy but at least could be carried by a strap-handle in a taxi. Shooting with sound meant travelling with severe hundred-weight of equipment in a van; it meant being down on expenses.

Paul Wyand (centre) filming Prime Minister Ramsay Macdonald for *British Movietone News* in the garden of 10 Downing Street, June 1929.

Fox-Movietone set up in Berners Street with half-a-dozen American cameramen, left-hand drive REO Speedwagons and an extremely handsome style of behaviour. Their first edition in Sound ('It Speaks for Itself') is undistinguished, but the second is interesting and the sound quality, to say the least, resonant. The commentary begins at funereal pace as if explaining a conjuring trick to a savage. 'In Living Sound and Graphic Action, Movietone Presents ...' There are items on rowing, Army horse-trials and a priest in a wind-filled surplice that effectively hides the Duke of York, later George VI. Finally, as a glory, Ramsay Macdonald introduces his second Labour Cabinet in the garden of 10 Downing Street: they seem to consist of midgets in gutta-percha collars and ladies waving as from a steamer excursion.

At first, wherever sound-vans stopped, crowds gathered and leaflets were given out to explain the system. The next to introduce the miracle was *Gaumont-Graphic*, as they had become, although prudently they carried on their silent edition for a time as well. Pathe were a fraction behind Gaumont but their sound was, as befitted the senior newsreel, beautifully mixed. One of the chief technicians in their changeover was Adolph Simon, who had returned to London from Shanghai, where he had been distributing Pathe equipment and running his own Oriental newsreel. He once pinched the Far Eastern Games from a competitor in Peking by standing on a table outside the ground and then escaping, with the table, by rickshaw.

Paramount were next with a sound system a year or two after Pathe; but Universal the newsreels' poor relation, who had replaced the old *Empire Screen News*, lagged far behind. They proudly called themselves *Universal Talking News* but, right into the Thirties, all their stories were shot silent and dubbed with a commentary by one R.E. Jeffrey, with a plum and pun in his mouth.

Pathe and Movietone took the lead, thanks to money and resources, with Gaumont-British under Castleton Knight acting as a horsefly on their expensive flanks. Movietone dropped 'Fox' from their name and became British-Movietone by association with the power-famished newspapers of Lord Rothermere; yet for a number of years they still used left-hand drive vehicles. Similarly, Pathe kept their Frenchness by calculating film in metres; while the commentators they used were so blah – indeed, some even had titles – that they mispronounced words of vital importance to the nation – *Betcher's* for Becher's Brook.

It would have been in Pathe or Movietone that there originated the legendary petty-cash entry 'Gratuity to Admiral for bringing Fleet closer inshore'. Gaumont-British, although their camera teams were sent out in Rolls-Royces, had a reputation for tightness over expenses. They rather expected their men to be tea-drinkers. Eddie Edmonds to this day smarts over the time the price of a Schweppes lemonade was crossed off his expense sheet. But ah, Pathe. Paradise: when Frank Bassill was sent to India in the early Twenties they gave him an advance of 100 guineas in gold sewn into a money-belt. By sale and resale of the mercurial rupee, he made almost that amount again. I have a copy of *The Man*

Upstairs by P.G. Wodehouse that belonged to him, and his uses for one job are worked out in florins and shillings on one flyleaf. With the total he could have bought a case of champagne or a new suit. Except you were no kind of a newsreel man unless after an open-air job you put in for a new suit as a matter of principle.

Often the warfare was not so much between newsreels as dynasties – there were strong families in the profession. Movietone had its air-acrobat Jack Cotter who finally crashed into a garden in Poole while bringing home pictures of the Dartmoor prison riots. He was also noted for having tried to photograph the 1927 eclipse of the sun through a 20-inch lens borrowed from Greenwich Observatory; his camera burst into flames. With him in balloon or monoplane was his cousin Terry Cotter, the sound-man. Terry was an uproarious practical joker whose favourite tricks were turning horses the wrong way round in their shafts, putting goldfish into beer, ferns into Belisha beacons; and offering his train ticket to be clipped with sixpence under it, so that the ticket collector's arm was jarred to the shoulder.

Of the Wyand family, Leslie was at Pathe with Frank Bassill before the First World War, and his nephews Paul and Pat both joined Movietone. Paul was immensely stout and a master of disguise; famous for the shot he took of Jack Dunfee's death crash at Brooklands when he was, illegally, only 20 yards from the car's final resting-place. He also claimed he was the first British cameraman at Beauvais after the R101 airship fell. Pat was quiet; on sound. Then there were Jock Gemmell of Pathe and Jimmy of *British Screen News*, then Paramount. Jimmy was noted for his impersonation of Gandhi and for having upset the tin commode that stood for 12 months on top of the Wembley camera-gantry without being emptied. People down below who felt the shower and licked their fingers swore it was vintage Scotch.

Pathe's circular and irascible Ken Gordon was always the man on watch if his company had bought the rights to an event: he was hopping mad, for example, when Eddie Edmonds pinched one big race from the cover of a bookmaker's umbrella and Jack Cotter stole a Cup Final at wonderful close quarters disguised as West Ham's chief mascot, with his camera inside the end of his ceremonial hammer. There was an immaculate freelance, George Plowman, whose entry into a bar was always signalled with the words 'a large Black Label and baby Polly'; and Leslie Murray of Movietone, who went to Universal, bought the rights to a set of quads and hung Universal placards round their necks at the christening; and Jimmy Taylor, who always had steak and Bass for breakfast and Frank Purnell of *Topical Budget* nicknamed Tatsie because of an impediment in his speech: that was the way he said 'taxi'. Tatsie was daring enough to parachute with a pretty girl to photograph her descent; but to his chagrin they floated down back to back.

There were great people too, in the aromatic, rubbery rooms where the cutting and editing was done: when Gaumont did their processing at Lime Grove, David Lean was a youth in the cutting-rooms. *Topical Budget*, before they collapsed, had titles and artwork done by Alf Skitterell, Frank Bassill's brother-in-law and by common consent the best optical printer the film industry ever produced. Movietone possessed a genius named Charles Ridley, the man who cut possibly the most famous piece of newsreel of all time: Hitler and Mussolini doing the Lambeth Walk. The genius of it reaches down the years.

Editors had to be able to out-talk and out-trick the cleverest of them all; they needed a touch of the Pirate King. Cameramen like Frank Bassill came to be editors: quiet individuals sometimes did as well; Henry Sanders of Pathe, for example, a soft-mannered man who always wore white socks and his trousers half-mast, and introduced the *Super Gazette*, an edition of twice the usual length. Sir Malcolm Campbell edited Movietone for a while in the Thirties and tried harder than most to wake the country up to what Hitler's plan for Europe was. However, the great jousting editors, the pair who tilted over and almost ruined the 1934 Test Match and other occasions, were Tommy Cummins of *Paramount News* and the demonic Castleton Knight of *Gaumont-British*.

Cummins's talent for thwarting his opposition was stick-like and humourless. In one year that Paramount had the Cup Final rights, he simply advertised blocks of contraband tickets, sold them to other newsreels when they applied, and then just ticked them all off on his own seating-plan, knowing exactly where the pinchers would be. Castleton Knight was the showman, the brilliant cuckoo: short and immensely dapper and compelled to wear a leg-brace. His greatest coup is arguable. Before he joined Gaumont (as producer rather than editorial head) he had been a cinema manager responsible for kidnapping Charlie Chaplin for a stunt, and director of the half-sound and wholly risible feature film, THE FLYING SCOTSMAN. His highly placed friends avowed Gaumont to be the only newsreel who ever set up their punishing arc lights inside Buckingham Palace *by command* of the Royal Family. But his most characteristic exploit was transmission of the first newsreel film across the world, after the celebrated arrival of the winners of the first London-Melbourne air-race. It was really nothing that Knight claimed: Gaumont had simply arranged for the race-winners Scott and Black to be photographed in Australia, having a drink, and a few frames were transmitted like ordinary still photographs. They made no more than a fingersnap of cinema-time; two men lifting their elbows with a jerk; but what Gaumont did with that! Knight produced it as a special item with fanfares and a whirr of drums and a commentary exultant even by their sherry-laden standards. Then came the tiny clip of film. After that the commentator said, '*Now* we will show it to you *again*'. After that he said, '*Now* we will show you how we did it'; and after that, '*Now* we will show it to you *again* ...' at which point audiences all over the country – the Empire – rose and cheered and clapped.

To most domestic stories the approach was cheery and unbuttoned, with an aggressiveness rather dictated by the weight of newsreel equipment. Despite the advances made in cameras, from the early handle-cranked models to the ponderous early sound cameras and tile Newman Sinclairs and American Mitchells with Mickey Mouse ears, nothing became very much less cumbersome; if the newsreels wanted to lay a sound-cable, very often they just dug up the road. Not that cameramen were by disposition very modest. One provincial hotel that annoyed a newsreel party found its foyer carpet rolled up and neatly stacked; and another that objected to the vans – which looked very distinguished – discovered a steamroller parked on its newly-raked gravel drive. An entire ground floor was thrown in a flutter on another occasion when a man in a loincloth came downstairs: it was Jimmy Gemmell who had been persuaded by his companions to do his impersonation of Gandhi and then found they had all disappeared.

They rather prided themselves, too, on acting cavalierly towards the gently-born. In the Wimbledon enclosure once, the Hon. Mrs Watt-Piper was photographed and then asked her name to he entered on the cameraman's fact-sheet. She replied, 'Watt-Piper'. The cameraman said, 'No, I'm with the newsreels'. Despite the tenacity with which they filmed Royal arrivals and departures – or rather, because of it – there was no great sweetness towards them at Buckingham Palace, especially in the years when the Prince of Wales, later the abdicating Edward VIII, was everyone's fair-haired darling. Edward sustained a running feud with the newsreels based, it

(Left to right) Norman Fisher (Movietone), Peter Cannon (Gaumont-British), Leslie Murray (Universal), Billy Jordan (Pathe) and Jimmy Gemmell (Paramount), filming Lord Mountbatten's return from India, Northolt, June 1948.

8

was said, on the cameramen's habit of assembling at the first jumps of Royal gymkhanas in the hope that HRH would be unhorsed there.

On Nice railway station one day Frank Bassill of Pathe was approached by a fair-haired man of modest height who truculently inquired why Bassill was following him. It was the Prince, and Bassill simply wished to catch a train. Some of the liveliest brushes occurred between Edward and Gaumont's Eddie Edmonds; possibly the least assertive newsreel employee of them all. Yet he was the man who drew forth a splendid example of a Royal oath when his camera made a noise at the start of one of the Prince's speeches; the Gaumont sound-recordist picked it up, immaculately, but it was destroyed by quick action from the Palace. History does not establish, however, which Royal personage it was who at an important occasion also near a Gaumont sound-unit remarked 'This is no job for a man!'

The cameramen collected in the same nest of pubs around Wardour Street – the Blue Posts, the Ship, the Crown and Two Chairmen – and in the same urn-steamy pull-up cafe, Hector's. The survivors declare they would like it understood that however intense the competition for exclusive pictures, it was always basically an amiable war. It couldn't have been, not if it combined the swift temper of Pathe's Ken Gordon and the inspired trickery of Castleton Knight *and* the gangs of specially-hired toughs who recur like a chorus throughout newsreel history, shaking camera-towers and thicking ears.

When Pathe had the Grand National rights and their rivals pinched shots from a barge moored beyond the Canal Turn, hobbledehoys appeared, holding a banner up that read 'See it all on Pathe News'. Swift negotiation by all sides ended with the displaying of the banner upside down. There was bidding in the same style over whether the toughs should or should not shake the camera-towers; while men at the top grabbed at their equipment and prepared to have their backs broken.

If a pinch was expected – as it always was – racecourse or stadium officials would patrol the stands with scouts from the defending newsreel. Anyone who was carrying an over-large shopping bag or wheeling a cripple with legs of particular bulk would be stopped and searched; if there was a camera in the oranges or leg-irons, the miscreants were escorted to the turnstiles without their film or, in cases of special friends, made to stand a horrifying round of drinks and then thrown out. Yet a peculiar kind of chivalry was accorded to successful pinches: no newsreel ever brought an injunction to stop a rival exhibiting pinched film. The one person who almost got himself put in jail was Terry Cotter, the Movietone sound man. Having sneaked with his cameramen into the 1931 Cup Final and helped in the stealing of fine shots, he was strolling back towards the exit when he met a lad carrying five cans of Pathe film: Pathe, as usual, had the rights. Cotter told him to hand over the film and the lad, thinking this was a Pathe senior, obeyed.

When Ken Gordon discovered this, he approached apoplexy and had Cotter taken in charge. Fortunately the Movietone cashier was in the stand and able to bail him out. The following morning he had to appear before a local magistrate in line with all sorts of villains: there were men who worked the lucky-dip racket with gold watches and custard-powder lids, and crooked charabanc drivers who brought people on champagne-and-lunch outings to the match, then abandoned them. It was only at this stage that Pathe dropped the larceny charges. Relieved, Cotter leaned on the dock-gate, which was unfastened, and fell straight on his nose in front of the Bench.

It need not have been all racing and Royalty: Pathe and Movietone in particular had foreign bureaus all over the world and Gaumont an affiliation with the Hearst Corporation's *Metrotone News* in America. By rights the newsreels should have been a seismograph of all that was getting ready to happen in Europe. One of the frankest items they ever showed about Hitler was his striking of a peg with a ceremonial hammer to launch a foundation stone, and the hammer flew to pieces. While the war noises were accelerating – from rifle to machine-gun fire to the noise of bombing planes – the newsreels were still gathering and giving headlines to a cavalcade of mind-stupefying trivia; like the man who tried to take flight with rockets attached to his trousers. All that happened was that he caught fire and had to roll about, screaming.

Another inventor believed he had devised the perfect device for releasing an unsinkable unit from the superstructure of a liner. This he demonstrated by means of a model hull on a string in Liverpool Docks, using paper bags full of five canaries to represent the passengers. All the newsreels were there in dinghies. Either the model hull sank and the birds were drowned, or the middle section failed to detach itself and, when the inventor recovered it and looked inside, they flew away. Finally, having used up all the canaries, he let go of the string, the model sank and he fell into the water himself.

In the late Thirties a touch of new blood was added in the person of an all-colour newsreel, National. Its commentator was Tommy Woodruffe, who later became a BBC radio immortal by exclaiming 'The Fleet's lit up!' But National was a doomed thing: the existing companies had a tourniquet hold on all distribution. And National were laughed out of Wardour Street because of technical misfortunes that may not have been entirely accidents. Colour news was no mystery; Jimmy Gemmell had been hand-tinting Pathe frames at the time of the First World War. Just the same, National's first edition was shown to the trade upside-down; and then a sequence of the Trooping of the Colour produced Grenadiers parading in tunics as white as lambs.

National folded, but the chuckling survivors had only a limited time to enjoy themselves. It was a paradox that the Second World War should have ended their grand tussle yet at the same time produced such brilliant 35mm reporting. Frank Bassill was with Churchill at Yalta; Eddie Edmonds, though by no means a young man, went with the Commandos to the Lofoten Islands, where he was said to have dictated the choice of landing-points according to what suited the camera. He and Bassill might have been working for the same reel. All the film had to be pooled and used for propaganda: in the end the newsreels were simply a national public-address system to remark 'Watch out, Adolf!' as ships full of grinning, waving Australians, New Zealanders and Gurkhas sailed off to be killed.

When the war ended, the world had a new phrase, 'public relations'. Even the Palace used its own staff cameraman, Graham Thompson, who was responsible for allocating Royal faces to the newsreels by six-month rotas. There could be no more bursting through hedges, as the bulk of Paul Wyand once did, to thrust a lens into Imperial perambulators. The newsreels came to a standstill as journalistic instruments. They were – as they finished up – like home movies; the voices of the commentators, Leslie Mitchell, E.V.H. Emmett, Bob Danvers-Walker, seeming to echo from lost rooms where men wore evening dress all day.

Television was the finish of newsreel; although, funny enough, television's first conception of news presentation was on a reel, and not a very much better one than Charles Pathé's original. Then, with the rise of instantaneous 16mm reports, it became financial heartbreak to produce 250 copies of a 35mm cinema reel that would be out of date before the projectionist even uncoiled it. Paramount finished in 1957, the united Gaumont-British and Universal companies were folded by the Rank organisation in 1959 and Pathe, its dynasty of cockerels having ended with one like a plaster fairground prize, closed in 1969. Only Movietone survives and expresses confidence in its future. News does not sustain it so much as a contract with the Government's Central Office of Information to make documentary films for more innocent worlds overseas; so there is still someone telling someone else, who believes it, how good we are as a nation. That was what the newsreels did in their squib-throwing days. At the same time, if they were blind and deaf to the real issues of life, they managed to give out more concentrated excitement than any TV film explained by a failed actor in a fleecy coat blocking the view.

Sunday Times Magazine, 10 January 1971.

My View of Things

'Nimrod'

The first British newsreel, Pathe's Animated Gazette, appeared in June 1910, when it was issued weekly. It was an off-shoot of the French Pathé-Journal, which had been founded in 1908. The film trade paper The Bioscope recognises the affinity with illustrated newspapers, and predicts a certain future for the new medium.

There is no mistaking the smartness of Messrs Pathe, and their latest achievement – the production of a weekly cinematograph paper, *The Animated Gazette* – has just about beaten all records for the interest which it has awakened among the great B.P. The daily Press has been devoting considerable space to it, with the result that curiosity has been aroused, and people are now busily discussing the latest thing in moving pictures.

Briefly the idea is to incorporate the usual journalistic methods of writing into filming, and to portray, in lengths of about 80 odd feet, the chief items of interest that have happened during the week. Thus the illustrated newspaper is being superseded by *The Animated Gazette*, which depicts the actual scenes of contemporary history in living and moving reality.

Mr Valentia Steer, a well-known journalist, is editor of this moving picture periodical, and he has a staff of photo-correspondents, who are stationed in all the big cities of Europe, besides another staff at home. Last week's news consisted of pictures of the cross-channel flight, Oxford University Eights' trial, Peary at Edinburgh, Roosevelt at Cambridge, besides many interesting 'glimpses' from home and abroad.

This week's contents bill announces motor-racing at Brooklands, the manouevres at Salisbury Plain, the departure of the *Terra Nova*, Chinese mission in Paris, quarrymen's strike, Caruso in the street, *Modes* in Paris, and other 'newsy' films.

That the idea will catch on is undoubted, and it is perhaps not looking too far into the future to anticipate the time when the weekly *Animated Gazette* will become an indispensable 'daily'.

The Bioscope, 9 June 1910.

The 'Animated' Newspaper

Frederick A. Talbot

F.A. Talbot's Moving Pictures: How They Are Made and Worked (1912) is an early and informative book on various aspects of the motion picture industry. His chapter on the only recently-formed newsreels gives us a detailed and observant account of early newsreel production in Britain, using the Gaumont Graphic as his particular example. The word 'newsreel' does not exist as yet, and Talbot uses a wide range of terms for the new phenomenon, including 'animated newspaper' and the most commonly-used phrase of the time, 'topicals'.

We have seen how the topical picture has developed into one of the most attractive and extensively appreciated phases of the art. Events of annual occurrence like the Derby or the Grand National, or those which have been advertised widely on all sides, such as an aeroplane race, are always anticipated with a keen curiosity.

At the same time, however, there are many incidents of daily occurrence which are of absorbing passing interest, such as the launch of a battleship, a railway collision, a big fire, or a public demonstration. Such subjects are not adapted to presentation as individual films of great length, being insufficiently momentous to grip the public for several minutes in the same way as the International Yacht Race, or some other dramatic item in our complex social and industrial life.

For some time occurrences like these were ignored. Sometimes weeks slipped by without any public event being presented on the screen, owing to lack of opportunity.

At this juncture one or two enterprising firms conceived a brilliant idea of turning these events to interesting and profitable account. Why not secure short lengths of film on various subjects of passing interest, and join them together to form one film between 200 and 350 feet in length, to provide a regular weekly topical feature? These little 'topicals' were secured – a few feet of this, and a few feet of that, subject depicting the most striking or interesting phases in each news feature – and joined to form a continuous miscellaneous moving mirror of the world's happenings.

When the idea was first carried into execution the film could scarcely be described as 'topical'. There was no attempt to serve up the pictures to the public in a 'red-hot' condition. The incidents portrayed in many instances had passed beyond the allotted nine days of wonder, and having been almost forgotten, aroused but a flicker of interest. The experiment recalled the days when newspapers first resorted to photographic illustrations; when the pictures were published often two or three days after the occurrence of the event to which they referred.

Yet the results achieved sufficed to prove that a new and promising field in cinematography had been tapped. Great possibilities awaited enterprise and energy. All that was required was to supply the pictures while the events were still fresh in the minds of the public. Haphazard methods promised only failure; a special organisation was essential to cope with the situation. In order to emphasise the motive of the undertaking, the topical film, which presented in tabloid form an assortment of news, was given a newspaper title; the animated 'Chronicle', 'Gazette', and 'Graphic' appeared; while to render the newspaper idea more pronounced, the exteriors of the picture palaces were emblazoned with placards drawn up in the most approved newspaper style.

In the course of a few weeks, as the operators displayed keener competition to outstrip rivals in securing the first pictorial representation of something of importance, and the pictures assumed a more and more up-to-date aspect, the moving picture newspaper established its significance. Showmen were tempted to assist in the enterprise by being able to purchase the newspaper film at a lower price than the ordinary subject. Although the animated newspaper has been amongst us for only a few months, yet it has already developed into an institution. Many people would as soon think of missing the 'newspaper' item as they would think of overlooking an opportunity to see the Derby re-run upon the screen.

From a cursory view no difficulty appears to be attached to the preparation of a film of odds and ends of topical interest; but as a matter of fact the task is quite as exacting and strenuous as the production of the morning newspaper.

The work can be handled successfully only by a firm having an extensive organisation, and with better chances of success if it has specialised in the ordinary 'topical'. There must be an editor to direct operations and to prepare the film. He must possess a large and scattered staff, so that no part of the world is left uncovered by a cinematograph. His scouts must be active and keen, always on the alert, and ready to secure on the instant a few feet of any incident of importance in their respective localities. In the offices a number of skilled operators must be ready to hurry off at a moment's notice to any desired spot.

The first-named emissaries constitute the special foreign correspondents, while the office staff feed the film in the same manner that the newspaper staff reporters supply the columns of the morning newspaper with material.

There is one feature in which the man with the camera holds an undisputed advantage over his *confrère* armed with notebook and pencil. He gives a truthful pictorial account of what takes place, not the garbled product of a vivid imagination.

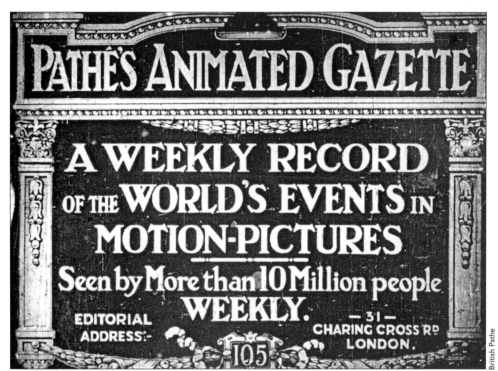

British Pathe

Pathe's Animated Gazette main title design from 1912.

As a result the editor of the animated picture newspaper is spared the menace which hangs always over the head of the newspaper director. He is immune from the pains and penalties of the libel law!

In order to secure a more intimate impression of the work of the moving newspaper, we will go behind the scenes of one of the most flourishing and successful of these animated news-sheets – *The Gaumont Graphic* – and follow it through its successive phases of production. When the proprietors of this pictorial record embarked upon this new development, they had the experience of some twelve years' work in the 'topical' field, and their machinery and staff had acquired the instinct to 'get there first'.

There is, of course, the editorial sanctum in which the presiding genius holds autocratic sway, and directs the many threads which control the acquisition of news. At his elbow the tape machine ticks merrily the livelong day. The telegraphic ribbon reels out the bald announcement that a big fire is raging in the City, that a devastating explosion has spread death and ruin somewhere in the north of Scotland, or that a Transatlantic liner has run on the rocks off some remote part of the coast. An operator is rushed to the scene, and there left to his own devices to secure a sensational few feet of film. He may succeed or he may not; it all depends upon the circumstances and conditions. Maybe he may have to wait four or five hours perched in an uncomfortable position, but if a few feet of film can be exposed to advantage he will not have failed.

The country is divided up into districts where cinematographic reporters are retained in readiness for any emergency, and they have command over a certain radius around that centre. For instance, if an accident happens in northern Scotland a telegram to the operator responsible for that locality hastens him to the spot. The editor of the *Gaumont Graphic* has branch offices at Newcastle – which covers the north-east of England – at Glasgow for Scotland, and at Liverpool and Manchester for the northwest of England, the Liverpool operators being ready to proceed to Ireland or the Isle of Man should the necessity arise. In addition, there are what might be described as sub-offices at Bristol and Birmingham, whence any point in the Midlands and the west of England can be gained, as well as another at Scarborough, so that the whole of Great Britain may be said to be mapped out and covered cinematographically.

As far as the foreign areas are concerned, owing to offices being established in all the large centres from China to Peru, no difficulty is experienced in gathering items of interest from all parts of the world. Operators are searching constantly for films of general interest from the industrial, commercial, scenic, travel, or some other point of view, and in the course of their work secure pictorial snippets of topical interest. As a result a steady stream of items recorded in animation pour in constantly from all parts of the world. The European and Asiatic items in the form of lengths of film pass to the French headquarters in Paris, while those of Canadian and Australian interest flow to London. A daily record of the films of a news interest received from foreign correspondents is received from France for the London editor to sift and select what he considers of interest. When this has been done, he telegraphs to Paris for what he requires – so many feet of this and so many feet of that film.

In addition, he has a tabulated statement of what may be described as 'fixed' functions, such as a race meeting, a motor competition, a flying-machine test, a society wedding, and what not, to which operators are dispatched.

In due course the small lengths of exposed film filter in by train and post. So soon as they arrive they are developed and printed. Proofs are handed over to the editor to be scanned and revised, sections which he considers the most suitable and likely to interest the public being snipped from each film-proof, by the aid of the indispensable scissors. Possibly much of the material when it reaches the editor's eye fails to win his appreciation, and meets an inglorious and premature end in the editorial waste-paper basket. A certain amount of wasted effort is unavoidable; for space, that is to say, length of film, is limited, and when the *Graphic* appeared only once a week, sifting was of a searching character. When a considerable amount of incident has occurred and has been cinematographed during the week, the selection process is by no means easy; many interesting items find themselves crowded out to be held over until the next issue, or destroyed.

As the pieces of each film are selected, they are 'pasted' together, and each incident receives its full explanatory title and sub-title. These revised proofs are connected up so as to form a continuous length of film, and copies are reeled off in the printing, developing, and drying rooms at tip-top speed, the operation corresponding with the printing machine room of the newspaper. The first complete proof is submitted to the editor's approval by being projected on the screen just as it will be submitted to the public. Further revision may be requisite, in which event the film undergoes another trimming process with the scissors, or possibly some late news has been received, and space has to be found for its inclusion at the expense of some other item.

The 'composition', or, as it is called, the 'make-up', of the animated news film is just as complex as that of a newspaper or magazine. It is essential that it should be diversified in its contents so as to appeal to the tastes of all classes of the community. There are the big items which stand pre-eminent, and which range from London to South America, and from Paris to China. Around these have to be disposed various other features of lesser importance.

Seeing that the length of the film newspaper is limited to between 500 and 650 feet, and is built up of from ten to seventeen subjects which vary in length according to their respective importance, careful discrimination is necessary. The public has become hypercritical in regard to animated pictures, and the appeal has to be made to the great majority. As a rule, endeavour is made to incorporate regular features in each issue. Sport is represented by some one or other of the many branches of athletics and racing; society finds itself displayed in a wedding, garden-party, ball, or other fashionable function; the woman's page has its equivalent in the animated portrayal of the latest Paris fashions as displayed by the mannequins – generally in order to give an enhanced effect this section is reproduced in colour – and so forth. Effort is made also to incorporate, if possible, a special function of some description performed by some personage looming prominently in the public eye. Variety is the keynote of success as much in the successful cinematograph newspaper as in its ink-and-paper contemporary.

The *Gaumont Graphic* has an extensive and influential foreign and colonial circulation, and accordingly special attention has to be devoted to the requirements of these readers, or rather spectators. The special topical films are ransacked, and little excerpts made. For instance, in the Coronation number of the *Gaumont Graphic*, two or three of the greatest features of the long Coronation film were cut out and pasted together to form a prominent item of news; the same applies to the inter-University boat race and other sports, the Derby and great race meetings, the Football Final; in short, to every important annual event. This procedure is necessary, for the animated newspaper reaches remote parts of the world, where perchance the complete film of an individual event may never find its way.

One noticeable feature is the friendliness extended to the cinematographic news-gatherer, who often meets with greater appreciation than his *confrère*, the Press snapshotter. The latter, armed with his small camera, often allows his zeal and enthusiasm to overstep his discretion – a fact that is particularly noticeable with regard to society and royal events. The cinematograph operator, on the contrary, being burdened with a somewhat cumbrous apparatus, is forced to remain at a fixed point. The apparent drawback is really a blessing in disguise, because special care is invariably taken to afford him an advantageous position. The outcome is that cinematographic portraiture ninety-nine times out of a hundred is far better than that secured by the snap-shotting fiend, who thrusts himself forward and catches his quarry, perchance, in an unhappy moment.

Yet the editor of the film newspaper is not relieved from worries and anxieties. Cinematography is dependent mainly upon a bright light; thus the success of a film, at least in Great Britain, is never certain beforehand. When the elements are adverse it is difficult indeed to collect the news. The operator may wait for hours to film a subject, or perhaps he makes his exposures in despair, and with a blind trust

Newsfilm pioneers Will Barker (left) and William Jeapes, founder of *Warwick Bioscope Chronicle* and *Topical Budget*. The cameraman is J.B. McDowell.

Luke McKernan

in luck. When heavy fogs hang like blankets over the great centres, passing events of importance defy recording, and it is a sheer waste of film to endeavour to secure pictures. As a result the film newspaper is much easier to produce in summer than in winter, and this climatic influence probably constitutes a unique feature in newspaperdom.

The animated newspaper even has its stop-press feature; that is to say, it can deal with pictorial records of events which occur after the paper is being printed off or has been circulated. A short film of some great incident trickles into the editorial room. It cannot be delayed until the next issue-by that time public interest in the item will have vanished. Consequently it is rushed through, and all subscribers scattered throughout the country are advised by telegraph that a record of such-and-such a topical subject has been obtained, and can be dispatched at once for display in the form of supplement to the animated newspaper now being shown. The late item is sent out, and upon arrival at the picture palace is attached to the end of the newspaper film already received, its inclusion perhaps necessitating sacrifice of some other item of less importance.

When the *Gaumont Graphic* first appeared, it was issued weekly, and accordingly corresponded to the weekly illustrated newspaper. Now it is published twice weekly, and with increased success. Indeed, the pictorial news film reaches its subscribers in the colonies and foreign countries contemporaneously, or even prior to the arrival of the illustrated weeklies, which are dispatched by mail.

In Australasia, Canada, India, and the smaller British colonies, the idea of giving the week's news in animation has met with a remarkably hearty reception, inasmuch as it serves to bring the world's happenings far more vividly before the public in those remote parts of the world than can be done in a brief newspaper cablegram or a single photograph published in the pages of the illustrated weeklies. The history of the world is re-enacted before them; they are brought to the localities where the episodes occurred – a miracle of transportation not to be effected by any other known scientific means.

How does the film newspaper affect the cinematograph theatre? What is the attitude towards the idea? Does the showman regard it with favour? These are questions which naturally occur to the mind. Opinion is best reflected by the success of the enterprise. Now that the picture paper is published twice a week, the expenditure of the showman is doubled; but this fact does not appear to have exercised a deterrent influence. When the *Gaumont Graphic* was published weekly, its circulation approximated 200 copies per week. In other words, 200 showmen subscribed towards this feature. This, by the way does not represent its full circulation, as a single subscriber may control two or more halls in one city, and very often the one film suffices for several picture palaces under one control. These 200 copies of the film newspaper, then, were seen, at a modest computation, by several millions of people weekly. Seeing that the subscriber is unable to hire the film newspaper for the week, but has to purchase it outright at a uniform price of 2½d. (5 cents) per foot, and that its average length is 600 feet, his outlay amounts to £6 ($30) for a subject, the exhibition life of which is restricted to three or seven days. As the average showman is a keen and shrewd business man, it is not to be supposed for a moment that the investment of such a sum every week is otherwise than remunerative from his point of view.

Will the cinematographic newspaper ever supplant its printed rival? By no means. It acts rather as an illustrated supplement to printed details; it renders the latter more comprehensive by bringing scenes and actors vividly and naturally before the eye, thereby causing a more living and detailed impression than can be obtained through the medium of words. On the other hand, it is beginning to rival the illustrated paper, which depends upon photographic contents, and this competition will be felt more keenly as time goes on.

The day is probably still far distant when a man, instead of giving a penny for a printed daily newspaper to see what has happened during the previous twenty-four hours, will spend the same sum to enter a picture palace, and devote a quarter of an hour to seeing in full animation what paper and ink merely describe. The modern business man acknowledges that he only has time to glance through the staring headlines of his morning newspaper; and surely comprehensive titles and a series of excellent pictures would perform the same service for him, and more besides. Producers would aid the development by giving careful attention to titles and headlines.

Thus the era of the daily cinematographic newspaper is not so remote as may be thought at first sight. The *Gaumont Graphic* is quite ready to appear daily if the demand should arise. The organisation is perfect so far as the news-film collecting, printing, developing, and other technical details are concerned. A complete paper could be turned out in four hours. That is to say, films could be received up to about ten o'clock at night, and the newspaper could be ready for projection by two o'clock in the morning. The early special trains which now leave the great cities at express speed for the delivery of printed newspapers to remote parts of the country may yet be called upon to carry small boxes of daily news-film for similar distribution. The manufacturing cost of the film is being constantly reduced; and once this essential is brought to a very low figure, enterprising showmen will not hesitate to spend a few shillings per day to reproduce in animation before the general public the chief episodes of the preceding twenty-four hours.

from *Moving Pictures: How They Are Made and Worked* (London: Heinemann, 1912).

A Criticism of the News-Film

Lester Ruah

The newsreels had settled into an easy formula, and there were six on the British market, when this article in a film trade paper criticised them for their reliance on the trivial, their predictability and uniformity of style. Such arguments would be directed at the newsreels over and over again, and here generated wounded responses from the newsreel editors (see page 24).

The recent remarks made by 'Stroller' with regard to the imperfections of certain news gazettes, budgets, chronicles etc, are to many cases very true, especially with regard to the short and 'snippy' nature of some issues. But there are other faults of quite as noticeable a kind as those touched upon, and mention of these in the pages of the *Kinematograph Weekly* will, perhaps, do something towards their elimination.

As mentioned by 'Stroller,' the short and unsatisfactory length of some items, which are flashed off just as one is becoming interested in the subject, form a legitimate ground for complaint. It would surely be better to leave out one item and lengthen the others, in such cases, or to cut down the sub-titling which is frequently on the screen three or four times as long as is necessary. The average person does not require a minute to read about fifteen words, of which half might easily be left out. The explanatory wording is often far too prosy and frequently contains a lot of quite unnecessary details. Of course, it means so much a foot, but that should not be the end to aim at; there should be an art to sub-titling news gazettes and budgets, even as there is in 'headlining' in the newspaper press.

The complaint of too short items, however, does not apply to all 'gazettes' (they will be called 'gazettes' here, though, of course, no special make is thereby indicated) for in some the very opposite is the case. We are shown long and drawn out picturings of the extremely unimportant doings of some village big-wigs in whom we have not the slightest interest whatever. We are shown dreary back-yard (the writer recollects one literary back-garden inspection) or 'Dulltown Market Place,' review of boy scouts and old age pensioners by puffed-up local nonentities; boring views of stone-layings and ship-launchings, with the greater part of the space allotted to the item occupied by self-important grocer councillors or brewery-mayors in their speech-making and hat wagging – interesting enough, perhaps, for a local topical, but quite out of place in a news-film which is shown all over the country. Why not simply show the actual laying or launching and omit all the ceremonial business – unless, of course, it stars someone who is really famous – say a prince, or a Cabinet Minister, or a music-hall artiste earning four hundred a week.

Touching on ship launching reminds the writer that the essential variety is not always particularly noticeable in some news-gazettes. One 'world's news' film is remembered which was occupied by four items ; (1) fashions (2) ship-launching at X, (3) ship-launching at Y, about twenty miles from X, (4) ship-launching at Z, about 7 miles from X. *World's* news in *variety* of subject.

There is a tendency in some gazettes to include, instead of news matter, items of general interest, such as views of a cat playing with a canary, of a house where King Charles slept, of a sign-post with a word spelt wrongly, how cauliflowers arc grown on Mr A.'s estate, a picture of Mr B.'s (the famous novelist) pigsties, or an intensely uninteresting view of an exceptionally large egg laid seven years ago by a three-legged chicken – and so on. These are often fairly interesting as they go, and would probably make excellent 'interest' films, but they are not news, and are certainly out of place in a news gazette.

The same criticism applies to the 'fashion plates,' with which many news-films are embellished. These are possibly of interest to some of the ladies, who, anyhow, form only a portion of the audience – but it is peculiar that many lady friends of the writer frequently vote the fashion items as being nothing to be pleased about, and sometimes, indeed, ridiculous; thus agreeing with the men. There is a most mistaken impression that these fashion items are eagerly welcomed by women because of the opportunities offered to copy the latest creations from Paris. But there are the considerations that the item is seldom on long enough for this to be done, even if it were desired, and in any case the ladies' fashion journals supply brilliantly coloured plates which may be studied and copied at leisure and which are quite as-up-to-date in design as the dresses shown on the news-film. If, as may be argued, the fashion item is useful in that it helps to satisfy the average woman's 'dress-mania' (which is doubtful) why not give the subject a news value by showing dresses worn by Personages at weddings, balls, plays and so on?

It may be pointed out that these general non-news items are of value in that the film is thereby given an interest beyond that of topical, so that it may be useful and effective even when shown at small halls, say, seven or eight weeks after release. But surely every endeavour should be made to prevent this undesirable lengthening of the life of films, which are, first and last, newspapers to be thrown aside when the topical interest is gone – and not necessarily worn out into film scrap? The tendency is for the news-film to approximate more and more the daily *news*paper and every effort to prevent this is simply an attempt to set back progress.

It is peculiar how the various gazettes, budgets, etc., are all of the same pattern. There is seldom anything specially noteworthy about any one which would single it out from the others. It would surely pay for an editor to try and give his gazette an individuality of its own, even if only in photography or make-up. And here is another subject which may be justly criticised – poor photography. Of course, with exceptionally important events, even poor photography and poor climatic conditions, such as fog or rain, may be often disregarded, as the public will expect to see the subject and will make allowances for blemishes. But to include items with such faults as the above to mar them, when the subject has no particular interest for the average person, is very bad policy indeed, though it is often done. The cameraman has many difficulties in his way, of course, to prevent him obtaining a perfect picture, and the poorly photographed item of average interest is far better left out of the news-film than included.

The writer is fully aware that the editors of most of the newsfilms know their business very well, and is also acquainted with the truism that every one can edit a paper (or film gazette) better than the editor thereof. Legitimate and useful criticism never did any harm to anyone, however, and it is to be hoped that a few of the faults and imperfections here touched upon will at least be partly remedied before long.

The Kinematograph and Lantern Weekly, 26 March 1914.

The article by Lester Ruah (see page 21) generated a strong response from the editors of the British newsreels. The Kinematograph and Lantern Weekly, the film trade-paper in which the original criticisms were published, gave space to the editors of Gaumont Graphic, Pathe's Animated Gazette, Eclair Animated Journal and Topical Budget (editor unnamed, but probably the owner William Jeapes) to defend their medium. Their defences are all based on practical considerations, generally reasonable in themselves, but which override any sense of engagement with the news itself.

The 'Criticism of the News Film', by Lester Ruah, which we printed a couple of weeks ago, has aroused quite an interesting and animated discussion among the Editors of the various news gazettes. We accordingly invited each of the gentlemen concerned to express their views on our contributor's criticisms, and below we have pleasure in printing a number of brief articles on the subject, which are full of suggestion, and will be read with interest by every Exhibitor who includes a news-film in his weekly program.

THE THEORIST AND THE NEWS-FILM

Alec J. Braid, Editor, *The Gaumont Graphic.*

No one welcomes the theorist more heartily than the practical man. He is a most delightful person. He tackles the problems of one's everyday life with complete assurance; bewails the other fellow's lack of enterprise; regrets his imperfections, and calls for individuality. That is just what 'Lester Ruah' did in a recent issue of the *Kinematograph Weekly.* As the editor of one of the newsfilms I am attempting a reply, not because I admit a tenth of the counts in the indictment, but for the reason that I regard the critic as more of a theorist than a practical man.

No one is more conscious of the shortcomings of the news film than the editor. During the dull weather and the slack season it is the bane of his existence. Week by week he has to find 600 feet of 'live' stuff. The picture-goer is blissfully unconscious of the difficulties of the man behind the camera, even when a 'job' has been found him. At home the editor is growling either because the subject has failed in interest or the negative is almost unprintable.

Just as we have left the leaden skits of winter behind 'Lester Ruah' holds us all up to be shot at. It is peculiar, he says, how the various gazettes are all of the same pattern, and cries for individuality in photography or make-up. How can such a critic be satisfied? Someone, certainly not myself, sought individuality by a picture of a famous novelist's pigsties; even the cat playing with the canary did not meet with his approval. What does 'Lester Ruah' require? Has he ever placed himself in the position of the unfortunate editor who struggles to meet the wishes of all his customers?

Let one take the serious criticisms in detail. The question of the title is important and difficult. Before I wrote the titles for the *Gaumont Graphic* I had written many thousands of headlines for newspapers and magazines. There is an art in conveying the story of the picture in a few words. But one has to be explicit. Even in these days of cheap and widely circulated newspapers it is not always safe to assume that four or five words will give sufficient information. As an experiment, 'Lester Ruah' will see that his criticisms have been considered – I paid even more particular attention than usual to the titles for the next issue. Try as one would it was impossible to compress the title of one picture into fewer than twenty words, but the other four subjects divided twenty-nine words between them. Detesting titles in place of pictures, it is my aim to give as few feet of explanatory matter as possible.

Regarding the length of the items constituting the film, no hard-and-fast rule can be laid down. As a rule the news value of a picture, and the negatives available, determine its length. It must be an event of exceptional interest to be worth more than 80 feet. It is, however, impossible to exclude the subject which is not worth more than 30 or 40 feet.

Another point for argument is the inclusion of the non-news item. Our critic sees that the inclusion of this feature is to extend the life of the film. Of course it is. While first-run customers are the chief consideration, the 'little man' has to be taken into account. Is he and his patron to be denied the attractions of the newsfilm as at present constituted? Interest, variety, and the quality of being up-to-date are the three essentials of the newsfilm, the first two being of importance because of the extended life of the film.

On the point of interest it must be remembered that the great news stories of the day are not always the best pictorially. Frequently a picture paper magnifies a topical story out of all proportion because it provides good pictures. The picture-goer, however, looks for the principal events. He also expects variety, and must, of necessity, be interested. Out of the thousands of picture theatres many cannot afford the luxury of a film direct from the producer; therefore the film has to do duty for weeks. Great news stories retain their interest because of their animation, but

William Jeapes filming for *Topical Budget* at Hendon air races, March 1913

Luke McKernan

leading events are not of daily occurence, and if the newsfilm is to fulfil its true mission the bulk of its contents must entertain until the end of its career. For this reason sections here and there partake more of the magazines than the news page of the daily paper. But is it less diverting or newsy because it brings to life out-of-the-way happenings?

One agrees that the tendency is for the newsfilm to approximate more and more the daily newspaper, but those who, like myself, are producing newsfilms, will agree that in the winter months this is an impossibility.

A JUSTIFICATION AND A GRUMBLE

Eric E. Mayell, Editor, *Pathe's Animated Gazette.*

The great fault of the news-film is its shortness. Even when the number of subjects is reduced to three or four, the average length is then only 75 or 100 feet, which means at the most two minutes on the screen. It is really a heart-breaking task to run through hundreds of feet of quite interesting negative, the greater part of which has to be rejected. Probably every patron of the kinema theatre would enjoy at least five minutes of Saturday's Ulster Demonstration in Hyde Park, but this would leave no room whatever for anything else. For years I have been urging exhibitors to take a news-film of at least 1,000 feet per week, as is done in practically every other country in the world.

Poor photography is, unfortunately, much too prevalent in some news-films. The art of taking good topical films is so difficult, however, that there is some excuse for this. The number of good cameramen regularly 'on the road' in the British Isles can be counted on the fingers of one's hands. Even with good photographers, however, the difficulties compared with ordinary snapshots for the press are enormous. The camera cannot be moved quickly; the angle of the lens is very small, making it often a matter of luck for any person, etc., to keep in the field more than a second or two, while no exposures can be taken at less than 1–40 sec. limiting work to outdoor and sunny scenes. I am often asked to take films by *flashlight*, though a few seconds' thought will show how ridiculous the request is.

The winter is the great dread of we poor editors. Very little is happening out of doors, and even then, more often than not, the light is too bad to take films. It is here, then, the general interest items are valuable, and indeed the only standby, unless items of parochial interest only are to be included.

One grumble I should like to make against exhibitors – they never complain. They pay the piper, but for some reason or other they do not call the tune. I can truthfully say that from one year's end to another I get scarcely a complaint, and I am not quite egotistical enough to believe that *Pathe's Animated Gazette* is the absolute 'it' of perfection.

IF UNSATISFACTORY – WHO IS RESPONSIBLE?

Val Steer, Editor, *Eclair Animated Journal*.

I have read with great interest Lester Ruah's criticisms of the average news-film, and consider them very fair, in fact, I am cordially in agreement with most of the views expressed. It must be remembered that the news-film is still in its infancy, and we are all learning things as we go along. For instance, there are certain subjects which I, as an old journalist, would formerly have thought a great 'scoop' for the journal, but which I now know to be totally unsuitable for kinematograph purposes. The public has already expressed a desire for more topicals, but many of the older school of exhibitors still refuse to recognise the trend of public opinion in this regard.

As regards the 'scrappiness' of some of the subjects, of which complaint is justly made, it is not fair to blame the poor editor or the manufacturer. The responsibility is again upon the exhibitor. I feel perfectly sure that the public would welcome a *good* news-film of 800 or even 1,000 feet. But the exhibitor will not pay for more

27

than 500–600 feet, and he wants it at a rock-bottom price which leaves practically no margin of profit to the manufacturer. In other countries firms are turning out these long news-films at 4d. and more per foot, but at present the topical department in Great Britain is the Cinderella of the industry, and has to be run on the cheap.

The complaint of your correspondent regarding unnecessary sub-titling, and the length of titles, I do not consider justified, at any rate so far as the *Eclair Journal* is concerned. We always reduce the length of our titles to the absolute minimum, but there are certain subjects which do not explain themselves on the screen at all, unless adequately sub-titled. The editor of a news-film has many little technical worries which are unknown to the sub-editor of an ordinary picture paper.

As regards the fashion pictures, this is a point on which it is difficult to find out what the public want. When I have left them out I have had many complaints for having done so – and I have also had complaints for putting them in.

In conclusion I feel certain that the news-film has not only come to stay, but to steadily improve in quality and importance until it becomes an essential adjunct to the ordinary newspaper press. And the sooner the authorities really grasp this fact, and grant to the news-film operator the same privileges and courtesies as are extended to the press, the sooner will the present service of animated news be improved.

A word from E.H. Montagu (of Selig's).

With reference to the article on the 'Newsfilm', I would like to concur in the criticisms of the writer, especially where he states that the majority of the items included in the news film are not really news at all.

It may be news to your readers to know that at the present time we are selling in the United States more topicals than any other firm, as we have an arrangement with the Hearst newspapers (the largest chain of newspapers in the States), by which their reporters are furnished with cameras and obtain real news items for the *Hearst-Selig Pictorial*. We find it, however, the hardest thing possible to obtain from England and the Continent real news items to make this pictorial complete, because so very few real news items are snapped. Also it seems to me that one of the reasons why the newsfilm in this country is not properly looked after, is because of the cheap price at which it is sold. I believe a good many are sold at 2d. per foot, less 10 per cent and how on earth anybody expects to be able to secure real good news at this price, I do not know. I can assure you that as long as the prices remain like this, you will never see a *Hearst-Selig Pictorial* over here.

WHOSE FAULT IS IT?

The Editor of the *Topical Budget*

We are in agreement with Lester Ruah with regard to the short section length of topicals, but whose fault is it? Certainly not ours.

We think that Lester Ruah and other critics place us in the same position as the publishers of the daily illustrated paper; but there is a great difference. The papers supply the public direct whilst the publishers of the news-film deal with the public through the kinema theatre proprietors, the latter deciding the length irrespective of the importance of the subject. Does any sane person imagine that the news-film producers would refuse to issue their budgets in longer lengths, if the proprietors would pay for them? A clear proof to the contrary is the long length subjects which are issued daily to the more important West-End theatres.

We can conceive some of our critics looking through their morning papers and exclaiming! Ah! If I were editor I would have filmed this. Now that is a news-picture. Yes, very likely it is, but how was it obtained? Taken by a local photographer at the expenditure of a few plates and half-a-dozen enlargements, from which he can recoup himself for his outlay (if it is not reproduced) by the sale of postcards. But the same photographer would think twice before filming the same subject with eighty or ninety feet of film to have same returned, 'The editor regrets'. There are not freelance kine news men wandering round the same as with presswork.

If one looks through the morning papers it will often happen that not a single picture reproduced is by their own staff men although they have been sent to cover the event. The art editor of these papers receives on an average four hundred photographs every day, and only uses about forty or fifty in his paper. Of course, those not used are not paid for; this would represent about *fifty or sixty thousand feet* of negative per week, for an average 300 feet bi-weekly.

Lester Ruah mentions the cat and canary sign-post, etc., but we do not think the news-film has been as great an offender in showing these 'events' as the illustrated press. We hope he will not forget the 'kid and flapper stunts' which are a feature of some of the papers. We have yet to see a news-film that ran to fifty or sixty feet for fifteen words; the average is about ten feet. We think Lester Ruah would find himself 'up against it' to 'tell the story' in the seven or eight words he mentions.

But there is still another aspect. The editor of a topical has not finished when he has found a story for his budget. Lester Ruah seems to think that when the editor sends off his kine operator the latter is received with open arms by the powers that be. Lester Ruah would be speedily disillusioned if he were the camera man. In eight cases out of ten he only secures his picture by dogged perseverance. To quote a case in point (one of many similar experiences) one of our operators was sent to cover the Royal Maundy ceremony at Westminster, and although he was in possession of a permit from the Abbey authorities, he was forbidden to take a picture under pain of arrest by a police inspector on duty, this in spite of having a permit, which was shown to the inspector. The camera man was not a novice but an old press-photographer with seven years Fleet Street experience before taking up kinematography. And the pictures of Prince Arthur of Connaught's wedding taken in the Mall were only obtained with the utmost difficulty by the kine news men detailed for this position.

The Kinematograph and Lantern Weekly, 9 April 1914 and 23 April 1914.

Adventures of a War Correspondent

Cherry Kearton

Cherry Kearton was a noted photographer and cinematographer of wildlife, the author of many books on this topic, who was best known for filming Theodore Roosevelt in 1910 on a big game hunting expedition in Africa. Kearton became owner of the Warwick Trading Company in 1912, and hence the producer of its newsreel Warwick Bioscope Chronicle. On the outbreak of war, Kearton established a 'supplement' to his newsreel, entitled The Whirlpool of War, and set out to join his cameramen in Belgium. Although, in common with all the other operators, he could get nowhere near the fighting, he filmed scenes of destruction and the distress of refugees in the Belgian cities. This account from his memoirs is an especially vivid and sensitive record of those times. Kearton's particular interests come through in the touching scene where he meets an African soldier, and his encounter with the animals trapped in the Antwerp zoo.

At that time I was a director and the largest shareholder in a small company called The Warwick Trading Co., which produced the first film gazette ever seen in this country. We took cinematograph films of all the principal topical events and although, of course, we could not manage the world-wide sweep of pictures that can be seen to-day in any news theatre, we managed to keep the gazette filled with items of interest.

For instance, when the King and Queen went to France shortly before the War, we arranged for Huck, the then famous airman, to carry one of our operators so that we could have pictures of the ship, taken from the air, as it crossed the Channel. First we got a picture of His Majesty inspecting the Guard of Honour at Dover. That was at twelve o'clock. Then there were views of the ship and escort in the Channel, and finally a few feet of film of the King and Queen landing at Calais. Then the aeroplane flew back to Hendon – and the film was shown at the Coliseum at half-past four the same afternoon. Even now, I believe, people marvel at the speed of the cinematographists when pictures of 'the great fight' are shown the same day: yet we were doing the same thing in 1914.

When the War came, we leapt at the chance offered to us and started a supplement to our gazette, called *The Whirlpool of War.* Of course, we had rivals, but we had experience and a readymade machinery, and I think it is beyond question that our films were the most successful – in speed of presentation as well as quality – of those which were shown to the public in the early days of the fighting, before the days of war correspondents came to an end. They were first shown at the Palace Theatre by arrangement with Sir Alfred Butt.

Of course, my own first idea when war broke out was to get into the thick of things. I heard that the Flying Corps wanted men who had had air experience and who were also good rifle-shots. That description fitted me, so I went to the recruiting-office in St Martin's Lane – only to learn that no more men were wanted. I then went on to the War Office where some optimist gave me the same reply. This seemed to me so astonishing that I promptly launched out into a prophecy of how long the War would last and how many men would eventually be needed. The officer smiled happily and bowed me out. I wonder how soon he ceased to be so sure.

But since it appeared that I wasn't wanted in the army, I returned to business and very soon I was myself taking an active part in the taking of films for *The Whirlpool of War.* I made a series of weekly trips to Belgium, making my way by car to various parts of the line and getting as close to things as I could – so close, in fact, that more than once I was in imminent risk of capture. Of course, I had to be unarmed and to remember that I was a non-combatant, so that if I had met the enemy surrender would have been my only chance. I reached the outskirts of Louvain and went into Namur just before it was captured. I worked down to Dinant and later, when all that territory was in German hands, I went out through Termonde and Alost with the idea of reaching Brussels – but, fortunately for myself, I received news when I was a few miles from the city which made me change my mind.

There were heartrending sights in Belgium in those days. One could seldom approach a town or village without meeting a long stream of refugees – young wives pushing barrows on which were piled all sorts of household possessions with one or two small children perched on top, while older children ran along clinging to their mother's skirts and the old grandmother and grandfather trudged behind, very likely pushing between them a perambulator across which a mattress would droop on either side. Some of these people had walked many miles, coming as they thought to safety and then finding, after a short night's rest, that the German advance guard had pressed quickly on, so that there was no haven of safety and they must trudge, trudge on. As I looked at their worn faces, I used to wonder in what they still found hope and to think how suddenly, how devastatingly, life had changed for them from the peaceful routine of life in small rooms behind shops or in the parlours of farms to this despairing flight. And then, from the dust-covered face of a young mother, weeping from sheer fatigue as she walked, I would glance up to the pyramid of household goods that filled the heavy barrow, and there I would see a little girl, excited with the novelty of adventure, laughing and chattering. But that was only when one of these families was still on its first day's march: after that, even the children despaired and youngsters of three or four would sit staring back down the long straight road by which they had come, with grime on their faces and fixed eyes and expressions which one hated, more than anything, to see in children.

On the day when I went to Alost, passed some thousands of these pitiable refugees and then as I came near the outskirts of the town the stream trickled out with long gaps between belated parties and finally one very old man, alone, who came uncertainly down the road, stopping twice to look behind him as if he doubted whether there was any point in trying to live.

So I came to the deserted town. I saw a mongrel dog sniffing at refuse thrown into the street outside a shop and a black and white cat very peacefully washing itself on top of a wall: and the bodies of two men and a woman, lying in the road where they had been killed by a German shell.

I hurried down the streets, making for the further outskirts because from there the sound of gunfire came and I had been told that I should find a Belgian battery at work. But I very soon found that what I was hearing was not gun-fire but bursting

Cherry Kearton

shells, for the German were shelling the tower of the town hall and several church steeples under the impression that they were being used as observation posts. And before I had been in the town for half an hour, I found that the German guns had moved nearer and shells were passing overhead in search of some further objective.

I got busy with my cinematograph camera and secured some fine pictures of shell explosions against a tower. Then I moved on, looking for fresh subjects for photography, but always with my eyes and ears alert for shells falling in the road around me. Once I came upon the body of a man lying across the pavement and something prompted me to go closer and peer down into his face ... and I started in amazement as I realized that this unknown Belgian was the exact double of myself – height, build, features and even clothes were exactly the same!

Perhaps it was that which brought me to full consciousness of the fact that if I lingered longer the chances were that in a few minutes I too should be stretching my length in the roadway. Or perhaps I could no longer stand the loneliness of that town. Never have I known anything to equal that feeling. I have been by myself in the heart of the African bush without any painful consciousness of being alone, and I have walked for hours on the Yorkshire moors without seeing or hearing a soul and have been completely happy. But in that deserted Belgian town, a great sense of loneliness came to me which was quite different from the loneliness of the moors or the bush. It came from the sight of empty houses and all the signs of abandoned homes. A broken chair outside an empty house in an empty street means not the absence of people – which may be peaceful and pleasant, but the departure of people which is cruel and sorrowful.

I had such thoughts in my mind as I turned back through those strange, silent streets – for there was a silence in them which persisted and made itself *felt* despite the crashing of the shells. And then, suddenly, I came upon a little square with a decorated bandstand in the middle of it, where doubtless young men and women had formerly held hands in the evenings and fat, elderly matrons had sat placidly listening to military bands – and there, quite startlingly, I once again found signs of life.

Drawn up beside the bandstand was a British ambulance, and two young men were going from house to house looking for casualties. The driver of the ambulance was a girl. She had taken off her khaki cap and stood unconcernedly tidying her hair while a shell burst with a great crash on the pavé in one corner of the square. In those days we weren't so accustomed to the coolness of women as we are now, and I expected her to dart into the ambulance or underneath it. Instead, she began very leisurely to stroll towards the place where the shell had dropped. Soon she picked up a ring-shaped fragment of metal, finding it still hot and passing it quickly from one hand to the other till it cooled. Then she came across the square to me and asked for a piece of string: she wanted, she said, to hang the piece of shell from her neck 'for luck'.

It was ordinary enough, that incident: but that was its charm. I had been thinking of death and deserted homes and silent streets – and then, suddenly, under the decorations of that homely bandstand I met a typical English girl, who smiled with unconcern and chatted to me rather as if we had met at a garden party. And somehow that made me realize that even war and all its horrors didn't stop all ordinary events, and that one day shells and bullets would be forgotten and that girl, older and more experienced but at heart the same, would return to some English country house and garden, while I, if the War left me unscathed, would go back to Africa and the lions and elephants and my beloved cameras. Somehow, the memory of that little incident stood me in very good stead during the next four years.

Just beyond that square, a shell burst close to me in the roadway, and I darted into a doorway, finding to my horror that what had appeared to be a deep porch ran back for no more than six inches. But I flattened myself against the wall – if a man who weighed eighteen stone can be said to flatten himself – and hoped for the best. Suddenly I felt something soft against my legs and looking down I saw a tabby cat which purred when I picked it up. And then a dog ran into the same shelter, too scared even to get excited about the cat. I carried the cat for a little after I left the doorway and the dog trotted at my heels, anxious for a friend; but I didn't see how I could keep them, so when we came to a butcher's shop I opened the door and let them both run in – surely no two animals ever enjoyed such a boundless feast.

Just outside the town, life completely swept down on me again. Here Belgian soldiers were throwing up hasty defences and cutting loopholes in cottage walls in readiness for a rearguard stand. Others were digging trenches, and now and again stopping to gnaw at unearthed turnips with every sign of ravenous hunger. I had left my car close to this clump of houses and now I was in a hurry to get into it and drive off: but a Belgian officer, who spoke very good English, asked me to lend it for bringing up ammunition. I agreed – and by so doing very nearly became involved in my first military action.

A report came in that the Germans were already through the town. The Belgian soldiers at once jumped to their loopholes while I, as a civilian, stood looking rather helplessly around, wondering what my position would be if a skirmish developed. But before I could make up my mind what to do someone pressed a rifle on me, said: 'You English? You shoot?' and pointed to a loophole in the corner of the building.

That seemed to me to decide the question. I didn't really bother any more about what would happen if I was caught in a civilian jacket with that rifle in my hands, and I knelt on the cottage floor, squinting along the rifle sights and getting an idea of ranges on likely spots. Then there was an uncomfortably tense interval, with no sign of any Germans. All, in fact, was very quiet, but I was struck by the sight of a civilian, making his way with great caution, not out of the town but towards it. He darted about in little short runs, like a man trying to keep under cover – but the odd thing was that what cover there was was always behind him and never between him and where the Germans were supposed to be. It was as if he didn't want to be seen – didn't want *us* to see him – and I grew so suspicious that if I had been more sure of my powers as a linguist I should have drawn attention to him.

Finally, I went outside just as a senior officer rode up. This man could talk English and I was just going to tell him of my suspected spy when I saw another civilian, this time mounted on a bicycle, trying to slip, in the same undemonstrative manner, past the side of the house. I said: 'That is the second man who has gone back into the town in the last few minutes', and I told my story.

It was too late then to apprehend the first man but the second was stopped: and I heard afterwards that he faced a firing party. The first apparently got through to the Germans and gave away our dispositions, for within a few minutes shells began to fall all round us with remarkable accuracy, so that we had to beat a hasty retreat. I don't suppose that retirement made any real difference to the outcome of the War; and I was certainly glad of it for it enabled me to put down that damning rifle. My time for fighting came a little later and lasted for four years: soldiering has its points, but fighting as a *franc-tireur* seemed a different matter altogether.

REFUGEES

During these months I had not been present at any serious military action although I had photographed war scenes innumerable. I had a pass which enabled me to go wherever I liked and several times Belgian officers had come to warn me that there was nothing ahead of me except the Germans. But most of my pictures had been of bursting shells and the throwing up of fortifications, together with scenes of pathos such as the exodus of refugees, the silent streets, and Cardinal Mercier weeping over his stricken cathedral at Malines.

In those first days of the War, such pictures seemed sensational enough, and my friends at home assured me that the theatres which were showing my films were continually crowded from stalls to gallery. Yet I always wanted to do more than that. I wanted pictures of a big modern battle.

My chance seemed to have come when the Germans swept forward towards Antwerp and it became clear that the Belgians, with our reinforcements, would attempt to stand there and save their city. Moreover, the presence of the British troops would put this section of the war into the forefront of British interest, so that this was clearly where I could be most usefully employed.

Getting into Antwerp was easy: indeed, I went in and out of the city several times during a fortnight. But I knew that if things went wrong to leave it finally might be another matter. But I didn't seriously bother about that. I rather thought that – being master of my own movements and able to choose my own moment for escape – I should probably be able to make my way into Holland. But that could wait till the eventuality arose. The great thing was to get into Antwerp and to contrive to be present with my camera at a modern big-scale battle.

So one day I took my car down the road from Ghent to Antwerp. Soon we overtook a long column of troops, accompanied by many armoured cars. They were our own men – the Royal Naval Division, sturdy fellows, keen for a fight, well equipped (certainly I saw no sign of strappings replaced by bits of string) and in the pink of condition. I contrived to leave my car and get a ride (together with some excellent pictures) on one of the armoured cars, just behind Colonel Wedgwood. And so, in the long convoy of my own countrymen, marching, as they thought, to the relief of Belgium, I crossed the bridge of boats over the Scheldt and entered Antwerp.

I went forward that same afternoon towards the firing-line, following our own fellows as they went hastily into action. My pass let me through and I had no difficulty in getting the photographs I wanted. But the guns were firing a bombardment and it soon became clear that further south very heavy firing was in progress. I tried to get news but no one seemed much clearer than I was as to exactly what was happening. Then I tried my luck with staff officers, but they were short with me, being apparently far too much preoccupied to consider my questions.

As the hours passed, however, I began to appreciate their pre-occupation. In a battle, news very quickly trickles into the back areas, telling the progress of the fight. It comes first with the wounded who are usually cheerful in their pain if their particular attack has succeeded, but silent if it has failed. On that day it became apparent that things were going ill. Little groups of weary 'walking wounded' limped past me, and when I asked for news they just shook their heads and limped on without an answer. Ambulances hurried by and the drivers' faces were set. Lorries were driven furiously down the road, back towards Antwerp or on towards the firing-line, and no one would stop to chat or sing out glad news in passing. An air of depression settled everywhere and it became certain that the day was lost.

The enemy shelling, too, increased and many bursts of shrapnel came near – too near – the road on which I waited. A little Cockney wagon-driver was waiting there too. What he was waiting for I don't know, and I rather suspect that he didn't know either. But that didn't matter to him. After a while I suggested that as the shelling was coming uncomfortably close we might do well to move. He answered: 'Well, my orders is to wait here, and here I wait if the whole blinking German army comes'. Fine discipline; but happily for myself I was not under orders. Besides, I had had my fill of photographing bursting shells and I wanted fresh subjects for my camera. So I moved off.

A little further down the road, in the middle of a bridge, I came upon a black soldier and addressed him in Swahili. His eyes stared and his mouth opened at that, for I don't suppose he had heard his own tongue for months. Then his face lit up with joy. He was waiting, too, and probably he knew no more why he was waiting than the Cockney had done, but he seemed very anxious that I should wait with him and converse with him in Swahili. He came from the Congo and knew Irimu, where

Adventures with Animals and Men

The exodus from Antwerp.

I had been a few months previously. 'Irimu very good', he said, 'Belgium very bad'. And as at that moment a shrapnel shell burst a few yards from us, just at the side of the road, I was definitely inclined to agree with him.

After that there seemed nothing for it but to go back to the city. And as things turned out that was my furthest advance from Antwerp towards the enemy. After that it was the enemy who advanced towards me.

There were several war correspondents in the city – Robinson of the *Times,* Fox of the *Morning Post*, Percival Phillips of the *Daily Mail,* Cleary of the *Daily Express* and many others. The representative of the *Evening News* was an Australian lady – I am sorry that I forget her name – whose pluck under shell-fire won my admiration. A month earlier she had disguised herself as a Belgian peasant and had managed to make her way into Brussels where she secured an interview with Burgomaster Max. And I think she was the last of the correspondents to leave Antwerp, for she stood in the crowd watching the German cavalry ride in.

Naturally enough the English Press representatives made a point of dining together whenever they could and of comparing notes. That evening, while several of us were at dinner, there was much discussion as to whether – and if so, when – the Germans would shell the city. The general opinion was that they would attack the forts but spare the city, but I, having seen Termonde and been very near to Louvain, was certain that Antwerp would come in for its share of destruction; and indeed, in view of what I had seen and heard on the road that day, I offered a bet that the shelling would start that very night, not later than midnight. Actually, it was at midnight exactly that the first shell, aimed at some oil-tanks and the bridge of boats, passed over the cathedral and burst near the river.

At that moment I was standing with the *Daily Mail* photographer outside my hotel, which faced the Square. I decided to walk across to the English Hotel on the other side of the cathedral and discuss matters with Cleary of the *Express,* who was staying there. Ten minutes before, that hotel must have presented the normal appearance of any hotel at midnight: a few 'late-nighters' would have been seated round the bar, others would have been in easy-chairs in the lounge discussing the affairs of the day, some people would have been in bed, many must have been in the act of undressing. But then that first shell had burst not far from the bridge of boats, dispelling all convictions that the city would remain unharmed, and immediately panic reigned. I met people rushing from their houses, half dressed: down the staircase of the hotel came a stream of people in their night clothes, some carrying strange assortments of clothes in their hands, others clutching jewel cases. The manager was darting about, stirring the scared servants into activity, assuring everyone that there was nothing to be frightened of, endeavouring to dissuade those who wanted to run out into the street and every minute dashing across the hall to show distracted people the way down the basement stairs to the cellars.

I found a young girl in the office, apparently torn between her terror of the shell and her sense of duty, which prevented her leaving. I tried to make her listen to me and at last got her to attend sufficiently to grasp that I wanted to know where Cleary could be found. Yes, she said, he was upstairs, in his room: at least he had been before this terrible thing happened. But now, who knew? Perhaps he was dead. People said that many hundreds had been killed. The city was in flames. In another minute the Uhlans would come, with their lances. They would kill everyone, everyone.

And so on. I stopped her at last. I pointed out that only one shell had fallen and that I had seen it burst across the river, harming no one. There was nothing, I said, to be frightened about. But I didn't feel sure of that.

I climbed the stairs, meeting many people coming down. As I passed along the corridors, searching for Cleary's room, I looked in at many open doorways and saw everything in disorder: clothes strewn on the floor, chairs overturned, trunks hastily ransacked for valued possessions, jewellery dropped on the floor and overlooked.

At last I found Cleary, in a small room at the back of the hotel, quietly going over a proof-slip with the editor of an Antwerp paper. It was a wonderful example of the advantage of concentrating on one's work. They hadn't even heard the bursting of the shell or the panic on the stairs. Indeed, when I told them the news they didn't believe it and when at last I persuaded them to come and see for themselves, and from the hall they heard the bursting of other shells, Cleary still persisted that the noise came from the firing of British guns.

I suggested that we should go to my hotel and hear what the other correspondents had to say. Before we had walked thirty yards, we heard the scream of a shell and saw it explode some distance down the road.

On the cathedral tower, the 'Peace Flag' presented by Carnegie was still flying in mute protest. In the cathedral itself, men were busy taking down valuable pictures and packing them for removal to safety. Across the Square came a crowd of refugees, dragging behind them great bundles of their possessions wrapped in blankets – there had been no time to pack – or pushing carts, wheelbarrows, bicycles, all laden high.

We reached my hotel and found it already deserted. The photographer from the *Daily Mail* was there – no doubt he was wishing as I did, that this scene could have happened in daylight when we could have used our cameras – and he and Cleary and I, finding that we could do nothing and having no desire as yet to join the swarm of refugees, stood in the porch of the hotel discussing the events of the day. Suddenly two British officers, who for some time had been walking to and fro past us, came up on either side and one of them seized hold of Cleary. When I tried to intervene, one of the officers said: 'This man is a spy. I don't know about you, but you were with him so I arrest you as well'. I told him not to make a fool of himself and suggested that he would do well to send for a staff officer. It was some minutes before one arrived, but I am thankful to say that when he did come he turned out to be a sensible fellow who admitted that our papers were entirely in order.

Cleary then went off to try to hunt for 'copy', but the other photographer and myself, being essentially daylight workers, did what we could to get some sleep on the floor of the porter's office, with our cameras for pillows. We did not sleep soundly. Again and again we were awakened by the crashing of shells, one of which actually hit the hotel. But if we didn't get much rest we at least passed the time till morning came – and with it the blessed daylight for our pictures.

But if we had rested it seemed that no one else had. Still the streams of refugees crossed the Square. Down every side street they came, leaving bare only one great island of paving near the side where several shells had recently fallen and turned the smooth pavé into a chaos of upturned stone and ominous-looking holes. The refugees thought – and they had only too good reason to think it – that this great square with the cathedral tower above it was a point of special danger; and in little knots they hurried across, too scared to stop if a bundle of their possessions tumbled off a cart, and shouting to each other to hurry whenever the stream threatened to become blocked by the slow progress of an ancient couple.

For some time I stood taking cinematograph pictures of this heartrending scene, and then – I suppose because of my special interest in animals – it occurred to me to go and see what was happening in the zoo: if shelling put Man into such a state of panic, how would it affect wild creatures in their cages? I went – and found scenes that to me were almost more terrible. The zoo was alongside the railway-station, and as that would naturally become a target for enemy fire it was thought that shells would fall also on the animals' cages, breaking them and setting loose panic-stricken animals to add to the horror in the city. Consequently, all the dangerous animals were being shot. Lions, tigers, leopards who had endured close captivity for years now ended their lives from bullets at close quarters. Keepers who had learned to love them came hesitatingly forward, gun in hand ... it was a horrible sight and one that I could not bear to watch.

So back I went to the even more terrible scenes of anguish in the streets. I went down to the bridge of boats across the Scheldt and found it hopelessly blocked with the swarm of refugees; a great crowd of whom was now gathered on the bank, fighting with one another to get nearer to the head of the bridge, women fainting in the crush, families becoming separated, children losing their parents, handcarts being overturned and perforce abandoned.

This sight convinced me that it would be madness to stay longer in the city. I had taken a thousand feet of film during the last twenty-four hours, and there was little more that I could do. By the next night, I felt sure, the Germans would be in possession.

I sent off my assistant early by car with the film, telling him to try to get away through St. Nicholas. I learnt afterwards that he had a narrow escape. Some German soldiers who had reached the road called on him to stop and when he accelerated by way of answer they opened fire on him. One bullet wounded an already wounded Belgian soldier to whom my assistant was giving a lift, and another smashed the lens of one of my cameras. But the car got through and the precious film was undamaged. Indeed, it was exhibited in London forty-eight hours later.

For my own part I lingered a little longer, taking photographs, and then in the late afternoon I made my way to the Scheldt. The rush there to get on to a steamboat was so great that many people fell between the side of the boat and the quay and were drowned. But many hundreds scrambled aboard, badly overloading the ship; and at last we pushed off. There were the same wild scenes at the Dutch frontier, where we had to transfer to the railway – indeed, I travelled to Flushing on the footboard, hanging on precariously with one hand on the frame of a window.

From *Adventures with Animals and Men* (London: Longmans, Green & Co., 1935).

Running the Topical Films

Anon

This informative article investigates newsreel production in the early months of 1915, as a maturing medium came to terms with working under war-time conditions. There is an excellent portrait of the operations of the editorial offices, their methods of newsgathering, the problems faced in getting the news, and the sort of stories – the visually unusual, stories produced at great speed, films of royalty – that were of most interest to them. The article notes how the newsreels sought to produce moving pictures of stories that had already been established in the illustrated papers, showing how the newsreels understood that they fell into a particular place among the news media available to the public.

In a good many respects the news film – which has nowadays become such a regular feature of all picture palace shows – is like a pictorial newspaper shorn of the greater part of its letterpress. Only, of course, the illustrations are put into motion, and consequently become far more realistic than those that appear in print.

It would, therefore, be accurate to say that the news film is the picture paper of the moving picture world; an animated record of passing events. And immediately it becomes natural that, like an ordinary picture paper, it should be edited, controlled from an office, and fed by representatives in all parts of the world.

As a matter of fact, the editing of a news film bears many points of resemblance to the editing of a daily picture paper. If you were to visit the editorial offices of *The Animated Gazette* at Messrs. Pathé Frères, or of *The Topical Budget* at the Topical Film Company (both in Wardour Street), you would find quite a number of people busily engaged in reading the day's papers with scissors in their hands. For this is one of the means by which subjects suitable for filming are found, and it results in quite a sheaf of cuttings being placed upon the editor's table for his consideration. At the same time, moreover, letters, telegrams, and telephone messages are constantly arriving from agents and employees in all parts of the world, describing events which have happened or which are about to happen.

UNDER THE EDITOR'S EAGLE EYE

The editor of a news film has to be a man with a 'nose for news', and a comprehensive mind. He has to decide, often in a few seconds, not merely whether a thing is worth doing, but whether it can or cannot be done in cinematographic form. And all day long he is considering and rejecting or accepting subjects suggested to him, and is sending expert operators off to diverse scenes of action in all corners of the kingdom.

In his room a tape machine ticks away the news of the moment, and every now and then this machine is consulted lest anything of value should have escaped attention.

Many events that have already happened are 'covered' without delay. The dropping of bombs on Southend, for example, was an outrage which naturally could not be recorded in the happening, but within a very few hours a whole tribe of cinema men were on the spot, photographing the visible signs of havoc caused by the bombardment. But the events which appeal most strongly to the editors of these news films are those which are advertised beforehand, for the simple reason that they can be photographed in the happening. Thus Lord Rosebery reviewed the Boys' Brigade the other day, in Glasgow, and within twenty-four hours the actual review was reproduced on the screens of hundreds of picture palaces. Messrs. Pathé Frères have a representative in Glasgow, and this representative informed the editor that the review was about to take place; whereupon instructions were given for it to be filmed.

THE PRESS AND THE CINEMA

All the film companies who go in for topical matters endeavour, as far as possible, to give each big town and district a pictorial turn. They know that local happenings have a tremendous appeal for local picture-palace patrons, and so, as the Editor of *Pathe's Animated Gazette* phrases it, 'they try to keep every place going, without sacrificing any of the big events for lesser ones'.

Operators are stationed in various parts of the country, the Continent, and, indeed, the world at large, in order that there may be no unnecessary delay; and, whenever possible, permits are obtained, and all sorts of fairly elaborate arrangements are made to ensure the best possible results. But with 'stop press' events an operator is sent off right away, more often than not from headquarters, and has to make the best speed he can on the journey and the best of things on his arrival.

The great aim of the editors is to have film reproductions of subjects which are illustrated in the daily papers; but many of these are not suitable from the film point of view. In some cases there is nothing to lead up to the event; in others the comparative darkness of the interior of a building defies the cinema camera, because it calls for flashlight exposures, which are utterly out of the question. The

Press photographer, moreover, has a tremendous advantage over the cinema operator, because he can use photographic plates that are considerably faster than the fastest film. And just now there are other difficulties.

THE SECRET MOVEMENTS OF THE MILITARY

'The present time', declares the Editor of *The Topical Budget*, 'is an extremely bad one for securing subjects, as to be topical they must be of a military nature, and nearly all the big military reviews are held almost in secret. Permits can, as a rule, be obtained, but the difficulty is to find out in time when and where they are being held.

'Even when you have secured the negative the trouble does not end there. The film has to be passed by the Censor. I'll give you an instance, we filmed H.M. the King and Lord Kitchener reviewing the Canadians on Salisbury Plain, but it was over seven weeks before this film was released for exhibition by the Censor. Of course, we quite appreciate that it is necessary to censor topical films, but that does not make the task of obtaining subjects any the easier. Just lately, however, the recruiting offices have realised the value of the topical film from a recruiting point of view, and therefore greater facilities have been granted'.

ROMANCE AND THE FILM

Abroad Messrs. Pathé Frères are enjoying a very great advantage in regard to military subjects. The Germans have taken so many films of the faked variety – in a vain endeavour to prove that they are most humane in their methods of warfare – that the French Government have appointed Pathé's official photographers to the French Army, so that they may help to combat our enemy's animated propaganda work. The result is that Pathé's operators are permitted to take their machines to the front, and to photograph almost when and where they please. But the films thus secured have to be submitted to the French Government for approval before any of them are published; and the work is not easy. Three of the French operators have been taken prisoners, and one has been killed.

Recently one of their men paid a professional visit to the internment camps at Groningen, Holland, and photographed the British prisoners there. The film thus secured was exhibited in various parts of the country, and the Editor of *The Animated Gazette* was promptly inundated with letters from relatives of the interned men, begging for pieces of the film. The firm actually printed thousands of feet of this film simply to give away to anxious people who had, as it were, discovered their husbands and brothers and sons and lovers on picture-palace screens.

WHEN THE LENS DIDN'T SEE THE KING SMILE

News film operators seek to rival the most famous of newspaper reporters in their ingenuity in securing films in the quickest possible time under the greatest possible difficulties, and the only adverse, circumstance that they really fear is bad weather. Many a topical film of importance has been ruined by fog or rain.

One film that should have been specially good was ruined not by rain, but by an unexpected effect of a rainy day. The King was to open a new hospital, and every film firm and illustrated paper had dispatched operators to the scene. Now, it is a very common practice for cinema operators to stuff their handkerchief in the front of their machine while they are waiting for 'copy' when it is raining, so that the lens shall not get spotted or the film spoiled.

An operator with his camera thus protected stood with the other men near the steps leading to the door of the hospital, but just as the royal party arrived he caught sight of a large flower bed in a better position, and immediately made for it. A number of wrathful officials yelled at him, but it was too late to interfere; the royal party was in sight. So the delighted operator began to 'turn', and the King, noticing him in his isolated position, very graciously bowed and smiled in the direction of his machine.

Subsequently the operator tore back to his office feeling that he had achieved a veritable triumph.

But when the film was developed it proved to have nothing whatever upon it. The operator had forgotten to remove the protecting handkerchief from the front of his camera!

HOW'S THIS FOR HUSTLE?

One often reads in the papers of the speed with which sundry topical events have been filmed and exhibited on the screen – especially the Derby; which, in addition to being a horse race, has in recent years meant a race against time for cinema men. But the following incident, related to me by the Editor of *The Topical Budget*, would take some beating.

'Two operators were sent up to Manchester to cover the November Handicap, the film being wanted for exhibition at The Palace, Shaftesbury Avenue, London, the same night. The operators arrived in Manchester to find the city enveloped in a dense fog, the result being that the race was postponed for over an hour. Instead, therefore of arriving back at Euston at 8.10 p.m., as planned, the operators arrived at 9.35 p.m. They jumped into a taxi, and arrived at the office at 9.40. Yet the negative was developed, dried, printed, and the film was delivered to The Palace at 10.25 p.m. – which allowed only forty minutes for the complete production'.

A LUCKY ACCIDENT – FOR THE OPERATOR

The editor has also given me an interest account of how an operator secured an a accident from start to finish.

The man was doing 'manoeuvre stuff' near Marlow in 1913, and in the village of

Medmenham he was told by the military police that heavy artillery was being brought over a pontoon bridge which had been thrown across the Thames.

He went down to the river and secured a pointy of vantage on the top of a house-boat. But the sky clouded over, and it started to rain very hard, so the operator decided that he would take the first thing that came over the bridge and then clear off.

The first troops to cross the bridge were the telegraph section of the Royal Engineers, and operator began to film their movements. They were about half-way across when one of the leading horses slipped on the wet wood, reared, and fell over into the river, dragging the other horses with him, as well as the wagon. The result was that the bridge was broken in halves, two horses were drowned, and several of the Royal Engineers had very narrow escapes of being drowned and of being kicked by the horses struggling in the water.

The whole film was secured by sheer luck!

Cassell's The Saturday Journal, 29 May 1915.

'The Supreme Moment of the War': General Allenby's entry into Jerusalem

Luke McKernan

Between May 1917 and February 1919 the British War Office took over one of the commercial newsreels, Topical Budget, as an outlet for Official propaganda film. It was issued first as the War Office Official Topical Budget, then later as Pictorial News (Official), when it came under the control of the new Ministry of Information. This essay considers the production and reception of the newsreel's most successful film, GENERAL ALLENBY'S ENTRY INTO JERUSALEM, and some of the problems of identification and authenticity raised by the multiple versions of the film that exist. The essay has been revised from its original 1993 publication to incorporate new information.

> If the cinema should win a place in the school it can gain much from the commercial cinema. Out of the Topical Budgets the films of some historical events are worth preserving, and teachers of history should be able to make good use of a National Film Library such as is, I believe, already in existence. Historic events like the founding of the Roman Empire and the Commonwealth of Australia would probably be filmed nowadays. Captain Scott's expedition and General Allenby's Entry into Jerusalem have left lasting impressions on my mind.[1]

The above statement, from a schoolteacher writing in 1931 for a report on the influence of the cinema on the teaching of history, records the impression made on one reluctant cinema-goer of one of the most celebrated and successful films of the First World War. I have encountered other such witnesses who, whatever else had passed before their eyes and been forgotten, remembered GENERAL ALLENBY'S ENTRY INTO JERUSALEM. This film, which exists today in several versions, came at a crucial point in both the war and the British campaign for filmed propaganda: a signal victory in each instance.

The aura surrounding Lawrence of Arabia has drawn attention away from the true desert hero of the day, General Edmund Allenby. Previously Commander of the Third Army in France, Allenby took over from the ineffectual Lieutenant-General Sir Archibald Murray to lead the Egyptian Expeditionary Force in June 1917.

Pugnacious, intelligent, considerate beneath a bluff exterior, and with a deep under-standing of war and soldiery, Allenby transformed the enfeebled desert campaign virtually overnight. Some inspired use of cavalry, mobile forces and general tactical manoeuvring in a succession of decisive battles against the Turks, led to a key victory at Gaza in November 1917. With considerable tactical resource and military panache Allenby was able to achieve Lloyd George's aim of 'Jerusalem by Christmas'.

On 9 December 1917, Jerusalem fell to the Egyptian Expeditionary Force. The Turks having retreated over night, the Mayor of Jerusalem struggled for some time to find someone to whom he could surrender. First encountering Privates H.E. Church and R.W.J. Andrew, two mess cooks who had blundered their way into the city in search of water in the early hours of the morning (who declined the honour), he surrendered unofficially to Sergeants F.G. Hurcomb and J. Sedgewick of the 2/29th London Regiment just before 9.00 am. However, they refused to accept the keys to the city or the formal letter of surrender. There then followed a near-farcical sequence up the chain of command, leaving the hapless mayor in a state of some desperation. Eventually Lieutenant-General Sir Philip Chetwode was contacted, and he sent Major-General J.S.M. Shea to accept the surrender on Allenby's behalf. The surrender was accepted at 11.00 am, ending 400 years of occupation by the Ottoman empire.[2]

It was an act with considerable symbolic resonance, apart from being a rare clear victory at a low point in the Allied war effort. It was chiefly the triumph of Christianity over the infidel, and the press were quick to refer to it as a new cru-sade, much to Allenby's discomfort.[3] The sense of a Christian victory was rein-forced by the closeness of Christmas. The British Official History of the war states:

> The capture of Jerusalem followed upon the Italian reverse at Caporetto, the collapse of Russia, the elimination of Rumania from the war, and the German counter-offensive at Cambrai. Coming at such a black moment, it had a heartening moral effect. The circumstances in which it was achieved, while incidents such as the bombardment of Rheims Cathedral and the destruction of the University of Louvain were still bitterly remembered, did high honour to British arms.[4]

Not a building in Jerusalem had been damaged by the fighting. Church bells rang out across the world. 'It was, after years of wretchedness and misery, an event which captured and held the imagination of the world. Allenby's name was on everyone's lips, as no other General's had been during the war', states Brian Gardner.[5] Allenby's good fortune even included the weather. It had poured with rain for days before Jerusalem was captured, but his entry into the city was to take place in bright sunlight – it would film very well.

Allenby was well aware of the significance of his conquest and the effect it would have locally and world-wide. It had been discovered that an Arab prophecy existed which stated that the Turks would be driven from Jerusalem only 'when a prophet of the Lord brought the waters of the Nile to Palestine', and Murray had already had a pipeline laid that reached to the boundaries of Palestine, the further construction of which was encouraged by Allenby. It was also noted that Allenby's name in Arabic could be read as '*Allah en nebi*', the prophet of the Lord.[6] His entry into Jerusalem was therefore stage-managed with consideration for the inhabitants of Jerusalem as well as propaganda. A crucial part of this latter plan, probably not realised at the time, was the adequate filming of the event.

In place at the entry into Jerusalem were two cameramen working for the War Office Cinematograph Committee (WOCC). The main operator was Harold Jeapes, British official cameraman in Egypt and Palestine. The identity of the second is not certain, but he is most likely to have been George Westmoreland, the British official stills photographer in Egypt and Palestine, who regularly accompanied Jeapes and took the still photographs of the event.[7] Their footage ended up in the British government's own newsreel, the *War Office Official Topical Budget*. In May 1917 the WOCC, which had been organising a programme of filmed propaganda since November 1915, decided to move away from the feature and medium length films it has been producing, largely on account of falling sales. A newsreel had been suggested by several people and the French had recently started up their own official newsreel, *Annales de la Guerre*. Thus the WOCC approached one of the four British newsreels then in existence, *Topical Budget*, with a view to using the newsreel as a vehicle for the material being shot by the various official cameramen. This coincided with an expansion of the numbers of these cameramen, including Harold Jeapes, brother of William Jeapes, the owner of *Topical Budget*, who was sent out to Egypt on 16 May 1917, shortly before Allenby himself was sent there. Knowing nothing of the newsreel business, the WOCC agreed with William Jeapes to allow him to continue to run *Topical Budget* as before, only now with exclusive access to official film of the war. The name of the newsreel became *Topical Budget: Official War News Film*, subsequently *War Office Official Topical Budget*. The first issue came out 30 May 1917.

However, it was soon discovered that there was more to running a successful newsreel than supplying it with exclusive film (no WOCC film was ever released to the other British newsreels). At the very time Allenby was advancing towards Jerusalem, the official newsreel was in crisis, with static sales and running battles between William Jeapes and the WOCC. Lord Beaverbrook, head of the WOCC, stepped in and bought up the Topical Film Company (producers of *Topical Budget*), marginalising William Jeapes and evolving a new company structure under the purposeful editorial control of Captain W. Holt-White. A marked turnaround in the newsreel's fortunes soon occurred. There was greater co-operation from the authorities, film was shot with the short time-span of a newsreel item in mind, a healthy balance between home and war front footage was secured, and intertitles were being increasingly used for comment as well as description. Within a short period sales had doubled and the *War Office Official Topical Budget* was now posing a threat to the market leader, *Pathe's Animated Gazette*. This success was marked by a change of name and crowned by the newsreel's most successful film when GENERAL ALLENBY'S ENTRY INTO JERUSALEM came to be released, 23 February 1918, issue 339–2 of the new *Pictorial News (Official)*.[8]

Allenby entered Jerusalem at noon on 11 December 1917. When the Kaiser had visited the city in 1898, part of the wall next to the Jaffa Gate had been knocked down so that he could enter by carriage. Allenby elected to enter the city on foot, leaving horses outside. No Allied flags were flown throughout the entire proceedings. Troops had occupied the suburbs of the city, but none went within the city walls before the official entry. Coming through the Jaffa Gate, Allenby headed a procession which included the commanders of the French and Italian contingents, Colonel P. de Piépape and Lieutenant-Colonel F. d'Agostio, the French diplomat François George-Picot (co-designer of the notorious 1916 Sykes-Picot agreement which sought to divide the Middle East between Britain and France), Commandants R. de Saint-Quentin and Caccia (French and Italian military attachés), and a select group of British officers, among them T.E. Lawrence.[9] They were followed by men of the 60th London Division. A proclamation was then read from the steps of the citadel, with a text supplied by the British government to be read in English, Arabic, Hebrew, French, Italian, Greek and Russian. Allenby later commented on the local reaction that 'great enthusiasm – real or feigned – was shown'. The cleverly-worded proclamation was as follows:

> To the inhabitants of Jerusalem the Blessed and the people dwelling in its vicinity.
>
> The defeat inflicted on the Turks by the troops under my command has resulted in the occupation of your city by my forces. I therefore here and now proclaim it to be under martial law, under which form of administration it will remain so long as military considerations make it necessary.
>
> However, lest any of you be alarmed by reason of your experience at the hands of the enemy who has retired, I hereby inform you that it is my desire that every person should pursue his lawful business without fear of interruption. Furthermore, since your city is regarded with affection by the adherents of three of the great religions of mankind, and its soil has been consecrated by the prayers and pilgrimages of multitudes of devout people of these three religions for many centuries, therefore I make it known to you that every sacred building, monument, Holy spot, shrine, traditional site, endow-

Photograph courtesy of the Imperial War Museum, London

General Allenby entering Jerusalem, 11 December 1917 (from IWM 13).

ment, pious bequest or customary place of prayer of whatsoever form of the three religions will be maintained and protected according to the existing customs and beliefs of those to whose faiths they are sacred.

Allenby then received various notables of the city and the heads of churches before leaving on foot as he had come. In the words of T.E. Lawrence, writing later in *Seven Pillars of Wisdom*, it was 'the supreme moment of the war'.[10]

Jeapes and Westmoreland (assuming that he was the second cameraman) were assigned to take both photographs and film. Jeapes had been accompanying Allenby since June 1917 and regularly supplying material to the *War Office Official Topical Budget*, while Westmoreland had been the Official stills photographer in the region since December 1916. From the evidence of the films and photographs they stood side by side for the march, while Westmoreland was positioned to the side and Jeapes directly above for the reading of the proclamation. The importance of the occasion led to the choice of two cameramen, but Jeapes was pre-eminent and took the bulk of the film material.

The film was sent to Cairo for processing and then on to the WOCC in London.

It would probably have been ready for exhibition in early January, but the decision was made to wait. One can only speculate why this was so, since it would seem most probable that they would release it while the news was fresh, but there are three likely explanations. Firstly, there was the opportunity to build up considerable interest in the film through trailer advertisements in the trade press (the film was promoted for many weeks before the release date of 23 February 1918). Secondly, they could exploit further Christian associations with the approach of Easter; the parallels with Christ's own humble entry into Jerusalem were there, and Palm Sunday would be on 1 April. Thirdly, the various battles that had taken place to unify the British propaganda campaign were to be resolved by the creation of the Ministry of Information (MOI) under Lord Beaverbrook in February 1918. The official newsreel, now a growing success, came under the control of the MOI, a change to be marked by the new name, *Pictorial News (Official)*, and the release of GENERAL ALLENBY'S ENTRY INTO JERUSALEM as the first film under the new title and regime.

The film was initially released in Britain as issue 339–2 of the official newsreel, being around 300 feet long (five minutes at eighteen frames per second), the standard length for a complete newsreel. Although the *War Office Official Topical Budget* had at this time only a limited distribution overseas (around four copies were being sent on a regular basis to a number of Allied and neutral countries), it was decided to produce an extended version, just under three times the length of the newsreel version. It was this version that had the greatest impact both in Britain and world-wide. Reports in Foreign Office files from British embassies for this period record the mixed reception allotted to the programmes of British official films that were sent to them, but GENERAL ALLENBY'S ENTRY INTO JERUSALEM seems to have been popular wherever it was shown. At Salonika a copy was shown with great success to the Grand Rabbi and Jewish community, with the intertitles in classical Hebrew being much appreciated. Among a programme of official films shown at fifty-one locations in China and Hong Kong it was the one film that roused genuine enthusiasm.[11] Scenes on the British home front did not appeal, the fighting was deemed disappointing, but anyone could appreciate the simple symbolism of the march on foot and the proclamation respecting individual beliefs. The basic film material was used and re-used in a variety of forms to the end of the war, and in compilations of War Office film thereafter.

GENERAL ALLENBY'S ENTRY INTO JERUSALEM therefore existed – and exists – in several versions, but essentially there is the newsreel version and the extended version. This latter film is best known through the copy held in the Imperial War Museum (IWM), numbered IWM 13. This copy, however, is problematic, as I hope to show, with reference to the newsreel version and an incomplete copy of the extended version with quite different intertitles which recently came to light at the National Film and Television Archive (NFTVA). From these I wish to suggest a reconstruction of the original, or rather to indicate the problems involved in positing such an original.

The short newsreel version itself is straightforward:

GENERAL ALLENBY'S ENTRY INTO JERUSALEM
Before the ceremony. The Commander-in-Chief conversing with Commanders of Allied detachments and attachés. Allenby talking to Piépape. Group of British officers and others outside the Jaffa Gate, with Allenby in foreground talking to various people (T.E. Lawrence in background). *General Sir Edmund Allenby, Commander-in-Chief E.E.F., entering the Holy City, accompanied by Allied Commanders and military attachés.* Allenby marches past at the head of a column of officers and men. *Reading Sir Edmund Allenby's proclamation.* High angle side-on view looking down at a crowded square and the proclamation being read. View looking directly down at scene, followed by side-on view again. *Reception of religious and civic dignitaries.* Various people being presented to Allenby in an open square, Piépape and d'Agostio beside him. *After leaving the Holy City the Commander-in-Chief mounted his horse outside Jaffa Gate and rode away through the streets of the suburbs.* Allenby and his party riding away from the gate. *In the streets after the ceremony.* Pan shot of a street thronged with people, including some British troops (318 feet).[12]

This is a description of a copy in the NFTVA. It contains the two key sequences, the march on foot and the reading of the proclamation, presented in a simple form designed for a British audience well acquainted with the story. It is in form and substance very much a *news* item – an actuality item of current interest for a specific audience – albeit somewhat longer than the average newsreel story.

The extended version uses the same basic film material but addresses itself to a wider audience. It is best known through the copy in the IWM:

GENERAL ALLENBY'S ENTRY INTO JERUSALEM
JERUSALEM 11th December 1917. Crowds in Jerusalem street. Camera pans from left to right, then tilts up for view along crowded street. Locals sitting by clock tower. Camera tilts upwards. *Commander-in-Chief received at the Jaffa Gate by the British Military Governor of Jerusalem.* View down street showing clock tower as troops march down it on either side. Close shot of waiting British troops, with locals sitting on roof. *General Sir Edmund Allenby, Commander-in-Chief, E.E.F, enterting* [sic] *the Holy City accompanied by the Allied Commanders and military attachés.* Allenby walking at the head of a column of officers, followed by a column of troops. *Before the ceremony. The Commander-in-Chief conversing with commanders of allied detachments and*

attachés. Allenby in conversation with Piépape, then talking to others and shaking hands with people. T.E. Lawrence visible in background. Allenby standing alone in the middle of a street lined with troops. Some men approach on horseback, then dismount. Allenby walks away from the camera to greet an officer. *Reading Sir Edmund Allenby's proclamation.* Side-on view at a group of officers, including Allenby, standing on a raised platform in front of a crowd fronted by a curved line of troops. A monk reads from the proclamation. View directly down at the scene, camera panning slowly left to monk reading. *Reception of the religious and civil dignitaries.* Medium close shot of Allenby shaking hands and talking to a succession of local dignitaries and religious leaders. Further shot of this from angle to the right. *Representative detachments marching through the streets.* Rear view of Indian and Italian troops marching down street. Cavalry ride past camera outside the Jaffa gate. Allenby talking to officers to right hand side of picture. Crowds milling over same scene, Allenby and officers still talking. Troops march through crowds. *The streets after the ceremony.* Group of children stare at the camera, and locals pass by in background. A horse and open carriage go past. British troops with horse wagons pass through archway. View of crowded street with people walking towards the camera. Rear view of this. *The departure of the Commander-in-Chief from the Holy City* [new title] *He and his escort mount their horses outside Jaffa gate and ride forth to lead the Army in further pursuit of the enemy.* Face-on view of Allenby and officers on horseback. They ride away from the Jaffa gate (724 feet).[13]

The appearance of this copy raises a number of questions. First, three different styles of intertitling are employed. After the main title, which is the same as the newsreel version, the opening intertitles are in white type on a plain black background; the succeeding titles are then white on a plain black background but in a slightly different type, but the last two titles feature the white type, black background with white border that characterises WOCC films of this period. Only these last two and the main title appear genuine. Surely only one style of intertitling would have been employed originally?

There are several scenes which are additional to the newsreel version: the clock tower, the waiting British troops, Allenby in a street greeting officers on horseback, extra shots of the religious and civic dignitaries, the representative detachments and following shots, and the street scenes at the end. But there are clear differences in the ordering of scenes. The street scenes that close the newsreel version are at the beginning here. The intertitle stating that Allenby meets the Military Governor of Jerusalem is followed by no such scene – might this be the scene where he is standing alone in the street instead? The title beginning *Before the ceremony* in the newsreel version precedes both march and proclamation; here it comes after the march. There are only two shots of the reading of the proclamation; in the newsreel version there are four. Assuming that the newsreel version is genuine (the original copy is on 1918 stock and there are no anomalies with the titles), then how did this copy get to be this way, and how accurate is it?

When the IWM acquired the original WOCC/MOI material in the 1920s, the decision was made in most instances to preserve the pictures only, for reasons of cost. Interest in the films at this period was in any case purely for their documentary worth, not as complete texts in their own right. Thus the original preservation copy, made in 1931, lacked intertitles. Dupes of these were only spliced in from the original negative material in 1963. This is now the viewing copy known as IWM 13. Records from the 1920s at the IWM indicate that the order of events in the film now is as they were when the film was first acquired. However, the IWM's shotsheet, which should be a record of the intertitles that matched these pictures, does not match them at all:

GENERAL ALLENBY'S ENTRY INTO JERUSALEM
The Commander in Chief is received at the Jaffa Gate by the British Military Governor of Jerusalem ... Reception of the religious and civil dignitaries ... Entering by the Jaffa Gate ... 'When the Nile flows into Palestine the Prophet (Al Nebi) from the west shall drive the Turks from Jerusalem' (Arab Prophecy) ... A proclamation by the C in C was read guaranteeing religious freedom to all. Representative detachments march through the streets of Jerusalem ... Allenby entering Jerusalem ... In the City itself the populace filled the streets. Expressions of joy that the city had been delivered from the Turks were evident on every side ... Two days later on December 11th Lord Allenby and representatives of the United States, France, Italy and the Allies made their formal entry into Jerusalem through the Historic Jaffa Gate ...

Although clearly out of order, with one or two probably the recorder's description of the action rather than the intertitles, this at first sight seems genuine, particularly the reference to the prophecy, even if it does not equate with IWM 13's titles, nor those on any other existing version of the film. But the last title at least was certainly written after the war, as Allenby was only created a viscount in 1919. This title has the feel of historical perspective anyway, and there was no representative of the United States who took part in the march. We therefore have IWM 13 with seemingly only two genuine titles, the rest deriving from some unknown source, and the shotsheet, which is either a draft text or record of a lost copy of a version of the film issued by the WOCC after the war.

All of these questions and confusion are brought into focus by another copy of the film which came to surface recently at the NFTVA. On 1918 stock, although incomplete and out of order, the intertitles are numbered sequentially. This of itself

Harold Jeapes filming General Allenby's proclamation.

would suggest a genuine original, but titles 6, 7 and 8 are in a slightly smaller type. One has to admit that there is no particular reason why all the intertitles in any one copy should be in an identical style, given the sometimes lax standards of actuality film-makers of the period, and to be looking for such consistency may be imposing anachronistic ideas of neatness and order. The pictures themselves are substantially the same, so the following description is of the intertitles only, put in their correct order:

GENERAL ALLENBY'S ENTRY INTO JERUSALEM
[Main title and opening two titles missing] … *Detachments of the Army passing through the outlying districts of Jerusalem … Crowds and Troops line the Route of Entry … The Commander-in-Chief is received at Jaffa Gate by the British Military Governor of Jerusalem … Leaving their horses outside the gates. General Sir EDMUND ALLENBY, Commander-in-Chief British Expeditionary Force, and Staff* <u>*Entering the Holy City on Foot*</u>*, accompanied by Allied Commanders and Military Attachés … Reading Sir Edmund Allenby's Proclamation, which is translated into different languages by interpreters. 'Lest any of you should be alarmed by reason of your experience at the hands of the*

enemy who has retired, I hereby inform you that it is my desire that every person should pursue his lawful business without fear of interruption' ... Receiving Representatives of the various Religious Sects and Civic Dignitaries. 'Every sacred building, monument, holy spot, shrine, traditional site, endowment, pious bequest, or customary place of prayer, will be maintained and protected according to the existing customs and beliefs of those to whose faiths they are sacred' (General Allenby's Proclamation) ... The British Commander-in-Chief, General Sir Edmund Allenby, conversing with Commanders of Allied detachments and attachés... The Departure of the Commander-in-Chief from the Holy City. He and his Escort mount their horses outside Jaffa Gate and ride forth to lead the Army in further pursuit of the Turk ... (720 feet).[14]

This is clearly better, with the intertitles in their numbered order matching the appropriate images. It moreover makes the most sense for at least part of the proclamation to be included in the intertitles, as it is on record that contemporary audiences were able to read it thus. Another characteristic touch is the underlining of *Entering the Holy City on Foot*, a literal expression of the metaphor. The wording is very close to that of IWM 13; the two WOCC-style titles in IWM 13 are exact matches. The title where Allenby converses with Allied commanders occurs at the start of the presumably genuine short version, but towards the end here, though it is clearly a scene taking place outside the Jaffa gate before the ceremonies. But a genuine version is not necessarily a chronological one, and obviously a number of the problems to do with this film come from the WOCC and MOI themselves manipulating the material in various ways. The proclamation sequence alone in the short newsreel version shows this: the first shot (side-on view) shows an officer reading the proclamation, the second (looking directly down) shows a monk reading, then there is a jump-cut to an officer reading, then a brief jump-cut to another officer saluting Allenby who prepares to leave, then the side-on view returns and it is the monk reading again. The only certain guide for the extended version here is the number sequence given on each of the intertitles.

It would be useful to set down the actual sequence of events on 11 December 1917. According to the Official History, guards representative of the troops in Palestine were drawn up outside the Jaffa Gate; Allenby was driven to Jerusalem, then entered the city on foot; at the Gate he was greeted by the military governor, Brigadier W.M. Borton, who conducted him to the steps of the Citadel, where he met some of the notables of the city; guards then formed up facing the steps and the proclamation was read out; the chief inhabitants of the city were then presented to Allenby, before he passed out through the Jaffa Gate once more.[15] It is not obvious from this account whether Allenby met the military governor before or after entering the city, and he appears to have met the city notables twice, but clearly the short newsreel version is correctly ordered. IWM 13 is equally clearly not in the right order, always assuming that this version was originally presented in chronological order. The title starting *Before the ceremony* suggests a confusion between the march and the proclamation; the officers are standing outside the Gate. But the NFTVA version, with numbered intertitles, is also seemingly wrong: as pointed out above, Allenby is seen conversing with his officers after the ceremonies. How can one say with any confidence what the true, 'original' version was like? It does appear that those editing the film in the first place were equally confused as to the true order of events, or were not overly concerned with chronology. It further appears that in going back to the original camera negatives for a new version of the film, the producers unwittingly reselected scenes with small variations each time.[16]

Any copy of any film has a history of its own, beyond the plain pictorial information it has its own special integrity. Original or duplicate, uncut, as released, re-edited, re-ordered, intercut with a different film, incomplete, damaged, lost: all have a story to tell. The history of a film's production is important; but so is the history of its distribution, exhibition and subsequent ownership. The various versions of GENERAL ALLENBY'S ENTRY INTO JERUSALEM bear witness to this. The newsreel version came to the NFTVA from a private source in 1973, the extended version came from the Norman's Film Library (a stock-shot company active in the 1930s and 1940s). The NFTVA also holds a 16 mm copy of the IWM 13 version, donated in the 1950s by Shell, still bearing the IWM opening title. IWM 13 itself was constructed over a period of years from material donated by the War Office; the full story of this copy's provenance may now be lost. Other versions of the film seem to derive from the WOCC, which existed in some form for a period after the war, continuing to make use of its holdings. One may perhaps point a finger at Sir William Jury, a major film distributor and both a member of the WOCC and Director of Cinematography at the MOI. Presumably there are copies in existence somewhere bearing foreign intertitles. It would be fascinating to know how they were translated, and by whom. The two main NFTVA copies are relatively uncomplicated, although I do not know why the long version is out of order or what the missing two titles were. But IWM 13 is a record not only of General Allenby's entry into Jerusalem but of eighty years of changing film archiving philosophy.

GENERAL ALLENBY'S ENTRY INTO JERUSALEM was shown across the world, with appropriate intertitling for each language, the constants throughout being the march on foot and the reading of the proclamation, with some of the words of that proclamation given as intertitles. The film's worldwide success can be put down to a number of basic factors. Firstly, the length of the film. At silent speed the long version would have lasted thirteen minutes. This is long enough to stand out from normal news footage, yet shorter than the other prestigious titles which the WOCC/MOI produced and continued to exhibit in programmes of film of which GENERAL ALLENBY'S ENTRY INTO JERUSALEM was a part. Few actuality films were made at this intermediate length, and one may guess that this length was enough to make the subject stand out, without making it wearisome or burying it within other material.

Secondly, there is the symbolism. There is no evidence that I have traced to suggest that the march was designed for the cameras, or that Allenby knew anything of film other than that Harold Jeapes was assigned to follow him. Yet there could hardly have been devised a better image for the cinema than the march on foot. The message is unmistakeable: humility with authority, respect for others with absolute conquest. What was designed for the people of Jerusalem, when suitably explained, made its mark on the world. The reading of the proclamation had less of a visual impact, but the message in the intertitles was powerful. Not only was it in individual people's languages, but it spoke specifically to them. Allenby had the gift of tongues. Ironically, the film is actually composed of two of the stalest newsreel formulae of the war: the march past and the voiceless speech. Here they are revitalised. Both the extended version of the film and the newsreel version are newsfilms. However, while one addressed the British audience, the second addressed the world – an actuality item of current interest for the whole wartime audience. The success of the title helped make the film memorable even after the war. Effective newsfilm depends on such memorable moments: the single image, action or phrase that expresses the story and its significance. One of the most eloquent gestures of the war became one of its most eloquent films.[17]

Historical Journal of Film, Radio and Television, vol. 13, no. 2, 1993 [revised].

NOTES

1. Frances Consitt, *The Value of Films in History Teaching* (London: G. Bell and Sons, 1931), pp. 286–287. The National Film Library, later the National Film Archive, and now the National Film and Television Archive, came into existence in 1935.
2. Details of Allenby's military campaign and the capture of Jerusalem taken chiefly from David L. Bullock, *Allenby's War: The Palestine-Arabian Campaigns, 1916–1918* (London: Blandford, 1988) and Brian Gardner, *Allenby* (London: Cassell, 1965).
3. Films of the period reinforcing this message include THE NEW CRUSADERS – WITH THE BRITISH FORCES IN PALESTINE (1918, IWM 17) and WITH THE CRUSADERS IN THE HOLY LAND – ALLENBY THE CONQUEROR (1918, held by the NFTVA). Allenby was annoyed by the Crusade references and was quick to point out that there were a number of Muslims among the troops under his command.
4. Cyril Falls, *Military Operations: Egypt & Palestine: From June 1917 to the End of the War: Part 1* (London, 1930), p. 264.
5. Gardner, *Allenby*, p. 160.
6. A.P. Wavell, *Allenby: Soldier and Statesman* (London: G.G. Harrap, 1946), p. 170.

7. Ministry of Information papers, Box Three, War Office, IWM Files no. 20, George Westmoreland personal file. There is nothing in Westmoreland's file to say that he ever operated a cine camera, but he is the most likely candidate. The Imperial War Museum catalogue has traditionally credited the Australian Frank Hurley as being Harold Jeapes' co-cameraman, but Hurley's diaries (held in the National Library of Australia) reveal that he was in Malta the day Allenby entered Jerusalem. On Westmoreland's stills photography, see Jane Carmichael, *First World War Photographers* (London/New York: Routledge, 1989), pp. 82–86.

8. Luke McKernan, *Topical Budget: The Great British News Film* (London: British Film Institute, 1992), pp. 35–48.

9. Lieutenant R.H. Andrew, Brigadier W.H. Bartholomew, Major-General Louis Jean Bols, Lieutenant-General Sir Philip Chetwode, Brigadier Gilbert Clayton, Lieutenant-Colonel Lord Alan Dalmeny, Brigadier Guy Payan Dawnay, Lieutenant-Colonel W.H. Deedes, Captain W.L. Naper, Lieutenant-Colonel A.P. Wavell and Major T.E. Lawrence, who was lent a uniform for the occasion and acted as Clayton's staff officer. The glimpses of T.E. Lawrence in GENERAL ALLENBY'S ENTRY INTO JERUSALEM have given the film an unexpected further value. Lawrence had recently returned from a raid on the Yarmuk bridge (and the notorious incident at Deraa) and was reporting to Allenby when Jerusalem fell. Borrowing from various people the necessary parts for a uniform, he took part in the march, and was in attendance at the reading of the proclamation. He is readily visible in both short and long versions of the film, among a group of officers standing near Allenby and taking part in the march. For the former sequence the cameraman seems to know more than he was aware of, as he pans left to keep Allenby in frame, only to settle on the diminutive figure of Lawrence in the background, who stares briefly at the camera, the people around him conveniently parting at just that moment.

10. T.E. Lawrence, *Seven Pillars of Wisdom: a triumph* (London: Jonathan Cape,1935), p. 462. Details of Allenby's entry into Jerusalem taken chiefly from Falls, Bullock and Gardner. The person who devised the whole ceremony, from the contrast with the Kaiser's mounted entry to an eye for such details as the posting of Indian Muslim guards at the 'Dome of the Rock' mosque, was British diplomat Sir Mark Sykes, the other half of the Sykes-Picot agreement.

11. Public Record Office FO 395/233 file 113861, FO 395/233 file 121197 and FO 395/269 file 003893. In America the film was included within a compilation of MOI Palestine-Egyptian released in August 1918 as a serial under the title BRITAIN'S FAR-FLUNG BATTLE LINE. Craig W. Campbell, *Reel America and World War I: A Comprehensive Filmography and History of Motion Pictures in the United States, 1914–1920* (Jefferson, NC/London: McFarland, 1985), pp. 91, 236.

12. This description, and those that follow, come from catalogue records for the film now recorded on the British Universities Newsreel Database (www.bufvc.ac.uk/newsreels). Titles on the films are given in italics.

13. IWM 13 concludes with a short sequence showing the Duke of Connaught presenting Allenby with the GCMG in March 1918. Obviously added on later, it has not been included in this description. Other versions of the film also included such later scenes – see note 16 below.

14. Each of the individual intertitles is numbered and are currently ordered 7, 8, 9, 10, 11, 3, 4, 5, 6. Given that the opening two titles and accompanying footage are missing, one may guess at an original length of just over 800 feet. There is one short sequence not in IWM 13: before Allenby meets the civic dignitaries, there is a shot of Jewish and Arab figures by a wall, with a group of British officers to their left.

15. Falls, *Military Operations: Egypt & Palestine*, pp. 259–261.

16. Another version of the film in the NFTVA is WITH THE CRUSADERS IN THE HOLY LAND – ALLENBY THE CONQUEROR (1918). Half of this is the same footage as IWM 13, the latter half footage of Allenby from 1918, but the proclamation sequence shows Allenby leaving the steps of the Citadel, a shot not in any other version.

17. The Jeapes-Westmoreland film was not the only one taken of the events on 11 December 1917. Pioneer of Israeli cinema Yaacov Ben Dov also took film on that day, though what he filmed is uncertain. Hillel Tryster, *Israel Before Israel: Silent Cinema in the Holy Land* (Jerusalem: Steven Spielberg Jewish Film Archive, 1995), pp. 30, 211.

'Chez Pathé': The Story of a 'Gazette' in the Making

Arthur Pereira

This article describes in some detail the day-to-day operations of the Pathe Gazette laboratories in the 1920s, showing the care and attention to detail that went alongside the inevitable need for speed that dominated the production of the newsreel.

There occurs twice weekly a veritable eruption of bright new tins of film which pour out from the Pathe building into Wardour Street and flow thence, on and on, until the final trickle stops incredibly far away – in China, maybe, or the further side of the Andes.

I have seen the 'Gazette' in a primitive theatre on the Sikkim border, where the cheaper seats were thronged with Gurkha hill people and the 'stalls' contained a sprinkling of tired-looking white men and their wives, watching with homesick eyes the happy revels, of their kin at home.

It has brought the world's doings to me in a mud-walled Arab town far up the Niger, where the French Engineer of the local wireless post eked out his salary with a weekly show of ancient and rainy films brought the last ninety miles from railhead in a transport wagon through lion-haunted bush, and shown in the open air upon a whitewashed wall. Though merely a news item to the picturegoer in town, to the exile who reads every scrap of a home newspaper, even to the advertisements, the advent of a fresh 'Gazette' film, months old though it may prove to be, at the wretched native kinema is an Occasion, and a fruitful topic in the club for days to follow.

But we are getting too far away from the office in which M. Touzé, the laboratory director, is waiting to receive us and hand us over to his second in command for a personally conducted tour behind the scenes of the Pathe organisation.

TITLING

We are first introduced to the titling-room where Pathe camera mechanisms are supported over small, brilliantly lit chambers, each furnished at its base with a sliding carrier which can be withdrawn to insert a title card, and, on replacement, slips into register with a 'click', bringing the wording into perfect alignment with the camera-gate above.

Before passing on to the printing machines however, there is a most important ceremony to be gone through – the grading of the negative: that is to say, the marking of each scene with the exact strength of light that will give on development the most perfect picture for exhibition; and the little grading machine, the work, I understand, of M. Touzé, is as ingenious as it is original.

THE GRADING MECHANISMS

The lights of the Pathe 'automatics' are capable of being dimmed down by exact resistances into twenty-one different degrees of brilliancy, according to the colour or density of the negative to be printed from, and the grading machine proceeds to make a specimen print only a few inches long, from each scene in the film, each specimen showing, by successive pictures, all differing slightly, the exact effect of printing the scene with every one in turn of the twenty-one light-strengths referred to.

It is then a comparatively easy task for the grader, who sits in a quiet corner with an illuminated ground-glass screen in front of him, to pick out from each specimen strip just that particular frame of film which best suits the subject and make a note of the light-strength used for it on his grading list.

Armed with this list, another worker taken the toll of negative and proceeds to punch out, with a small hand tool, a long, narrow notch in the film edge at the commencement of every scene where a change of light has been ordered by the grader.

We shall return to these notches directly; meanwhile, there is one more operation to be gone through before printing can start, and that is the preparation of what we will call control cards, which secure that the correct amount of light, as settled by the grader, shall be used on each scene as it rushes through the printer gate.

PRINTING CONTROL CARDS

These cards are ruled horizontally all the way down, one line for each film notch punched out.

Each line, again, is divided into twenty-one squares, corresponding to the variations of light obtainable. Now then, let its imagine that the grader has chosen light No. 3 for tile first scene, No. 7 for the second, and No. 5 for the third, etc.

All that has to be done is to punch a hole about a third of an inch in diameter in the third space of the first line, the seventh space of the second, and so on, all down the card.

The latter is now fixed on to the printing machine in front of a close mass of electrical contacts, coinciding in number and position with the rows of squares on the card.

Only one contact in each row, and that the one which happens to be underneath the square with a hole in it, can come into action to reduce or increase the printing light, and the signal for it to function is given by a device put in motion by the notch in the film-edge referred to just now.

In the production of a news film there is an outstanding need for speed. Now comes a problem. The negative is ready at last, and a couple of hundred or more prints have to be got out for the morrow

Obviously, if printed singly, there will not be time, and so clever brains have evolved a machine with *four* printing gates, each with its separate feeding spool of positive film, and the negative is threaded through each of these gates in turn, so that it is really being copied front in four different places at once.

Assuming that it takes ten minutes uses to print from end to end, this means that a complete print is being produced every two and a half minutes – pretty good going, as one must admit. Of course, with four gates and four printing lights, there must also be four cards, each with its own group of electric contacts, so that the post of machine-minder is no sinecure.

It will probably have occurred to the reader that, unless all the printer lights are of equal intensity with one another, and with the test light in the grading machine, the elaborate pains taken to secure the best result will have been in vain. Twice a week, therefore, an inspection takes place, and all lamps are submitted to a photometer for candle-power measurement

CHECKING LIGHT STRENGTH

Again, one of the notches may 'miss fire', and so put out of order all the ensuing light strengths. Miles of film might then be wasted but for a smart warning device. Whenever a title should be running through, a signal flashes out. The operator glances at his gates, and if these have not all the same luminosity, which can readily be seen through the practically clear film of a title negative, the machine is stopped and readjusted.

Such accidents are rare, naturally, but the precaution is one more instance of the foresight everywhere displayed.

Now we will follow the printed film to the developing-room. Here, ranged in a row, are eight machines, each consisting, in brief, of long and deep, though narrow, developing and fixing tanks arranged in line with one another, with a smaller washing tank between and through all three of which the film is constrained to pass in a series of hoops controlled by steering rollers and driven by sprocket wheels moving at one common speed.

To obtain uniform results the developer must be maintained at an even temperature and it is replenished, filtered and kept in constant circulation by means of a system of pumps and storage tanks.

On emerging from the fixing bath, the film is led through a slit in the adjoining wall and passes into the daylight, where it is treated in a series of washing tubes, on leaving which it is gently squeegeed through soft, thin rubber lips, which, aided by powerful suction tubes, remove all surface moisture.

HARDENING AND DRYING

A chrome-alum bath is also encountered on this journey, and serves to harden the emulsion in readiness for the drying cabinet. This last is a long, tall glass clipboard, about eight feet high, with a double set of driving sprockets above and below respectively.

The film, on entering the cabinet, is threaded around these, and its slow passage through the drying unit takes, perhaps, half an hour.

Hot air is admitted to the lease of the cabinet, and its temperature can be variably controlled at different stages of the film's progress to prevent a undesirable curling, whilst an exhaust fan provides for the necessary, renewal of moist air.

Arrived at the farther end of the apparatus, the now dry positive emerges through a slot and is wound on a take-up spool.

Its adventures are nearly over, and when the whizzing cleaner-belts shall have removed from its plain side the last traces of the handling it has undergone, it will disappear into the joining-room, there to be finally arranged, measured and boxed for transport. The skilful planning shown elsewhere is typical of the joining-room as well, and the separate steel tables, with their side-by-side winders for the easy comparison of print with show copy, boast time and labour saving gadgets calculated to rouse envy in the worker of an earlier day (not so long ago), when makeshifts were the rule.

THE NEGATIVE DEPARTMENT

There is much more that can be only briefly touched on in the course of this survey: the negative department, for example, with its old-time array of flanks and drums (still employed the world over for the development of negatives, and unlikely to be supplanted while they embody so many advantages).

A glimpse of the positive store-room showed shelving and floor space alike heaped high with glistening tins of plain and coloured base, all ready for the printers.

In the basement are the boilers, and here my attention was drawn to the heavy electrical installation, all being in duplicate to make the chance of stoppage more remote. I noted that the printing-machine lamps were fed from a separate transformer to guard their voltage from fluctuations happening outside.

Kinematograph Weekly, 26 August 1926.

Why Not a Socialist Newsreel?

Benn

'Benn' was the film critic of the Independent Labour Party's weekly journal The New Leader. His identity is uncertain, but he is thought to have been the Left-wing intellectual Gary Allighan. Benn is one of the first writers to identify the important role that the newsreels now played in moulding opinion, not only in what they showed ('sport and royalty, royalty and sport') but in what they chose not so show. In 1930 the Federation of Workers' Film Societies was to produce Workers' Topical News, but only three issues were made, and it was never seen in cinemas. Worker's Newsreel, produced in 1934–35 by Kino, showed advances in technique and ran to four issues, but again was restricted to Left-wing groups.

It is rather surprising that in film criticism practically no attention is made to the newsreel. *The Topical Budget, Pathe's Gazette, Fox News, Eve's Pictorial Review* and the rest are regular features of every movie programme, and by the mere fact of their regularity must play a large part in the forming of popular ideas and in the moulding of public opinion. If it is the little daily dose that does it, it is worthwhile examining the composition of the pictorial daily dose, so as to find out how it is made up and what are the effects at which it aims.

LICKSPITTLES AND JINGOES

Take as an example the newsreel I saw last week. It consisted of the following items: first, two school boy football teams playing for some trophy or other; second, Princess Mary opening a building; third, the erection of a stand on a racing track, and racing ponies engaged in trial runs on the track; fourth, the Prince of Wales opening the Newcastle Exhibition; fifth, Captain Campbell failing in his attempt to beat Major Segrave's motor-racing speed record; sixth, the King being removed from Bognor to Windsor on his recovery from illness. Six items – three devoted to sport, and three showing the movements of royalty. No mention of the General Election of May 30, 1929, (perhaps it is not considered an item of news value at such a time as this), no mention of the industrial troubles in Yorkshire and Lancashire, no hint that there is a mill strike in Bombay, or a strike in North Carolina, no pictures of the Russian trade deputation. Nothing about art or music or industrial development of slumdom or the breakdown of the efforts towards international agreement on disarmament.

Simply sport and royalty, royalty and sport. And this newsreel that I have selected is only exceptional by reason of the moderation of its choice of events. Usually, one has pictures of Mussolini reviewing the Italian troops, of tanks in action somewhere in England, of gas-mask parades, of aeroplanes practising bombing raids, of naval manouevres – pictures of the whole paraphernalia of slaughter, but never a picture aiming at the development of the will to peace and at the inculcation of the spirit of internationalism. Always militarism, jingoism, sabre-rattling or sport – never internationalism, peace, scientific advance or any matters likely to raise the intellectual and moral standards of the people.

This, then, is the newsreel. Its object is not to present news, but to breed a race of society gossipers, sport-maniacs, lick-spittles and jingoes. There is room here for a Workers' Film Society to photograph events of interest to the workers. We could have a newsreel showing industrial and political demonstrations; the social causes leading up to strikes; co-operative activities; the effects of the miners' eight-hour day on the miners and their families; the contrast of a nine-to-a-room in workers' homes with one-in-nine-rooms in the homes of the upper class, etc. It could be fairly easy to film such events, and, if done internationally, we could have a newsreel that would act as a real educational weapon on behalf of Socialism and world peace, and a defence against the dope with which the cinemas are now flooded.

The New Leader, 31 May 1929.

Beating the Press?
Reporting the R101 Disaster

James Taylor

This specially-commissioned article takes the news story of the crash of the R101 airship at Beauvais, France on 5 October 1930, and shows how the newsreels vied with the newspapers and the photographic agencies to be first with news of the disaster. It shows how the news was carried forward by new technologies, new forms of transportation, and by a growing sense of competition across the news media. It also recreates in detail the sequence of events surrounding the crash, and the actions of the cameramen, photographers and reporters involved.

> For what in all probability is the first time in the history of news reels, the Press have been 'beaten to it' in pictorial journalism. (*The Bioscope*)[1]

> R101 Pictures: news reel effort that beat the Press. (*Daily Film Renter*)[2]

> The Press beaten. (*To-day's Cinema*)[3]

In this age of 24 hour live global TV news, satellite links, videophones and broadband transmission it is increasingly hard to picture a world where the newspaper pictured the world, premiering the nation and the globe's big events. Today, most often, we will see the moving image testimony of a local, national or foreign news item on the evening news and read about it in the next morning's papers – where the story will be illustrated with still photographs of a scene we already recognise. Go back however, before television, before satellite transmission, before the Internet to a period when your moving image testimony was restricted to visits to the cinema and the newsreels featured in the twice-weekly programme change – and the tables are turned in pictorial journalism. With a spread of newspaper titles, daily output, several editions including many evening titles, over twenty picture agencies supplying the papers, mutual agreements between the press agencies and photographic agencies of different countries – it was the newspaper that not only brought the story to the public first but the pictures to accompany it too. In fact the cinema newsreels were not in the business of being first with the news, or of breaking stories – they were supplementary and dependent on their audience already being aware of the story to which their images referred. As Luke McKernan has written, 'newspapers came out first and determined news stories and news trends. Newsreels followed in their wake, supplying the moving pictures to an audience already informed of the subject matter. The news is made by who gets in first'.[4]

The 1930s saw an unprecedented competition for supplying the news, the economics of the depression had led the newspapers into a circulation war as the market struggled to support so many titles. At the same time the newsreels were locked in what Anthony Aldgate describes as 'the newsreel war',[5] kick-started by the arrival of American corporations with the finances to support sound newsreel production, eventually forcing the smaller British companies, unable to afford the conversion, out of business. The newspapers and the newsreels were not in direct competition however, and the press seems to have felt no challenge from news film, being concerned far more with the threat of being 'beaten' posed by a broadcast medium. The newspaper barons had forced severe restrictions on the news service of the fledgling BBC radio both in terms of where it got its news from and when and how it could report it.[6] So, not being in competition, the newspapers and newsreels were not in the habit of racing each other for the news, nor indeed for news pictures. While newspapers would often race each other for news and photographs, and newsreels would sometimes race each other for news footage – they were competing in different leagues. Even in terms of pictorial journalism, the Press got in first and had all the advantages in getting pictures to the public. Between major cities photos could be sent by 'photo-telegraphy' making use of the latest wireless transmission and facsimile technologies to transport images across large distances, and internationally, while news-film would have to be physically transported. Also, while the production of a newsreel shared much of the chemistry of still news photography, it was nevertheless more time-consuming and involved. Similarly the distribution of a newsreel was more difficult and prolonged, while papers 'hot off the press' could be on sale on the streets in minutes, news reel prints 'fresh from the baths' must first travel to the theatres for display in the cinema programmes. While a single projection could show the news to a massed audience of hundreds in one sitting, outside the auditorium hundreds of papers were being hawked, passed on, and read by people waiting in cinema queues.

The opening quotes from the cinema trade papers therefore present an exceptional achievement. They boast proudly that the press were 'beaten', thereby suggesting a victory for the newsreels over the newspapers in a race we would not have expected them to be having. Such an exceptional achievement could only be the product of extraordinary circumstance, and the news story that provoked these claims was far from everyday. In the early hours of the morning on Sunday 5 October 1930, the British airship R101 crashed into a hillside near Beauvais in Northern France, seven hours into her maiden voyage from Cardington Bedfordshire to Karachi. The crash resulted in the destruction of the million pound airship, the deaths of 48 people onboard including a Cabinet Minister, and effectively ended the British airship programme. The story was of major importance for both newspapers and newsreels. However it was the timing and location of the incident which were critical to how news and news pictures of the crash site were communicated to the British public, and which placed the newsreels with an opportunity to be first. The location of the accident, being overseas but only two hours' plane ride from London meant that the site was reachable, but was outside the area the newspapers would regularly cover. Reaching the site and bringing back pictures therefore required unconventional action and offered equal difficulties to both. The timing of the accident, the early hours of a Sunday morning, meant that it occurred after the last editions of the day's papers and on the only day of the week that did not also have evening titles. So, while the newspapers were already in the process of distribution, the newsreels were preparing for the Monday edition and were still in a production phase. If notice of the crash reached the newsreels soon enough they would have a chance to get the first pictures to the public.

From contemporary reports in the newspapers and cinema journals, from the memoirs of those involved, and elsewhere, it is possible to put together a picture of events on 4 and 5 October, of how notice of the crash made its way to the British media and how the news and news pictures of the disaster were acquired. Some of the information is contradictory or fits together uncomfortably. The competition in both newspaper and newsreel industries encouraged an institutionalised exaggeration in their staffs' feats, as all the companies tried to prove their own pre-eminence. Also, as some of the incidents are recounted decades later by those involved it is perhaps not surprising that a little personal exaggeration may slip in here and there, and events may not be recalled with the clarity and exactness which they may have done earlier. The following section attempts to collect this information together.

SATURDAY, 4 OCTOBER 1930

18.36 GMT (19.36 BST) The R101 launches and begins its journey from its base in Cardington. British Summer Time ends that evening and the clocks on board are adjusted to reflect Greenwich Mean Time. Several journalists, photographers and newsreel staff are in attendance, including cameramen from British Movietone, Pathe and Universal, and Movietone and Pathe sound teams.[7] The photographer Edward Dean takes pictures from the air as he is piloted about the airship in a hired plane.[8] The late launch was inauspicious for the moving image photographers, as was the inclement weather. The arrival of dusk and the cloud filled sky at the moment of launch, combined with the slow film stock of the time made recording an image of the actual departure impossible. Only Pathe appear to have persisted, and their publicity in the following week stressed that their *Pathe Super Sound Gazette* and *Pathe Gazette* were 'the only news reels to give actual scenes showing

British Pathe

Pathe Gazette film of the wreckage of the R101 airship.

the Airship commencing its ill fated flight'.[9] The use of the word 'showing' is deceptive here however as no image was registered, and the *Super Sound Gazette* shows only a black screen while the commentator says 'Well it's, absolutely pitch black … It's quite uncanny standing here in the darkness, not able to see a thing, but just hearing her go slowly away'.[10] Edward Dean writes that he and his pilot Captain Schofield followed the airship by plane. The first editions of the Sunday papers had already gone to press.

20.21 At this time the R101 is over London, the crew sends a wireless message stating their location and 'Course now set for Paris. Intend to proceed via Paris, Tours, Toulouse and Narbonne'.[11] Later editions of the Sunday papers report its ghostly appearance as it passed over London, invisible except for its lights penetrating the clouds.

21.47 R101 sends a wireless message: 'crossing coast in vicinity of Hastings'. At this point according to Dean, he and Schofield cease following the airship and turn back to London: 'We escorted her over London and out to the coast, and I took my pictures as daylight stole away'.[12] Even with the extended day afforded by altitude and the benefit of travelling south, light suitable for photography must surely have long passed.

23.36 R101 sends a wireless message: 'Crossing French coast at Point de St. Quentin'.

SUNDAY, 5 OCTOBER 1930
00.18 R101 sends a wireless message to Cardington, giving the ship's location at midnight as 15 miles SW of Abbeville and a message:

> After an excellent supper our distinguished passengers smoked a final cigar. And having sighted the French coast have now gone to bed to rest after the excitement of their leave-taking. All essential services are functioning satisfactorily. The crew have settled down to watch-keeping routine.

This was the last message the R101 sent to Cardington.

01.00 The R101 was seen by observers at Poix airfield.

01.28 The R101 sends a directional wireless signal to Cardington.

01.45 The R101 sends a directional wireless signal to Valenciennes and Le Bourget (Paris), locating it exactly by cross bearing.

02.00 R101 is sighted flying low over the town of Beauvais. The noise of its engines attracted attention and several people were woken. The secretary of the Police Station is among those who noted its passage overhead.

02.07–02.09 The R101 crashes near the village of Allonne, a couple of miles from the centre of Beauvais.

The few survivors stumble away from the burning wreck. Local people start rushing to the accident site. Arthur Disley, the R101's Chief Electrician and wireless operator, is found wandering near the wreck by a French man. He refuses to go to hospital until he has telephoned the Air Ministry and attempted to get help.[13] It cannot have been easy to make an international telephone call in rural France in the early hours of a Sunday morning in 1930. The nearest village Allonne may have had no phones at all, the French telephone system was underdeveloped and had been shattered by WW1. Disley is unlikely to have spoken much, if any, French, the Allonne locals little English. Disley had burns to his hands, arms and legs reducing his mobility and basic ability to handle a phone (photographs of him in hospital show his hands ballooned by bandages).[14] The prompt arrival of the gendarmerie probably brought more useful aid, but even after communicating his intentions, travelling to a phone (probably in Beauvais) and receiving physical assistance in its use, making an international call would have been no easy business. An international call would probably have been routed through Paris, and an operator would have rung back when a connection could be made. That Disley was a communications professional was in his favour, nothing else was and that it only took around an hour to get through to London is quite an achievement. Elsewhere, the news was travelling faster.

02.16 Le Bourget aerodrome sends out a wireless message to all stations: 'GFAAW a pris feu', GFAAW (the R101's call signal) has caught fire.[15] Commander Girardot, the Officer in charge of Le Bourget had been anxious about the lack of communication from R101 and made enquiries discovering the truth.[16] All of France's aerodromes had been instructed to 'stand to' on account of the bad weather that night.[17] London's aerodromes must have been some of the first places in Britain to learn something had gone wrong, as the night duty staff heard the message.

03.00 At this time or a little after Arthur Disley eventually gets through to London. At the Air Ministry offices in Kingsway London, the resident clerk on night duty answers the phone, to hear a faint and anguished voice:

> R101 has crashed in flames bear Beauvais. Nearly everybody has been killed. This is Disley, the wireless operator.

The clerk then proceeds to telephone and awaken Cabinet ministers, members of the Air Council and high officials in the Air Ministry with the news.[18]

03.05 Between 02.16 and 03.05, the news agencies become aware of the R101's situation, those with a Paris office obviously having the advantage (Reuters chairman Roderick Jones listed the crash as his 'top story of the year').[19] Monday's papers featured first hand accounts provided by the agencies British United Press, Central News,[20] and Reuters.[21] Michael Wynn Jones reports that it was '3.05 am precisely when news reached Fleet Street over the wires'.[22] From the point of view of a newspaper this was just about the worst possible time for a major news story to break, all the Sunday papers had been 'put to bed', the final editions laid up and already rolling off the presses. Solomon Levy, the 'late stop' at the *Sunday Express*, reads the news coming in and rings Assistant Editor Arthur Christiansen, who rushes via foot and cab from his home in Pimlico to Fleet Street and takes charge of getting a new edition out. Christiansen stops the presses while the new edition is made ready, between now and 08.00 three updated editions are put together and issued.[23] The actions of the *Sunday Express* lead the Press back to work and 'belatedly the other Sunday's followed suit'[24] producing their own special editions. The newsreels appear to fall immediately behind, with no responsive action being taken for over two hours. Most of the newsreels had working arrangements with the news agencies, and in 1936 Gaumont claimed 'Two tape-machines provide a twenty-four-hour-a-day service in the London office',[25] a model no doubt repeated in the other companies. The question is, who was minding shop? Gaumont staff would work on the Monday release over the weekend 'editing on Saturday night and printing on Sunday'[26], the delay here suggests no-one was watching the wires in-between and the news may not have reached the newsreels until Agencies contacted the editors by phone.

04.00 *Express* newspaper photographer Bill Tovey is awoken by the Night Duty Officer of the Sunday Express (presumably the 'late stop' Solomon Levy) and informed of the crash. He drives from his home in Barnes to Fleet Street, a journey he says he made in fifteen minutes.[27].

c.04.15 Tovey arrives at Fleet Street, he is told to proceed to Croydon aerodrome where a plane has been hired and he is to meet the Aviation correspondent Harold Pemberton.

05.30 Tommy Scales of *British Movietone News* telephones and wakes cameraman Paul Wyand with the news. Wyand asks for more information, but Scales cuts him short:

> Leave the chat until later, Paul. Get over there right away. We've chartered a plane for you at Croydon, and we want the film on show in London to-night.

Then rings off. Wyand dresses and stows a camera and 10 rolls of film in his car.[28]

06.00 The *Express* team Tovey and Pemberton take off from Croydon, directing the pilot of their hired plane to Beauvais. Maurice Wallenstein of the Planet News photo agency telephones photographer Edward Dean and tells him to get to Fleet Street, they already have a plane waiting to take him to Beauvais.[29] About this time Bert Garai head of the Keystone picture agency is telephoned by the American agency Associated Press and informed of the crash, he drives to Fleet Street and makes arrangements to fly a photographer to Beauvais.[30] A little after 06.00 Ramsay Macdonald is telephoned at Chequers and informed.

06.45 Wyand arrives at Croydon Aerodrome.

08.00 H.W. Bishop, production manager at *Gaumont Sound News,* hears about the crash and starts to contact staff. In the following period Keith Ayling, the news editor rounds up laboratory staff and calls in editors Roy Drew and David Lean who rush in to work to try and assemble a story from pre-existing footage.[31] Arthur Christiansen decides to put out another edition of the *Sunday Express,* 'a Sunday Morning Special to sell on the streets of London'. Bishop may indeed have found out about the crash from one of the earlier editions of the *Sunday Express* that would have already been in distribution. The first story put together by Drew and Lean opens with a shot of a Sunday paper with a crash headline and photos of the victims, it is the front cover of the *Sunday Express* (framed so the banner is not seen).[32]

08.20 Tovey and Pemberton must reach the Beauvais area at around 08.00, but then they circle for 20 minutes searching in vain for the crash site before landing at Beauvais aerodrome. There they hire a car, the chauffeur knows where the crash site is but there are 'thousands of men, women and children flocking along the roadside, making anything like speed impossible'. Eventually they leave the car and start to walk across rain sodden ploughed fields towards where they believe the crash site to be.

08.30 Wyand writes that his pilot spots the crash site from the air and lands nearby, and that he arrives at the crash site and starts shooting at 08.30, but the flight alone would have taken around 2 hours, and he says he had to squelch through mud for a quarter of a mile from where he landed to reach the site (carrying his camera and tripod). It is more likely after 09.00 before he reaches the site. At whatever time he arrives, he finds French cameramen and the Paris Movietone sound team already there. Tovey and Pemberton also eventually reach the site and Tovey takes pictures of the wreck before they head back to Beauvais to interview and photograph the survivors in the hospital there.

10.00 Wyand boards his plane again and begins the flight back to London. By this time H.W. Bishop has dispatched a cameraman to the crash site. Dean must also have started his journey back at about this time.

SUNDAY MORNING

At Biggleswade exchange, Maria Bailey a telephone operator takes a call reporting the crash, which she translates from the French and passes to Cardington.[33] At unspecified times on Sunday morning a whole raft of other media personnel travel to Beauvais: a French contingent of newspapermen, photographers and reporters, and newsreel men from Fox-Movietone, Gaumont and Pathe. The Paris correspondents of British newspapers, including Victor Console of the *Daily Mail,*[34] George Renwick of the *News Chronicle*[35] and H.J. Greenwall of the *Daily Express.*[36]

Also arriving from Paris by motor car for the *Daily Mail* are Special Correspondents Harold G. Cardozo, C.J. Martin and Roger Fuller.[37] Other Newspaper reporters and photographers fly by chartered aircraft to the site including J.C. Cannell of the *Daily Sketch*,[38] the Special correspondent of the *Times*,[39] an unnamed *Daily Mail* reporter and photographer,[40] and an unnamed *Daily Mirror* photographer.[41] Planes for hire between London and Northern France must have been getting thinner on the ground, and the price of travel rising, 'the *News Chronicle* without hesitating to count the cost, chartered an airliner'.[42] Agency photographers are also on site, including: Jimmy Sime of Central Press;[43] S.R. Gaiger and J. Gaiger of the Topical Press Agency;[44] the photographer for Keystone;[45] and a Press Association photographer.[46] At some point that morning the other British newsreels make efforts to obtain pictures: Harry Sanders at Pathe 'dispatched' a cameraman; while a *British Screen News* cameraman films at the site 'a few hours after the disaster';[47] the actions of the *Topical Budget* are not reported in the trade journals but they too film the wreckage.[48] The *Universal Talking News* 'commissioned Mons. Nicolas and Mons. Duteriez of Paris, to take an aeroplane to the scene of the disaster, and secure what pictures they could',[49] whether they chose this option for speed or because there was no longer any planes to be hired from London is not clear. Any advantage in sending men from Paris was diminished though, when those men took the

A *Gaumont Sound News* van in Soho Square, London.

footage back to Paris with the material not reaching London until the Monday morning.

12.00 Wyand arrives back at Croydon, a waiting car rushes his film to the labs. Shortly after midday Edward Dean lands back at Hanworth and is met by Maurice Wallenstein who rushes Dean's plates to the office for developing. Tovey and Pemberton arrive back at Fleet Street, they expect there to be plenty of time to produce their story and pictures for Monday's *Express*, but discover that the *Sunday Express* wants to put together a special edition, with Tovey's photos, to publish and distribute that afternoon. Despite the delay in Movietone hearing about the crash, the *Express* men faced delays in reaching the site and also had to get interviews for the paper while Wyand could shoot the site and leave. The initial time advantage for the press is lost.

12.30 Arthur Christiansen and his staff of journalists leave work and go to the pub. Christiansen makes not one mention of Tovey, nor of the expectation or the provision of photographs. His account of events says there was no time to send 'photographers from London'.

13.00 Wyand's film arrives at the lab.

SUNDAY AFTERNOON
According to Bert Garai the Keystone photographer arrives back in London 'early on Sunday afternoon when, for the first time since World War One, special editions of the Sunday papers appeared and several of them carried our pictures'.[50]

14.30 Tommy Scales looks at Wyand's negative.

18.30 The *British Movietone News* coverage of the accident is shown in London cinemas, with prints put on a train to Birmingham for the last performances there.[51] The Gaumont cameraman is reported to have returned to Heston aerodrome at dusk (presumably around 18.30). H.W. Bishop has flares laid out to expedite the landing. The negative is rushed to the labs in Shepherd's Bush, where the works manager Mr Hitchcock personally develops and prints the film, while Keith Ayling and H.W. Bishop prepare titles before helping to turn out a number of prints.

SUNDAY EVENING
Pathe put on a special edition of their newsreel including launch and crash stories in the 'principle West End and Suburban cinemas'.[52] This claim crucially does not state that their crash story features footage of the crash site. The issue sheet for *Pathe Super Sound Gazette* 30/37, dated the next day 6 October 1930, which does

feature footage of both 'launch' and crash site – credits two cameramen: 'Wyand' (presumably Leslie Wyand, Paul's uncle, Pathe cameraman at this time) and 'Jones' (perhaps Pathe cameraman Harold G. Jones), but also lists 'P Cinema', perhaps a reference to Pathé Cinema and the French Pathé newsreel.[53] Did Pathe wait another day for footage from their French colleagues? The British Pathe library holds a French item on the crash titled LA CATASTROPHE DU DIRIGEABLE BRITANNIQUE,[54] the description of which contains many items recalling images in the *Super Sound Gazette*, but then all descriptions of wreckage read much the same. If Leslie Wyand had filmed the crash site, surely Paul Wyand would have mentioned the fact in his account.

20.50 The time of the scheduled BBC radio news that day. Events may have led to an earlier scheduling, but the restrictions on news coverage forced by press interests, prevented news being broadcast before 18.00.

22.00 Gaumont story put on screen at the Capitol Haymarket and the Shepherd's Bush Pavilion. These screenings are reported in the trade press as occurring shortly after 10.00, but Gaumont's achievement also makes it to the Monday's *Daily Sketch* where a line reads: 'R101 FILM IN LONDON. Pictures of the R101 crash taken by *Gaumont Sound News* were shown at the Shepherd's Bush Pavilion at 10.30 last night'.[55]

So who was first? Who beat whom? There are discrepancies in the accounts. Evidence points to the *Sunday Express* presenting the first pictures of the crash to the British public but the physical evidence is hard to locate, The British Library only preserves an edition of the *Sunday Express* of 5 October 1930 which predates the news of the crash. The absence of any mention of Tovey or of his photographs in Christiansen's account of the *Sunday Express*'s output that day is problematic and creates doubt about what happened. We must note that Christiansen was writing thirty-one years after the event, Tovey only ten, and that Christiansen's account gets crucial timings wrong. But while memory is surely to blame for getting timings wrong, to omit mention of Tovey's photos (if they *did* appear) could only have been intentional. Perhaps the edition featuring the photographs was produced after Christiansen had gone home and thus not mentioned because it did not contribute to his achievement. A photograph of the top half of a later edition of the *Sunday Express* in *Headlines All My Life*, and a different reproduction, similarly cropped, of the same edition in Michael Wynn Jones's *Deadline Disaster* show library photographs of the R101 at its mast, and the victims Sefton Brancker and Lord Thomson. This edition is marked 'Last London Ed' on the banner, and has 'Afternoon Special' written after the headline. There are no photographs of the crash site, nor an indication of them being on the pages within. Monday's *Daily*

Express however features many pictures on its front and rear covers, including an aerial shot, a picture of a survivor in hospital, a photograph marked '"Daily Express" exclusive picture', and the photograph of the site reproduced in Tovey's auto-biography here marked 'Special "Daily Express" Picture'; they are all clearly Tovey's photographs. The front page also features the article written by his companion, the correspondent Harold Pemberton.[56] The British Library copies of *The News of the World, Sunday Chronicle, Sunday Dispatch, Sunday Graphic, Sunday News* and *Sunday Pictorial* for 5 October 1930 are all editions prior to the news of the crash and can offer no pictorial competition or substantiate Garai and Dean's claims.

British Movietone News appears to have been the winning newsreel according to Paul Wyand's account, but interestingly this claim is not made in the contemporary trade press where Gaumont is heralded as being first. No mention is made of a 18.30 showing on Sunday evening for the Movietone story. A trade journal dated Tuesday 7 October 1930 writes only that Movietone had gained pictures of the site and 'As a result, it was reported yesterday, all West End customers were enabled to include the R.101 tragedy in their programmes'.[57] A report on Wednesday 8 October 1930 says 'Public interest in *British Movietone News* pictures of the R.101 disaster has been so great that more than 4,000 people have already seen the film at the Shaftesbury Avenue News Reel Theatre which is a 500 capacity house'.[58] A full page advertisement trumpeting Movietone's R101 coverage makes 6 statements of achievement, but being first to show the disaster is not one of them.[59]

Gaumont has an advertisement that clearly stakes its claim 'Something Like Service!! THE GAUMONT SOUND NEWS Screened genuine pictures with authentic sound of the R101 disaster, on Sunday evening in the West End. CAN YOU BEAT IT?'[60] No other company, including Movietone suggests that they did. It is Gaumont that receives the largest amount of coverage in the trade press, and that makes it to the front page of a Monday newspaper. It has been suggested that Gaumont actually sent no cameraman of their own and that 'Movietone allowed them to dupe their footage',[61] but it seems unlikely that Gaumont would phrase their advertisement this way if that were true. And in the newsreel war it seems unlikely that Movietone would have let them get away with it. The physical evidence is unavailable; the *Gaumont Sound News* story that survives is the version that Drew and Lean constructed on the Sunday morning and contains no footage of the crash site at all. The take off and landing at Heston rings true though, the proximity of Heston aerodrome, the laboratories at Shepherd's Bush and the Shepherd's Bush Pavilion create the most convincing geography for speedily getting the film from the crash site to the screen. By 1936 Gaumont-British had 'its own office at Heston aerodrome with a plane and skilled pilots permanently standing by'[62] and agreements with the plane hire company Air Commerce.[63] Whether Gaumont screened pictures with 'authentic sound' is another matter; certainly they would not have transported 1,400 pounds of sound equipment to the site, and unlike Movietone they could not benefit from their French equivalents' sound team, as the French Gaumont newsreel did not convert to sound until 1932.[64] Movietone's full-page advertisement for its R101 coverage stated that it gave 'The *Genuine Sound News Reel* pictures of the wreck of the R101', and the italics seem to be there to stress the '*Genuine Sound*' element.

While the newspapers struggled directly for circulation amongst the public, the true audiences for the newsreels' efforts were the exhibitors. The exhibitors were the customers for who they fought and whose attention they needed to attract. In the trade journals that the exhibitors read Gaumont was the clear winner, its advertisements may have been smaller and fewer than its competitors, but it gained the most space in the articles and it was heralded as the one that 'beat the press'. This was in any case a race for an audience almost completely limited to London for both the newspapers and the newsreels. With several editions already printed, distributed and recalled that day, economics and practicalities would have limited both the number of papers carrying pictures of the crash printed on the Sunday afternoon, and their subsequent distribution. As the staff of the Dailies had been in since the Sunday morning preparing Monday's editions it seems likely that efforts must increasingly have concentrated on the weekday papers. Arthur Christiansen made his 8.00 am edition 'to sell on the streets of London'. Copies of the Movietone reel may have been put on trains to Birmingham, but it was a London audience the newsreels were aiming for, as Tommy Scales told Wyand: 'we want the film on show in London to-night'.

It is unlikely that the press were beaten to picturing the event by the newsreels. Despite the lack of physical evidence it seems fairly certain that there were newspapers carrying photographs sometime that afternoon and, with no newsreel claiming a showing before 18.30, these would have been out first. But it was close; maybe a couple of hours separated the distribution of a newspaper with pictures of the crash from the exhibition of a news film with *moving* pictures of the crash. If it had not been so close the claim could not have been made. No doubt at least some people would have seen their first images of the wreckage sitting in a cinema audience, and those moving images with 'authentic' sound must have conveyed the devastation all the more strongly. The limitations of communications technology had given the newsreels a chance to compete. If the R101 had crashed just outside Paris, photographs could, and would, have been sent direct from Paris to London by photo-telephony[65] on the Sunday morning and the newsreels would not have stood a chance. In rural France, without nearby transmission equipment, the photographs had to be physically transported over distance just like the film. But as this technology for relaying images developed, it also increased the threat of the moving image: in 1930 the BBC made its first experimental television sound and vision transmissions. It would still be several years before the emergence of contemporary television news, but here already was modern news making in genesis. Staking its claim, threatening to beat the press, edging towards being first.

NOTES

1. 'R101 Disaster in the Reels. Amazing Speed: Films by Air', *Bioscope*, 8 October 1930, p. 40.
2. 'R101 Pictures: news reel effort that beat the Press', *Daily Film Renter*, 7 October 1930, p. 1.
3. 'The Press beaten: Gaumont sound news feat: the R101 disaster', *To-day's Cinema*, 7 October 1930, p. 2.
4. Luke McKernan, 'Witnessing the Past', in James Ballantyne (ed.), *Researcher's Guide to British Newsreels Vol. III* (London: British Universities Film & Video Council, 1993), p. 35.
5. Anthony Aldgate, *Cinema & History: British Newsreels and the Spanish Civil War* (London: Scolar Press, 1979), p. 23.
6. Asa Briggs, *The History of Broadcasting in the United Kingdom, Vol. II: The Golden Age of Wireless* (London: Oxford University Press, 1965), pp. 153–155.
7. Footage shot by these newsreels on 4 October features in: *British Movietone News* no. 70 (release date 6 October 1930); *Pathe Super Sound Gazette* 30/37 (6 October 1930) and *Universal Talking News* no. 26 (9 October 1930). The date for the *Universal Talking News* is based on date given on the issue sheet, but this footage must have appeared on the 6 October issue (replacing much if not all of the R101-free no. 25 scheduled for issue that day), and is described as appearing at noon showings on 6 October in *To-day's Cinema*, 7 October 1930, p. 2.
8. Edward J. Dean, *Lucky Dean: Reminiscences of a Press Photographer* (London: Robert Hale, 1944), p. 31.
9. Full page advertisement, *Daily Film Renter*, 7 October 1930, p. 5.
10. It is unclear whether this sequence appeared in all editions of the newsreel as it is not mentioned in the description of the item on the British Pathe database (under TRAGEDY MOST PROFOUND, Tape PM0747), but it certainly appears in the copy of *Pathe Super Sound Gazette* featured in a compilation reel held by the East Anglian Film Archive under the title THE R101 STORY. The temptation to cut in library footage of an earlier R101 launch must have been as strong for Pathe, as it was for the other companies who 'recreated' the launch this way.
11. The times and text of all the R101's wireless communication are taken from: John Simon, *R101: The Airship Disaster, 1930* (London, The Stationery Office, 1999), abridged edition of *Report of the R.101 Inquiry* (1931 cd.3825); Sir Peter G. Masefield, *To Ride the Storm: The Story of the Airship R.101* (London: William Kimber, 1982), pp. 389–396.
12. Dean, *Lucky Dean*, p.32
13. *Times*, 6 October 1930, p. 14.
14. See Nick Le Neve Walmsley, *R101: A Pictorial History* (Stroud: Sutton Publishing, 2000), p. 123 and *Daily Mirror* 6 October 1930), back cover.
15. *Daily Mirror*, 6 October 1930, p. 4; *Daily Sketch* (6 October 1930), and elsewhere.

16. *Daily Mail*, 6 October 1930, p. 14.

17. Revealed in a communiqué issued by Laurent Eynac, French Minister for Air, issued 5 October and reported in *Daily Express*, 6 October 1930, p. 3.

18. *Daily Mail*, 6 October 1930, p. 11.

19. *World's Press News*, 1 January 1931, quoted in Donald Read, *The Power of News: The History of Reuters 1849–1989* (Oxford: Oxford University Press, 1992), p. 201.

20. *Daily Express*, 6 October 1930, p. 11 and *Daily Mail*, 6 October 1930, p. 14.

21. For example, *Daily Express*, 6 October 1930, p. 3.

22. Michael Wynn Jones, *Deadline Disaster: a newspaper history* (Newton Abbott: David & Charles, 1976), p. 96.

23. All reference to Arthur Christiansen come from Arthur Christiansen, *Headlines All My Life* (London; Heinemann, 1961), pp. 68–72. Christiansen's memory of the timing of events has to be questioned however; he says he was woken with news of the crash shortly after 01.00, but the crash did not happen until 02.07.

24. Jones, *Deadline Disaster*, p. 96.

25. 'Aeroplanes and Tape Machines cover the World for News-Reel', *World Film News* vol.1, no. 3, June 1936, p. 22.

26. Roy Drew in a letter to the *South Bank Show* (7 August 1984), quoted in Kevin Brownlow, *David Lean* (London: Faber, 1996), p. 69.

27. All references to Tovey and Pemberton, and the timings of their activities come from P.H.F. 'Bill' Tovey, *Action with a Click* (London: Herbert Jenkins, 1940), pp. 86–91.

28. All references to Wyand, and the timings of his activities come from Paul Wyand, *Useless if Delayed* (London; George G. Harrap, 1959), pp. 51–53.

29. All references to Dean, and the timings of his activities come from Dean, *Lucky Dean*, pp. 32–33.

30. Bert Garai, *The Man from Keystone* (London: Frederick Muller, 1965), pp. 172–173.

31. Information on the Gaumont newsreel's activities comes from the reports in the journals *Bioscope*, *To-day's Cinema* and *Daily Film Renter* as well as Brownlow, *David Lean*, pp. 69–71.

32. *Gaumont Sound News* issue held by the NFTVA under the title R.101 DISASTER; *Gaumont Graphic* no. 2041 (9 October 1930).

33. Reported in the *Daily Telegraph*, 6 October 1980, when Mrs Bailey attended the fiftieth anniversary memorial.

34. See Walter Rogers' account in Ian Ormes and Ralph Ormes, *The Sky Masters* (London: William Kimber, 1976), p. 77.

35. *News Chronicle*, 6 October 1930, p. 1.

36. *Daily Express*, 6 October 1930, p. 3.

37. *Daily Mail*, 6 October 1930, p. 13.

38. *Daily Sketch*, 6 October 1930, p. 3.

39. *Times*, 6 October 1930, p. 14.

40. A *Daily Mail* reporter and photographer were flown by Captain Wilson, *Daily Mail*, 6 October 1930, p. 13.

41. *Daily Mirror*, 6 October 1930, p. 2. The photographer was piloted by 'Lawrence Hope, the famous pilot', probably W.L. Hope of Air Taxis Ltd, who in the following week would also

pilot Tovey to cover the return of the dead to Britain, and transport photos from London to Manchester for the Sunday Despatch.

42. Michael Wynn Jones, *A Newspaper History of the World* (Newton Abbott: David & Charles, 1974), p. 124.

43. Photographs of the site by Sime are held in the Hulton Getty collection, image nos. HP4546, HN7323, JD6375.

44. Photographs of the site by this team are held in the Hulton Getty collection, S.R. Gaiger: image nos. JD6644, JE4522; J. Gaiger: image no. HU5389. A further two images in the Hulton Getty collection are credited to Topical Press Agency, without naming the photographer, image nos. HC4080, HJ7946.

45. A photograph of the site credited to Keystone, without naming the photographer is held by Hulton Getty, image no. HN1059. A newsreel cameraman can be seen in the background.

46. Photographs of the site by a Press Association photographer are held by PA Photos, negative nos. V1247, V1249, V1251, V1252 (an aerial shot).

47. *Daily Film Renter,* 7 October 1930, p.6. *To-day's Cinema*, 7 October 1930, p. 8.

48. THE TRAGIC END OF R101, *Topical Budget* 998–1 (6/9 October 1930). The NFTVA also holds two reels of offcuts for this item both titled R101 DISASTER, these are 240 feet and 300 feet in length.

49. *To-day's Cinema,* 7 October 1930, p. 2.

50. Garai, *The Man from Keystone*, p. 173.

51. Presumably *British Movietone News* no. 70 (issue sheet lists release date as 6 October 1930), or a variant of the same footage.

52. *To-day's Cinema,* 7 October 1930, p. 8.

53. See record on British Universities Newsreel Database, http://www.bufvc.ac.uk/newsreels.

54. Tape PM0476.

55. *Daily Sketch*, 6 October 1930, p. 2.

56. *Daily Express*, 6 October 1930, pp. 1, 11.

57. *Daily Film Renter*, 7 October 1930, p. 6.

58. *Daily Film Renter*, 8 October 1930, p. 1.

59. *To-days Cinema*, 9 October 1930, p. 6; *Daily Film Renter*, 9 October 1930, p. 3.

60. *Daily Film Renter,* 7 October 1930, p. 2.

61. Brownlow, *David Lean*, p. 71.

62. 'Aeroplanes and Tape Machines cover the World for News-Reel', *World Film News* vol.1 no. 3, June 1936, p. 22.

63. Tim Sherwood, *Coming in to Land: A History of Hounslow, Hanworth and Heston Aerodromes, 1911–1946* (Hounslow: Heritage Publications, 1999), p. 119.

64. *L'Histoire de Gaumont*. Available at: http://www.gaumont.fr/cinematheque_2002/histoire_gaumont.asp?v=f2d1ee2z&n=4&nc=52tgddklliheoighfibpHHZFD332 (accessed 16 March 2002).

65. The daily papers had time to arrange getting photographs to Paris and to transmit them from there. In the following week they included pictures by 'telephony'.

The News-Theatre

C.A. Lejeune

Caroline Lejeune was The Observer film critic. Here she welcomes the emergence of specialist cinemas for the exhibition of newsreels, and enthuses over the particular human qualities of the newsreels. She calls for a wider range of newsreels, similar to newspapers, to match the widely differing tastes of the cinema-going public.

I believe that one of the most hopeful signs for the future of the cinema is the establishment of news-reel and magazine theatres in various big cities throughout the world. It shows a salutary breaking-away from the old slogan of 'Bigger and Better Pictures', which suggested that entertainment should be reckoned in terms of mathematical ratio, and that the ten-reeler must inevitably provide better value for money than the 'short', however richly and fully conceived. It shows that the industry has grasped, at last, the overwhelming force of the movie as a modern narrator and propagandist. And it opens out a province of entertainment in which tersity and directness of speech, reticence and drive – qualities which have not generally occupied the cinema – will have to be studied and mastered if it is to hold its place in the hustle of modern life.

The institution of specific news-film theatres is likely to prove the solution of many long problems, and I am convinced that they will, if they are rightly handled, come to fill a very definite place in our civilisation. Not only has the topical camera-man of to-day reached a high pitch of skill and ingenuity, and learnt to get his effects in the teeth of the most overwhelming odds, but the addition of sound, even in its most primitive form, has gone a long way towards popularising and pointing the news service of the screen. The presentation of fact has always a fascination of its own, and the presentation of fact in pictures has to many people an added conviction that the printed word can never quite achieve. In a good newsreel there is always something to touch one's personal experience, some point of contact with individual occupation, some special answer to a special curiosity. The news-reel, like the newspaper, can rely on a large and multiple audience, because in it there is always something that seems to have been chosen for each individual alone, and in the new combination of sight and sound, of image and comment, foreign face and foreign tongue, the cinema has provided a universal bulletin that can bring, as no newspaper can, the nations of the world together in knowledge and wonder.

But the very fact that such theatres are coming into existence suggests that the news-reels and short-film programmes will have to be chosen with much greater care and intelligence, and arranged with much finer sensibility, than they have been in the past. The editors of film news-reel have taken for granted, and we have never disputed them, that any event, from the eruption of a volcano to the display of a Paris gown, is unassailable film news, just as any picture of an expedition crossing a stretch of waste land may be regarded as a travelogue, and any series of animated drawings with gyratory flanks and goggling eyes can be accepted as a comic cartoon. But the fact that a Mayor, or even a Lord Mayor, shakes hands with a beauty-prize winner, is not in itself a just excuse to get out the movie camera and shoot. The itemised scenes in a news-reel must be both well chosen and well presented if they are to catch and hold attention. Each must have unity and finish, breaking off at its climax only for a specific purpose, and given its full measure of natural timing. If the topical camera-man has had the bad luck to bungle or miss the end of his sequence, the man in the cutting-room is always there to put the job to rights; not touching its truth, but shaping its form and so assuring its content. A news-reel must be regarded exactly as a full-length film, of which each unit and each frame is a separate brick for construction. It must be in fact a true film newspaper, with a carefully chosen make-up, not in space but through time, so arranged as to hold the attention of the audience and give it the right proportions of rest and concentration.

The first thing that our news-reel editors will have to learn, when they have pulled, as they must, the old dummy to pieces and started making up the pages over again, is that the modern cinema has developed a new technique of journalism, as different from the pictorial statement of the old-fashioned 'topical' as our daily papers are from the *Spectator* of Addison's day. The propaganda films of Soviet Russia have, rather ironically, influenced the technique very much more than the thought of modern life; they have offered us a method of quick emphasis, of exhortation and persuasion, that suits very fully the needs of our film journalists and publicity men. The economy and punch of the good trailer, and the poster boldness of the good advertising film, are derived alike from the modern cinema of constructive cutting, and the news-reel man who knows his job will soak himself in these new applications of photography, and learn from them a system of journalism that will give his material the very maximum of pace and thrust.

That the cinema is the natural journalism of to-day, cannot be denied; ours is not a reading age; words are too tardy for us; but the very pace of life that gives the image precedence over the sentence involves also the selection of that image. It is a day of specialisation, and I see no reason why the news-reel should not be composed for specialists by specialists. Why should we look for everything in our

Gaumont Sound News van outside Lime Grove studios, 1929.

news-reels? Why should we expect a bit of every topic, a touch of every style? When we open our national newspapers, we know exactly what sort of goods we have bought with our money. If we want the style of the *Manchester Guardian*, we do not order the *Daily Mirror*; if we want the material of the *Daily Express*, we hardly dally with *The Times*. I see no reason why a chain of film newspapers and journals should not be established all over the country, each with its special features, its characteristic make-up, its peculiar circle of readers; nor why there should not be as clear a distinction between news-theatre and news-theatre as there is between the different organs of the national press.

There will always be, I know, a large proportion of foreign news-reels in the programmes of every magazine theatre, for the love of travel is rooted in the very essence of the cinema's popularity – its power to provide by proxy sensations that the picturegoer cannot himself enjoy. Just as the cinema has flourished for thirty years past on passion by proxy, courage and sentiment, riches and sophistication, it is ready to prosper to-day by its ability to bring every experience of travel to the compass of an arm-chair. The news-reel from foreign countries is the poor man's holiday, the busy man's escape into leisure. There is no part of the world that it cannot touch, no place too secret or dangerous for it to penetrate. But it cannot afford to go too far afield too constantly, to devote itself exclusively to the distant and extraordinary. We want, as well as travelling in foreign countries, to see ourselves: we want to see on the screen the reflection, although not quite the humdrum reflection, of our homes and our lives, our sports and our pleasures. We want to see ourselves as we hope we look, as we think we might look, if our ships came home; ourselves in 'ideal' homes and 'ideal' costumes; which is, after all, what the majority of newspapers try to show us every day.

And it is this shifting and balancing of material, this adjustment of a common stock to the needs of a highly differentiated public, that must concern the news-reel men of the future. They will have to compile, out of the stuff of life, a number of characteristic organs that will present to each section of the public the right aspect of material in the right way. One may have political views of a certain marked order; one may have satiric leanings; one may plump for red-hot news still pulsating over the wire. A news-reel may specialise in serials, or in competitions; in the home page, the sportlight, the fashion survey; in the nature diary, documentary and meticulous in the style of the Ufa jottings, or seductive and lyrical, as we shape it in our Welwyn studios; in the hints to England's countless animal lovers and horticulturalists; or it may take its authority from a comic strip, a critical section, or a 'correspondence' column, where news-letters from amateur photographers can regularly be shown.

In an industry of this kind the news-reel editors of to-morrow will be as important as the great directors, and the topical camera-man will come into his own at last. Many of the best photographers of the screen have in their time been newsmen, but their names have meant nothing to the public until they were news-men no longer. In the future, I think, celebrity will come to them while they are still on the job, and we shall have signed articles in topical photography, each with its own style, its own perspective, and its own visual criticism. We shall have to distinguish between the different photographers, as well as between the different editors; to know the men who work best in sound and the men who are more fully themselves in silence; the man who can best handle the individual interview and the man who best knows the value of the massed or impersonal scene. It is one thing to observe, and another to report, and still a third to edit that reporting. And from recognising the men who can best do these things, we shall gain, I hope, a new fruitfulness of observation, discovering how to go straight ahead to the vital point in any given moment of vision; to see in our own daily experience with the clarity and selection of our film travels, learning from men whose job it is to record, but whose virtue it is to use every record as a basis for the creation of something personal and new.

From *The Cinema* (London, Alexander Maclehose & Co., 1931).

Pirates of the News-Reel

Enne Fisher

This is a contemporary article from a popular weekly journal about the lighter side of the newsreel wars: the energetic competition to secure, and then to defend exclusive rights to key events by the newsreels. Many of the standard anecdotes of the newsreel pirates and the 'pinching' of stories are here, though inevitably it does not touch on the struggle for business dominance which lay behind the tales of comic disguises, lights shone in camera lenses, and smuggled cans of film.

A scoop! The news-reel men were delighted. At enormous expense their firm had secured the exclusive right to film the Cup Final. Equipment worth thousands of pounds was installed in the stadium, every vantage point was covered by cameras, and over six thousand feet of film were exposed. The 'takes' were rushed to the laboratories by racing motor-cycles, developed, printed, edited, titled, and dispatched to the cinemas. Within a few hours of the end of the match the news-reel was being shown to the public.

Then came an anti-climax. Just as the hustlers were patting themselves on the back, they were astonished to learn that the very same scenes, secured by pirate cameramen from rival news-reels, were being shown in the opposition picture theatres. The scoopers had been scooped!

To add to their annoyance, upon reviewing their own film they made a strange discovery. One of their best 'shots' showed a cheery supporter of West Ham United waving a huge mascot in the shape of a hammer, decorated with the team's colours. On closer inspection they recognised the 'supporter' as one of the rival cameramen in disguise, and discovered that the hammer was really a film camera, cleverly camouflaged!

'Never mind. We'll get our own back next year', they said. And they did!

Ever since then there has been a fierce battle of wits between the news-reel men to steal pictures from beneath the noses of their rivals, particularly at the Cup Final and the Grand National, which are the two principal bones of contention. With each successive year the efforts of the owners of 'exclusive' rights to protect their interests are increased, but the pirates have always gone one better in devising ingenious tricks to outwit them.

Pathe's Jack Cotter, disguised as a West Ham United fan for the filming of the 1923 FA Cup Final.

British Pathe

Perhaps the most undaunted and unashamed of all the picture stealers, are the men of *British Paramount News*. Maintaining the principle that all news events are public property, they have steadfastly refused to bid for exclusive rights and have openly avowed their intention to secure pictures whether permission is granted them or not. And so far they have been remarkably successful, despite the most elaborate plans to frustrate them.

Let's go up to Aintree and see the fun during the running of the Grand National Steeplechase.

Right up to the zero hour there is not an unauthorised camera in sight, but as soon as the magic words 'They're off!' echo through the crowd, and the excited spectators press forward to watch the race, pirates pop up in all directions.

Look at that fellow on top of the refreshment booth, holding a tray of fruit. Quite natural that he should ask his employer's permission to watch the race from there, but why has he taken his tray with him? You've guessed it. He is a pirate cameraman who has actually obtained a job as a refreshment peddler in order to obtain access to this private grandstand – and his tray contains a camera.

A 'spotter' is already on his track. Dashing through the crowd he climbs after him and tugs at his ankle, but by the time he succeeds in dislodging him the horses have gone by. A struggle ensues. The tray of fruit crashes to the ground. The 'spotter' makes a grab for it. But where is the camera now? It is hidden beneath the coat of that small boy over there, who is vigorously pushing his way through the crowd towards a waiting motor-cycle!

Did you notice what happened at the canal bend? Just as the horses were approaching, a coal barge drifted slowly by. And from amidst the grime an astute cameraman, who had hired it, was securing an excellent picture of the race.

And what's the excitement over here? Just outside the course is a steam shovel, engaged upon some building operations. The shovel is raised just above the level of the fence – and there is a cameraman sitting inside it.

CAMERAS, CAMERAS EVERYWHERE

A 'spotter' has caught sight of him, but cannot get near enough to stop him filming. Suddenly he gets an inspiration. Turning to a young lady by his side he borrows a mirror from her handbag, holds it up, and flashes the reflected light in the pirate's lens.

'That's spoilt his little game', he says, as he hands the mirror back with a grin.

Special attention has been given to the grandstand, for this is an important vantage point which the gate-crashers will almost certainly try to storm. Detectives posted at the entrances have scrutinised the face of every person entering the stand, and they feel confident that no rival cameraman has gained admission.

But just as the horses are passing the post a man in chauffeur's uniform is seen in the act of putting a film camera back into a luncheon basket which he had previously carried in for a well-dressed lady, presumably his employer. When challenged, the 'chauffeur' protests indignantly in broken English that the basket contains only refreshments. The basket is opened, however, and the camera is found. But there is no film inside it! Meanwhile the 'lady' is beating a most unladylike retreat with a suspicious bulge beneath her skirts.

See that 'bookie' over there? Right up to the beginning of the race he was shouting the odds and taking bets. Now he has suddenly produced a movie camera from his satchel and is getting some excellent shots of the horses passing the post. Oh, yes, he's a genuine bookmaker. But the movie pirates have been giving him lessons in the use of a hand camera and he has undertaken to steal a picture for them. Unobserved, he passes the little camera to a runner – who vanishes in the crowd – and turns his attention to the more familiar job of paying out to those who have secured another kind of 'scoop'.

There's another little incident alongside the rails. A young man on the roof of a motor-coach is seen to be operating a camera; and some way in front of him, close to the thundering hoofs of the horses, a girl is holding a small suitcase. One of the 'spotters' has just observed a suspicious trail of rubber-covered cable running from the suitcase to the coach. The case contains a microphone, and the coach has a complete sound-recording apparatus hidden beneath the seats!

And so the battle goes on. As each successful 'take' is completed by the pirates, it is smuggled out of the ground and taken to a secret rendezvous, whence it is rushed to a high-speed aeroplane and flown straight to the laboratory at Acton.

As soon as it is developed, the film is projected in negative form, while the Editor-in-Chief makes a rapid selection of best shots. Titles, previously prepared from news received by tape machine, are joined in; portions of sound track, consisting of a descriptive running commentary and noises recorded on the course, are added to those scenes which were filmed by 'silent' cameras; copies are printed four at a time in a special high-speed machine, and dispatch riders are rushed off to the leading cinemas where eager audiences are waiting to see the race on the screen.

'And that's that,' says Mr C.T. Cummins, head of the *British Paramount News*, with a smile of satisfaction.

He has reason to be proud of his 'boys'. Last year they were well ahead of their rivals in releasing the Grand National film to London cinemas, and, despite the vigilance of the 'spotters,' they lost only 200 feet of film in the fray.

Two particularly striking 'shots' were included in their day's bag. One was a panorama of the entire field, complete with sound. It was secured by two of the staff who climbed over the fence with their apparatus during the night and dug themselves into a rubbish heap, in which they remained hidden all day. After securing the picture they were spotted, their apparatus was detained and their film confiscated. But their captors were astonished to find that the film they had seized was blank and that, by some mysterious means, the valuable 'shots' had been smuggled away beneath their very eyes.

The other scoop showed a spectacular spill at one of the jumps. The cameraman who obtained it got past the detectives at the gate by disguising himself as a messenger boy and carrying a large horseshoe bouquet, presumably ordered for presentation to the victor, but actually designed to camouflage a camera.

THE 'WAR' GOES ON

All the episodes described above occurred last year. Very soon the war will break out again. Exclusive rights to film the Grand National and the Cup Final have already been secured by two of the leading news-reel organisations, and secret plans to steal unauthorised pictures have already been devised by all their competitors. At each of these events, rival cameramen – who are generally on the most friendly terms – will again become enemies for a day. And there is no knowing what tricks they may get up to next!

Pictorial Weekly, 31 March 1934.

Newsreels Show Political Bias: Editing of Spanish War Scenes Discloses Partisan Views

Brian Crosthwaite

The Spanish Civil War began in July 1936 and was duly covered by the newsreels. The war was fought between the Republican forces of the legitimate Spanish government, and the Nationalist forces led (after October 1936) by General Franco. It was not a subject on which it was possible to be neutral, and critics soon detected in some of the newsreels' coverage a bias towards the Nationalists in their avowedly impartial coverage. In particular, Gaumont-British News's notorious 'Blonde Amazon' story (on British schoolteacher Phyllis Gwatkin Williams) comes in for particular criticism here.

The newsreel cameraman is the new war-correspondent. He represents all the bravery or the great journalists of fifty years ago, who sketched – for they had no cameras – scenes of fighting on the battlefield itself. He brings to life, more vividly than any words, the plight of common people whose daily life has been suddenly spotlit by the drama of war.

But what happens when the material he has shot gets to the editorial cutting-bench? A check on recent newsreel tendencies shows that the old impartial presentation of news is disappearing. A partisan spirit has arisen. There is a strong measure of political bias. And it is time to face tip to the implications behind this vital change of style.

The brilliant work by the newsreel companies on the Abyssinian invasion and now on the Spanish civil war was at first sufficiently sensational in its presentation of the violence and grimness of the modern battlefield to be simply the highspot of every issue. But as time goes on, it is a little depressing to find such material pushed down to the lower level of baby-shows and beauty parades. On such vital situations this banal and negligent treatment should he avoided at all costs.

But the question of partisanship raises a much more serious problem

Up till quite recently the Newsreels presumably regarded themselves mainly as entertainment and information caterers (chiefly entertainment). Their aim was to serve up a popular hors d'oeuvre of the week's sport and any other items of snob-value, thrill-value, or amusement-value. They would indignantly have repudiated accusations of propaganda or the deliberate plugging of controversial issue in a one-sided manner.

But almost imperceptibly the new racket has started. In recent newsreel issues about Spain the pro-rebel bias has been too obvious to escape notice, as witness ... the fact that the Rothmere-controlled British Movietonews blatantly uses the terms 'Red' and 'Anti-Red'.

This propagandist clement in the newsreels is bound to have a telling effect on the average audience. Shots of unkempt militia-man contrasted with Mola's smart regulars, backed by a carefully worded and tendentious commentary, impel the innocent middle-classes to side with the better-dressed. And when the film uses its subtle technique of assertion by implication, the cumulative effect of atrocities and desecrations (nearly always by Government forces), becomes terrific. Many people have noticed the fact that newsreels which in previous issues had been well sprinkled with 'Red' atrocity stories presented the fall of Badajoz without reference to the mass executions of prisoners which took place there.

With typical guilt-complexes several newsreels have been careful to proclaim their impartiality. Items complimentary to the Government forces are indeed not unknown. But this does not alter the fact that no intelligent person can fail to notice the bias and political partisanship which is so rapidly establishing itself on the newsreel screens. Whether this bias is to Right or Left, it is in any case something to he regarded as dangerous. The public must be warned. And, what is more, impartiality must be regained. If the newsreels themselves are unwilling or unable to re-attain it, there will very soon – if there is not already – be a crying need for a truly-balanced newsreel, which will give both sides of the picture with equal fairness, avoid violent political lobbying on public screens, and in general keep a check on the more unscrupulous of its contemporaries.

If cinema is to have its Yellow Press, it must also have its 'Times' and its 'Manchester Guardian'.

The whole problem is recommended to the newly formed Film Council for its early attention.

THE 'BLONDE AMAZON'

The *Gaumont British* newsreel in its issue of August 13th has, I think, made a new and very dangerous departure from the rule of impartiality, which we are led to believe they have imposed on themselves, in its presentation of a witness of the Spanish rebellion. The lady interviewed, described for us as the 'Blonde Amazon', was looked after by Government troops and recounts the stories with which they regaled her – of burning 4 fascists in a car, executing 70 officers with a machine gun, and so on. She herself had seen a church burned down in front of her hotel; and she tells how the women-fighters were the worst of all.

Now we have no right to doubt this particular lady's word: but it must be pointed out that although she was selected from some hundreds of refugees from Spain, many of whom have an entirely different story to tell, she was not a witness at first hand of the most important part of her story and had apparently no knowledge of Spain to give any importance to her account.

The choosing of an unreliable but sensational witness is deplorable but perhaps understandable. The *Gaumont British* newsreel editor has however gone to considerable pains to give verisimilitude to her story by cutting in, at the appropriate and telling moments, shots of a car burning, a church burning, fierce-looking civilian soldiers their fists raised in salute, women fighting and the noise of machine guns, which in conjunction with the interview has become straight anti-government atrocity propaganda. This method of cutting to stock shots is the normal method of giving reality to the fiction film; but when it is used to give reality to what is only a witness's statement in a newsreel film which we are in the habit of accepting as objective it becomes deadly dangerous.

World Film News, vol. 1 no. 7, October 1936.

Newsreel Man in the Firing Line: The Adventures and Misadventures of Richard Butler, Pathe Cameraman in Search of Newsreel Pictures on The Aragon Front

Richard Butler

Butler was a cameraman with Pathe Gazette. He filmed in Spain at the time of the Civil War, and was assigned to the Government, or Republican side. He filmed for nine days and provided this breezy account of his experiences ('packed full of adventure, interest and ... pleasant moments'), covering the perils of filming in war-time and the problems he faced from censorship.

I produced my papers – showing them how much money I was bringing into the country. I was allowed to pass on. I reported to the British Consulate and was advised to get out of Spain without delay as they did not consider it safe for me to attempt to take photographs.

I got to an hotel and dumped my equipment and then sat down to partake of a Spanish breakfast, which to an English appetite fell far short of what I had hoped. I had a walk round the town. Almost everyone was in some sort of military uniform – or shall we say dress, as a Sam Browne over an ordinary suit of clothes, revolver in holster and the militia cap made a well-dressed soldier of the Red Army of Spain. Flags and banners flew from every car, private and otherwise; and every car had roughly painted on the initials of the organisation to which the owner belonged – P.O.U.M., F.A.I., C.N.T., U.G.T., P.S.U., and others too numerous to recall with ease, and there appeared, of course, the sickle and hammer painted on somewhere. Everyone appeared to be in high spirits, and by the look on people's faces one could not help acquiring confidence.

That night – and on most nights, so I was told – the streets were crowded with people listening to the loud-speakers giving forth the news, propaganda, etc., mingled with the 'Internationale'. This sort of thing continues to about 1 a.m. the following morning.

The next day I started making enquiries how to get to the front. Some people to whom I spoke about this regarded me with interest; others thought I was crazy. After a lot of suggestions I concluded that to visit some of the organisations would be a good idea. I first of all visited the Commission of Propaganda; then the F.A.I. headquarters; and after receiving little satisfaction I approached the P.O.U.M. I could not get a start. Everyone seemed to want to shift the responsibility of giving me papers. However, I was finally given the first encouragement from the propaganda people, who were most helpful, giving me several addresses to which I should apply for permission to take photographs in Spain.

With these papers of recommendation I thought I was fairly safe to make a start, so engaged a car to go to Madrid. Everywhere the roads are in a bad state and desperately in need of repair. We had not gone far, and everything seemed to be going well, when we were halted by a road sentry, who drew his revolver and kept it pointing steadily in my direction, while I gave him all the papers I possessed to read. He mumbled something in Russian and then called up a comrade, and together they decided that I should about turn. The driver of the car tried his best to explain, but this only served to make the guards more excited; they were madly gesticulating, and waving their arms about in the air. That revolver did look pretty threatening, so late that night I arrived back in Barcelona feeling fed-up at having apparently wasted a day and about 200 pesetas.

But this first set-back only went to prove how important it was to have every paper that was procurable before starting off again. The reason for these difficulties, I discovered was due to the fact that two Continental cameramen had taken pictures at the Government fronts and that films containing military information of an important character had found their way into Rebel hands.

The Commission of Propaganda now came to my aid in a whole-hearted manner, after I explained that I was out in Spain to obtain pictures of an impartial nature and to show the British public the Government as well as the other side to the question. So many Rebel pictures had been shown, I pointed out, but very few of the Government side.

Two days later more papers were obtained, and in one of the Commission of Propaganda cars I set off for the Aragon Front. But twenty miles out, owing, I inferred, to the excessive vibration of the car caused by the bad roads, an oil pipe burst and ran the engine out of oil. I waited with the car while the driver went on in another car to the next village, returning an hour later with the necessary oil and accessories for repairs.

During his absence I visited a farmhouse about one hundred yards off the road, and was given wine and bread by two old peasants who cried like children when the war was mentioned – their two sons were fighting somewhere on the Aragon Front. I thanked them in bad French and a little Spanish; however, they seemed to understand. It is dangerous to drink water out in the country, and so if you get too much of a thirst you must be able to carry your liquor well, or there will be two wars going on.

I arrived at Barbastro that night about forty miles away from the Front, and had to sleep in a small bed with the driver, the town being full up with troops on their way to the Front. Next morning I set off at eight a.m. for 'the bloody hell', as some called it in the town billets. On the way the back axle snapped. I hired another car and so on to the Front, arriving in what was once a town, but now a mere heap of bricks. I reported to the Committee and officer in charge, and proceeded on foot to the Front-line trenches where spasmodic ride and machine-gun fire was going on. No one took much notice except myself, but I soon became accustomed to it.

It was not long before I unpacked my camera, and started getting a few shots – some excellent scenes of sniping, etc. I spent the day here. The night before, I was informed, there had been an attack by the Moors, their front line being only 350 yards away. I was told in the trenches that priests encouraged and blessed the men before they went into an attack – giving them crosses to carry round their necks and promising them that should they be killed in battle they would go straight to Paradise. My informant told me that five to six hundred Moors had been shot down the night before, but I could not see any from the Government lines. So I decided to investigate, and, under the protection of a ditch, crawled out about eighty yards and got several shots of dead Moors – all around on every side I could see the countryside strewn with these corpses. I counted up to 500; then lost count. I did not see any 'Spanish Rebel' corpses on this part, only Moors. Every now and then

British Pathe

Bomb wreckage in Barcelona, from *Pathe Gazette*.

the dust would be raised by a rifle bullet, and I was glad of the cover afforded by the ditch I was crawling in. I slept that night in a place that was once a house – straw on the floor and huge holes in the roof and walls.

Next day I visited another battery behind Tardienta and took several 'shots' of the troops. They all seemed cheery souls, and the camera caused quite an amount of interest. During the time I was there, an unexpected flank attack was commenced by a small body of Rebels, which was soon repulsed by the men of the battery with rifle fire. Often the Rebels broke through the line at some weak spot and got lost and endeavoured to fight their way back to their own lines. After one has seen the country, this is quite easily understood.

I travelled the following day to Septimo, miles further up the line, and reported to the Committee and officer in charge. My food supplies were limited, so I sent the driver back to get more stock. He took the best part of a day to get some tinned provisions and bread, having to go about thirty to forty miles inland for it. I slept that night in a room with about a dozen soldiers on straw, all of them in high spirits and very merry and bright. My cameras caused much interest, and everybody wanted his photograph taken. Up at dawn, I was glad to get out away from the straw, which I am sure, from my discomfort and the state of my underclothes, was lousy. I took some 'shots' in Septimo all in ruins, and got permission to go to Huesca Front line, some 2,000 yards away. The driver arrived at a part of the road where sandbag barricades were to be seen all around.

Here was a good picture, so I started getting the cameras out of the case when there came a voice in good English, 'Get down, you bloody fool! Get back!' The driver backed the car and I took the advice received.

I met an Englishman commanding one of the Government batteries. He explained that we were right in the front line, and where the driver had stopped the car was a spot well covered by about four or five Rebel machine-guns; fortunately no shots were fired and we proceeded with more caution. I went into the trenches with the Englishman and got some more photographs, and it was here I was amused at the following incident. Rebel trenches were only fifty yards away, and Government men and the Rebels would shout across to each other insults of every kind. As they were in Spanish I cannot repeat them, but I could use my imagination.

Going to the battery just behind the front line, which is well covered by a thickly wooded stream, I sat down by one of the gun pits and had a chat. A couple of bullets cut off a twig and some leaves hardly a yard off, so I shifted to a safer spot in the gun pit. No photographs are allowed to be taken of the guns or the activities of the gunners. Returning to Septimo, I had some grub and came back that evening to the front line to talk with the Englishman, who gave me some photographs. I drank Spanish wine till I thought I had better get back while I could.

Next day I visited front line kitchens and the War Hospital at Tiers, a little village about five hundred yards behind the line. My companion and myself had to take cover from 'planes on several occasions. They were very active and would circle overhead menacingly and keep flying round as though to depart, but would reappear when least expected.

I got good shots of a Government attack through a rifle firing hole. They ran into a machine gun and got cut up badly; the pictures show them falling and retiring in rather bad disorder. The shortage of arms and ammunition was certainly evident. Visiting Tiers again, I took some shots of the Rebel lines through a tele lens, but had them cut out by a censor as they showed the Government position in relation to the Rebel lines. I returned to Septimo for a night and had a sing-song with the Government soldiers; they certainly could sing, a quartet putting on a Mills Brothers act to perfection.

I was off at dawn to a heavy battery position. They were giving me a position to the right of Huesca. I took two hundred feet of film going; then I moved to a new and more comfortable position and made several shots of shells bursting on Rebel positions. After a few hours I returned to Huesca Front line, and had lunch with the P.O.U.M. I got some good shots and during lunch several rifle bullets hit the top of the wall in the room – or what was once a room. It had no roof, but we were covered by a wall in front of us, and were some six feet or more out of the line of fire. Under the conditions, I didn't enjoy my lunch as well as I could have done. Nobody else took any notice, so I endeavoured to disregard the firing, but was nevertheless glad when lunch was over.

Next day I left for Siriema and discovered before I had journeyed many miles that it was necessary to buy a new tyre for the car; it was not exactly 'new', but better than the one that had cut up badly on the rough roads. Arriving at Siriema I reported at the Air Field for permission to take pictures of the British Red Cross and Air Field – the general here commands the whole of the Aragon Front – but my papers were not good enough for him and he graciously had the driver and myself put under arrest and shoved into prison. Although we did not possess firearms, we had an armed guard with us all the time. My cameras and films were all taken and things looked pretty black. I spoke all the French and Spanish I knew, but of no avail.

However, that night we were removed to a house and given a bed to sleep in. There were literally thousands of bugs; it was a most vile and filthy place. The bed was damp and I was indeed grateful to see the dull grey light of morning, after lying awake through the night.

I was still finding it difficult to get someone to understand the English language. At last I was understood in French, and was told that the police had telephoned Barcelona. This sounded better. Our guard was glad of a drink, so I let him have what he wanted – he soon became quite jolly and obliging, and I eventually managed to get to the police head quarters. Here I 'phoned Barcelona myself, and found out that papers were on their way from the Commission of Propaganda.

That night I left for Barcelona, managing after difficulty and much signing of papers to regain possession of my cameras, but the films had gone to the aviation field. I found out later that they would be developed in Madrid, censored and returned to Propaganda, and as no one seemed to be in any hurry at all I became almost desperate trying to hurry things up and get hold of the films

Just before leaving for England I learned that the films in question would be shown to the various censor committees, who, if they considered it prudent to release the films, would instruct the Commission of Propaganda to have them dispatched via express transport to Paris.

The censoring problem is the biggest 'headache' of all. During the Abyssinian War, one Committee was sufficient to enable one's films to be either rejected or released but six or seven and even more censoring organisations have to be considered before Spanish war films can leave that country without further interference.

So ended nine days packed full of adventure, interest and, I must also say, some of the most pleasant moments with some very fine types of men – confident, happy, but terribly handicapped by the shortage of arms and ammunition.

World Film News, vol. 2 no. 12, March 1938.

Newsreel Scripts: A Case Study

Anthony Aldgate

The documents created by the newsreels as part of their production process – commentary scripts, assignment sheets, cameramen's dope sheets, shot lists – are an important means of understanding how the news medium was created, but their relative inaccessibility has, until recently, prevented the use by historians that they merit. Anthony Aldgate here analyses some of the commentary scripts of Gaumont-British News during the Spanish Civil War, noting not only what was said and what was omitted, but what was amended by commentator/editor E.V.H. Emmett before the commentary was recorded. Many such documents are now available online from the BUFVC's British Universities Newsreel Database.

The interest shown by historians in cinema newsreels as a primary source for historical study has centred upon the actual newsreel issues, as they would have been shown in the cinemas, with particular regard being given to the individual stories which made up those issues. Historians have tried to determine what message and information permeated each story by an examination of the newsreel editors' juxtaposition of picture, spoken commentary, musical accompaniment and sound effects. It should not be forgotten, however, that the spoken commentary to an individual story generally went through several drafts before being finally accepted and laid over the edited film. Even a cursory perusal of the drafts of a commentary, where they exist, throws interesting light on how a newsreel company decided where its emphasis should lie.

The scripts of the commentaries for all the major newsreel companies are available in their respective archives, though they are frequently incomplete and rarely catalogued. The *Gaumont British News* is perhaps the best of the newsreels upon which to conduct such an exercise, mainly because its editor and commentator were one and the same person, E.V.H. Emmett. It would appear that Emmett was particularly prone to amending and redrafting his typewritten scripts and the scripts to all the Gaumont stories from 1934, with Emmett's handwritten amendments and rewrites upon them, are kept in chronological order in part of the Visnews Film Library. The short survey which follows gives some ideas, albeit tentative and speculative, on the sort of material thrown up for the consideration of the historian.

In 1937, for example, the *Gaumont British News* prepared a story for inclusion in its issue no. 338 which was to be shown in the cinemas on 25 March. The commentary, written by Emmett, originally read as follows:

> Mr Anthony Eden, the Foreign Secretary, has discussed with the T.U.C. the question of non-intervention in Spain, and our news pictures this week from the land of Civil War include these of British prisoners. Some of Britain's army of unemployed enrolled for road-making under the Spanish Government at wages of £5 a week, but they were captured by the Insurgents. Here they are in a detention camp, being served with food, of which there is no scarcity.

Emmett was evidently not very happy with three points in his typewritten script as it stood, for he proceeded to make changes to it. The phrase 'has discussed with the T.U.C.' was crossed out and replaced with the handwritten insert 'is again discussing'. The word 'Britain's' in the phrase 'Britain's army of unemployed' was underlined, presumably with the intention of being dropped. Most of all the phrase 'at wages of £5 a week' was circled and scored in the margin with the comment 'Out'. It is possible of course that these small excisions and changes were to be made because the story was considered to be marginally over-long and because it was felt that more breathing space was needed in the commentary. It is equally possible, however, to speculate that by the very nature of the changes he intended to make, Emmett was indulging in a common enough Gaumont bias in the selection and presentation of the news. Gaumont was a newsreel company of decidedly 'Conservative sympathies', as Nicholas Pronay has recently reiterated.[1] And those sympathies would have been reinforced at the editorial conferences which were held every Friday and presided over by Castleton Knight, the production chief who controlled Gaumont's policy making. They would have been acted upon at the level of production by Emmett, a one-time insurance agent who trained for the Stock Exchange before entering journalism and then the newsreels, among others. It might be suggested, for instance, that by deleting the reference to the T.U.C., Emmett was hastening to point out that the Government was acting very much on its own initiative over this matter; or that by dropping the direct references to Britain, when mentioning unemployment, Emmett was simply omitting a point which he felt did not merit undue emphasis; or that the mention of a sum like '£5 a week' earned working in Spain would appear to be quite lucrative and worthwhile, and therefore once again should be dropped. After all the scripts emphasized that the men shown had only been 'road-making' in Spain; there was purposely no mention of their being engaged in any fighting. And even by 1943 the Wartime Social Survey in its inquiry *The Cinema Audience* considered that those people earning a weekly sum 'up to £5' constituted the lowest income group in the country and 75% of the sample population. In the end the whole story was dropped completely from issue no. 338 and was not shown on the intended date of 25 March.

It was used, however, in Gaumont's next issue, no. 339, on 29 March in an amended version:

Mr Anthony Eden the Foreign Secretary is again discussing the question of non-intervention in Spain, and our news pictures this week from the land of civil war include these of British prisoners. Some of the army of unemployed enrolled for road-making under the Spanish Government, but they were

```
SIR KINGSLEY WOOD ON PENSIONS.
                                                      Mrs
        The Mother of Parliaments is going to play/Santa Claus, and
we have askedSir Kingsley Wood to tell you how.
TROTTING AND JUMPING.
        Lyndonville, Vermont is crazy over horses and any excuse for a
race is considered better than none.   By way of a change they
had the trotters out on a snow-clad Main Street --- and if that
isn't a good excuse they just race anyway.
        Mexico City had the cavalry out too --- not for racing but
for training.   They say that cavalry is out of date --- but the
cavalry won't admit it.
EDEN AND BRITISH PRISONERS IN SPAIN.
        Mr Anthony Eden the Foreign Secretary is again discussing the
question of non-intervention in Spain, and our news pictures this
week from the land of civil war include these of British prisoners.
Some of the army of unemployed enrolled for road-making under the
Spanish Government, but they were captured by the insurgents.
Here they are in detention camp , being served out with food,
of which there is no scarcity.   In the fighting line our cameraman
is on the spot, securing the first sound-film interview in
the trenches.   And then --- the deluge -------- Taking some of
his pictures from a ruined building and some from an armoured
car, our cameraman secured this grim record of an attack on the
village.
```

Gaumont-British News no. 339 commentary script.

captured by the insurgents. Here they are in detention camp, being served out with food, of which there is no scarcity. In the fighting line our cameraman is on the spot, securing the first sound-film interview in the trenches. And then, the deluge. Taking some of his pictures from a ruined building and some from an armoured car, our cameraman secured this grim record of an attack on the village.

This script is interesting for several reasons. First of all it still maintains that the men who went to Spain from Britain were unemployed. Even now, there is of course much debate about this point. A.J.P. Taylor, for instance, states that 'Of the 2,000 odd British citizens who fought for the Spanish Republic, the great majority were workers, particularly unemployed miners'.[2] Yet in his book *Britain Divided*, K.W. Watkins holds that 'The best estimate is that only somewhere between an eighth and a quarter were unemployed, the rest relinquished their jobs, often secure ones, in order to go'.[3] Wherever the truth may lie on the unemployment issue, the fact remains that the pecuniary motive alone was not, as Gaumont's commentary implied, the compelling factor which sent men to Spain. Idealism and ideological commitment provided just as strong a motivating force, but Gaumont made no mention of them. Secondly, this report suggests once again that the prisoners had gone to Spain to make roads, though there can be little doubt that as members of the International Brigade they would have contributed most to the fighting. It is a notable feature of the script that it makes no mention whatsoever of the title 'The International Brigade'. Finally the commentary goes out of its way to mention how well they were looked after in detention by Franco's forces, at the same time making it clear that the Insurgents were amply supplied with provisions to sustain at least one part of their war effort.

Having made the points they wished to make in this script about the British contingent of the International Brigade, Emmett and Gaumont adhered to a similar line throughout the course of the Civil War, manifesting on several occasions the same capacity for bias and selectivity, both in what was cut out in the final draft stages of a commentary and in what was left in.

The final script for one story in issue no. 358, for example, which was released on 3 June, 1937, read:

Looking strangely criminal with their cropped hair, these men were unemployed when they went to Spain to work on road-making and other such occupations. They became part of the International Brigade under the Spanish Government; they were taken prisoner by Insurgent troops and placed in a Franco detention camp where they were given food and a few cigarettes.

This commentary made advances as well as further retreats. Once more there is an insistence upon unemployment, road-making and the good care received from Franco's troops, this time extending to cigarettes in addition to food. The introduction of a comment that the men looked 'strangely criminal' was a particularly significant addition to the script. But for the first time at least these prisoners were correctly acknowledged to be members of the International Brigade.

The penultimate draft of this script had in fact stated categorically that these men were actually 'fighting under the Spanish Government', but the word 'fighting' was of course omitted in the final commentary. Presumably the use of that word would have undermined the point that they were given comparatively menial jobs to do. In any case, at a time when the British Government was reluctant to acknowledge openly the presence of fighting troops in Spain, other than the Republican and Insurgent protagonists, it was too much to expect the British newsreels to do the Government's job for them and to reveal the extent of foreign intervention on Spanish soil. The newsreel issues show that to be the case, and the final drafts of the newsreel scripts simply endorse such an opinion.

History, vol. 61, 1976.

NOTES

1. Nicholas Pronay, 'The newsreels: the illusion of actuality', in Paul Smith (ed.), *The Historian and Film* (Cambridge, 1976), fn. 24, p. 118.
2. A.J.P. Taylor, *English History 1914–1945* (London, 1965), p. 396.
3. K.W. Watkins, *Britain Divided* (London, 1963), p. 168.

Newsreel

C. Day Lewis

Cecil Day-Lewis puts into poetry what many on the Left felt, that the newsreels and the cinema-going experience were anaesthetising the public against the realities of the Spanish Civil War.

Enter the dream-house, brothers and sisters, leaving
Your debts asleep, your history at the door:
This is the home for heroes, and this loving
Darkness a fur you can afford.

Fish in their tank electrically heated
Nose without envy the glass wall: for them
Clerk, spy, nurse, killer, prince, the great and the defeated,
Move in a mute day-dream.

Bathed in this common source, you gape incurious
At what your active hours have willed –
Sleep-walking on that silver wall, the furious
Sick shapes and pregnant fancies of your world.

There is the mayor opening the oyster season:
A society wedding: the autumn hats look swell:
An old crocks' race, and a politician
In fishing-waders to prove that all is well.

Oh, look at the warplanes! Screaming hysteric treble
In the long power-dive, like gannets they fall steep.
But what are they to trouble –
These silvery shadows to trouble your watery, womb-deep sleep?

See the big guns, rising, groping, erected
To plant death in your world's soft womb.
Fire-bud, smoke-blossom, iron seed projected –
Are these exotics? They will grow nearer home:

Grow nearer home – and out of the dream-house stumbling
One night into a strangling air and the flung
Rags of children and thunder of stone niagaras tumbling,
You'll know you slept too long.

From *Overtures to Death, and other poems* (London: Jonathan Cape, 1938).

The News-Reel

Robert Herring

This essay was first published in 1937 as 'Notes on the News-reel' by Charles Grinley in Life and Letters To-day. Curiously, it was republished the following year as being by Robert Herring, in a collection of essays on the response of the Left to the rise of Fascism, In Letters of Red, edited by E. Allen Osborne in 1938. Robert Herring was film critic on the London Mercury, and edited Life and Letters To-day. Whoever the true author maybe, this politically-informed criticism argues that 'the news-reel isn't news, but a screen in front of it', and points out that it shies away from the kind of committed filmmaking shown in some documentaries.

The news-reel has five units devoted to it in this country. It appears twice a week. On special occasions 'flash editions' are sent out, followed by longer versions. It has its own ways of getting the pictures, and its own ways of delivering them. It has its own theatres and its own public. During the last few years the issues at stake in world events have made that public increasingly news-minded. The news-reel has become news.

Events that empty ordinary cinemas, such as a big fight or Jubilee, fill the news-theatres. For this box-office privilege, the news-reel pays. If its pictures fail to do justice to a happening, as many thought the Coronation films failed, there is an outcry. If they do more than justice, as some thought the reel of King Alexander's assassination did, there is an outcry. Recently Paramount and Universal were so impressed with their respective reels of the war in the East that they did not censor them. This was found surprising and, in some quarters, outrageous; Mr Jeffrey Bernerd, of *Gaumont-British News* (which did not have so full a record), stated: 'I disagree entirely with Mr Cummins, editor of *Paramount News* ... The exhibitors of this country run their theatres with the idea of entertaining the public. To show the ghastly destruction of human beings in the most horrific form is, I contend, letting down the exhibitor'.

The remarkable thing about this seems to me not that the pictures were uncut, but that it created comment that they were. Indirectly it is thereby admitted that we have become used to news-reels being deleted or doctored. Film-fan and film-maker have for long boasted that one of the cinema's gifts was that it allowed us to see, with the vividness of visual impact, what was actually happening. Yet now it has become remarkable if a news-reel shows what the camera took. For this reason it is high time that this product of what is still sometimes called the candid camera should be considered in some detail. News-films have been with us from the very start of moving pictures, but, as far as I know, their history as a separate branch of the cinema has never been traced.

I make no claim to be a historian. I am doing no more than providing some notes on the news-reel. I hope their incompleteness may be atoned for by their topicality – and that word may well serve as a starting-point.

News-reels were the first films. Though they were not called that, there they were – rough sea at Dover, boot-black in the street, and the famous train which ran towards the audience (in consequence panic-struck). These were actual happenings and it may be remarked in passing that the French still call the news-reel *actualités*. Other early news-reels were the Corbett-Fitzsimmons fight, the Diamond Jubilee of Victoria, her funeral, and that of President McKinley in 1901. Not long after, Cherry Kearton was filming London from an airship, Tolstoi was 'turned on' and pictures of George the Fifth's coronation were shown that same night in Paris. In those days, if my memory is not at fault, the reels most familiar to filmgoers were *Pathe Pictorial* and the *Topical Budget*. Since Pathe was French, it perhaps followed that fashion played a prominent part. Certainly no less well known than Bunny and lamblike Little Mary were those rather liverish-looking ladies who displayed hats, as I see them now, too big for their heads in dresses too tight for their busts. The 'tints' were usually watered pink and the kind of uncompromising green in which railings are painted. The ladies manoeuvred on to a set fraught with palms, one would sit down at the same time skilfully opening her coat. As soon as seated, she would arise – because the other lady walked in front of her, as likely as not twirling a parasol. In revenge for this, the first lady, with an air of abandon, would either remove eight hatpins very fast or slowly revolve her head, thus showing that whereas her colleague undoubtedly had bats in the belfry, she herself had a couple more bird-wings on her own brim than anyone else could support. In which she was right …

These tarnished ladies, with the sickly smiles, were the forerunners of the bathing mannequins and Miss Day of Judgment who now 'crash' the cine-magazines. Let it be noticed that as the 'budget' developed, it split into sections, the cinemagazine, the news-reel, the instructional, and, later, the documentary. But already there was evident the format and make-up which militated against the true reporting of news. True news-reporting does not consist only of presenting facts. It consists of presenting them so that they make their full impression. In a reel of five items, you can present appalling shots of an earthquake. But you can make it seem unimportant, even irrelevant, by glossing it over and surrounding it with four others of, say, a cricket match, Ascot, a ceremonial parade, a royal drive.

I criticise the news-reel, for I think their editors do not fulfil their responsibilities as journalists, as do editors of newspapers. Heaven knows there are enough editors apparently unaware of any save that of pleasing the boss who sets circulation figures. But there are others, and that gives not only respect but variety to the Press. I do not find that variety in the news-reels. We know the reason. It's the audience. That, of course, is to say the picture people's idea of the audience. I'd bet a Mickey to a Movietone that they still refer to a married woman who has children as 'materfamilias' – and materfamilias has to have her item. She has, say, the Duchess of Hog's Norton at a bazaar, or scenes at a poultry show; something to appeal to her shopping instincts. Paterfamilias likes to remember his young days, so we have a beauty parade (commentary – *'bird show of another kind, let's hope they ARE kind'*), and a sport item. Pater-to-be is still interested in sport, so we have a bit more, and as the 'rising generation' is mechanically-minded, we have airplanes or cars. The young man's girl has to be considered (that's why he bought two seats) – she gets a giggly bit about sunbathing or 'Eskimo Eve chews Greenland Gable's shoeleather'. Then, to encourage all of them, there's another military parade or

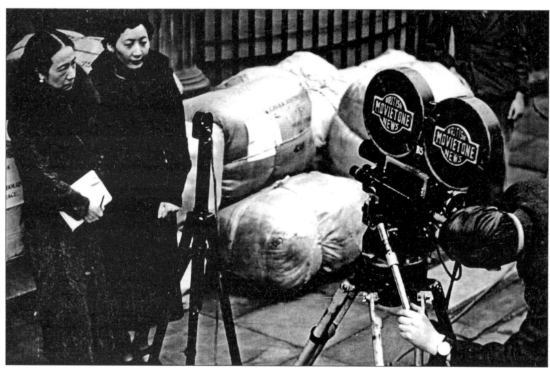

British Movietone News cameraman filming Madame Chiang Kai-Shek.

BUFVC

'naval occasion,' it doesn't matter which, so long as the male can feel he's one of the men and the females can impose on their own man their fantasy-thrill from the others, while bands blare over the whole show.

There's your reel. And there it has to be, because the cinema caters to that audience. Say it shouldn't. But that's its audience; in press-terms, its 'readers'.

Now, in fiction films, you find a different type of audience for Arliss, Dietrich, Spencer Tracy. Each appeals to a different section of the public. You'll get people who stay away from a cinema if Shirley Temple or Cagney is showing. But you don't get people staying away from a news-reel because it contains a crèche item or dirt-track scenes. They may complain after. They do. The news-reel answers back by putting in a little to please in case a little should annoy. It plays Safety First – that's the joke – while it's meant to be showing the world to-day.

The news-reel's political or propagandist aspect is patent. Certain reels are under the control of those from whom unbiassed news is hardly to be expected. For varying reasons, different news-reels stress different sides of human activity. Mr Sanger, of British Movietone, has answered the criticism that his reel concentrates unduly on sport and militarism with the reply that these are two of the subjects richest in that movement which is the essence of movie. Not much of an answer, you may think – hunger marches have as much movement as an inspection – but it's safe (for the time being), and news-reels play for safety, and we might as well admit that the editors of the news-reel know, probably, more about their audiences than you or I.

Political considerations apart, it isn't just chance that the 'gazette' has to try, in its limited compass, to be all things to all men – and women. It has to remember not only our Alf, who's paid for his Maisie's seat, but the mood he wants Maisie to be in afterwards. It has to remember that maybe Alf's dad and mum have gone out, so as to leave the parlour free, and it has to remember that there are lots of Alfs, without a Maisie and vice versa. It has to remember such a hell of a lot that you can't blame it if a little matter like the world outside gets left – well, outside. For the news-reel, on the whole, and with notable exceptions, can't show us the world as it is. For one reason. It is coming to terms with the world as congregated in cinemas.

No news-reel has yet had the courage to set up as the equivalent of a Liberal or Labour twopenny daily. With the exception of Paramount, the only reel to cover Mosley's East End March, none have the courage to be a little more complete or considered in what they chronicle than the rest. Now that the news-reel is news; it is essential that it should wake up to the sense of duty which has, believe it or not, for long animated the better sections of the Press. When we see how little effect that has we must agree with someone roughly like Nurse Cavell and say even the best is not enough.

In the beginning, it may have been. But now we have to admit that the only way to achieve what is good is to change the standards of what was once certified best. At the start, news-film, like any other movie, had the advantage of novel presenting of new matter. Like any other unfair advantage too ruthlessly used, that balloon has been popped. The news-public has got back to the first simplicity of expecting a news-film to be news with a capital 'N'. The news-film-folk don't know it, won't admit it, or must not. But the result is that all the terrific costs of covering, camera-ing, commentating, developing, dispatching, directing a news-reel are, in final effect, nullified by *The March of Time,* which sets out to be not topical but contemporaneously historical, reminding that history, like Anna Neagle, marches on.

The news-reel is carried a step farther by *The March of Time.* We may remark that this particular reel would be nowhere if it hadn't the cuteness to nip in, mouse-like, on the cheese of documentary, just as documentary learnt how to get the Gruyère front the double-teethed trap of 'news' and 'interest' cinema.

Theoretically, I am taking no sides, I am merely observing that the result of more than thirty odd years of news-reel reporting has ended in some clever guys realising that there is enough news not reported to make it worth while reconstructing some. I say nothing against *The March of Time,* which has given us adequately interesting and informative screen-articles on many subjects of which it is essential to know. I am grateful for much knowledge of Hawaii, Colonel la Rocque, the Irish Free State, China, the Western Plains. *March of Time* may be okay. But supposing there were a *Mark Time o' Time?*

The news-reel has won great facilities for reporting major events. Its power to preserve for posterity is recognised by authorities. Yet it has been beaten at its own game. On paper, the news-reel exists to show what happened at the time and in the place at which it happened. Experience has taught us that, in fact, we only see, first, what the sponsors wish, secondly, what the cameramen are there to record. We know by now that a commentary can tip the scales, as witness the American film, THE DEAD MARCH. Banned by the English censor in its original anti-war version, it is passed with a new commentary which gives a new angle to the shots, and creates the effect of a recruiting picture. We know what happened about the film of Alexander's assassination, why the *Krassin* pictures were withdrawn, why the Windsor wedding was not shown in this country.

We know, in fact, what's behind the news. So the news-reel isn't news, but a screen in front of it. *Just when the news-reel is, journalistically, most 'news'.* We've got used to that happening in the worse sections of the Press. But the dopey quality of screen-entertainment (and the screen is still assumed to provide that more than information) prevents the majority from observing that it is happening in the cinema. I am reminded of the patient who refuses food through the ordinary channels and is too exhausted by his effort to notice his involuntary assimilation by injection.

The news-reel 'lasts', as they say, for a quarter of an hour. I may seem to overrate its importance. But look at the effect it has had on every form of film, not excluding the fictional – after all what else is VICTORIA THE GREAT but nostalgic news-reel in reverse? The early 'budget' or 'gazette' incorporated 'interest' shots. Peeps at distant lands, and birds on nests crystallised into travelogue (Fox's *Magic Carpet,* Fitzpatrick's *Travel Talks),* and scientific film *(Secrets of Life,* etc). When both of these grew – by reason of their acceptance in the newsreel – they left it. They became the documentary. The hen-on-nest became Buy British Eggs. The travelogue, either a pamphlet for cruises or ballyhoo for the Empire. *This is why the Strand has Bananas.* Substitute tea, coffee, stamp-paper, or anything else that happens to be sponsored. For though the documentarian claims directness and facts without fiction, the fact remains that he is liable to be as much at the mercy of his financiers as other film-makers. The difference up to date – and thank God it is a big difference – is that he usually believes in the propaganda of his bosses, or else finds it so weak, he can turn it to his own uses.

The result of this freedom has been many admirable films. They have brought a new light into the cinema. And a new life. They have resulted in several of the more prominent documentarians being hauled, not unwillingly, to America. They have in part produced – I really don't think it's unfair to say this – those 'commercial' Hollywood pictures such as FURY, CRIME DOESN'T PAY, ZOLA, PASTEUR, THEY WON'T FORGET, etc., as it seems, *ad lib.* Between writing, I have seen the American documentaries shown at the Paris exhibition – even London appears to have room for LAND WITHOUT BREAD, MILLIONS OF US, THE WORLD TO-DAY, which are American 'social problem' pictures. Commercial films (Fidelity) produce pictures on KEW GARDENS and DANGER AT SEA, a survey of the English lighthouse system. Even now, Gaumont British Instructional produce fifty pictures a year. There are the *Three-Minute* series of Zenifilm, the shorts of Painlevé, and many others. There are also such compositions as FORGOTTEN MEN, THE WORLD IN REVOLT, and all the rest in which old news-items have been used in conjunction with recent, usually retrogressive, sound-tracks. It can be argued that these have nothing to do with the news-reel, because they're documentary. That is a favourite argument. It is also my own best answer. That answer is – the documentary, the travelogue, the interest and the instructional, as opposed to scientific or purely educational, film developed from the news-reel. It was bound to develop. So was the news-reel. But that didn't develop as much as its offshoots. The Gas Light and Coke Company make a film on the question of NUTRITION, a subject of national importance. They follow it with one on CHILD-REN AT SCHOOL. Hounded newsreel editors may remind me that these films are not for commercial distribution. I reply, that is the fault of the news-reels. These are their subjects and they either ban or ignore them. It remains for a business undertaking not specifically concerned with either film or feeding to step in.

113

There should be no need for them to step in. I am not being rude to Gas Light and Coke. I admire and am vociferously grateful. I merely point out that their films stand out because they deal with things that are 'news'. It is news, say what you like, if forty million people in the United Kingdom are below par on diet. It is news, like it or not, to know that one teacher has to control, let alone instruct, a class of fifty children for whom both lavatories and heating are inadequate.

These things are not stated so forcibly in the newsreels. Life as seen by 'the eyes and ears of the world' is a series of parades – mannequin, military, monarchic. The Pope and Perry. New Pier at Folkestone, Old Peer in New York, Marlene Dietrich says 'Nuts', Pet Monkey beats her by Three Syllables, and so on. The great proportion of important events are not recorded, or at most given cursory notice. So for all its apparent 'service', the news-reel isn't giving us the real news. A pity. But it is more a pity that, in consequence, audiences don't give the news-reel the whole of their attention. They drop in, notice the items they want, doze through the rest. They don't study how it is put together or what outlook it expresses. And so, by degrees, slogans can be dinned into the audiences' ears till they become familiar with them, the first step towards accepting

Gaumont-British News Camera team at Croydon Airport, 1937.

them. A viewpoint can be presented until it seems the natural one. Subtly, the propaganda of the news-reel can sink in – without anyone asking whose propaganda it is.

During elections we have seen the screen used by politicians. Do we imagine that's the only time they are the voice behind the screen? THE GAP, that air defence film which told us where we got off if we didn't join the Territorials, is only one film of news-interest made by the National Government as propaganda. The implications are obvious.

All right if you like that. All right if you don't; you can't do anything about it. But realise what isn't done. Realise what is done. And realise what might be done in the way of nose-leading public opinion during what are politely referred to as 'times of emergency'.

The news-reel has, therefore, led to the reconstructed news-reel. It must be admitted as a joke that the reenactment of events should produce an impression nearer the truth than that given by screen-reporting. What conclusion is reached? 'The governments of the world know that with the movie you can propagandise and persuade and, perhaps even more important, you can distract attention away from what is significant and towards all that is trivial. What will happen from the desire not to please but to propagandise the people? ... We have to face the possibility that the moving picture ... may even cease to be a form of entertainment' (Gilbert Seldes, *Movies for the Millions,* Batsford, 7s 6d).

But I think that years hence it will be found very entertaining – when more is known of the world to-day than we may now know – to look at the news-reel of to-day. The news-reels will seem the comics, and it will be the Marx Brother films that seem more truthful, less distorted in their picture of a civilisation which has found ways of preserving everything but itself.

Originally published in *Life and Letters To-day*, vol. 17 no. 10, Winter 1937.
Republished in E. Allen Osborne (ed.), *In Letters of Red* (London: Michael Joseph, 1938).

The News-Reel Cameraman

Robert Humfrey

Robert Humfrey had been a cameramen prior to the First World War. In his book Careers in the Films, he gives a light but not uninformative account of the sort of qualities a newsreel cameraman should possess. 'News-reel work is a strenuous job, but it should appeal to a robust youth fond of an open-air life and of travel with a spice of adventure thrown in ...'

Though in the earlier days it took some time for exhibitors to grasp the fact that the public vastly preferred the topical item to the sickly second-rate drama prevalent at the time, to-day the news-reel item occupies a very important position in the cinema programme, almost equal in interest to that of the second feature film. This is hardly surprising, since it enables patrons to watch in comfort news events taking place all over the world, and to vizualize the news about which they read in the papers. In addition to scenes from overseas, important home events take a big part in news-reels.

Nowadays when important events such as Jubilee or Coronation processions take place, it is not uncommon to hear people remark, 'I'm not going to be jostled about in the crowds, I'm going to wait and see it comfortably at the pictures in the evening'. This attitude is not surprising, because the average person must either pay a high price to watch such processions from an elevated position, or else chance his luck at one point on the ground amongst a seething mass of people, and run the risk of seeing nothing at all, as happened to hundreds during the Silver Jubilee procession. Compared with this, the big news-reel organizations present the event as seen from perhaps a dozen or more commanding positions for which they have paid big money, thus enabling the cinema patron to watch a far more complete ensemble than he could possibly hope to obtain from a single vantage point. In addition, the advent of sound has made these spectacles so realistic on the screen that it is difficult to realize that one is not present on the occasion. The news-reels, without a doubt, enable many thousands to watch these events who would otherwise never have a chance to do so. This branch of film work is now highly specialized. Paul used to drive back from his historic Derbies in a wagonette with his apparatus and precious film. Conditions are very different to-day, when the classic race and its incidental scenes are probably covered by as many as a dozen cameras working from different angles. In addition, aerial views are taken from a plane. As soon as a scene is complete, the negative is rushed back to the laboratories by waiting motor-cycles, whose riders are often dirt-track racers. It is probably necessary, owing to pre-arranged contracts, to deliver a certain number of copies to the more important theatres by 7 p.m., a quick business now that sound has to be added, and which can only be accomplished by elaborate and efficient organization.

News-reel work is a strenuous job, but it should appeal to a robust youth fond of an open-air life and of travel with a spice of adventure thrown in. The news-reel cameraman may find himself suddenly ordered to fly to the Arctic or to Africa; almost certainly he will be sent to any European country where serious trouble is going on. The work is intensely fascinating, and often exciting. Although sound has made the job rather more difficult, it has the advantage that the cameraman now has the company of his sound engineer, who as a rule drives the truck that carries them both, together with the equipment. The roof of the truck is very often used as a convenient means of elevation for the camera when the occasion demands. The cameraman and the sound man work as a unit and, provided they pull together well, the work is very pleasant and of ever-changing variety.

The qualities needed in a news-reel man are a thick skin, indomitable push, and boundless ingenuity and resource to help him in the tight corners in which he will inevitably find himself; and, most important of all, plenty of tact and patience to deal with all sorts of authorities, both reasonable and unreasonable. On his tact will depend very often whether he can get permission to operate. Some men by their manner will quite unintentionally upset high officials or the police, upon whose good will so much depends.

Needless to say, the ability to make a quick decision is essential, as also is a certain flair for what is of news interest. On many stories, the class of material to select and take is obvious and presents no difficulty, the main points being the angles chosen and camera technique.

The best chance a news-man has of showing his ability is when he is sent on a weak story that needs building up to make it of any value to the reel editor. He must be prepared to take jobs as they are allotted to him, and some are very unpromising. It is surprising how differently two men will treat a story that needs nursing. The camera work of each may be excellent, but whereas the one will give it a good public appeal, this may be entirely lacking in the work of the other, so much depending on the angles from which the story is viewed. In fact, the building up of a weak and perhaps uninteresting story is really difficult, and the cameraman does not always get due credit.

The corporations producing news-reels generally employ a capable news editor – often a Fleet Street newspaper man – whose job it is to select suitable

Norman Fisher of *British Movietone News*.

BUFVC

news stories and allot them to the cameraman to cover. He has a very responsible and arduous job, from which he can seldom relax, and on his ability and vision depend to a great extent the interest and appeal of the reel. There are five or six news-reels produced twice weekly in Britain, and, needless to say, as with news-papers, there is intense competition to secure the best stories and give them the best presentation.

Working in conjunction with the news editor are usually a couple of contact men who, when the stories to be covered have been chosen, set off to make contact with the authorities concerned, get the necessary permits, and arrange the best viewpoints, and thus relieve the cameraman of such work in order that he may concentrate more readily on his job. Certain important stories, such as a Jubilee or Coronation, where every news-reel is anxious to secure the sometimes limited viewpoints, have to be contacted and organized weeks or months ahead to ensure that a news-reel does not get 'left'.

When, owing to lack of space, it is impossible for all the firms to work together, an arrangement is sometimes made whereby one firm only operates and supplies the other firms with prints of the event. These stories are called 'rota' jobs, because the different news-reels take it in turn to work on them exclusively. In many cases it is the only arrangement that allows of a job being filmed and presented to the public.

Installed in the news editor's office, are the tape machines of one or more news agencies, which ensure that all hot news, such as wrecks or train disasters, may be dealt with at once. Very often the cameraman is bundled into a plane and flown to the scene. A good example of the use to which a plane can be put was when the French liner, the *Atlantique,* was burnt out. As soon as the news came through, all the news-reel planes flew over the burning ship, circled round a few times to get pictures, and then flew straight back to the laboratories with the material, thus getting a vivid picture in a record time and with a minimum of effort. A few years ago such a feat would have been impossible.

The news editor has also to keep an eye on individuals who suddenly burst into the news, such as inventors, or air pilots who break records. Such people are invited to the laboratories, where perhaps they make a short speech or answer a few questions.

Sporting events naturally occupy a big portion of the news-reel programme in the course of the year. These events recur so regularly that they are termed 'hardy annuals'. The first of the season is the Waterloo Cup coursing meeting at Aintree in February. Then comes the Lincolnshire Handicap (first flat-racing event), closely followed by the Grand National, probably the most thrilling and spectacular event of the year. Then comes the famous Cup Final, now barred to the news-reels because they refuse to pay what they consider an exorbitant sum for the film rights. And so the year progresses, bringing the classic Derby, followed by the Ascot meeting, and the Wimbledon Championships.

By this time the news editor is beginning to mop his heated brow. Whereas in the winter months he was feverishly looking for stunts, now he is literally snowed under with material. The cameramen also feel the strain and their nerves perhaps get a little frayed, but they know that after the peak time of mid-June the pace will slow down. The Henley week is not too strenuous and is rather pleasant. Then comes the fashionable Goodwood meeting followed by Cowes week, a pleasant pick-me-up for the tired cameraman, who by now is beginning to know by sight all who matter in Society circles.

The hectic rush is now over, but a few hardy annuals still remain. A stray man or two are sent up to the grouse moors to take Society behind the butts, a not very exciting story which needs carefully building up and which relies more upon sound than scene. The tail end of the racing season still remains to be dealt with, and the 'Classics', the St Leger, Cesarewitch, and Cambridgeshire, are important. But before these are over, the football season has begun, and the F.A. cup rounds must be carefully watched for early surprises. The Manchester November Handicap finishes the serious racing events and the news-reel man is lucky if he gets it clear of fog. The first week in November sees the opening meets of fox-hunting all over the country, and with the aid of sound, realistic and pretty scenes of the English country-side may be secured.

The news editor now once more has to rack his brain to keep the reel interesting, and he welcomes any good 'stunt' suggested by a cameraman. Field events are now comparatively scarce, but several indoor evening events, such as boxing matches, and ice-hockey, come to help out the programme. On these occasions the various firms often take down their own lighting installation. The pace is definitely slower, but the panorama of life never stops and the news cameraman must always be ready, for a big story may crop up at any moment. As likely as not he finishes up the Old Year and sees in the New Year working from the top of a sound-truck outside St Paul's on a hilarious mass of celebrating Scots. The next day, if he is lucky, he may be leaving London fogs and speeding south to the Riviera.

A good story told of the late Admiral Beatty illustrates the methods the news-reel man may have to adopt. During the War, an American cameraman surreptitiously got aboard his ship, fully determined to secure a close-up at any price, knowing full well that he would be summarily evicted from the ship. He set and prepared his camera ready to crank, and walking up boldly, planted it two yards in front of Beatty. 'Smile, Admiral, smile,' he said. Beatty was so taken aback that he smiled for three seconds before starting to hold forth as he was well able to do. The cameraman apologized, but Beatty goodnaturedly admitted he deserved his picture for his 'damn cheek'.

From *Careers in the Films* (London: Sir Isaac Pitman & Sons, 1938).

Censorship and The Restriction of Liberty

Parliamentary Debate

On 22 September 1938 British Paramount News included an item on the Munich crisis, entitled EUROPE'S FATEFUL HOUR, in its issue no. 790. The item was then withdrawn on the day of release. The item included a discussion between the journalists Wickham Steed and A.J. Cummings, and the taxi driver Herbert Hodge, who was a popular 'man-on-the-street' commentator on BBC radio. Their discussion was strongly critical of the Government's policy of appeasement. Paramount said that the withdrawl of the item was its own decision, but the matter was raised in the House of Commons on 23 November by the Liberal MP Geoffrey Mander, who secured the information that the item had been withdrawn on official request, as it might have a 'prejudicial effect upon the negotiations' (i.e. Prime Minister Chamberlain's negotiations with Hitler at Godesberg). Mander raised the matter again on 1 December and for a third time on 7 December. The extracts from the House of Commons Official Report below are from the 7 December debate, which ranged widely over press freedom and various examples relating to film censorship, including the Paramount newsreel. Mander tabled a motion on the importance of press liberty, but the amendment was added that the House was 'fully satisfied that His Majesty's Government have maintained these traditions unimpaired'. Mander is supported by the MPs Dingle Foot and F. Montague, and challenged by MPs N.A. Beechman, E.L. Granville, and Home Secretary Sir Samuel Hoare.

Note: The symbol *** indicates where sections of the debate have been excluded from this selection, which concentrates on the subject of newsreels.

Mr Mander: I beg to move,

> That this House, attaching the utmost importance to the maintenance undiminished of British democratic traditions of the liberty of expression of opinion, both in the Press and in public meetings and also in other media such as cinema films, would greatly deplore any action by the Government of the

day which tended to set up any form of political censorship or which exercised pressure direct or indirect.

***

... I now pass to the subject of news reels. This is a very important new medium. There do not exist with regard to it the same traditions as those which have been established with regard to the Press over a long period of years in this country. Some of those responsible for news reels try to realise their usefulness as a very important organ of information. Others are not so careful about that side of it, and are perhaps interested more in the purely commercial side. There is no doubt that the difficulties with regard to alleged censorship which exists here are not altogether, but very largely, the fault of the cinema people and the exhibitors themselves. If they would only show a little more courage, if they would only stand up and say, 'We are not going to be interfered with by the Board of Censors on political matters', they have, to a large extent, got the matter in their own hands. I hope that in future they will take a firmer line when any attempts are made to interfere with them. But I do assert that there is, in connection with the news reels, a definite political censorship which is hostile to the Opposition and friendly to the Government. I do not necessarily say that the Government themselves are directly influencing it, but I say that such a thing exists and that there is no question about it.

***

I now come to the last but most interesting case. During the crisis four out of the five news reel theatres played down the Czechoslovakian point of view, but Paramount gave it space and gave a number of pictures of happy life in Czechoslovakia. One hon. Member of this House told me that he had seen it and that he had immediately notified his friends and had urged them to see it, because, he said, 'I do not suppose this will be tolerated for very long'. It was not tolerated for more than one day. In order to give the point of view of Czechoslovakia – because, after all, I suppose the people of this country have some right to hear that side – Paramount invited Mr Wickham Steed and Mr A.J. Cummings to speak during the reel. The film was issued on the evening of 21st September, and it was withdrawn on 22nd September. A telegram was sent by *British Paramount News* to all its theatres, saying:

> Please delete Wickham Steed and A.J. Cummings' speeches from to-day's Paramount news. We have been officially requested to do so.

Later on they denied that they had been officially requested to do so and said they had done it at their own discretion, but, unfortunately for them, the Chancellor of the Exchequer had given the whole show away, and I would remind the House of what took place. I asked the Prime Minister on 23rd November:

> Why representations were recently made by His Majesty's Government to the American Embassy for the withdrawal from a Paramount news reel of items contributed by Mr Wickham Steed and Mr A.J. Cummings?

> Sir J. SIMON: His Majesty's Government considered that certain passages in the news reel referred to, which was being shown at the time of the Prime Minister's conversations with Herr Hitler at Godesberg, might have a prejudicial effect upon the negotiations. The Ambassador of the United States, I understand, thought it right to communicate this consideration to a member of the Hays organisation which customarily deals with matters of this kind and which brought it to the attention of Paramount News, who, from a sense of public duty in the general interest, decided to make certain excisions from the news reel.

He was asked various other questions, but the only relevant reply was:

> I do not know of the other cases, but in the present case His Majesty's Government are grateful to the Ambassador of the United States, and I am glad that the Ambassador and ourselves were in complete accord. – [OFFICIAL REPORT, 23rd November, 1938; cols. 1727–8; Vol. 341.]

It is very interesting to find such an accommodating Ambassador – very remarkable. The matter was raised again by me later, and the Prime Minister then gave the impression to the House that no such incident had ever taken place. He said, however, at the third time of asking

> The attention of the American Ambassador was drawn to certain items, and he was asked to look into the matter. [OFFICIAL REPORT, 1st December, 1938; col. 584, Vol. 342.]

There you get a perfectly clear and open case of political censorship by the Government of the day in the interests of the foreign policy that they were pursuing, and it was a foreign policy which was detested by probably half the nation It is not as if you were dealing with a case where you had national unity and 95 per cent. of the people thinking one thing. That would have been very different. [HON. MEMBERS: 'Why?']

If hon. Members say 'Why?' I will agree that it is not desirable to have any censorship at all, under any circumstances, but I submit that you must have a sense of proportion. If they wish no censorship at all, I am fully in agreement with them.

What were the words that were withdrawn? What was it that was said by these two gentlemen? I will tell the House. In the course of an objective narrative of events Paramount introduced Mr Wickham Steed as a former editor of the 'Times' and a friend of President Masaryk. We know that he is one of the most distinguished journalists in the world to-day. He then introduced Mr Cummings in the following terms:

> British Paramount News, seeking still further independent and informed opinion, interviewed the famous foreign affairs journalist, Mr A. J. Cummings; and for the man-in-the-street's viewpoint sought the popular broadcasting taxi-driver, Mr Herbert Hodge.

That is what Mr Wickham Steed said:

> Has England surrendered? Who is 'England'? – the Government or Parliament or the people? The British Parliament has not surrendered for it has not been convened, and still less have the British people. Our Government, together with that of France, is trying to make a present to Hitler – for use against us when he may think the time has come – of the 3,000,000 men and the thousands of aeroplanes that he would need to overcome Czechoslovak resistance. Hitler does not want to fight – oh, no! He only wants to get without fighting more than he would be able to get by fighting. And we seem to be helping him to get it. And all this because British and French Ministers feared to take a risk when they could have taken it successfully and believed they could diminish the risk by helping Hitler to gain a triumph – when he was at his wit's end – instead of standing up to him.

I turn to Herbert Hodge and A.J. Cummings, and the dialogue went in this way:

> Hodge: Well, Mr Cummings, what do you think of the news? Everybody's saying to me that England has surrendered to Hitler. Do you think that's right?

> Cummings: Well, beyond a doubt, Hitler has won an overwhelming diplomatic triumph for German domination in Europe. Nothing in future will stop him but a mass war.

> Hodge: I think most of us, although we want peace with all our hearts, would be prepared to go to war if it was a case of either going to war or allowing Hitler to dominate Europe.

I thought that was the policy of the Government. The dialogue continues:

> Cummings: The fact is our statesmen have been guilty of what I think is a piece of yellow diplomacy.

Perhaps that is what the Government did not like.

> If in good time we had made a joint declaration with France and with Russia making clear our intentions, and stating emphatically and in express terms that we would prevent the invasion of Czechoslovakia, I'm certain that Hitler would not have faced that formidable combination. If we were not prepared to go to the extreme limit we should certainly not have engaged in a game of bluff with the finest poker player in Europe.

> Hodge: What worries me about it all, Mr Cummings, is whether we've simply postponed war for another year or two against a much stronger Hitler of the future.

> Cummings: I am afraid we've only postponed war; and frankly, I am very

Gaumont-British News camera team on display.

fearful about what is yet in store for millions of young men of military age in all the countries of Europe.

I can see nothing improper in these statements. They represented the views of a very large proportion of people in this House and the country, but the Government censored them. They would not allow them to be said. They took every step in their power to prevent the opposition point of view being presented. The other side of it was not interfered with. We could have plenty of pictures of the Prime Minister and we could hear all the 'try, try and try again' slogans, and things of that kind. There was no limit to that, but anything that represented the opposition point of view was not to be allowed to be shown in the cinemas of this country. That was a most improper action by the Government.

I hope that the ventilation of this subject to-night, even if the Government try to make out that a great deal of it is not quite as represented, must do a great deal to stop the growth of censorship, direct or indirect, and to prevent it arising in future. I venture to hope that we shall show, in spite of the spread of dictatorship in so many great countries, that we are still a true democracy, that we are prepared to hear all views and to have every aspect of political matters laid before us, and, to the best of our ability, choose that which we think is wisest. If ever this country were to be gagged and bound and our centuries-long liberties interfered with, we may have peace, but it would not be England. I hope that by passing this Motion to-night unanimously we shall show we are the freest people in the world …

***

Mr Beechman: I beg to move, in line 5, at the end, to add:

but is fully satisfied that His Majesty's Government have maintained these traditions unimpaired.

***

My hon. Friend dealt rather particularly with the Press, and I should like to begin by making it clear that there is no censorship of the Press in this country, just as there is no censorship of the British Broadcasting Corporation. They are both free agents, and they collect their news in precisely the same way. I think my hon. Friend almost suggested that it would be an insult to the Press to suggest that they would be subject to improper pressure of the kind to which he was referring. I do not believe, either, that the great magnates of the Press, still less, perhaps, those working journalists who have such a respect for their profession, and such a keen perception, would allow themselves to be influenced in any such ways. If it can be suggested that there is any limitation upon the Press it is to be found far more in limitations imposed by the Common Law and by Statute Law in regard to libel and proceedings in contempt. I should have thought that the supreme danger to the

Press in regard to the satisfactory presentation of news might be the fact that it is a commercial venture, but I think we owe it to the Press to say that in spite of that fact they do certainly run their business as a social service.

There is a further danger, and that is the partisanship of certain papers. It has already been referred to by my hon. Friend. Again I think there are two cures for that. First of all if we have enough papers they cancel each other out; unlike that incident on the films to which my hon. Friend referred where one distinguished journalist, Mr Wickham Steed, was addressing another distinguished journalist, Mr Cummings, and both of them were taking the same point of view at a crucial time. I am going to leave it to my right hon. Friend to deal with matters of which he must obviously have far more knowledge than I have. Nevertheless I called his attention to the fact that there was a film at a crucial time which transgressed that doctrine to which I have referred, that there should be freedom of choice. There you had two different men, both with their great skill and influence advocating the same point of view.

Mr Mander: The point is that there were five news reels whose reels are being shown every night and that while four of them were consistently showing the Government point of view there was only the fifth which attempted for one night to show the opposition point of view. Surely the hon. Member will see that his argument is all on one side.

Mr Beechman: I gathered that the hon. Member was referring to only one news reel in a particular cinema as the one in which that particular comment was to be found.

Mr Mander: There were four others.

Mr Beechman: I was not in that theatre and I do not know the facts ...

***

Mr Granville: I hope the hon. Gentleman the Member for West Islington (Mr Montague) will forgive me if I do not follow him on the lines of his interesting speech, because I desire to speak for only a very few minutes ... On the whole, I think the news reels of this country are of a high standard, and are impartial. I have no connection with news reels, but after all, they have been showing for some considerable time this country. A news reel has to bring some sort of photographic evidence that the news story it is presenting is true, because, quite obviously, any fake will be detected by an audience. The same sort of check cannot be obtained in the ordinary Press. I think it will be found that most film audiences in the ordinary cinemas – not so much in the news cinemas – dislike the talks and tit-bits by Cabinet Ministers and others. They go to the cinema for entertainment, and not for politics.

I think that the same body to which the hon. Gentleman referred as having recently passed a resolution were making strong representations some years ago, at a time long before these political talks began, to have these talks deleted from the ordinary news films.

Mr Mander: That body was started only in the last two months.

Mr Granville: Well, I think it was a larger body, which embraced the whole of the cinema exhibitors in the country, including some of the news theatres. But the moment you bring on to a screen anything like propaganda you are up against the cinema proprietor. I think the cinemas are trying very hard to establish the real difference between news and propaganda. The hon. Gentleman referred to a particular case – that of a talk by Mr Cummings and Mr Wickham Steed. He also referred to the pro-Government bias in a number of news films. But when the Prime Minister returned from Munich that was news.

Mr Silverman: It would have been news if he had not returned.

Mr Granville: When he returned from Munich he was the Prime Minister of this country, and the people of this country, whether they agree with his policy or not, are interested to hear what he says and to see pictures of him. The same would be true of any Prime Minister. The people who go to see such a film are ten times as numerous as the crowd which goes to see the Prime Minister at Heston Airport.

Mr Mander: We do not want that and nothing else.

Mr Granville: All right. What I am going to suggest is that when Mr Wickham Stead and Mr Cummings, who represents a newspaper with a strong bias, want to put their point of view, that is propaganda, it is not news, and this House is the place to debate two propaganda points of view. If you make the news reels available for that purpose, I believe you will have disturbances in cinemas all over the country.

As to the question whether an individual is wise in privately and unofficially suggesting that people should have the opportunity of putting forward propaganda on the films, my view is that in Hyde Park you can get all the debate you want. In the newspapers you have the 'Letters to the Editor' column, and at the B.B.C. you get the presentation of a variety of views. In the cinema, when you are presenting a news film it is a take or leave it presentation. There can be no repudiation, except such a repudiation as that of the hon. Member opposite, which was so emphatic that he was nearly turned out of the cinema.

Mr Montague: It was not the news that I objected to, nor the picture of the Prime Minister, but the comments that were made.

Mr Granville: I must confess that I went to cinemas to see and hear the news reels, and I had to listen to remarks which I did not like. I also went to cinemas where there was complete uproar. In one, the first 20 rows were packed with Nazis and the back rows were packed with the oppositionists, and it became a shouting match. I wanted to hear the news film, but I had no opportunity of doing so.

To return to the point whether there should be Government supervision, taking all the facts into consideration I think there should not be Government intervention. It should be left to the good sense of the cinema organisations themselves. There is no Hays Organisation in this country, whereby you could create a sort of co-operation between the film industry as to what type of film they should show. I would prefer an organisation similar to the Hays Organisation of America, which would represent the film industry in this country. If you are going to have complete freedom to show all these news reels, you must be free to show all films. You may show the films of Leni Riefenstahl, of the Nazi Congress at Nuremburg, and films showing what Hitler has done for Germany. If you give that complete freedom and those films were shown in London, you would have the cinemas in complete uproar. This should not be the responsibility of the Government, but it should be the responsibility of the film industry itself.

The hon. Member for East Wolverhampton also referred to the case of the American Ambassador and the news reel where representation was made by the Chancellor of the Exchequer by communication to the American Ambassador. As I understand the facts, there was a representative of the Hays Organisation from America in this country, and the American Ambassador, in an unofficial, friendly and private capacity, pointed out to this individual, as a result of this communication, that the presentation of this American news film created a problem for them, and that they would have to face up to the problem and settle it in the best interests of all concerned. That is what the American Ambassador did, no less and no more.

We should remember that the American Ambassador is a great personality and that he goes a long way towards linking up America to this country. He also has had vast experience in the film industry, far more than most people, and his knowledge of cinema audiences and films is unique. In making this contact he considered that he was doing something which was a contribution to the peace of the world. It was one of his many activities, the basis of which is to create a feeling of friendship between the people of America and Great Britain. Therefore, I would suggest to the hon. Member that he should not make his criticism of this great Ambassador too carping.

***

Sir S. Hoare: Ever since I have been in the House – and it is now nearly 30 years – there has always been some hon. Member who has been the champion mare's-nester. I remember that when I first came into the House the right hon. Gentleman the Member for Gorton (Mr Benn) was also in the House at the time and he will remember it – there was an hon. Member on the Government side – I was then on the Opposition side – who had this childlike passion for mare's nesting whom we, on our side of the House, used to call the 'Mad Hatter'. I am inclined to think that the mantle of the Mad Hatter has fallen upon the shoulders of the hon. Member for East Wolverhampton (Mr Mander). We had an example to-day of his passion for mare's-nesting. He came to the House with his Motion. He told us it was a very harmless Motion that we ought to pass unanimously, and he then proceeded to support it, not with direct charges based upon facts, but by a series of innuendoes, a whole number of tentative questions, all of them obviously directed to attempting, to discover something, all of them obviously showing to any impartial Member of the House that once again the hon. Member for East Wolverhampton is looking for mares' nests.

I propose to deal first of all, I will not say with the hon. Member's charges, for he did not make any charges, but with those of his innuendoes that were a little bit more definite than most of the other ones. I will begin with some of his innuendoes about the films and the Press. I will not disguise from the House that at one moment I was inclined to think that they really did not need an answer, but that it would probably be more convenient to the House that we should ignore them – [HON. MEMBERS: 'No!'] – and that we should go into the Lobby and pass the Amendment which has been moved by my hon. Friends. As I listened to the hon. Member, however, I remembered what was said yesterday by the hon. Member for Bridgwater (Mr Bartlett) in his very interesting maiden speech. I do not know whether it surprised other hon. Members, but it surprised me when the hon. Member for Bridgwater said that of all the criticisms against the Government, that which had carried the most weight at the Bridgwater by-election was the criticism that the Government were trying to suppress the expression of public opinion in this country. I rubbed my eyes and wondered what justification there was for a criticism of that kind. None the less, according to the hon. Member for Bridgwater, it was a criticism that carried some weight with the electors at Bridgwater, and for that reason I had better deal with it to-night, and deal. with it quite specifically.

Let us put an end once and for all to this whispering campaign that a great many people have started in the country. They go from one to the other, and they say, 'Oh yes the newspapers will only put in what the Government wish; they would have taken a very different attitude in the crisis if it had not been for Government pressure; I have heard of this or that case of the Government threatening this or that newspaper, or bringing pressure to bear with regard to this or that film'.

Tonight, let me begin by stating quite categorically that there is no foundation whatever for the innuendoes in this whispering campaign.

There never has been any justification for any suggestion that the Government are exercising a censorship either upon the Press or upon the films. There has never been any justification for the suggestion that we wish to suppress the expression of opinion that does not support the Government's view, and I challenge any hon. Member, as I challenged the hon. Member for East Wolverhampton in the course of his speech, to bring any definite evidence to refute the statement I have just made.

Let me now pass to some of the cases mentioned by the hon. Member for East Wolverhampton. [An HON. MEMBER: 'Fetch him in'.] Yes, the hon. Member has gone.

Mr Foot: I would like to explain that my hon. Friend the Member for East Wolverhampton (Mr Mander) had not realised that the right hon. Gentleman was going to speak at this time; otherwise he would, of course, have been here; and he will be here in a moment.

Sir S. Hoare: It is the hon. Member's Motion, and I should have thought that he would have stayed in the House during the course of the Debate. I hope that the hon. Member opposite will report to his hon. Friend the answer I have been making. Let me deal with the story of the Paramount film. My right hon. Friend the Chancellor of the Exchequer clearly explained the position to the House, and subsequently my right hon. Friend the Prime Minister gave certain additional answers to the questions which were asked on the subject. Let hon. Members remember the actual date on which this incident took place. It was on 22nd September. It was brought to the notice of the Foreign Office on the morning of 22nd September that a news reel was being exhibited, with two speeches, both of which the hon. Member for East Wolverhampton quoted this evening, made in connection with a film LIFE IN CZECHOSLOVAKIA and the incidents that were taking place in Czechoslovakia. It probably was the most critical day in the whole course of the crisis. It was the day on which the Prime Minister went to Godesberg. If ever there was a day on which it was necessary to exercise. caution and to say or do nothing that was likely to stir up dangerous reactions, it was the 22nd September. We were faced, as hon. Members will remember, with the urgent danger that a European war might take place within a comparatively few short hours. It was brought to the notice of the Foreign Office that this film was being exhibited and that these speeches were being made. I ask any impartial Members who were in the House tonight, when the hon. Member for East Wolverhampton read extracts from those speeches, whether they were not the kind of speeches which would have inflamed the atmosphere at that particular moment.

Hon. Members: Where?

Mr Montague: Does the right hon. Gentleman mean then that speeches of that character must be censored, while all propaganda on the other side must be allowed to be shown? Why not censor the lot?

Sir S. Hoare: No, Sir. I certainly have no such meaning, as the hon. Member will see when I have finished dealing with this point. The Foreign Secretary was definitely of the opinion that it was undesirable that those two speeches should be heard while the talks at Godesberg were actually in progress on that particular date, 22nd September. There was no general kind of censorship. It was his view, with reference to that film, during the time the talks were going on at Godesberg, that, while he did not wish to apply any pressure – and he did not apply any pressure – and there was no question of censorship, those speeches might compromise the chances of peace.

Mr Mander: Defeat the Government's policy.

Sir S. Hoare: No, it had nothing to do with the Government's policy. I would ask hon. Members to believe me when I say – though I dare say the hon. Member for East Wolverhampton will not believe it – that on 22nd September, faced with one of the greatest crises that ever confronted the world, we were not thinking of the fortunes of the National Government. We were thinking of much graver issues.

Mr Mander: Trying to get out of the mess you had got into.

Sir S. Hoare: Nothing of the kind. Accordingly, my right hon. Friend informed the American Ambassador of his views and asked him to look into the question. The American Ambassador said he would do so and would communicate the Foreign Secretary's views to the managers of the Paramount Company and, on that, the managers of the Paramount company withdrew that particular film, at that time. There was no censorship, there was no undue pressure.

***

Mr Foot: The right hon. Gentleman began his speech by accusing my hon. Friend the Member for East Wolverhampton (Mr Mander) of being the champion discoverer of mares'-nests. He proceeded to deal with the principal charge which my hon. Friend had brought and to substantiate practically all the facts that my hon. Friend gave. I am referring to the question of the Paramount news film. The right hon. Gentleman admitted that this was brought to the notice of the Foreign Office – he did not say by whom – on 22nd September. He said, of course quite frankly, that it was one of the most critical days of the crisis. He said that what the Government did did not amount to a censure. Of course, formally that was perfectly true, but the effect was precisely the same as though there had been a censorship of the Press. Are we seriously asked by a Minister of the Crown to believe that the conversations which were taking place on that day, or may be the next day, at Godesberg, between the Prime Minister and Herr Hitler would really have been affected by the news films displayed at a London cinema? Is that the proposition which the right hon. Gentleman is seriously putting before the House of Commons? I do not suppose that any hon. Member will believe it for a moment.

The Home Secretary did not dispute any part of the narrative of the film as given by my hon. Friend. The film was concerned with what had been done at Berchtesgaden. What was done thereby this country was a matter of acute political controversy. There was the greatest feeling about it. The point which the right hon. Gentleman did not attempt to meet was that all the time there were other news films – news films which supported the Government, news films which extolled the Prime Minister; but no sort of check was put upon them. Every kind of propaganda through the news film could be used in support of the Government, but, when there was one film which was critical of the Government, steps were taken to prevent it from being shown to the public. So far as that, which was the principal charge made by my hon. Friend to-night, is concerned, it is admitted in substance by the Home Secretary ...

***

Question put, 'That those words be there added'.
The House divided: Ayes, 171; Noes, 124.

House of Commons Debates, cols. 1261–1319, Vol. 342, 7 December 1938.

The Industry's Front Page

J. Neill Brown

Newsreels were seen not only in conventional cinemas, but in many specialist news theatres, often located at railway stations. These showed not only newsreels, but cartoons and other short films. The article describes their numbers, the leading names and news theatre circuits, and the sort of audiences they attracted. It also reveals that some news theatres compiled their own reels out of the newsreels issued to them, a practice unlikely to have found much favour among the newsreels themselves.

The crisis – the Premier goes to Godesberg – Parliament reassembles – B.B.C. news bulletins in French, German, and Italian – last minute intervention – Munich – thankfulness of a world that can expect its Christmas in peace. Front page news in every corner of the world. Sleepless reporters each giving another angle on the events of the day. News-hawks of all political parties interpreting the news to suit their readers.

And along with them, in every corner where the events of the crisis were taking place, was another news-hawk, but without the power to translate the news into the appropriate colour of individual parties – the news camera. The Premier speaks to the people as he leaves Heston. The camera photographs, the microphone records. Just that and nothing more. And because the public were excited and wanted to see just that, the busiest cinemas in London during crisis week were the newsreel houses.

There are about 22 of these small 300 to 500 seater halls in the country, 16 of them in London. They are planned on the same more or less general principle, and though in most of them the news takes up short of twenty minutes of the hour's program, that twenty minutes forms the most important item of the program. During that week of the crisis they clearly demonstrated their position as the front page of the cinema in no uncertain manner, practically all of them playing to 'standing room only' all day. Most of them found that the great public events of the day always increase the takings, and consequently it behoves us to look for a moment at this very important section of our industry.

In the first place it may be questioned why people should select a special news cinema in order to see the newsreel when they can see exactly the same news in the major halls and a couple of features along with it, to say nothing of a cartoon or a stage show. Well, it so happens that there still is a small percentage of the people of this country who do not like the pictures. They just would not go to an ordinary cinema for fear of mistiming their arrival and having to sit through two or three hours of Greta Garbo or Ronald Colman before coming to the item they want to see – possibly Lloyd George feeding his pigs at Churt or that hardy weekly item of the march past of a brass band. Indeed some people don't even like all of the newsreel and frequently phone up the news cinema and ask when does the news come on, and does the bit about the mayor opening the sewage works come at the beginning or the end and if so just *exactly when* will that be. Then they drop in to see that little bit and go out again. Such discriminating individuals form as much as ten per cent of the news halls' clientele. The other ninety is drawn from the passing public, the folks who are in town for the day and have an hour or two to spare, too short to go into a full feature show and too long for a cup of tea. You will find most news cinemas managers very proud of the type of patron they cater for, not for them the ordinary sensation seeker of the west end, but rather the thoughtful, 'man-in-the-street,' the artisan who takes an interest in public affairs, the educated man who wants to get an even broader outlook on current events than he can get from the daily papers. It is, in the main, the news without comment. And there are those who go so far as to want the news without the commentator. His is a difficult job, for if he is at all interested in certain aspects of public life, it must put a keener edge on his commentary to talk of those things. News cinema managers have told me that they can frequently tell the political opinions of a commentator by the enthusiasm he displays. Some managers would like their reels to be a little controversial so that they could then present more than one side of a problem to the customers and let them draw their own conclusions. But others regard this as a dangerous practice and tend to avoid any political slant whatsoever. They usually make up their own reels from bits and pieces of others, taking good care to include only the sections that are likely to give no offence to any section of the audience. Their general policy is to do nothing to antagonise the Government in power in case it should bring a stringent censorship to bear on the newsreels, which at the moment do not have to be submitted to the censor. Mention of the 'bits and pieces' plan reminds me of a small objection I have frequently felt to their lack of foresight in this matter. It is nothing unusual to see a reel starting with the leads of the 'G.B. News,' followed by the leads of Paramount and having a section from Movietone as its first item. I cannot see why they should not have their own special lead, as they have at the Empire, Leicester Square, acknowledging the reels from which the excerpts are taken, and their own end title instead of what I once saw, four separate play-outs.

The fact that there are as many as 16 news cinemas in London and very few in the whole of the rest of the country tends to suggest that this type of cinema is only

Waterloo News Theatre, Waterloo Station, designed (1934) by Alister G. MacDonald.

Royal Institute of British Architects

really suited to the metropolis. The experience of the London halls does tend to show that a very large floating public is necessary before even the small numbers that go to the news cinemas can be collected. It has been thought in some quarters that the news cinemas on stations, as at Victoria and Waterloo, would be excellent paying propositions owing to the large numbers of people to be found standing about the platforms at all times of the day. Personally I'd as soon open one at a football ground on the assumption that with so many people about it would be bound to pay. The folks who stand about the stations, however, are not there individually for long enough to make it worth while to spend all hour in the cinema. I should imagine that they only get to the station about five or ten minutes before their trains go. I notice that in the most recently published report of the trading profits of 'Capital and Provincial News Theatres, Ltd,' the company that owns the two station cinemas mentioned, there is a net loss of £1,752, although they add later that the company's properties are now all paying their way.

Among the London news cinemas there are three within a stone's throw of each other that demonstrate the different ways in which these theatres call build up their own special public. At the top of Charing Cross Road is the 'Tatler,' which has specialised for a long time in a general sort of program, built up of about 15 minutes of news, a cartoon (sometimes two), an interest picture, occasionally a comedy, and nearly always a documentary. The last time I was there they were showing that excellent American documentary by Pare Lorenz, THE RIVER, the finest thing of its type I have yet seen. Round the corner from it is the 'G.B. Movietone' theatre, which is claimed to be the only genuine NEWS theatre in London. It shows nothing else *but* news, except a travel film now and then. They have a special reel made up for them by Movietone which includes all the items in the general release, and a lot more besides. Not only so but it is fuller on each point it deals with than the major cinema copy. The manager there tells me that he has the best and most intelligent audience in all London. It has been open continuously for eight years and during that time its programmes have been seen by no less than six million people. Back in the Charing Cross Road, but at the bottom end, is the 'Cameo,' which has built up a regular clientele by the showing of comedy as its main item. In the same week as I saw THE RIVER at the 'Tatler' (and the hall was almost full at 3 o'clock in the afternoon), I saw the show at the 'Cameo,' which was running a program entirely made up (except for the news) of comedy shorts by MGM who had won the Academy prize for the best continuous run of comedy shorts for the year. It was a fairly good program, though I considered that I had seen better individual shorts before. The hall again was about as full as the 'Tatler' had been for the same time of day.

The 'Monseigneur' circuit finds that a program somewhat like the 'Tatler' is the most suitable balance. About 15 to 18 minutes of news, a single reel travelogue, a general interest film of two reels, a cartoon (usually Disney), and sometimes a comedy; and they say that that is roughly the order of public appreciation. If there were more news they would give more of their time to it, and if it were interesting enough to run the full hour they would leave the other things out.

In a short review of the situation like this it is quite impossible to deal with the problematic future of news theatres. They may expand, they may not. They may leave out the other shorts and concentrate on the news; again they may not. But whatever they do I hope they will continue to exist if for no other reason than for the use of the shorts producers. In the major halls the short is, as Wardour Street correctly puts it, a 'fill-up'. It provides a good opportunity for the boy-friend to get the girl-friend an ice, complete with spoon, which he usually drops on the way back to his seat and spends the time of the short under a neighbour's seat. In the news theatre it is regarded as of as much importance as the rest of the program.

The news theatre supplies all urgent need for the shorts producer in providing a place, indeed the only place, in which the short is really taken seriously.

The Cine-Technician, March-April 1939.

British Newsreels in the 1930s:
Audience and Producers

Nicholas Pronay

Nicholas Pronay's two essays on the British newsreels in the 1930s are key texts. Published in History in 1971 and 1972, they established a critical understanding of the newsreels as a subject and a tool for the historian, and they have influenced most subsequent work in this field. The two essays, 'Audiences and Producers' and 'Their Policies and Impact', are reproduced here as originally published, with a single-word emendation. As originally printed, a line stated that cameramen were expected to 'shoot fact and above all else dispatch the exposed film double fast'. The phrase should have been 'shoot fast...', a remarkable case, the author states, of a misprint giving almost entirely the opposite meaning to that which was intended.

The extensive screening of archival films during the last decade as part of television programmes such as THE LOST PEACE has helped to dispel some of the claims which have been made, from time to time, for the value of film as an historical record. Although these programmes, as well as some of the educational films based on archival material, are interesting as well as useful, both for the general public and for undergraduates, they were disappointing in terms of sheer information. They have demonstrated, in fact, that the film archives do not have the answer to all that which we may wish to know about the period. Apart from a few speeches which were not known in writing, some additional physical details and the undefinable contribution of mannerisms and expressions, there were very few 'hard facts' in them which were new. Much the same may be said for the 'Scrapbook' series of sound recordings issued by the BBC. Does this experience suggest, however, that historians may now avoid the technological complications of working in these 'non written' archives, and that these expensively preserved records – some 200 million feet of non-fiction film is held in the six main British archives alone – are of peripheral value only? In one sense the answer is clearly in the affirmative, because of the very nature of film. Film (and radio) was a means of communicating, not a means of note-taking. Films were made to be shown as widely as possible and as soon as possible, not to be kept confidential. Hence, the information which they contained was more akin to what the newspapers of the day had printed than what

was being filed in Westminster and Whitehall. As sources of primary information about the events which they portrayed, films like newspapers are therefore only of peripheral value. It is in fact pointless to look to them for this kind of primary information because, as we shall see below, they were not set up to even try to preserve it.

On the other hand, and as in the case of newspapers, they are records of what the public was told about the events, the politicians and the policies of the day. It is as records of the media of public information, in the century of the common man, that they are of historical importance and utility. It is in the size, social composition and the attitudes of the audience of the newsreels that the strongest case for studying them is to be found. It is possible to argue that because by the 1930s two new media of mass-communications, broadcasts and newsreels, had joined the newspapers as suppliers of the sum of information and the range of interpretation upon which public opinion formed itself, the acquisition of the uncongenial technology required for studying their records is necessary for the full understanding of the period.

The cinema, of course, developed long before the 1930s. It had been the foremost example of the 'application of technology to entertainment' and could be accurately described, long before 1930, as mass-entertainment. Before the introduction of the sound-synchronized 'talkies' it could not, however, also become a medium of mass-communication.[1] The range of social and political information which could be conveyed by pictures and monosyllabic captions alone, was obviously too restricted. The change-over to sound-film began in Britain in 1930 and was substantially complete two years later, by which time all the newsreels were also available with soundtracks. These enabled them to cover any subject which was news-worthy irrespective of whether it was pictorial in nature. Soundtracks also enabled the newsreels not only to show something but also to interpret it. There is, for instance, a great deal of difference between the back of Neville Chamberlain disappearing into an aeroplane and the same shot underlined with music and synchronized with the words, *Mr Chamberlain never wavered in his determination to secure Peace. We know that no man can do more than he*. With the arrival of the Talkies the men of Wardour Street became as fully fledged journalists as their friends in Fleet Street. Between the acquisition of their 'voice' by 1932, and the Second World War, that is during those same difficult years of uncertain loyalties and leadership, there falls the first period when the newsreels were in a position, technically, to contribute to public opinion. During the war, of course, the cinema was integrated into the structure of wartime information, which is a subject on its own.

The first thorough survey of the cinema-industry was carried out during the course of 1934, by the distinguished statistician, S. Rowson. He used the figures provided by the Board of Trade and by the Industry itself which covered the years immediately preceding 1934. To these he added those which resulted from his own survey. The resultant paper, presented to the Royal Statistical Society[2] has been

accepted as the basis of all subsequent work. He found that in 1934 there were 4305 registered cinemas in England, Scotland and Wales (no figures were obtainable for N. Ireland), and that these provided 3872 million seats.[3] The average weekly admission figure was 18.5 million: there were seasonal variations ranging from 13.8 million in June to 21.8 million in January.[4] As the corresponding population figure stood at 4509 million, and since the very young neither went to the cinema nor need to be considered in terms of public opinion, the least which these figures indicate is that by 1934 the circulation figure for the cinema was already 43% of the population.

In 1939, five years after the Rowson survey, the film trade estimated that the cinema audience had increased to a weekly average ranging between 20–23 million.[5] This figure cannot be accepted as fully as Rowson's figures, but if we consider the findings of the Board of Trade Enquiry of 1941, then it appears that the Trade was not far wrong, if at all.

In 1941, as part of an attempt to find sufficient numbers of trained projectionists for the Ministry of Information's huge network of 'public' cinemas, the Board of Trade surveyed the cinemas which were still open after the Blitz and the closure of some of the one-man rural picture-houses.[6] They found that there were 4618 cinemas – of which a mere 173 were in fact closed – and that seating capacity of those which were open, stood at 4.21 million seats. At the outbreak of war, thus, there must have been at least 4.3 million seats available, a growth factor of nearly 15%. Since the published accounts for distributing companies and cinema-chains all show that they had a very good year, we may accept that the increased seating capacity was no worse utilized, which would indicate average weekly admissions in excess of 21 million. In other words, in 1938–9, over half the population, excluding the very young, saw each week what was communicated by means of the screens. Arguably, the twelve months during which the public had to accept at the hands of its government both the humiliation of Munich and yet another European war, as well as failure to solve unemployment, was one in which the inter-relation between public opinion and the government was of crucial importance.

A statistical figure of over half the population being admitted to the cinemas in an average week is in one sense less important than the answer to the question 'which half?' Rowson's survey of 1934 shows that the distribution of cinema seats in relation to the density of population was very uneven. But perhaps contrary to expectations, the highest concentration of cinemas was not in the prosperous regions of the metropolitan south, but in the industrial areas of Scotland, Lancashire, the North of England, South Wales, Yorkshire and the Midlands, in that order, while the fewest were to be found in the Eastern Counties, the Home Counties and the West of England respectively. There were in fact more cinema seats per head of population in bitterly hit North-Wales with its dying slate industry than there were in the London area.[7] The same sociological implication may be found in the distribution of seat prices; in Rowson's words: '43% of the entire cinema

Very working class pursuit!

admissions were in respect of seats for which the charge did not exceed 6d. Nearly four out of every five persons visiting the cinema did pay not more than 1 shilling including duty'.[8] The President of the Society, in appraising Mr Rowson's paper, pointed out that these figures explained the quality and kind of programmes one was to see in the cinemas. It was clearly connected to the working class.[9]

The Social Survey of Merseyside was one of the many surveys which recorded the extent and the nature of the working-class affiliation of the cinema. Carried out at about the same time as Rowson's statistical work, the Merseyside Survey confirmed the implications of his statistics: about 40% of the adult population went to the cinema each week, the manual working-class went more frequently than those immediately above them (Registrar Generals' Groups 4–5) and the professional and upper classes frequented the cinema the least. The sociologists from the University of Liverpool also found two new and very important aspects of the relationship between the cinema and the working class: 'It was evident that the majority of those who attended regularly go to the cinema more than once a week' – and that 'Working-class children ... nearly all attend the cinema at least once a week'.[10] At the age when they left school and began to work, at 15+, '80% went to the cinema at least once weekly'.[11]

The pattern of the relationship between the working class and the cinema which was already shown by the Merseyside Survey at the very beginning of our period, was echoed all through it by the many other social surveys of this period.[12] During the war years of 1942 and 1943, and then after the war, a series of surveys carried out by the M.O.I./C.O.I. Social Survey and the Hulton Readership Survey[13] all confirmed the continuation of this special relationship. They also showed that despite the increased middle class acceptance of the cinema, partly as a result of the war, there was still an essential difference in their relationship with it. While the 'lower income groups' had the largest proportion of 'regulars' (once or more a week), in the upper income groups there were practically no 'regulars' at all. It was also shown that the children who became 'regulars' in their early teens (as we have seen the great majority of the working class) remained 'regulars' until about the age of thirty-five.[14]

Thus the evidence indicates that not only was the cinema 'exceptional among all the products of twentieth-century technology in that it reached the poorer elements in the community first before spreading upwards to those who at first affected contempt for it'[15] but also, that it retained a special and powerful relationship with them. The distinguishing features of this relationship, early conditioning, habitual attendance and communal participation, were especially significant in terms of the potential effectiveness of the media. The abundant information which we possess about the relationship between the cinema and its audience emphasizes the singular hold which the cinema had over most of the industrial working class during their most impressionable and active years.

It is important to see the figures for the cinema-attendance in comparison with the penetration of the other two media of communications, the newspapers and broadcasting. In 1938–9 the circulation of daily newspapers averaged 10.48 million; the Sunday papers 13.59 million[16] and there were 8.95 million radio licences.[17]

There are, of course, many obvious qualifications one has to bear in mind in comparing these sets of figures. Many people bought more than one newspaper. The whole household may have had access to the newspaper which one of its members had bought. There were some who read only the business or the sports pages as there were those who bought sweets while the newsreels were on the screen. Most of these kinds of qualifications, which hardly need listing here, cancel each other out, but clearly some upward adjustment to allow for multiple family use has to be made. Nevertheless, the circulation figures do nothing to lessen the significance of the cinema. If we look at the position in terms of class-affiliation, then we must bear in mind the fact that the middle classes took more than their share of papers. *The Times*, the *Daily Mail*, the *Daily Telegraph* or the *Observer* were rare indeed in working-class homes, while even the *Daily Express* can only be described as a cross-section paper.

In the case of the radio too some obvious adjustments have to be made: not all radios owned were also licenced; the whole family may have had access to the set; on the other hand, some used theirs for music only – Luxembourg was already a hated rival of the BBC. In relation to the working class, we should recall that the Merseyside Survey had found that: 'In the slum areas in particular and amongst the working-classes in general the wireless is almost unknown'.[18] In the intervening years, by 1939, the number of radio licences had trebled and, no doubt, the penetration of broadcasting below the middle classes had very greatly increased. But there was no 'Volksempfänger' manufactured in this country and the Voice of Britain was not obliged by vulgar competition to lower its tone.[19] A great deal more work is needed on this subject, but it appears that the BBC continued to broadcast only on middle-class wavelengths and thus failed to become the mass-medium which, in terms of technology, it could have been already. In contrast, competition was the key-note of the cinema. With more than half of the cinemas owned by small individuals, and with the remainder owned by a number of competing chains, no one could afford to try and 'educate' the customers. As in all small leisure-businesses, whether pubs, fairs, or 'pics', the first rule was that you must please the regulars, for on them depended the business. Therefore, working-men and their wives, from adolescence to about middle-age, were better placed to get the kind of product which they actually wanted in the local cinema than anywhere else. For once it was they who paid the pipers and were seen to be paying them too. The cinema-owners made their living from the tickets they sold and neither advertising nor any other revenue came to obscure their direct dependence on their working-class customers.

British Pathe

Newsreel sound recordist.

Turning to the suppliers of this market, and remembering that with the arrival of sound virtually all cinemas found that newsreels were a well-received way of making up the programme, but that there was no obligation on them whatever to take them, we find that the market was held by the same five firms all through the period.[20] They were all more or less self-contained offshoots of major feature production companies, British or American. The newsreels themselves were wholly made in this country for the British market and by British personnel. In fact if the normally international character of the film business is considered, particularly in Britain during the 1930s, they were exceptionally 'British' in personnel and character. The following five companies produced the newsreels: Gaumont-British (owned by *Gaumont-British* UK), Movietone (jointly owned by *20th Century Fox* USA and by Lord Rothermere UK), Pathe (jointly owned by *Associated British Picture Corporation* UK and by *Warner Bros.* USA), Paramount (*Paramount Pictures* USA) and Universal (owned by *General Distributors* USA).

These five companies produced by 1933 an average of 520 newsreels per annum, two a week by each of the companies for twice-weekly programme changes were becoming the norm. In addition some of them also produced a weekend edition, a sort of Sunday paper, and they all produced occasional special editions. It was a very

143

large industry. It produced the equivalent of a full-scale feature film every week – with international ramifications and a financial structure which was peculiar and very complex. The full details need not concern us here.[21] What is of significance is that the newsreel companies were run by their parent-companies as a break-even advertising unit to keep their names before the cinema-goers and to keep off others who would undoubtedly have filled their time span on the screen. There were other aspects to this arrangement, but the point is that there was more than the normal degree of commercial pressure upon them to give the public what it, or rather what the cinema-owners said it, wanted. The newsreel companies also indulged in a kind of competition amongst themselves which was reminiscent of the Wild West.[22]

The structure of the industry ensured that it would model itself upon the popular press. While it can be argued that the differences were at least as important as the similarities, there is no doubt the newsreelmen saw themselves as doing the same job in much the same way as the newspapers.[23] The wish to become the Northcliffe of the newsreels was habitually expressed by newsreel editors; the critics also sometimes hoped a 'Northcliffe' would take charge of the newsfilms.[24]

The head of the operation was the editor. He decided what to cover or not to cover, on the advice of the news-editors and upon information received from the ticker-tape to which the newsreel companies were subscribers. The introduction of sound reduced the importance of the cameramen to exactly the same role as that of the reporters in the newspapers. They were dispatched to 'cover a story' sometimes with a member of the editorial staff, and were expected to shoot fast and above all else dispatch the exposed film double fast. As in the case of the popular press the most important achievement was neither accuracy nor balance, but to scoop others. The companies measured their abilities according to the speed with which they could get a sensational event on to the screen. As a matter of fact they were capable of remarkable speed: the Belgrade funeral of King Alexander was on the screen in London by the same evening. Of course there was sufficient warning in this case for the special arrangements which made this 'feat' possible, but also clearly the state of technology was sufficiently advanced to allow the newsreels to compete with and sometimes even to outmatch the newspapers.

The emphasis on speed and the subordination of the cameramen were both aspects of the changeover to sound. In the last resort it did not matter what was actually filmed; the audience was told what happened and even what they were seeing. The pictures were there primarily to back-up the 'voice'. Even if the film taken failed to make sense, or even did not arrive in time, the newsreel carrying the 'story' could be, and often was, issued.[25] On the sound principle that one knocked out tank looks much like another, or that a town's panorama was not likely to change from last year's, the newsreels succeeded in providing their viewers with the illusion of as full a news-coverage as the newspapers provided.

The second main item which the newsreels contained were scheduled events such as football-matches, military parades, state visits, major political speeches and the like, including their beloved ship-launchings. These scheduled events allowed them to set tip their cameras in advance and to provide good, genuine, illusion-restoring coverage often using original sound as well. Remembering that very few political speeches lasted the mere 4 to 5 minutes which the reels chose to allocate to them at the most, it is in these parts that the newsreels might occasionally have preserved a nugget of primary information not available in writing.

The third main item in all the reels contained magazine items of general interest, corresponding again to those of the popular press, such as Universal's *Do You Know?* series.

The newsreels were being made continuously. Cameramen were sent to cover local stories based on the reports of the several thousand 'correspondents' on whom they relied – many of whom were the local cinema owners or managers – to keep them in touch with the little events and the little people whose medium they knew themselves to be. The exposed negatives of these and the other stories were developed and cut into rough sequences by the cutters – often on no information other than what looked like a 'good sequence' – and then projected for the staff to view. These screenings were the central gatherings of the whole operation. It was then decided what to do with the rough-stories: to use it as it was, to augment it with stock-shots, or to put it into the library for the time being. The selection was made on the basis of news value. Once the dead-line was reached the editor assembled as coherent and balanced an 'issue' as he could, containing all three kinds of items. At the very last possible moment the words were finalized on the basis of the latest information. The commentaries – it is a misleading term, so often were they the only intelligible part of the story – were made up of whatever information they had had from the correspondents, from the cameramen and above all from what was available by then from the press or the radio. The sound-track was then 'mixed' using music, sound-effects (chiefly made in the studio, though only Universal altogether eschewed the use of original sound as a matter of policy) and the recording of the commentator's voice was laid over it. The finished negative and sound-track were then reproduced in as many prints as the finances allowed.

It was at this printing stage that one of the special problems of the newsreels emerged: prints were very expensive, accounting for much of their budget. Hence only about one third of the cinemas received a print of the newsreels when they were issued. These, first-run houses, showed it for three days and then passed it on to the next rung down the ladder until, in about three weeks, the newsreel worked its way down its appointed circuit. This system emphasized again the importance of the editor, who had to possess some of the editorial skills of both the daily papers and the magazines. It also provided a good reason why the newsreels could not be made simple topical pictorial records – even if the thought had attracted their editors, which it did not – and why editors had to opt for the interpretive and more journalistic approach. Technically they were capable of discharging the same functions as the newspapers. They served a very large and very susceptible audience. Their policies and editorial attitudes are therefore every bit as important as were the editorial policies of their newspaper colleagues. These will be discussed in the next article.

History, vol. 56 no. 188, October 1971.

NOTES

1. These terms are used here in the sense, and with the qualifications, of Asa Briggs' *Mass Entertainment: The Origins of a Modern Industry* (University of Adelaide, 1960) and *The Communications Revolution* (Leeds University Press, 1966).
2. *Journal of the Royal Statistical Society*, vol. XCIX, 1936, pp. 67–119, 'A Statistical Survey of the Cinema Industry in Great Britain in 1934 by S. Rowson, M.Sc.'
3. Rowson, p. 76, table IV.
4. Rowson, p. 74, table III.
5. *Kinematograph Year Book* for 1939, p. 9.
6. Published in *Board of Trade Journal*, 13 May 1950, p. 980. Table VI and note j.
7. Rowson, p. 85.
8. Rowson, p. 71.
9. pp. 119–121. Sir Perchy Ashley, the President, when at the Board of Trade, was instrumental in bringing in the Cinematograph Act of 1928. He was one of a group of leading Civil Servants who perceived early the potential significance of the Cinema as a medium for information, and who were responsible for the far-sighted and imaginative sponsorship which brought this country to the forefront of such use of the medium. This lead paid handsome dividends both before and during the war. For the relationship with the Government the wartime and foreign use of the cinema, see my forthcoming book, *The Coming of the Mass-Media*.
10. *The Social Survey of Merseyside* ed. Caradog Jones (University of Liverpool, 1934), vol. III, pp. 280–2.
11. Ibid., p. 219.
12. There were, as Professor Marwick remarked, 'a lot of them'. See for example: *Report of the Birmingham Cinema Enquiry Committee*, (Birmingham, 1930). *The Edinburgh Cinema Enquiry*, by ... John Mackie (Edinburgh, 1933). *The Film in National Life being the Report of the Enquiry ... into the service which the Cinematograph may render to education and social progress* (London, 1934). Birkenhead Vigilance Committee, *The Cinema and the Child*, (Birkenhead, 1931). Almost all the well-known town-surveys – London, York etc – contain similar information.
13. For the 1943 Social Survey see J. P. Mayer, *British Cinemas and Their Audiences* (London, 1948), Appendix III. For the post-war surveys, their comparability and value see: P.E.P. *The British Film Industry* (1952), pp. 181–6.

14. Submission by Social Survey to the Wheare Committee quoted P.E.P., op. cit., p. 186.

15. Arthur Marwick, *Britain in the Century of Total War* (The Bodley Head, 1968), p. 186.

16. D.H.E. Butler and S. Freeman, *British Political Facts, 1900–1960* (Macmillan, 1968) pp. 213–14.

17. Ibid., p. 218.

18. *The Social Survey of Merseyside*, vol. 111, p. 247.

19. Z.A.B. Zeman, *Nazi Propaganda* (Oxford University Press, 1964), p. 51.

20. Except, of course, in the cinemas which were owned by companies making newsreels, such as the Gaumont-chain or the ABPC-chain.

21. See: Peter Baechlin and Maurice Mueller-Strauss, *Newsreels Across the World* (UNESCO, 1952) which is the only, but quite detailed, survey of the structural and financial aspects of the newsreels.

22. There is an entertaining account of their antics by one of the surviving 'Newsreel Boys' of the 1930s in the *Sunday Times*, Colour Supplement, 10 January 1971.

23. They sometimes referred to themselves as the 'Fourth Estate'. *Manchester Guardian*, 10 October 1942.

24. e.g. Donald Fraser in, *Sight and Sound*, Autumn 1934, p. 90.

25. On 9 November 1936, most of the cinema-audiences could 'see with their own eyes' the fall of Madrid and the entry of Franco's troops. The editors acted on the best information available, which was that the city was falling, and they knew that there was no chance of footage actually from Madrid arriving in time for the dead-line. When Madrid did eventually fall, in 1939, they 'showed it again', unabashed. Also in 1936 it took Captain Halse 18½ hours to fly from Portsmouth to Khartoum during his record-attempt – Pathe showed him 'flying past Khartoum' less than 14 hours later!

British Newsreels in the 1930s: Their Policies and Impact

Nicholas Pronay

Pronay's second essay on the British newsreels in the 1930s covers the editorial policies of the newsreels, and their impact upon a predominantly working-class cinema audience. He concludes that the newsreels provided a 'direct and effective illusion of events', and their value to the historian is not as records of events, but of events as they were presented to a mass audience.

The Newsreels of the 1930s belonged much more to the world of journalism than to the film-world. The film-makers fully realized this, though they often resented some of the implications of this separation, such as the absolute control of an Editor in the place of a film-director and the use of incessant soundtracks instead of more artistic techniques. Despite the fact that the Newsreels produced a greater footage and were seen by a larger audience than probably any other product of the British film industry, the Newsreels have been virtually excluded from the standard film-histories.[1] Their contribution to the age has to be assessed alongside the newspapers of the period, but it is essential to realize that they operated under quite different conditions. For all the apparent competition between newsreel companies, which paralleled or even exceeded the competition in Fleet Street, there was little difference between them in matters of editorial policy. The five newsreel Editors met regularly to decide on their policies concerning 'touchy' subjects and they abided by the agreements. Thus it is appropriate to deal with a general policy which operated through five outlets rather than to deal with five separate policies. The reasons for this practical unanimity in broad policy matters derive from the combined difficulties of presenting news in the technical and naturalistic medium of film, and from the ever-open question of censorship.

It was far more difficult to get the necessary equipment and men to the place where the news was going to happen than it was for the illustrated newspapers to do so. 'Ten cameras, sound, silent and hand were specially made, while motor-trucks with protection compartments were purchased together with a fleet of side-car equipped motor-cycles. Miniature laboratories for taking tests on the ground were designed and built' ... These were just some of the preparations involved in Movietone's coverage of the expected war in Abyssinia. Paramount, at great expense, placed camera-teams in the entourage of both General de Bono and the Emperor. They also set up permanent bases in Libya, Somaliland, Khartoum, Djibouti and Addis Ababa and also sent some aeroplanes under the charge of Paramount's veteran pilot-cameraman, F. Purnell.[2] Although tropical wars were a somewhat extreme case, nevertheless the technical encumbrances, which were not substantially reduced until after the Second World War, imposed upon the Newsreels a set of priorities which differed markedly from those of the Newspapers. 'Foresight', wrote the editor of Paramount, 'is one of the principal factors involved in Newsreel organization and today (1935) the Newsreel editor has to work ahead – sometimes many months ahead – in order that his men are on the spot when the story breaks'.[3] It was inevitable that when they at last obtained *their* story, they felt tempted to make it appear as being the only event of importance. Newspapers themselves often exaggerated the relative importance of particular events as a result of editorial judgements and policies, but the much wider coverage of a newspaper, and the fact that there were always many other papers available side-by-side, made this news-manufacturing much less effective in the case of the newspapers.

Another peculiarity of the relationship between the newsreels and the events which they were supposed to portray became apparent in the mid-thirties. It was widely believed, at least in America, that the showing of newsreels, and even the mere presence of camera teams at certain types of events, made a material difference to the events themselves. When the Newsreels decided, after some hesitation, to cover the strike at the Republic Steel Works, a Senate Committee banned, in advance, the exhibition of the resultant newsreels until three months after the strike.[4] The Senators were concerned lest showing the newsreels would lead to a drastic worsening of the situation and hoped that the ban would stop the Companies from sending their teams to the steel works in the first place. The story of Paramount's 'scoop' of the Memorial Day riots in Chicago underlines the reality of the fears. Despite a considerable delay imposed on the company before the reel was released, and despite the fact that people had already read and heard the story, the showing of the film, even in an extensively cut version, caused such unrest that it was banned again in most of the affected States. In recent years the effect of newsreels, shown by television, on the events themselves has been increasingly recognized and much attention has been devoted to this phenomenon.[5] The newsreel-men of the 1930s were fully aware of this mass-media problem, and their consciousness of it affected their treatment of the events to an important degree.

The political conditions under which the newsreels had to operate were, perhaps, even more fundamental in determining their policies. Both the aims and limitations of the newsreels were different in kind from the editorial newspaper policies. G.T. Cummins, the editor of Paramount believed that: 'The daily life of the whole civilized world is to be told in pictures, nothing must be omitted. But nothing must be included which the average man will not like. We do not hope to satisfy these conditions – they represent an ideal – but we have got to get as near as possible'.[6] The newsreels believed that their survival directly depended on discerning what the 'average man' did not wish to see and hear. The commonest outcome of the meetings which the Editors held over 'touchy' subjects was the decision not to cover them at all, so concerned were they with the repercussions of a misjudgement. For the one fundamental difference which distinguished Newsreels from newspapers was the general unsureness whether to extend to newsreels the traditionally accepted norm of the freedom of the press; or whether to place them under the traditionally accepted norm of the lack of freedom of the stage.

All films were, in accordance with the second norm, subject to censorship by the local Councils who were advised, in a manner of speaking, by the British Board of Film Censors, a body maintained by the industry. By the early 1920s it was decided by the Courts, that local Councils could not only enforce regulations relating to *cinemas,* but that their consequent power to grant licences entitled them to enforce their will relating to individual films shown in them also. Through a small and formally unsecured loophole, the newsreels were not subject to separate licences,

Cameramen from the five main newsreels outside Epsom, early 1950s.

hence to censorship. This was, however, certainly not a right which could be taken for granted, subject only, as in the case of newspapers, to the laws of libel and good faith. On the contrary, all through the period there were demands for the formal introduction of censorship – in fact each small step away from the principle of 'nothing which the average man will not like' resulted in a shrill chorus demanding censorship, often by the same people who would not have dreamt of diminishing the freedom of speech or of the press. For instance, after a showing by the Newsreels of the Japanese air attacks on Chinese cities, the Hereford County Council complained that 'scenes of war, sudden death, and violence were included from time to time in the Newsreels'. The Executive of the County Councils Association then formally requested the Home Secretary to make it an offence to display films depicting suffering or loss of life and to make all films showing events more than a week old subject to censorship.[7] The conflict of deeply felt principles, and muddled thinking to which it led, could hardly have been expressed more clearly. The Government would have none of it, of course. But this attack demonstrated to the Newsreels the special conditions under which they operated, quite unlike the Press.

Even more complex was their position in political matters and here again they found themselves in a very different position to their colleagues in Fleet Street.[8] There was great sensitivity about the presentation of *any* political issue through the medium of film. Correctly or not, the contemporaries of the newsreels regarded the cinema as an exceptionally potent means of communication – and of propaganda for that reason – with the result that the newsreels had to evolve an entirely different pattern of behaviour from the newspapers. The extent of this sensitivity is hard to recapture, yet without fully grasping it neither their history, nor the newsreels found in the archives, can make full sense.

In 1928, for example, there were 345 films to which 'exception' was taken by the British Board of Film Censors. There were 86 separate 'reasons' for this listed under 9 categories: 1, *Religious*; 2, *Political*; 3, *Military*; 4, *Administration of Justice*; 5, *Social*; 6, *Questions of Sex*; 7, *Crime*; 8, *Cruelty* and 9, *Titling*. The following specific reasons for objections were listed for example under Category 2, 'Political': (*a*) *Reference to HRH Prince of Wales*; (*b*) *Libellous reflections on Royal Dynasties*; (*c*) *British possessions represented as lawless sinks of iniquity*; (*d*) *Themes likely to wound just susceptibilities of Friendly Nations*; (*e*) *White men in a state of degradation amidst Far Eastern and native surroundings*; (*f*) *Equivocal situations between white girls and men of other races.* The following came under Category 3, 'Military': (*a*) *Officers in British uniform shown in disgraceful light*; (*b*) *Conflicts between the armed forces of a State and the populace*; (*c*) *Reflections on the wife of a responsible British official stationed in the Far East.*[9] Eisenstein's BATTLESHIP POTEMKIN was banned under: *Conflicts between the armed forces of a State and the populace* and so was INSIDE NAZI GERMANY' under: *Themes likely to wound just susceptibilities of Friendly Nations,* a decade later.[10] One reason why the more 'advanced' and controversial *March of Time* series was unsuccessful in England and was not followed by British newsreels, was its frequent brush with the censors.[11]

The Newsreels rightly regarded the continuance of not being under the censors as their highest priority. Nevertheless, one result of this censorship was that their presentation of domestic political issues took on a peculiar form. The complaint of the manager of the Tatler News Cinemas in Cheshire in connection with the resignation of Eden, fairly sums up the situation: 'Cinema audiences allowed in the Press to read forthright expressions of opinion … have been treated by the newsreel companies to the baldest statement of fact coupled with some shots of the leading personalities'. 'In some cases, even this "Bald and unconvincing narrative" was delayed by three days, possibly in the hope that something would turn up to relieve the embarrassment of the commentators. This hush-hush reporting was true of all but one firm (Paramount) who were so indiscreet as to allow a prominent critic of the Government to speak his views to the camera. Within a couple of hours of delivery of this reel to exhibitors, urgent orders were issued that the item must be deleted'.[12]

The views of the cinema-owners were equally important; they had no wish to have their patrons upset. 'It is not the job of the newsreels to show customers where they are wrong and put them right. There is room for such "propaganda" films but not on the cinema screens. It cannot be too strongly stressed that the cinema's primary business is to entertain'. The editorial in the cinema-trade's official organ went on to argue that the Newsreels must steer a course between the Scylla of dullness and the Charybdis of controversy. 'Even the playing of the National Anthem can be controversial', it added, 'as many Managers in Irish territories could testify'.[13]

The Newsreels themselves were fully aware of these feelings. Apart from making declarations such as 'British Movietone News never has and never will abuse its influence as a news publishing medium to distort the significance of events or to give them propagandist flavour …', their solution was to depart from one of the more basic tenets of popular journalism. They featured and played up the ordinary, the orderly, the well-arranged aspects and events of the society around them, rather than the truly sensational. The Newsreels laid stress on the points of similarity, identity of outlook and interest between the world of the government and that of their working-class regulars. Above all, they stressed the points of consensus rather than the points of conflict. The majority of Newsreel editors, it should be added, did so by inclination as well as necessity.

This policy of the newsreels infuriated the concerned, radical and usually well-born, hence guilt-ridden, cognoscenti who made up both the Documentary Movement and the PEP – Political and Economic Planning. The organ of the Documentary Movement stated in 1937, for example, that 'World events conspired to show up the British Newsreels at their most cowardly and incompetent', for 'the failure to face the issue of the year's labour disturbances' and, for their 'boycott of the century's most amazing story,the Abdication'.[14] In 1947 the PEP Report on the *Factual Film* believed that 'the content of the average British Newsreel before the War was trivial'. They also claimed that 'the Newsreel Editors shirk their responsibilities to the public'.[15] Yet there is little doubt that the working-class regulars hardly needed to be shown 'the plight of the unemployed', nor the 'disturbances' in Paris and in the United States or the London bus strike, which was the kernel of the particular complaint quoted. We also know from the Jarrow Crusade how they resented the intrusion and the implications of the Abdication. They could read about all these events if they wanted to read about them.

In real and practical terms the Newsreels served well their regulars who wanted to hang on to what they believed were the basic decencies of their situation: a belief in the good intentions of their rulers, the belief that things would get better without violence in Britain, and that they should bravely meet their present plight with a laugh. In all they felt, and the Newsreels helped them to feel it, that they must avoid despair. That way lay the salvaging of their self-respect. What good would the other approach have done *them*? It could have brought militancy and further embitteredness which might have appealed to their self-chosen champions, but hardly to the ordinary people who, as their votes showed, had no such intentions. As for the Newsreels, it would have led to the loss of their public, and long before that, to the loss of their freedom from censorship, such as it was.

While the Newsreels infuriated the cognoscenti and were contemptuously ignored by the educated classes in general, their consensual approach and their years of learning 'about the tastes of that perverse and fastidious entity, the average man',[16] allowed them to build up a capital of trust which stood them, and the country, in good stead from 1939 to the end of the war. It allowed them to 'editorialise' freely when the BBC could not. In a national crisis such 'propaganda' was essential for morale – especially amongst the 73% of the population who qualified as 'working class' under the provisions of the 1936 Act.[17]

The change-over to this new role began with the sudden possibility of war during the Munich crisis in September, 1938. Some were quicker off the mark than others: British Gaumont, in many ways the most successful in gaining the affection of its regulars and in developing its 'common touch', went on to declare by picture and sound '*Mr Chamberlain, our great Statesman, who has brought to politics the commonsense point of view of the ordinary man in the street … on whose sane judgement we place our hopes of peace and happiness*'. They never looked back after that and presented the policies and issues of the next seven years with equally little restraint on 'editorialising'. Paramount, on the other hand, unwittingly demonstrated the special position of the Newsreels: they interviewed Wickham-Steed and three others who were somewhat critical of the Munich Settlement. Thereupon the Foreign Office approached the US Government who contacted the parent company in America. The result was that the offending reel was at once withdrawn; subsequent questions in the House were handled by R.A. Butler with characteristic tact and skill and Paramount learned its lesson. Although they remained the most middleclass orientated in attitudes, they too played their part in preparing the country for war.

The reaction to Paramount's excursion into controversial journalism raises what is the most intractable problem of the Newsreels as a medium of communication: how can their effect on their huge and regular public be assessed? The problem is not confined to visual media, but applies also to broadcasting and the newspapers. The whole question needs as yet fundamental work, perhaps along the lines which in the contemporary context is being done on the influence of television, by Dr J. Blumler and others. Some external, and only preliminary evidence may, however, be adduced.

Contemporaries, such as the editor of the *Daily Sketch* who might be expected to know the business of communicating to a lower-class readership, thought in 1934 that there was a 'tremendous audience' which followed the Newsreels.[18] His recipe for improvement – more human stories – seems to have been adopted. Film-magazines, such as the *Picture Goer,* which did not care for Newsreels, commented that: 'Newsreel is assuming a new importance compatible with its reputation of being an essential and extremely popular section of the programme'.[19] Certain newsreels, such as the bombing of Shanghai, had considerable pulling power, rivalling the main feature in attraction. The steady growth in the number of specialist news-theatres such as The Times chain also indicates their popularity.[20] Even the criticisms of the socially motivated Documentary group might be cited as evidence of their success. Much of what the Documentary film-makers thought was wrong in the approach of the newsreels reads today like an extract from Professor Richard Hoggart's description of working-class attitudes to politics and society; that is the personification of political issues and the directly personal style;[21] by way of contrast, the cult of impersonality adopted by the BBC[22] and by the Documentaries, appealed to the middle class. It is evident that the newsreels appear to have been in the van of many facets of the *mass-media* as it broke to the surface in the 1950s. There is little doubt that they 'got through' to their working-class audience. After the Second World War came warnings about the effects of Newsreels on, for instance, the popularity of the government in power, and their effect on the public's understanding of the issues which the government wished to see appreciated. There were renewed efforts to control them.[23] Often these warnings were hysterical[24] and derived from the fear of propaganda which experience during the War had engendered and they derived ultimately from the growing realisation of the possible difference between the effects of reading and viewing, or at any rate, from the then current theories on that subject.

Whatever one may think of the more fanciful theories of audio-visual perception, or of the extent to which people become highly suggestible sitting in a dark

BFI

British Movietone News commentator Leslie Mitchell.

auditorium subject to powerful light and sound effects, there are undeniably some characteristics which distinguish the cinematic reception of 'news' from reading newspapers. In newspapers, it is possible to re-read a piece, to compare it with another version side-by-side and, to read as fast or as slowly as individually necessary for a full understanding; and above all, it is possible always not to read parts of a page. None of these aids to the critical faculty were available to film-viewers, but only partly because of the obvious technical problems. The Newsreel companies themselves went out of their way to avoid giving any aids to critical viewing. The 'stories' were constructed to move as fast as possible. It was, and still is, a fetish of the industry that nothing must be 'held too long'. The cutter's skill lay in knowing the minimum time required for getting a point across; he would then cut it a few frames short, moving the viewer across to the next item while he was still in the process of assimilating the information in the first. The professed reason for this technique was to cut before anyone in the audience became bored. It was, however, also another way of saying 'cut' before anyone could have had a chance of going over the story again in his mind.

This was *not* the general cinematic technique. On the contrary, the provision of lingering dissolves, slow fade-outs, and long pans were the normal ways of the cinema designed to provide thinking pauses and time for emotional involvement. It was peculiar to, and part of, the special techniques of the Newsreels that they eschewed any 'thinking pause' whatever. Much the same applied to their soundtracks; the points were made to sink in through speed, loudness and repetition. Some commentators, such as the very able and likeable E.V.H. Emmett of Gaumont British, fired away at nearly twice the speed of normal speech. This combined barrage for getting the points 'installed' was clearly the more effective the less the viewer was used to quick mental moves – i.e. the most effective on precisely the social and educational groups who were their regular audience.

The breakneck speed of the Newsreels helped further to accentuate what in any case was the most difficult aspect of this medium and which distinguished it from both broadcasting and the newspapers. In the case of the newspapers, it was clear to even the least alert reader that what was before him was what *somebody* had written, that he only had that man's report, that man's word for it. In the case of the cinema, however, it required constant mental effort to remember that what was on the screen was also a mere report; that it was in no sense what the viewer might have seen had he been where the camera stood. Or to be precise, that it might or might not have been *some* part of what took place in front of the lens, but that he had no way of knowing whether it was and which parts, if any. The intellectual effort involved in grasping the very difficult concept of 'montage' – whereby a sequence of photographs can be made to evoke *in the mind of the viewer* images which none of the photographs actually portrayed – was in any case beyond the powers of the great majority. They believed that in the case of feature films they saw what the actors actually did in the studio. In the case of newsreels and documentaries they believed that they saw, 'with their own eyes' (as television audiences still do) what actually took place in the faraway scenes of these 'actuality' films. After all, they went to the cinema precisely in order to come under its illusion.

The documentary film-makers made elaborate attempts at true 'authenticity' by trying to square the images evoked in the mind of the viewer with what they took to be the facts at the time of filming. The Newsreels were not concerned with such intellectual games – they saw their job as telling their customers news – stories from the world around which would interest them. Their 'language' was sound-film. They made no claims to being a recording agency. For one thing they knew their medium too well not to know that a photographic process can only record an object, but not an event. For another, they did not think that their customers would have preferred records to stories.

What gave this 'language' sufficient vocabulary and flexibility was the central treasure-trove of the Newsreel companies: their libraries. Without them it would not have been possible to issue regular newsreels twice a week, given the technical conditions of the age. Without a firm grasp of the function, of these libraries, we can neither understand what the Newsreels contributed to their own age, nor what use they might be to historians.[25] The fact is that it was a rare newsreel which did not contain footage shot sometime in the past or at a place other than where the preceding or succeeding sequences were filmed. There is no certain way whereby these, essentially stock-shots, can be distinguished from the others – at least not as a matter of routine. Of course, one may recognise a shot which has been seen before, or notice that the season appears to be wrong or that somebody is wearing last year's medals but there is no generic difference. In fact the whole point is that the Newsreels were made up from assorted footage in any case and it made no real difference whether a small part or even the whole of a story came from the library, because, in most cases, the shots which *were* taken at the scene were filmed usually long before the cameraman had much idea of what was going on.

In the case of demonstrations, for example several cameras at various points along its route shot footage without any idea of how the whole thing was going. It would be hours before anyone knew whether it could be fairly described as peaceful or violent, successful or not – whether to show smiles or scuffles, both of which could be filmable in any demonstration. The shots which were taken, as quickly as possible, where then sent to the cutters, usually without any detailed chronology. The story itself was finally made up when the editors became reasonably sure as to what in fact could be said to have 'happened', by selecting from the footage the appropriate visual ingredients and by describing with them – as if they used an Identikit – what they believed was a fair representation of what had taken place. If it transpired that they did not have the appropriate shots, a sequence could always be made up from the library, which with the aid of the 'voice' of the film told the audience as clearly, or more clearly, whatever they, as responsible journalists, believed was the truth and significance of the events. Not to use stock-shots, sometimes, would have led to untruth.

In the case, for example of British Gaumont 545, THE CRUCIFIXION OF CZECHOSLOVAKIA, there were a host of shots chiefly from UFA and Czech sources showing German troops and armoured vehicles in various parts of Czechoslovakia including some in Prague, and one of Hitler looking out of the Hradsin window – taken at least one day later, of course. That is what the pictures actually show, but the *Newsreel* itself was about a great deal more. After the title, the sound-track started: *'Once again the rattle of a German army on the march echoes through Europe. Where that march may end, no-one can foretell, but here before our eyes unfolds the drama of a nation dying. Hitler's troops enter Moravia. At Munich, the Fuhrer gave his words that he wanted no more land in Europe. These pictures show you what his words are worth'.* After a relatively long section 'showing it' with skilfully cross-cut music, shots and the 'voice', which were all built into a fine and powerful piece of montage, the point is made: *'You have seen the map changed once again. Be warned and offer yourself for National Service. Ask yourself the question asked by the British Prime Minister: "Is this the last attack upon a small state, or is this to be followed by others? Is this in fact a step in the direction of an attempt to dominate the world by force?"* Chamberlain's voice coming over shots of armoured cars and marching troops was recorded, of course, during his speech at Birmingham, three days after the event.

This combination of live shots with stock shots (in this instance no one even in Wardour Street could possibly know which was which) and live sound with stock sound, was the essence of the Newsreel. Together they created a direct and effective illusion of events and the woven-in editorial opinion was all the more effective because in style and approach it was so clearly pitched at the classes whose education stopped before the age when critical concepts and methods could be taught. Neither effort nor literacy was required for assimilating the message of the films. Once in the cinema, the film could not be turned off. It was indeed a powerful new means of communications.

There is thus a case for the historical importance of the Newsreels. The fact that, because yesterday's *Issue* was tomorrow's library footage, the Newsreels have been preserved by their owners in unbroken series enhances their usefulness. They are important historical evidence which deserves study. Not as records of events, but as records of what a very large, socially important and relatively little documented section of the public saw and heard, regularly from childhood to middle age.[26] They are also primary evidence for the history of those wider developments which are brought about by the application of modern technology to communications and which have been once described by Professor Asa Briggs as: 'the changes in the ways of seeing and feeling and forms of perception and consciousness'.[27]

History, vol. 57 no. 189, February 1972.

NOTES

1. e.g. Paul Rotha, *The Film Till Now* (Spring Books, London, 1967). 'They are simply a record in which the interest lies more in the speech than in the visual image ... They are an elementary form of the cinema "without joy" and considered as such, are only of casual and historic interest', p. 408.
2. *Kinematograph Weekly,* Supplement, 14 November 1935, p. 11.
3. *Kinematograph Weekly,* Supplement, 14 November 1935 p. 12.
4. Peter Baechlin and Maurice Mueller-Strauss, *Newsreels Across the World* (UNESCO, 1952), p. 31.
5. For a consideration of this phenomenon in a contemporary context see J. D. Halloran, P. Elliott, J. Murdock, *Demonstrations and Communications: A Case Study,* Penguin Special 1970. More generally see: *Sociology of Mass Media Communications,* ed. P. Halmos. Sociological Revue Monograph No. 13.
6. *Kinematography Weekly,* Newsreels and Shorts, 25 October 1934, p. 8.

7. *Today's Cinema, 24* November *1938*, p.1. *Today's Cinema* was the official daily organ of the Trade.

8. On this subject see the somewhat (though openly) tendentious, but factually reliable book: Ivor Montagu: *The Political Censorship of Film* (1929).

9. Montagu, op. cit., pp 33–8.

10. R. Manvell, *Film* (Pelican, 1944), p. 143.

11. Ibid., p. 144.

12. *Today's Cinema,* 1 March 1938, p. 2. The author was P.W. Dennis.

13. *Today's Cinema, 2* March 1938, p. 1.

14. *World Film News,* vol. 2. July, 1937, p. 29. *World Film News* was edited by John Grierson's sister and was, for all practical purposes, his and his movement's official organ. It was, also, a brilliantly written and produced journal.

15. PEP *The Arts Enquiry: The Factual Film,* 1947, p. 25. Members of the Committee were H.L. Beales, G.D.H. Cole, Mrs L.K. Elmhirst, Professor B. Ifor Evans, Miss M.C. Glasgow, F.A.S. Gwatkin, Mrs M.A. Hamilton, Dr Julian Huxley, C.C. Martin, A.D.K. Owen, E.W. White, K.W. Wilkie, with A.P. Cox as Secretary.

16. *Kinematograph Weekly,* Newsreels and Shorts. 25 October 1934, p. 8 by G.T. Cummins.

17. Housing Act. Schedule 11. cf. Arthur Marwick, *Britain in the Century of Total War* (1968), p. 228.

18. *World Film News* Autumn 1934, p. 31.

19. *Picture-Goer,* 19 October 1935, p. 24 by W.A. Pullan.

20. By 1938 there were approximately 50 in existence. All towns of medium size and above had at least one News Cinema. There were Newsreel shows on some mainline trains too, such as Leeds-London, and some of the bigger hotels provided Newsreel shows for their guests. This latter development was brought to a stop by the protests of cinema-owners who regarded it as unfair competition.

21. Richard Hoggart, *The Uses of Literacy* (1957), especially ch. IV.

22. Asa Briggs, *Golden Age of Wireless,* OUP 1965, p. 40.

23. PEP, *The Factual Film,* p. 26. 'A change in the present system by which news reaches the British cinema audiences is essential … The need for a change of attitude is particularly necessary if the crucial events of the reconstruction period arc to be adequately and fairly represented', i.e. as 'crucial'.

24. *Tribune,* 5 August 1949, presents, on the front page, a particularly choice example under the title *'Beware of the Newsreels'.* The article begins: 'Socialists fighting the next General Election will not only have to contend with the Opposition but with an even more powerful weapon – the Film. While there is a healthy distrust of what is read in the Newspapers a myth still exists that the camera cannot lie. But, if all goes according to plan – the camera will lie …'

25. For the use of stock-shots and the related problems of identification see Jay Leyda, *Films Beget Films,* 1964. The author, however, views the problems from the mistaken belief that, provided the 'authentic' shots can be sifted from the 'unauthentic' shots, they will become records of events. For an interesting discussion of the whole question of visual evidence and history, see J.A.S. Grenville, *Film as History: the Nature of Film Evidence,* University of Birmingham, 1971.

26. During the autumn of 1938, a survey was carried out amongst the 150,000 children who attended the Saturday morning 'Mickey-Mouse Club' run by the Odeon chain – as to their reaction to the Newsreels. 83% declared that 'they liked them as a whole'. It was also reported that '88% dislike the Dictators and 53% boo when they appear'. The survey was carried out by the Trade themselves and gives an interesting sidelight on what *they* thought they were doing. For this survey see: *Today's Cinema, 2* November 1938, pp. 1–3.

27. Asa Briggs, *The Communications Revolution* (Leeds University Press, 1966), p. 13.

The Cinema. News Reels.
At Various Cinemas

Graham Greene

The author Graham Greene was the film critic of The Spectator in the 1930s, and wrote some of the finest film reviews of this or any other period. A few weeks into the Second World War, Greene cries out for a new sort of newsreel that will lose the timidity of the past, learn from the techniques of the documentary movement and the German propagandists, and to recognise that 'this is a people's war'.

War always seems to surprise somebody; a year after Munich trenches which were begun that autumn are still being dug on the common outside; even the news-reel companies have been caught unprepared. They must have expected the temporary closing of the cinemas; they must have been prepared for censorship, and yet, like the newspapers, they have to rely on Germany as their chief source of supply an admirable picture of the siege of the Westerplatte, and another of the war in Poland. What have they got ready for us from the home front, and how have their commentators risen to the great occasion? One remembers what Hemingway did for SPANISH EARTH, and one hopes ... Even a war of nerves has its heroic angle.

As we fumble for our seats the too familiar voice, edgeless and French-polished, is announcing: 'The Queen has never looked prettier'. Royalty is inspecting something or other: `Royal interest inspires them to redoubled efforts'. Women bus-conductors climb aboard: 'For men passengers it will make going to work almost a pleasure'; they wave holiday-girl hands. Mr and Mrs Chamberlain walk in the Park; complete strangers take off their hats – an odd custom. The Duchess of Kent, instead of going to Australia, makes splints: 'We never thought we would live to be grateful to Hitler'. Very slowly we approach the violent reality; the Expeditionary Force marches to the coast, whippet tanks move through the woodlands, and the voice remarks something about 'shoulder to shoulder in this death struggle for liberty'. Surely by now we should realize that art has a place in propaganda; the flat and worthy sentiment will always sound hypocritical to neutral ears beside the sharp and vivid statement. There was much that Hemingway had to slur over in his commentary: his cause was far more dubious than ours, but the language was much more effective. Let us hope that Germany is not employing a commentator of his standard, for I cannot believe that neutral opinion – or home opinion if it comes to that – will be impressed by the kind of words we listen to shoulder to shoulder, liberty, baby-killers ...

The siege of the Westerplatte provides the best few minutes in any news cinema. It would have been interesting to hear the German commentary, for the picture seems to make the same odd psychological mistake as the Italian film of the Abyssinian War. The emphasis is all on power directed towards an insignificant object – we cut from the belching guns of the Schleswig-Holstein to the huge bombers taking off, from the calm complacent face on the Captain's bridge to the pilot's face at the wheel, sweating shadowy, intent: it is all smoke, flame, blast, inevitability. Nobody, we feel, can stand against this for an hour, and the mind answers quickly back that two hundred men stood it for a week. It was an astute move to show this film in England.

From Poland come some pathetic scenes of mob enthusiasm. Colonel Beck and the British Ambassador bow from a balcony: the faces of the crowd are excited, enthusiastic, happy ... The German film of the advance into Poland is beautifully shot and well staged – so well staged (the cavalry cantering in broken sunlight through the woods, the machine-guns rushed to the edge of the meadow grass) that one suspects old sequences of manoeuvres turned and mounted at leisure. Only the huge smashed bridges – like back-broken worms writhing in water – carry the stamp of real war. The same effect is given by the French films cleverly cut in with shots from the pre-war German film of the Siegfried Line: the balloon falling in flames is too tidy.

None the less, fake or not, these war pictures from the East and West are impressive, well directed, and edited with imagination and there is no reason why pictures from the defence front should not be equally effective. A different conception of news is needed – shadows of gold keys and cut ribbons and beauty queens linger. But news no longer means leading figures; we want the technique Anstey used in HOUSING PROBLEMS; America is more likely to listen with sympathy to the rough unprepared words of a Mrs Jarvis of Penge, faced with evacuation, blackouts, a broken home, than to the smooth-handled phrases of personalities. Above all, we don't want the old commentators, with their timid patronizing jokes; this is a people's war.

The Spectator, 29 September 1939.

We Lived in the Presence of History: The Story of British Movietone News in the War Years

Gerald Sanger

Gerald Sanger was editor of British Movietone News from 1929 to 1954. This unpublished account of Movietone's war years is probably the manuscript for a talk given shortly after the war. Sanger proudly recounts Movietone's service to the public and to the Government, but is also revealing on the newsreel's attitude towards censorship and propaganda, and has much useful information on practical operations in war-time. Sir Gordon Craig was the managing director of British Movietonews and chairman of the Newsreel Association.

In early 1939, when it began to be crystal clear that Britain was inevitably to be involved in a new war, the forms and magnitude of which it was difficult to visualise, a provisional plan had to be made for the release of *British Movietone News* to be continued under new unpredictable conditions. The formulation of such a plan was further complicated by the fact that the scope and policy of the new hush-hush Ministry of Information was not to come into existence until war started. It might well be that the Ministry under powers secured to it by Parliament might close down all independent commercial newsreels and issue instead its own propaganda reel, which all theatres would be compelled to exhibit.

 In spite of this uncertainty, very practical steps were taken by Sir Gordon Craig (supported by the Board of the Company), to forestall the emergency measures which would be forced upon us. *British Movietone News* is ordinarily produced and printed in one compact building in Soho Square, located literally in the heart of London's West End. As London was expected to be the immediate target for Germany's fleets of bombers, Sir Gordon, with the assistance of Tommy Scales and Pat Sunderland, made contingent arrangements for the transfer of *British Movietone News*' editorial offices and laboratory work to Denham, where the Laboratories were no then owned by Mr Rank, while the Studios were in fact under the control of Sir Alexander Korda. These arrangements enabled the news-reel to operate completely clear of the expected centre of destruction; they were parallel to the dispositions made by all Government departments and big business, but curiously enough, they were not duplicated by any other news-reel. If the blitz had materialised at that time on the scale generally anticipated, *British Movietone News* would, alone of British news-reels, have been prepared for it. We had a further reserve in a recording installation at the Finsbury Park plant of Kay Film Laboratories.

The war came on September 3rd, 1939, and *British Movietone News* moved out lock, stock and barrel to Denham, leaving only the News Department and camera staff in Soho Square. Tommy Scales and the make-up party got down immediately to producing a news-reel under unfamiliar conditions and with unfamiliar collaborators. It was a terrific undertaking which might have daunted men of less hardy confidence and experience. The task was to produce a worthy record of what seemed a turning-point in national history; and how well they did it, can be verified from the cans in *British Movietone News* library. The testimony is there to screen, and to admire. Cecil Burge's admirable commentary, pungent as ever, never over-stressed; Leslie Mitchell's delivery of it; Pat Sunderland's recording; Sid Wiggins' deft cutting, Stanley Wicken's skilful matching of sound and music, and Tommy Scales' perfectly assured control of the whole proceedings – all these separate and equally important ingredients emerge for me from that first news-reel of the Second World War with a vividness which I capture from no other reel. Later, we reissued a digest of the first two news-reels of the War under the title WAR COMES TO LONDON, and it was the first *British Movietone News* 'short' of the war to be translated into all the languages under the sun for propaganda distribution overseas.

Sixteen issues of *British Movietone News* were produced at Denham. Then, as the Luftwaffe's blitz had not matured, we moved back to Soho Square and resumed our printing at Kay West End Laboratories.

In the meanwhile, the Ministry of Information had established itself in the Senate House of London University and was exercising its first mortifying influence on Press and news-reel. It was an accepted principle of that confused period that nobody with commercial experience could be appointed to posts in Government departments for fear that the temptation to favour their former associates might prove too strong for them. A few journalists – not many – found their way into the Press Division; but the Films Division began its career with nobody who knew anything about news-reels. Which was unfortunate, because news-reels were about the only commodity that the Films Division were able to show for their appointed task of giving film support to the national effort.

However, the lack of experience in the Films Division did bring one mighty benefit. No attempt was made at that time to fuse the commercial news-reels into a single Government propaganda reel, and the five companies (Movietone, Gaumont-British, Paramount, Pathe and Universal) were allowed to pursue their separate existence. The temptation of instituting a Government reel was, of course, never far from official minds and later assumed the proportions of a threat, which was successfully withstood. But, in the early days, incompetence at the Ministry of

Information made it manifestly impractical, and the project was only mentioned as a talking-point.

On the other hand, actual production of news-reels was done under great and cloying embarrassments. A 'Security censorship' had been clapped on us with the first signal of war. Its operations were at first weird and unintelligible. Our cameramen seemed to be prevented from taking any shot which had any bearing on the war. This impression grew not only from our own incomprehension of some of the regulations but also from the censors' hesitating interpretations of them. Amazing restrictions appeared to emanate from the R.A.F.'s desire not to give the enemy any hint about Britain's weather. Ten days had to elapse after the first snowfall before you might show any picture with snow in it. And this, although the dreaded German spy might be walking into the cinema out of a street mushy with trodden snow! So anxious was the War Office not to reveal to the enemy our Order of Battle that we were not allowed to take any shots of soldiers anywhere unless there was literally no background in the picture and unless their regimental badges were not visible.

The effort of the authorities was primarily to prevent incriminating pictures being taken. Cameramen, therefore, found that their Ministry of Information passes were not valid in the view of the Army, Navy and Air Force and sometimes not even in the

British Movietone News editing rooms at Soho Square, London.

eye of the Police. They were times of 'official jitters', even though we were living through the months of what was known in America as the 'phoney war'. Gradually, common sense began to obtrude into the bureaucratic mentality. There was substituted the policy of allowing cameramen to shoot questionable material and of intercepting it before publication, as trust in the news-reels' integrity and discretion grew. In the end, the British news-reels were taken into the confidence of the Government in advance of many important developments, and secrets were imparted to the principals of the news-reel companies in a way which would have horrified the early guardians of national security.

There were one or two cases where an exasperated news-reel, in order to force the hand of a Government department, took action which that Government department was able to represent as prejudicial to the national interest. These reckless incidents reflected on all news-reels and brought us as near to complete Governmental control as at any time during the war. It is pleasant to record that *British Movietone News* was never the perpetrator of any such irresponsible conduct. In fact, it is true that our news-reel set the standard, and the prestige of news-reels as a whole rose during the war to an unprecedented level, very largely thanks to the wise and forceful handling of our public relations by Sir Gordon Craig.

It was Sir Gordon who had nursed the News-reel Association along the way it should go. The Association, which had been born before the war out of necessity to make joint arrangements for rota, pooling of 'rights', and resistance to crushing taxation on filmstock, began to assume a preponderant importance in wartime. The authorities would not deal with each news-reel individually; they required to deal with bodies representing an industry. Thus, the Newsreel Association became the recognised negotiating agency of practically every assignment. Either the Government department channelled its interpretation and suggestions through the Secretary of the Association, or one company acted as liaison company for the others. A routine was established of screening all five news-reel issues on Mondays and Thursdays at the Ministry of Information; and on Mondays a conference was held immediately afterwards with the Director of the Films Division, at which news-reels and representatives of Service Departments exchanged information and requests.

All our younger cameraman did well. Graham Thompson covered the landings in Madagascar, North Africa and Sicily, and was present at the attempt on Dieppe. Norman Fisher did a long spell in Singapore (just before its fall), in Java, the Middle East and Tunisia, culminating in the liberation of Greece; while the wanderings of Alec Tozer would fill a book and indeed look like doing so – for Alec has written a delightful and amusing volume on his experiences, which include the 'miraculous' overwhelming of the Italian Army in Libya by Wavell and his 30,000, the Retreat through Burma and its subsequent reconquest, a journey through the Himalayas to Tibet, an assignment in Chunking, the suppression of the Iraqi revolt and the meeting of Russians and British in Northern Persia. His casual remark 'I took a taxi through Persia' rated a leading article in the London 'Times'.

It is unnecessary to mention that it was not entirely an 'overseas' war for us. The 'blitz' came to Britain in July 1940, and all our cameramen were engaged in recording at some risk to life and limb the havoc inflicted on London and other great cities by Goering's squadrons. They recorded, too, the havoc inflicted on Goering's squadrons by the gallant fighters of the R.A.F. The winter of 1940/41 was the greatest ordeal to which the population of Britain has ever been subjected. Americans, who saw our pictures of that ordeal, as re-edited for America by our New York associates, will find no difficulty in imagining the hazards and stresses to which our cameramen and organisation were exposed during that period. Many cameramen shared the credit of this nerve-racking coverage. In particular I remember some amazing pictures of fired buildings, walls crashing and firemen working amid a blazing inferno turned in by Dick Harris at Plymouth in March 1941 and by Jim Humphries in Liverpool.

The headquarters of the organisation stayed in London. Having made the experiment of migrating to Denham in the previous year, we did not repeat it, though it requires an effort of memory to recall why. One reason was that the outskirts of London seemed no safer than the centre. I think, however, the real truth is that after Dunkirk a sort of bemused fatalism inspired everybody; we stayed put, worked hard and crossed our fingers. In the outcome, we were extremely lucky. Although large areas of London were devastated, no bomb fell in Soho Square; and only once was our building evacuated – when a delayed action bomb was located in Charing Cross Road. We migrated to Kay's other laboratory in Finsbury Park, but within twelve hours we were back in Soho Square, a small bomb having been extracted from a mysteriously large crater. Three years afterwards they found by chance another bomb on the same site – a huge unexploded fellow who had been the actual cause of the debris. Any time during those three years, 22 Soho Square and a lot of other property might have been damaged by a shattering explosion.

The blitz ceased suddenly on May 10th, 1941, and for the three years already mentioned there was comparative peace in London, broken only by sporadic incendiary raids and by alarums and excursions, which were more alarm that excursion. 1944 opened with the 'February blitz' which was Hitler's retaliation for the pasting that German cities were getting from Lancasters and Fortresses. A stick of bombs fell along filmdom's Wardour Street, and one of our competitors (*Universal News*) had its offices and laboratories wrecked – the only casualty suffered among news-reel buildings during the whole war. Mr Rank accommodated the unlucky victim in the premises of his other news-reel (*Gaumont British*) at Shepherd's Bush.

Then after D-Day came the Buzz-bomb or V.1 or Doodlebug; and once again the mentality of blitz days returned to London. There was this difference, however: it was so plainly a last throw, and having survived the vicissitudes of a long war, no-one wanted to get bumped off in the last stages by a buzz-bomb. Therefore, in a way it was even more nerve-wracking that 1940–1941. The terrible suspense 'when the engine stopped' was something that tens of thousands of Americans then in South-East England will vividly remember, and there were many times when the diabolical sound seemed to stop right over Soho Square. However, Movietone's luck remained good and neither V.1, nor its successor V.2. made any descent upon us.

The end of the war in Europe found us intact and confident, if a little doubtful of the new era into which we were heading, for the General Election followed very quickly on V.E. Day and new political horizons began to reveal themselves. Looking in the reverse direction – backwards – we had a record of which we could be proud. *British Movietone News* had never ceased to produce its two news-reels a week through all the perils which had assailed our 'embattled isle'. Regularly Mondays and Thursdays our news-reel issues had been delivered to customers from Cornwall to the North of Scotland. They had carried the pictorial record of Britain's resistance and fighting come-back to the screens of every city and town, and allied to Leslie Mitchell's heartening commentary these pictures must have played their considerable part in sustaining the national spirit and will to win. We had in fact been powerful propagandists for the national cause – all the more powerful for being unofficial. This was a point of which the Ministry of Information and the other departments concerned with us gradually became appreciative.

Overseas, the same pictures, regularly shipped to associates in New York and Sydney, were providing material for treatment by Lowell Thomas, Ed Thorgerson and Jack Davey, adapting to American and Australia audiences under the friendly eyes of Edmund Reek and Harry Guinness; we were also shipping negatives to South Africa, the Middle East and India, and translated versions were going to such countries as Iran and Greece.

Mention should be made of the very activities made by us in translating and scoring foreign versions of shorts made by the Ministry of Information. In fact, this operation was not limited to 'shorts'. We converted DESERT VICTORY, TUNISIAN VICTORY, TRUE GLORY, and over 70 other films into nearly every language from Sanskrit to Choctaw. Mr Robert Gibbon was in charge of this work; marvellous was the patience exercised by him with foreign commentators and truly amazing was the speed with which he got through the sessions. It is a matter of incontrovertible mathematics that he presided over the making of 482 foreign versions of short films, and 478 editions of foreign news-reels.

We also made a number of short films in the English language. It would be false modesty, and a little disingenuous, if I suppressed all reference to myself in this account of *British Movietone News*' war record. My main undertaking, apart from filling in for Tommy Scales occasionally and keeping a watchful eye on our production activities generally, was to attend to the making of short films, in

British Movietone News viewing theatre, 1940s, Gerald Sanger second from right, middle row.

conjunction with Raymond Perrin and Peter Whale, for various Government sponsors. The chief sponsor was the Ministry of Information who took delivery of 35 films edited by Raymond Perrin, including three long compilations in the nature of 'war history', which were translated into European languages for the liberated peoples. Another big sponsor was the War Office, for whom we produced Tank Identification films for the instruction of the Army, and Aircraft Identification films for the Army and Royal Air Force. Peter Whale specialised in work for the National Savings Movement; and we also executed commissions for the British Council, Red Cross, Ministry of Fuel and Power and the Admiralty. We never refused a job, and never failed to complete it.

However, these side-lines, important as they were, took second place to our chief concern, that of turning out 'G.R.' (General Release) regularly and to time and with the greatest effect for audiences. This was the principal wartime occupation of Tommy Scales as Make-up Editor, with the assistance of Commentary-writer Cecil Burge, Chief Cutter Sid Wiggins, Chief Sound Engineer Pat Sunderland, Music Librarian Stanley Wicken and Chief Projectionist Jack Cross. Necessarily, the contents and form of the news-reel changed with the war. The purely 'entertainment' content became less and less. There were periods indeed when the very grimness of the outlook argued for the inclusion of light-hearted items (if they could be found), and not a few of the brighter items emanating from the United States before Pearl Harbour were brought in to relieve the solemnity of our own coverage. But it became accepted by the public that the news-reels' function was to report the war, and as the war became world-wide, the stream of other items dried up.

The restriction of filmstock also acted in the same sense. The length of the news-reel was reduced in two bites, first from 850 to 800 feet (early in the war), then from 800 to 700 feet when the Board of Trade called for a saving of 30 million feet per annum. We faced this second cut with gloomy forebodings, wondering how we could be expected to turn out a good news-reel with only 700 feet to play with. We saved 20 feet by adopting a shorter main title, but the remainder of the economy could only be achieved by dropping stories or sequences.

We found that it was no solution to resort to quicker cutting or speeding up the tempo. The visual reporting of war needed, in fact, a slower tempo. That was our conclusion, and the number of stories in an issue of *British Movietone News* tended to decrease. The usual practice was to let at least one story run about 300 feet, and complete the reel with three or four others. Moreover, we produced a considerable number of one-subject reels in the course of the war. We also turned *British Movietone News* into a one-voice reel, Leslie Mitchell delivering the entire commentary, with Lionel Gamlin coming in to replace him one reel in four.

All these changes helped in the evolution of the wartime product, which I suppose is now truly a little bit of history. Before we cut down our main title, I had used as part of it a slogan 'We live in the presence of history'. The reels on which that slogan ran are now recorded history themselves.

Unpublished manuscript for talk delivered c.1946.

The Faking of Newsreels

Len England

Mass-Observation was a social research organisation founded in 1937, which monitored ordinary people's lives by a system of reports produced by unpaid 'observers'. Cinema-going was included among its social surveys, and during the period 1939–1945 it monitored the newsreels, producing an invaluable picture of cinema audience's reactions to the newsreels in war-time, particularly for the early years of the war. Data from the original observers' reports were collated into File Reports, of which three are reproduced in this Reader. All the film File Reports were compiled by Len England, and in File Report no. 16 of 7 January 1940, England reports on a subject of particular interest to him, the use of fakery in the newsreels.

The impression created by any film upon an audience is the result both of the actual photographs and of the sound and commentary. Both of these elements can be made misleading. In the question of newsreels, where a great deal of the sound is added from material in their libraries a completely false interpretation of the evidence can be conveyed. A picture of a burning building, for instance, may be accompanied by the sound of bombs exploding and by the commentator saying 'This is but one of many buildings which have suffered'. A further false impression may be gained if the building is photographed from many different angles with the result that it seems on first sight as if the shots are all of different buildings. The audience cannot concentrate at the same time on both commentary and pictures and the tendency is to merge the two together, believing the evidence of the eyes and therefore of the ears.

In this direction nothing can be proved as the details of how a newsreel is made are the closed secret of the newsreel companies. There are examples, however. The *Gaumont British* news (18.1.40, seen LE, Gaumont, Streatham) contained a shot of Indian troops in France and prefaced it with the words 'India stands with Britain to a man'. The *Pathe Gazette* (21.12.39, seen LE, Regal, Streatham) contained shots of a destroyer in action; obviously here there could have been no sound equipment and all the explosions and so on had been added later. The newsreel men in Finland naturally wish to travel light and carry no sound equipment (evidence: Ralph Bond) and so all the sound of these shots is superimposed. Some houses in Finland have been photographed from several angles to give the impression of several houses (evidence: Sidney Cole). Commentary gave the impression that a whole train load of Swedish volunteers was leaving for Finland; but an observer noticed women and children also in train and volunteers only in one part of it (Sidney Cole). One sequence of a burning Finnish village was syndicated to the newsreels and Pathe said that it had been fired by a retreating Red Army and Paramount that it had been set alight by the retreating Finnish army (evidence: Christopher Brunel).

In some cases the sequences show signs of being 'prepared'. A cameraman told an observer (LE, before special study) that a regiment of soldiers had been marched backwards and forwards over a hill for a whole morning for the benefit of a newsreel; on another occasion a tank was shot being loaded on to a ship for France, but as soon as the cameras had stopped it was taken off again as the ship was never able to carry such cargo. The evacuation of Dulwich College was taken; one boy walked in and out of a house many times before the newsreels were satisfied that the shots were sufficiently 'natural' (evidence: LE from boy at the school). An appeal by Madame Gripenburg contained the story of a woman in a fur coat coming to the door of the Embassy and handing in some money (Sidney Cole). The newsreels showed this scene meaning either that they knew before that the woman was coming or that they reconstructed it afterwards. Many of the shots of the Finns sniping released to all reels have been taken from a position in front of the Finns so that the cameraman must have been standing with his back to the enemy. G.B. (13.12.39, seen LE, Academy) showed shots of air raid havoc including women sheltering under a wall; some of them, however, were laughing and there were 'feet' walking about on top of the wall quite unconcerned; the shots in Pathe (8.1.40, seen LE, Brixton Pavilion) on the other hand showed the children crying as they went into shelters. In shots of action on the front (Paramount 30.11.40, seen LE, Astoria, Streatham) a cameraman focused the camera on a spot and a second later a shell burst right in the middle of the section covered. And finally in none of the action shots (except those at sea taken by naval officers) has the camera jolted or been out of focus.

A third method has been to 'reconstruct' events. *British Paramount News* (20.11.40) cut shots of crashed bombers with violent action pictures prefaced with some remarks such as 'this is what it would have looked like'; at Eros News Theatre, Piccadilly Circus, an observer heard one man say 'of course this isn't real' and at the Paramount, Tottenham Court Road the next day, some laughed at the sequence. The Cameo News (G.B. and Paramount) on 4.12.39 contained a sequence of a submarine being sunk after a depth charge had hit it. A G.B. news early in the war (seen LE privately) contained a shot of the Kiel ships being bombed before THE LION HAS WINGS did the same. G.B. News (1.2.40, seen LE, Gaumont, Streatham) contained description of patrol; only scenery was a tree, barbed wire and snow and the camera accompanied the patrol even when it inspected a blockhouse, presumably in enemy lines. The whole action took place in broad daylight. The commentary gave the impression by inference that this patrol was the actual one on which the first DSO (?) was awarded; it ran something like 'this is a patrol of one officer and three NCOs; Captain – won DSO on patrol.' Obs. knows this deceived at least one person.

It must be re-emphasised that nothing can be proved conclusively unless one of the newsreels makes a big mistake. All of the 'editing' is done by the newsreels in secret, and there can be no proof that sound track was added afterwards, that commentary was intentionally misleading, or that actions were posed or reconstructed.

Those mentioned in report
Sidney Cole; editor of The Cine Technician
Ralph Bond; of Realist Films
Christopher Brunel; son of Adrian Brunel, very interested in the propaganda value of film
Leonard England; Mass observer doing special films work since early November, including reports on 26 news reels

File Report 16, LE 7.1.40

EDITORIAL NOTE

File Reports 16, 22 and 314 have been reproduced in this volume. These reports, and the remaining File Reports nos. 141, 215, 334, 444 and 524, all from 1940, are available online via the British Universities Newsreel Database, www.bufvc.ac.uk/databases/newsreels/resources/texts.html.

Newsreel Report

Len England

In this report for the Mass-Observation social research organisation, Len England provides a detailed account of the newsreels from the outbreak of war to the date of the report, 28 January 1940. England documents both newsreel content and audience reactions to the newsreels. This was the period of the 'phoney war', before Dunkirk, the Blitz, or Churchill's premiership. The newsreels struggled to find material to report on the war, both through a lack of footage and the strictures of wartime censorship. The report illustrates their use of 'fakery' and comedy, an increased tendency to make pointed comment, and a greater degree of 'horrific' material being shown. Audience reactions to personalities, chiefly politicians and royalty, is analysed, and individual voices are heard expressing opinions concerning the newsreels themselves, their style of delivery and their propagandist content. Comparison is made with England's report on THE LION HAS WINGS, a British propagandist feature film made by Alexander Korda with Ministry of Information support early in the war.

CONTENT OF NEWSREELS

Subject matter

Naturally as soon as the war broke out the whole emphasis of newsreels became centred on war news; in the first six months, less than 15% of their news has had no connection with war (see Appendix A) either in this country or in Finland. But the lack of activity after the collapse of Poland forced the newsreels to look beyond Europe for their shots. They could not indefinitely show sequences of the BEF on manoeuvres or in their trenches, and by the middle of December the British Army in France began to fade from the newsreels; between the beginning of November and the middle of December seventeen observed newsreels contained shots of the BEF. Since that date there has been one.

At sea more was happening, but the difficulty here was to get action pictures; with the *City of Flint*, for example, the newsreels could do no more than take pictures of the stationary ship when she docked at Bergen, while when the *Rawalpindi* was sunk by the *Deutschland*, the newsreels showed shots of each ship firing their guns and cut them with one another. The same difficulty occurred with the work of the RAF. In both cases some attempt was made to enliven the sequences by the introduction of faked shots of submarines sinking or of air battles with the remark 'this is what it would have looked like'. On one occasion the audience laughed at an RAF fight and it seems that these reconstructions have been given up. But a dangerous precedent has been created in false news.

No shots of action on the Western Front were released until the 11th of December and it was another ten days before action at sea was obtained. Neither of these sequences were more than a muddled picture of bombs dropping and shells firing – and the one of the navy was taken by an officer of the ship – the audiences were not impressed. But when, just before Christmas, the *Graf Spee* was scuttled, cameramen were on the spot and on the 2nd January newsreels contained a long sequence of the sinking battleship. At the end of it the audience at the Cameo, Charing Cross Road, as a rule most unresponsive, clapped loudly and even a fortnight later a suburban audience applauded.

But an event such as the scuttling of the *Graf Spee* was too rare for the newsreels to depend upon it for interest. When the Polish resistance was finally crushed and no activities on the Western Front were forthcoming, the newsreels turned elsewhere for shots of fighting. One long sequence dealt with the war in China and caused more comment than anything else in observed newsreels. For some time manoeuvres in America were the mainstay; these were staged on a large scale with tanks being blown up, aeroplanes bombing ground troops, and above all a night attack with tracer bullets which the Gaumont British commentator admitted to be 'America's gift to the cinema, to make up for the war in Europe'.

Then on November 30th 1939, Russian troops invaded Finland, and there were immediate air raids. Since that date eighteen newsreels have been observed, and in thirteen of them shots of the war in Finland have been included with an average length of over two minutes. Six of these thirteen newsreels have caused comment, once the Finns have been applauded. This exceptionally high degree of response seems to indicate that the newsreels have been right in emphasising this element, but the number of people who in answer to the questionnaire said that they objected to war in newsreels, together with the 'God's and 'horrible's of the comments, tends to indicate that they are not effective propaganda.

Here again, however, there is evidence to suggest that the newsreels have been 'reconstructing' events. Some of the shots, it is said, bear a marked resemblance to those of bombed Spanish towns; women supposed to be rushing to shelter in an air raid were laughing; of a picture of a burning village, the Pathe commentary said that it had been fired by the retreating Red army, while Paramount argued that the Finns had burnt it after them themselves.

Before the war, even in the last weeks of August, the only response to shots of soldiers was laughter. On not one occasion since the war has any soldier been laughed at with the exception of two French soldiers riding a tandem, a sequence that was intended to be funny. The Women's army has, however, created some amusement due in part at any rate to facetious remarks in the commentary; Universal, for instance, with shots of Land Army girls on a turkey farm produced remarks about 'nice birds'. On other occasions bad marching has produced titters.

Though there has been no laughter, there has been a good deal of clapping at the sight of soldiers and sailors. At the beginning of the war the sight of a sailor leaning out of a window was on one occasion sufficient provocation for general applause, while on another French troops marching were clapped. About 10 per cent of the appearances of allied forces have been greeted by clapping; otherwise they have been watched in silence.

Mention has already been made of the inclusion of faked news in newsreels. Yet another way in which the companies have tried to make up for the lack of any interesting information is by the introduction of items which are topical but have no direct news value. At the beginning of the war, for instance, the Crazy Gang became

Pathe Gazette title design from Second World War.

British Pathe

an admirable substitute for news. On one occasion Bud Flanagan portrayed a soldier in a dug-out dreaming of French girls and Blighty; on another, in an item called THE WORST WRESTLING MATCH, the Crazy Gang did a fight in slow motion. On this occasion no attempt at all was made to connect it to any item of news and the audience was at first mystified; a week earlier the Crazy Gang had been seen wrestling, but this time it was for the troops and soldiers were seen in the shots. Cartoons were used in short epilogues; in the same news as THE WORST WRESTLING MATCH a cartoon addressed to Hitler pointed out that 'we've got the money, we've got the guns, so what are you going to do?' The next week Pathe included an illustrated poem on the value of 'Keep it Dark'. The inauguration of the keep-fit classes on the wireless prompted Universal to depict a fat woman trying to touch her toes, while Pathe has now instituted a whole series of 'Nasti News'. One was seen by an observer:

Lord Haw-Haw enters with large moustache and monocle. By his side is a 'lie-making machine' (laughs 1)

Remarks about Goering and his medals (laughs 2)

'Next Tuesday a British ship was sunk at Tiddleywinks on Spee' (laughs 2)

A man who has been painting a wall at the back turns round; it is Hitler (laughs 2)

He awards Haw-Haw with an Iron Cross (laughs 2)

'To facilitate scuttling, German ships are being made without bottoms' (laughs 3)

Fade-out with Hitler saluting (laughs 3)

It will be seen that there is a high degree of audience response to this comedy. At the 'Keep it Dark' sequence there was even some applause. And while this is not a post-war development – it was used quite extensively by Movietone before the war – nevertheless in newsreels observed since the war, nearly 30 per cent contain a comedy.

Personalities

There follows a comparative table of the appearances of famous figures in pre-war and post-war newsreels.

	Pre-war (12 newsreels)		Wartime (38 newsreels)	
	No. of appearances	No. of times applauded	No. of appearances	No. of times applauded
British politicians				
Anderson	3	0	0	0
Baldwin	5	3	0	0
Cecil	4	0	0	0
Chamberlain	10	1	4	2
Churchill	0	0	5	3
Eden	0	0	2	0
Lloyd George	5	(2 laughs)	0	0
Halifax	11	1	0	0
Henderson	8	1	0	0
Hore Belisha	3	0	6	3
Hoare	0	0	1	0
Simon	0	0	4	2
Runciman	1	0	0	0
Kingsley Wood	4	0	0	0
Total	54	8	22	10
Royal family				
The King	8	0	11	2
The Queen	5	0	11	3
Queen Mary	3	0	1	1
Duke of Kent	2	0	0	0
Duke of Gloucester	0	0	4	1
Duke of Windsor	0	0	8	6
Duchess of Kent	1	(1 laugh)	0	0
Duchess of Windsor	0	0	1	0
Total	19	1	36	13
Other figures				
Daladier	5	0	3	0
Hitler	0	0	1	0
Roosevelt	4	2	1	0
Stalin	0	0	2	0

It will be seen immediately that the emphasis in wartime news has shifted from personalities to events. The numbers of well-known people in thirty-eight newsreels observed since the war are hardly greater than the number in twelve pre-war newsreels. It has also shifted from politicians to royalty and within those groups from one figure to another. Finally, the audience now responds to different figures.

Before the war, the appearances of the King and Queen were less frequent than those of either Chamberlain or Halifax; since the war both of them have appeared more than twice as often as anyone outside the royal family, and whereas on no occasion formerly were they applauded, now they have been clapped on 20 per cent of their appearances. The Duke of Windsor was not seen at all before the war, since he has appeared eight times and been applauded on six of them, or on 75 per cent of appearances. The Duke of Gloucester has not been seen at all since the war, though one of his four appearances since has been clapped.

Before the war, as has been mentioned, Lord Halifax and Mr Chamberlain were more frequently seen than any personality; since the war Lord Halifax has not been seen at all and Mr Chamberlain was not observed until three days before Christmas, while on his tour of the front. On this occasion he was not clapped, but after the resignation of Hore Belisha, when Mr Chamberlain was photographed making his Mansion House speech, he was applauded on two occasions though in both cases very feebly. Hore Belisha, on the other hand, has made six appearances since the war, four times before his resignation; on one occasion he was clapped. After his resignation he made two very brief appearances but each time he was immediately clapped. Mr Chamberlain, in brief, in two appearances of four minutes and three minutes, in which he made many remarks that caused clapping from his Mansion House audience, was applauded very feebly. Hore Belisha, in two appearances of half a minute, in which he did not speak a word, was clapped more vigorously.

Of other politicians the two that have made most appearances have been most clapped. Mr Churchill has made five appearances, including a five-minute reconstruction of a broadcast which constituted the entire news at the Gaumont, Haymarket, and on three occasions was clapped. Simon has made four appearances and was clapped twice; neither of these politicians appeared at all before the war.

On the other hand, there are many politicians as well as Halifax who have not appeared at all since the war. Sir John Anderson, Lord Baldwin (clapped on 60 per cent of his appearances pre-war), Viscount Cecil, Lord Chatfield, Lloyd George, Sir Neville Henderson, Lord Runciman, and Sir Kingsley Wood, none have appeared in observed newsreels since the war. Roosevelt who was clapped on two of his four pre-war appearances has been seen only once when the audience showed signs of boredom.

Military leaders have not been featured to any great extent. Lord Gort has made three appearances; on no occasion was he clapped and when he gave a Christmas message – 'the first time in newsreel history that a commander-in-Chief has spoken' as the *Pathe Gazette* announced – the only response noted by an observer was one woman who remarked 'silly, isn't it?' Gamelin has made one appearance and Colonel Lane in charge of the Army Mail made an appeal at Christmas. A brief shot of the

General who signed the Anglo-Turkish agreement was greeted with immediate, loud applause.

A sequence of the burial of the victims of the Munich bomb explosion, obtained through neutral countries, included a long shot of Hitler – there was no response at all. At the beginning of the Russo-Finnish war sequences of Stalin were included; at the Cameo, Charing Cross Road, one man called out something fairly loudly and another muttered 'urcha'. At the Regal, Kennington, there was no response at all.

The appearances of the Crazy Gang have been mentioned before, but it is worthy of note that Gracie Fields has appeared as often. On none of her four appearances has she been clapped, but there has been general laughter at all her jokes. On each occasion she has appeared on the newsreel just after a broadcast, and every time she has been photographed actually entertaining the troops, not specially engaged by a newsreel company.

Summary of content

The newsreels appear to have well judged public taste. Since the war the public figures who have appeared most in the newsreels are those that have been most applauded. The shifting of emphasis from politicians to the royal family may indicate that the public now prefers the uninterfering royalty to troublesome Members of Parliament, though the popularity of Sir John Simon, even after the announcement of his war budget, is surprising.

In subject matter the tendency is directly on war themes; though until Russia's invasion of Finland there were few 'action' shots. Shots of the BEF were frequent until all aspects of their life had been exhausted, and much the same applied to the navy. Nevertheless the newsreels are very far from succeeding in making all their contents vital as the number of criticisms in the questionnaire on the grounds to 'no news' or 'repetition' show.

Finally, a new tendency is appearing to produce in newsreels both faked news and reconstructions of events that could not be filmed, and also comic interludes that have no direct connection with any item of news. This must be a direct consequence of the absence of news, or the difficulty of getting it, and while they are well received, they must be regarded as a dangerous inclusion. In their true form newsreels can be regarded as a record more accurate than any other, but once reconstruction or faking appears, their whole value is lost.

Other general tendencies

As well as the general tendencies in newsreels that have been noted under 'Subject matter', there are one or two general points that must be observed. Before the war the newsreels portrayed the official view of events on most occasions though at the time of the Munich crisis one of the companies was asked to withdraw a

British Pathe

Pathe's Terry Ashwood filming in North Africa during the Second World War.

speech by Wickham Steed which was considered to be out of keeping with the Government's plans. Later, however, at the time of the film tax, the newsreels argued that they provided the Government with excellent propaganda free of all charge.

Since the war the newsreels have continued to contain much propaganda, a little too much, judging from the questionnaire. Shots of Dominion troops are almost invariably an excuse for the expression of patriotic sentiments, while even the arrival of Indian troops in France provoked the remark that India stands behind Britain as one man. Among the political figures on the screen, no Opposition speakers have been seen and no opportunity has been missed to pour invective on Germany or on Russia. The feature 'Keep it Dark', mentioned elsewhere, was an even more obvious case of propaganda.

But for all this the newsreels appear to have found a little more initiative in the war. At the resignation of Hore Belisha, Paramount came out openly on the side of the departing Minister, and in so doing reflected public opinion; 'so leaves one of our ablest men' ran the commentary. On this matter a question was asked in the House.

The same company, a few weeks previously, had provoked another Parliamentary question over their item on the return to this country of Miss Unity Mitford:-

Lord Denman described as a fake that part of the film showing battleships manoeuvring, troops on parade, a strong force of police, a royal guard of honour, and aeroplanes flying in formation.

To magnify Miss Mitford's return into a matter of national importance as this film seemed to do was really absurd. Far more objectionable than the pictures was the running commentary. The commentator proceeded to make rather cheap jokes at the expense of Lord Redesdale and his daughter.

In peace time no newsreel would have dared to express an unconstitutional opinion as strongly as this.

Another tendency that may be said to be due to the war is that which is producing 'horrific' shots. Before the war shots of the burning of the Graf Zeppelin were cut on the grounds that they were too horrible for the general public. Yet in one newsreel recently a whole series of shots showed dead Russians lying in the snow, and it was followed up almost immediately by a sequence on the Turkish earthquake which included a picture of a man pulling at a leg that was emerging from a shattered house. At both these shots there was considerable comment from the audience and at the second, a number of 'oh's, but there was no sign of any general revulsion, as there was at the first photos of the bombing of Helsinki, a sequence which little imagination was necessary to translate into an event which might happen to any member of the audience.

Questionnaire

Two hundred people, equally divided into class, age, and sex groups, were asked, among other questions, 'What do you think of the newsreels?' Their answers, in brief, can be classified as follows:

Like them very much	Like them	Doubtful	Dislike them	Dislike them very much	Don't know
24%	37½%	19%	12½%	2½%	4½%

This large majority who like the newsreels is fairly evenly distributed among all groups, as will be seen from the more detailed analysis that follows:

	Like them very much	Like them	Doubtful	Dislike them	Dislike them very much	Don't know
CLASS B						
Men over 30	36%	44%	4%	8%	4%	8%
Men under 30	4%	24%	20%	44%	4%	8%
Women over 30	36%	44%	16%	–	–	4%
Women under 30	32%	32%	24%	12%	–	–
CLASS D						
Men over 30	36%	20%	24%	12%	–	8%
Men under 30	4%	48%	16%	24%	8%	–
Women over 30	32%	36%	28%	–	–	4%
Women under 30	16%	52%	20%	4%	4%	4%

It will be seen that the only group that shows any strong objection to newsreels are the men under 30 of the middle classes; men under 30 of the lower classes have no greater number among them who like the newsreels greatly, but practically half their number showed no objection to them. Not a single woman over thirty had any criticism to make of newsreels. Of these two hundred people only sixty, or 30 per cent, gave any further comment. Nearly 10 per cent of these criticisms were on the grounds that the news was merely repetition:

> They're pretty interesting except that the 'somewhere in France' descriptions of what is happening come over and over again (Man, 20, working class)

> They're good when you have only seen them once but after two or three times … (Man, 20, middle class)

> They are the same thing over and over again; but I suppose that it's all right for some people (Man, 40, worker)

Even more complained that they contained much too much propaganda, men under 30 of the middle classes being particularly critical of this aspect:

> I hate all propaganda of any kind (Man, 20, middle class)

> Well, for instance, they will show you the navy and they say 'isn't it superb?' and its object is to defend freedom while the German navy wants to destroy everything. And that's that (Man, 20, middle class)

> They are all right when they are not saturated with propaganda as they invariably are (Man, 25, middle class)

> There's much too much glorious Britain, triumphant Britain about them (Man, 25, worker)

> They are trying to boost the royal family (Man, 40, worker)

Many complained of the lack of news:

> They are all right most of them. There's not much news in them, of course (Woman, 20, middle class)

> I don't think they give very interesting news nowadays (Man, 20, middle class)

> Let's have real news. Same trouble as that of the press (Man, 20, middle class)

Six per cent could not believe what they saw, even though a newsreel is supposed to consist entirely of photographic records of actual events:

> I think the news reels are hooey, they tell you what is dished up every five minutes on the wireless, with the same Nazi planes crashing and our men not all coming back, but they don't tell you how many don't. I don't believe a thing, honestly (Woman, 20, working class)

> They only show the light side of war and the enemy trying to be destructive (Man, 40, worker)

While one woman complained that there was not enough war pictures in the news, many others thought there was too much. This objection to shots of actual fighting is borne out by newsreel observations.

> You get a lot of destruction in them and my lady doesn't like it (Man, 40, worker)

> It doesn't give me personally much pleasure to see bombs dropping and houses falling down (Man, 50, middle class)

> The bombing of Helsinki was a bit too realistic. It's all right showing war, I suppose, but that was a bit too much (Woman, 20, working class)

Many people, on the other hand, added most complimentary remarks:

> They are the most important part of the show, I go there for that (Man, 50, worker)

> They are interest number one for me (Man, 50, middle class)

> They are best of all sometimes. I go sometimes to see them (Woman, 20, middle class)

> I enjoy them, I wish they went a bit slower and were a bit longer (Woman, 50, working class)

Despite the fact that many of the newsreels sequences are common to all five companies, five people mentioned the name of one particular reel that they liked or disliked. One man chose Paramount, another Pathe and GB, two more mentioned GB. One woman, on the other hand, said 'We always enjoy them, but I don't like the man with the too dramatic voice, you know the man I mean', presumably meaning Emmett of the Gaumont British.

In brief, over 60 per cent of the people questioned liked the newsreels, and, unlike those who said they liked THE LION HAS WINGS, many of them gave reasons or comments on their approval, one man going as far as to wish that the newsreels were a feature; that there is a genuine interest in them is borne out by the number who showed a preference for one newsreel in particular. Many of the criticisms, on the other hand, concern matters that are not the fault of the newsreels. The largest number of complaints was directed against the inclusion of too much war news; but a newsreel by its nature must be concerned with topicalities and therefore the war. Others argued that there was 'no news'; but this is due to the Censor not to the companies who would obviously be delighted if there was more news released to them.

Most of the remaining criticism was directed against the propaganda element in newsreels; this complaint appeared with equal regularity on THE LION HAS WINGS questionnaire where it was established that any propaganda to be successful must be concealed. The newsreels with their 'glorious Britain, triumphant Britain' are not masking their propaganda sufficiently to give it the most effect. It would be as well for the newsreels to remember in this connection that the only class of the public that shows any marked opposition is the men under thirty of the middle classes. Of these 48 per cent dislike the newsreels, half of them giving as their reason that 'there is too much propaganda'.

GENERAL CONCLUSIONS

1. The newsreels are genuinely popular
2. The newsreels have to some extent earned this popularity by discovering public opinion and altering subject matter to taste
3. Emphasis has changed in wartime
    (a) from people to things
    (b) from politicians to royalty
    (c) from one politician to another
4. Emphasis is now entirely on war matters
5. Newsreels still contain much propaganda
6. But this propaganda is a little too obvious
7. The newsreels are developing character of their own
8. General tendencies in newsreels are
    (a) the inclusion of faked news

(b) the inclusion of 'comedies'

(c) the inclusion of 'horrific'

9. Audience now applauds royal family more than politicians

10. No longer thinks that soldiers are funny

APPENDIX A
Content of newsreels (divided into subject matter)

	Pre-war	Wartime
Soldiers	7% of shots	71%
War (except soldiers)	21%	14%
Non-war	62%	15%

The emphasis has shifted naturally from non-war subjects to war subjects but there is also a shifting from the effect of the war on the private citizen to its effect on the soldier as soon as war is declared. The very small percentage of shots of soldiers pre-war may be due to the laughter caused by their presence.

APPENDIX B

Statements and criticisms (made by 60 out of 200 interviewed on newsreels)

CRITICISMS	Class B				Class D				Total
	MO	MU	WO	WU	MO	MU	WO	WU	
No News		3	1	2	1			1	8 (12%)
Restricted		2			1			1	4 (6%)
Propaganda	1	4			1	2			8 (12%)
Disbelief		1			1	1		1	4 (6%)
Repetition		1			1	3		1	6 (9%)
Too much war	3	1		2	1		1	1	9 (14%)
Too little war								1	1 (1½%)
Too short							3		3 (5%)
Too slow					1				1 (1½%)
Uninteresting		1							1 (1½%)
COMMENTS									
Look forward to them most of all	1			1	1		1		4 (6%)
Lot of news							1		1 (1½%)
Should be a feature						1			1 (1½%)
Educational							1		1 (1½%)

Liked particular one:	Man over 30, B – Gaumont British
	Woman over 30, B – Pathe and Gaumont British
	Man under 30, D – Paramount
	Woman under 30, D – Gaumont British
Disliked particular one:	Woman over 30, B – 'Man with dramatic voice'

APPENDIX C

Observers, Cinemas, etc., of Newsreels Since the War

No	Observer	Date	Cinema	Time	News
1	LE	30.10.39	Leicester Square	12.30	GB
2	LE	1.11.39	Cameo, Charing X Road	2.00	GB & Paramount
3	LE	2.11.39	Granada, Tooting	3.30	GB
4	LE	8.11.39	Regal, Marble Arch	1.30	Pathe
5	LE	9.11.39	Gaumont, Streatham	3.00	GB
6	LE	11.11.39	Regal, West Norwood	3.00	BMN
7	LE	13.11.39	Monseigneur, Trafalgar Sq	2.00	BMN
8	LE	14.11.39	Regal, Streatham	3.00	Pathe
9	VD	15.11.39	Tatler, Charing X Road	–	–
10	BC	16.11.39	Empire, Leicester Square	–	–
11	BC	16.11.39	Academy, Oxford Street	–	–
12	LE	18.11.39	Gaumont, Haymarket	11.30	GB
13	MK	18.11.39	Queen's Hall, Rushey Green	5.30	–
14	LE	20.11.39	Eros, Piccadilly	2.00	BMN & Paramount
15	LE	21.11.39	Paramount, Tottenham Court Road	3.00	Paramount
16	BC	24.11.39	Tatler, Charing X Road	–	–
17	BC	25.11.39	Regal, Marble Arch	Evening	–
18	WL	25.11.39	Grand, Hanwell	9.00	–
19	BC	26.11.39	Empire, Leicester Square	7.00	–
20	BC	27.11.39	Paramount, Tottenham Court Road	afternoon	–
21	LE	1.12.39	Astoria, Streatham	3.00	Paramount
22	WL	2.12.39	Grand, Hanwell	9.00	–
23	LE	5.12.39	Cameo, Charing X Road	7.30	GB & Paramount
24	LE	6.12.39	Regal, Kennington	5.30	BMN
25	LE	9.12.39	Gaumont, Streatham	4.30	GB
26	BA	11.12.39	Tatler, Charing X Road	6.00	BMN
27	LE	12.12.39	Astoria, Streatham	2.30	Paramount
28	LE	13.12.39	Academy, Oxford Street	3.00	GB
29	AH	16.12.39	Lido, Worktown	2.30	Universal
30	LE	20.12.39	Moulin Rouge	1.30	GB
31	LE	21.12.39	Regal, Streatham	3.00	Pathe
32	LE	22.12.39	Stoll, Kingsway	3.30	GB, Par & BMN
33	LE	2.1.40	Cameo, Charing X Road	6.30	GB & Paramount
34	WL	6.1.40	Tatler, Charing X Road	6.00	–
35	LE	11.1.40	Gaumont, Streatham	3.00	GB
36	LE	13.1.40	Astoria, Streatham	3.00	Paramount
37	LE	18.1.40	Gaumont, Streatham	3.00	GB
38	LE	27.1.40	Regal, Streatham	3.00	Pathe

File Report 22, LE 28.1.40

Memo on Newsreels

Len England

*A report for Mass-Observation from August 1940. The newsreels'
problems with insufficient war material at this time is noted, also their
tactic of producing some longer films similar in style and tone of
Ministry of Information shorts. Changes in trends over audience
applause are noted, especially their preference for people who are seen to
be 'doing their bit'.*

As at the beginning of the war, the newsreels are faced with the difficulty of
producing a thousand or 1,500 feet of film a week, when in the course of that week
very little of interest happens. During the short period of actual fighting the
problem must have been to decide what to cut out, and nine-tenths of the material
used was 'action' shots, ships bombed, aeroplanes shot down and so on. Now,
perhaps once in every two weeks, an action shot is obtained of a battleship of a
convoy being attacked by air. For the rest of the time the reels have to do the best
they can with inspections, armament making, and all the various other stopgaps that
were used in the first few months. Much of the news shown now comes from other
countries; one Paramount reel, for instance, devoted four out of seven items to news
from America with two long sequences, one in the comeback of Jack Dempsey, and
another on Election Riots in Mexico.

Even with such out of the way news as this, the necessary footage cannot always
be made up. At the beginning of the war the companies introduced comedies that
had little or no relation to the war. This time their supplementary items have more
direct bearing on the situation. Often, they take the form of direct appeals to the
public to become nurses, save their scrap iron, join a National Savings Group, take
cover in air raids, and so on. On a few occasions these appeals have been worked
out to link with an item of news: for example, a scrap ironheap in London leads to
an appeal. Sometimes they have been made up in the studio with a speaker and
direct appeal. Occasionally they have consisted entirely of words flashed on the
screen (e.g. 'JOIN THE W.V.S.' – Go to your local centre' etc.) with a sound
commentary consisting of a man reading the words as they appear.

On occasions news has had to be held up a day or two before being shown to the
public. This was the case with the Dunkirk evacuation and Pathe took the opportunity to cut the shots they had and mould them into a unity. This technique was

carried farther until finally newsreels came to include occasional items that were very similar, though shorter, to the Ministry of Information's propaganda films. GB, for instance, showed a long sequence of England at play before the war, went on to point out how all our simple desires had been crushed by the will of Hitler and rounded it off by pointing out how necessary it was to use all the qualities that we possessed for games in the harder battle of war: from this the shots cut to a sequence of the King presenting medals to the RAF heroes, and so was brought up to date. This was called THE LAND WE DEFEND. Pathe, a week later produced an item OUR ISLAND FORTRESS. It is not a new development in newsreels – compare Movietone's treatment of Armistice Day 1939, but it is being more than usually exploited.

There is still practically no criticism of any feature of the war. Paramount, always the most anti-Government newsreel, said that the postponement of the Overseas Evacuation scheme has disappointed thousands of mothers, but this is the only example of criticism noted.

To uninspired newsreels, audience response has naturally not been considerable. The last time there was any big demonstration in a newsreel was at Italy's declaration of war. Applause is still heard frequently but it is very half-hearted. At the moment there is no outstanding personality or Service. Churchill has not been seen recently but probably he would get an exceptionally good reception. It seems that the audience now applauds anybody who is doing 'their bit'. For example a recent list of applause points were for these people:

A man awarded the VC
Dominion troops (particularly the Indians)
Polish troops
Czech troops
Dr Rewcastle, first Navywoman doctor
The woman who captured a German airman
General de Gaulle
The RAF

On no occasion was the applause very loud – the longest was for a brief shot of Indian troops – but other figures seen, the Royal family, Cabinet Ministers, and so on, have received no applause at all. All those applauded are *doing*, not merely *saying*, or *watching*.

Very recently however there seems to be a trend away from this opinion. Both the King and Queen have been applauded this week, though each time the applause was very faint. There had been no other clapping at all for them for them for nearly a month. Also a sequence of the Democratic convention gained slight applause.

<u>Footnote</u>. It seems certain that an audience unless very deeply moved, will applaud only at 'applause points', that is to say, unless the commentator makes such a remark as 'Well done the RAF' or 'she is a very gallant woman', or if the sequence showing an airman or a Pole or a heroine, the audience will not respond. This had already been noted over the Dunkirk evacuation and reappeared very clearly in the handling of an air battle off the coast. This was observed in three reels (Pathe, G.B. and Paramount.) In two of them there was little or no applause: these two had Charles Gardner's BBC commentary, and showed the film just as it had been taken. Pathe cut the action shots with stock of RAF planes and the like, and the commentary, instead of stopping short, was worked out to a conclusion. This resulted in considerably more applause.

File Report no. 314, 2.8.40.

Newsreeler at Dunkirk

Charles Martin

Pathe's Charles Martin tells how he came to be the only film cameraman to get pictures of the British withdrawal at Dunkirk, images that have become among the most familiar and frequently-used newsreel shots of the Second World War.

I was enjoying a few quiet days back in England after being over eight months filming with the B.E.F. in France, when I was sent to relieve one of our cameramen at a British port, who was taking films with the Navy. He told me on arrival that things up to then had been very quiet, so I settled down for an easy week-end. He went on his way, and after lunch, as soon as I got down to the quay-side, I met a naval commander who told me that a ship was leaving immediately for Dunkirk and this would probably be our last opportunity of getting any pictures. Would I care to go? And then I realised it might not be such a quiet week-end after all. Within a few minutes I was on board with my cameras and away. The ship was an old Clyde paddle-steamer which had already made several trips across, and had brought back a great number of the B.E.F. and they had had a pretty hectic time of it, what with being harassed and bombed from all sides. All this they broke to me gently on our way over – just to cheer me up.

We arrived off Dunkirk in the very early hours of the morning and in the distance could be seen fires and a great pall of smoke. I tried filming this but unfortunately the light was not strong enough. All during the night the enemy were bombing the towns around this area, and the foreshore where our troops were waiting to be taken off was being constantly shelled. Our poor old ship was shaking from end to end and I wasn't feeling too steady myself either. When dawn came, I saw thousands of troops standing at the water's edge waiting for us to take them off. All around us were warships and craft of every shape and size waiting to evacuate the troops. Fortunately our ship, being a paddle-steamer, was able to actually run ashore, and as soon as we did so, the men swam out, some of them without their clothes. A great many tried to reach us with their full equipment on – so I seized a megaphone and shouted to them to throw off everything they'd got. It's the instinct of the soldier to hold on to his equipment to the very last – and even then we hauled a sergeant-major aboard who still had his equipment on, including a great coat. I'd never known before how heavy water-sogged clothing can be. I'd started to take some pictures, but again, unfortunately, on development of the negative the light proved not strong enough, as this was about 5 a.m. All the material was shot on a Newman Sinclair, the same that I had used on the battle fronts in France. (Incidentally it was the only camera I was able to bring back – we lost all our other equipment and film, including several thousand feet of negative stock). It had a 2-in. lens with f.1.9 aperture. Stock used was Kodak Super XX.

After taking a number of pictures, I had a very busy and hectic two hours helping the crew get the men aboard. We pulled them up over the side of the ship by ropes as fast as we could, and threw over lifebelts to those who had to wait their turn.

We then drew away about half a mile from the shore and took count of how many we had. We found the number to be approximately four hundred. Naturally the men were very cold. And many of them drenched to the skin. We were sending them down below to get what warmth they could, when we heard the noise of approaching aircraft. Within a few seconds, out of the sky came droves of German machines power-diving in all directions and machine-gunning the ships and the troops on the foreshore. I was on the bridge at the time and was fortunate enough to get a shot of the German aircraft approaching with our anti-aircraft shells bursting all around it. But I'm afraid that the public won't see any dramatic pictures of them starting to make their dive on our ship; I ducked down and flattened myself out as best I could, whilst they sprayed the ship with tracer bullets. The effect of these dives is terrifying. The terrific roar of the engines get-

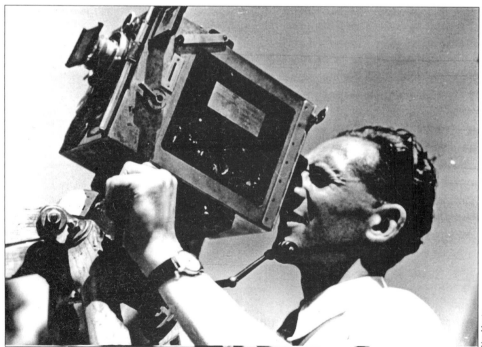

Charles Martin.

Alan Martin

ting nearer and nearer, the rattle of their guns spitting fire and our own machine-guns replying, the still greater noise of our warships firing, all makes you think the end of the world has come and you wish you could make yourself the 'Invisible Man'. All these machines diving and zooming in every direction seemed like the Hendon Air Pageant gone crazy! They came out of the sky like a swarm of locusts, to fly up into the clouds again and re-appear within a few moments to repeat their performance.

When I was able very cautiously to poke my head over the side of the bridge I saw an amazing sight. A few seconds previously I'd seen tens of thousands of men standing on the shore; when I looked again the whole beach was like a place of dead men. At the same time as German machines had power-dived on us, three others in quick succession had machine-gunned the beach. The whole mass of troops had thrown themselves flat down on the ground. I waited, and much to my relief saw them stand up again. Only just here and there a few figures remained on the sand.

The skipper, finding we could still take some more men, decided to run on to the beach again. We rescued a corporal who by his age was evidently a war veteran. He swam to the ship and was absolutely soaking wet. All he had on was a coat and trousers, with no boots or stockings. In spite of this he somewhere on deck picked up a rifle, and all the time we were there, and throughout the voyage back, he never once put it down. At the approach of enemy aircraft, however far away they were, he cracked off at them. It must have relieved his feelings.

I was fortunate enough to bring back pictures out of all this chaos and turmoil. Ships of all sizes and shapes, fully laden with our troops going back to England; burning Dunkirk with its great pall of smoke; in the foreground some of our ships which had been sunk in this effort of rescue; our men wading or swimming out to us and being hauled aboard; and on the trip back the same men, so shortly after their rescue, once more bright and cheerful. My one great regret is that my early dawn pictures were unsuccessful, and that I couldn't bring back with me more material to show what every man jack of them had to endure. When we started rescuing these lads there were many sights which it was not humanly possible to film, because no one could stand by and see these things going on without making some attempt to help. It became difficult to remember that one was there to take pictures at all; this grim event was so obviously a fight against time. Every moment of hesitation might mean someone's life.

I was the only cameraman lucky enough to cover the evacuation of Dunkirk at close quarters. My stuff was used by all the newsreel companies, so I hope whoever sees it anywhere in the world will feel as I felt then, and that my pictures will convey to them something of that truly great event – the Evacuation of Dunkirk.

The Cine-Technician, August-September 1940.

The Newsreels

Edgar Anstey

Anstey, a leading figure in British documentary filmmaking, praises the skills of the cameramen evident from British Paramount News' review of the year for 1941, but still more praises a new-found political urgency in the commentary that is 'neither infantile nor reactionary'.

1941 closed and 1942 opened with two of the war's best newsreels. Paramount British celebrated the passing of the old year with an annual review which was motivated by sweet reason rather than the sound and fury which is more usual in these compilations, whilst the newsreels of the Commandos' raid on Vaagso represented a first halting answer to two years of complaint about the inadequacy of British war-reporting for the screen. It is possible that the newsreels may yet succeed in adding their due quota to the enormous propaganda power of the film of fact. In a review of the year in this column last week I had no space to write of the very real contribution to the war effort which has been made by many non-fiction films. Amongst studio features only 49TH PARALLEL can compare in propaganda value with a long list of fact films memorably headed by Harry Watt's TARGET FOR TONIGHT and Jack Holmes's MERCHANT SEAMEN. And the extra-theatrical distribution of documentaries by the Ministry of Information (whose weekly live-minute theatrical films are becoming commendably broader in conception) represents the most important development in the cinema to be found anywhere in the world – besides being a new instrument of public information and education which will long outlast the war. But the newsreels, unhappily, have not yet fitted into their war-time place. It is encouraging to find evidence in the Commando item that if they are provided with facilities or material they will make use of them. And there is evidence in Paramount's annual review that at least one company has imagination and a sense of political realities.

The Vaagso raid material was photographed partly by Army Film Unit personnel and partly by a newsreel cameraman. The War Office is to be congratulated on providing the opportunities and the cameramen upon taking such excellent advantage of them. For although there may be a little disappointment amongst those whose expectations had been aroused by the written accounts of the fighting, there is evidence that the cameramen photographed with admirable coolness and skill everything that came within the range of their lenses. It would be unfair to regard this film as anything more than a very important beginning from which everyone concerned will learn much for the future. The set faces of the men as they go ashore, the precision and caution with which they advance upon a blind street corner, the leisurely character of the re-embarkation and the obvious relief and jubilation of the returning men – all these make up the first convincing picture we have seen of the British Army as being efficient – even ruthless – and yet essentially human.

Paramount's review of the year consists pictorially of familiar scenes skilfully re-edited. But its commentary is one of the most remarkable statements of forward-looking liberalism ever to be widely made in the cinema, or, come to that, through any other medium of communication in a country at war. The commentator talks of the 'money-changers' whose pre-war capitalist system would not permit the present free flow of raw materials and manufactures amongst the allied countries and whose system had consequently to be changed. 'It will never return', he says. He talks of the ridiculous nationalisms perpetuated by the Treaty of Versailles, and points out that this Treaty denied to certain countries an access to the world's raw materials which is promised by the Atlantic Charter. He indicates the dangers of post-war oppression of the German people. The political sentiments expressed are not always developed to their logical end; but whether or not the politics are sound, it is most invigorating to find a newsreel whose approach to the great events of the day is neither infantile nor reactionary.

The Spectator, 9 January 1942.

D-Day as the Newsreel Boys Saw It

The British newsreel cameramen present at D-Day each describe their experiences: Jock Gemmell, Bob Colwyn Wood, Alec Tozer, Jack Ramsden, John Turner and Jimmy Gemmell, Jock's brother. All speak of their pride in being a part of the invasion, and express the admiration for the troops, but they also comment on the censorship imposed on some of their footage afterwards. Jock Gemmell confesses to self-censorship, declining to film that which was 'too gruesome', and criticises himself for cheering an airborne squadron: '...very foolish – cameramen shouldn't be emotional'.

JOCK C. GEMMELL (PATHE)

D-Day Minus X

We are summoned to a Naval Rendezvous. There are, I suppose, not less than fifty British War Correspondents present and the Newsreels are represented by five cameramen attached to the Royal Navy and one to the Merchant Service They are: Jack Ramsden (Movietone) John Turner (Gaumont), R. Colwyn Wood (Universal), Jimmy Gemmell (Paramount), myself for Pathe and Alec Tozer for the Merchantmen. We are transported to the ports where we are to embark in our various ships, and as we shake hands and wish each other 'Goodbye' and 'Good luck' perhaps we have a wee lump in the throat – we've all been in action before, and you never know.

D-Day

Bad crossing – am aboard a ship that doesn't take it. Many soldiers bad. Full marks to a Major of Signals who was sick many times but who always came back to his job every time. Am on deck at dawn – make pictures. The most amazing sight. Have seen part of the Invasion Fleet the previous night, but now no adjective can describe the scene. To the left, that is to the East, the Battle wagons are blazing away, and to the West the same thing – the din is terrific. In the meantime, the cruisers and destroyers are having a go at the batteries to the East. No pictures. Too far away to film. Astern, that is to the North, there is just a procession of all kinds of craft with

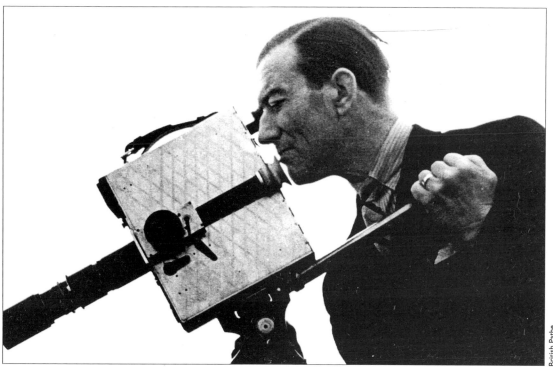

Jock Gemmell.

British Pathe

balloons attached heading southwards. Nothing but craft and balloons us far as the eye can see. Ahead the landing craft are still going in – brave blokes.

There never was such an Armada – never such a spectacle.

The ship that I am aboard is so placed that it does not present any great opportunities at the moment but by now I know that she has a special mission – can't tell you about that. Make all kinds of pictures, and then see my brother Jimmy's ship coming up and film her escort going into action.

Infantry landing craft comes alongside – a gory sight. Don't film it – too gruesome! It's what remains of our gallant young boys.

Later, the Airborne Glider Troops arrive – coming in squadron after squadron, wave after wave, in broad daylight, with impunity – the sheer impudence of the whole thing. Make pictures and think 'That's that'. But I am wrong. They are still coming in wing after wing. Newsreel cameramen all over the world have seen many awe-inspiring sights in their time but I am sure that nothing could equal that. I cheer them – very foolish – cameramen shouldn't be emotional.

We move forward until we anchor right inshore – so close, in fact, that I am able to film scenes ashore – houses set alight by our landing parties; gun boats racking with small fire, buildings still holding snipers. Wise Guy says 'Now we're for it'.

Apart from the night bombing, which was expected, we weren't 'for it' – smoke screens and AA prevent that.

D plus 1

Up again at dawn. Discover that the enemy are bombarding the beaches from the elevated ground to our left. Not pleasant. When shells fall short of beaches they are too perilously near the ship. Most annoying – can't get pictures. Nobody knows when Hun is going to fire, or what at.

D plus 2

Boarded a Rhino Raft, coming off-shore with about 700 of the first German prisoners to leave France – good story. After tying up the LST 1st Officer shouts down from fo'castle, 'Sergeant, are you sending your guards aboard with these bastards?' 'Sorry, sir, we ain't got no bleeding guard' was the reply.

D plus 3

An audacious attack by low-flying enemy aircraft on the beaches – a huge dump is set alight – good pictures, but to us all a very distressing sight – so many men have lost their lives getting that stuff ashore. Still, as an old RFC man, appreciate technique.

After several days returned to UK and was very pleased to see the old shores again.

The Naval organisation for getting the material back home was really first-class: full marks to Commander Dillon Robinson and his staff. From information received, the public gave the Invasion editions a wonderful hand, so although this is only my own little story I do think that all cameramen who took part in D-Day have just cause to be proud of a good job of work well done.

R. COLWYN-WOOD (UNIVERSAL)

I was luckier than some in the crossing, being aboard a Flagship which took small heed of a sea that brought crews of little ships near blasphemy and made so many passengers sick unto demonstration. Our ship bulged with personnel and I snatched some rest on the floor of a cabin designed for one man and now housing five. I too remember the Infantry Landing Craft and the sights that chilled and humbled one. Yet an exalting, indelible picture remains – a Tommy with a head wound, blood pours down his face rapidly turning his battle dress a dirty plum colour. He struggles to his feet when the MO goes aboard and, grinning, holds up his tin hat and proudly draws Doc's attention to the gaping rent in it – seems oblivious of his wound. On the deck propped against an ammo' case a Sub-

Lieutenant, his left arm shattered, an ever-widening crimson circle forms beneath. He looks up, catches my eye, notes the camera and raises a grin. Another man lies on the steel decking, a blanket scarcely hides the heavy, near-sodden dressing about his stomach. His face is green but his eyes are bright, with little success he tries to smoke but finds the breath to say: 'We've blasted Jerry to hell on that beach, lad'.

I took a poor view (literally) of Jock's 'audacious attack by low-flying enemy aircraft' being about fifty yards from the ammo dump when the egg was laid! I had gone ashore with Colonel Langley (inventor of the Rocket-ship) to obtain special shots for Combined Ops. I heard the plane, and more important heard the bomb. Reckon I hit the sand 1/5th second before bomb hit dump! A lucky strike for Jerry if ever there was one.

What goes up has to come down, and that was a biggish dump, so I hug my camera thinking of the two I had lost in previous action, wonder if this is to be the third. A trooper takes cover at my side, nurses his trophy – a German automatic rifle with ring sights, nice weapon. A scream, a rush of air, I look at companion – with lugubrious expression he eyes what he grasps. It bears little resemblance to his prized trophy for sights and breach have been sheared off cleanly. Better a Jerry gat than my Eyemo I think.

When I got off-shore in a Duck the dump was still putting on a fair imitation of Vesuvius writing finis in lava across Pompeii. I transferred to an Infantry Landing Craft waiting for our Admiral, who was carrying out a beach inspection despite the hail storm. An enemy battery, attracted by the dump, ranged the beach and included our craft in its arc of fire, then a cheeky ME tried a little machine-gunning. Strong evasive action whilst standing on bridge with Col. Langley and using shelf as snack counter to partake of corned beef and cabbage followed by Christmas pudding washed down with whisky … the British at war are a strange people!

I came to regard the Colonel as Combined Op's gift to the newsreels – till I got back to London. I was able to accompany him in the observation craft and secure breath-taking shots of rocket ships in action, but despite my caustic comments and a nice line in co-operation from the Colonel, SHAEF Censorship remained adamant. About D-Day plus 6 I found comfortable accommodation sharing a cabin with that companionable and conscientious worker F.W. Perfect (*Daily Telegraph*). Jock Gemmell spent a night aboard the Flagship on his way back to UK and I retain happy (tho' hazy) memories of the select little party in our cabin. Jock took a short (but deep) sleep on an Ante-Room settee, pushing off on a ML a little after dawn – I still wonder how he managed it …

It was good to find, on getting back, that our stories had been so well received and I feel, with Gemmell that no one should object if we cameramen sometimes apply a spot of gentle pressure to our own back. What a pity that the biggest story is sometimes the one that got away! I made some pictures I'm not allowed to talk about, and the censors have seen to it that they got away from the public gaze. A bit galling sometimes.

When in action I'm scared (who isn't?), but somehow it's an inspiring tonic-like brand of fright. Back home again I'm restless, often bored – deflated. D-Day was something of a nightmare ... on D-Day. Now, D-Day seems to have been the real thing, and this life (I write from my home set in pleasant country near Cardiff) a dream-like existence!

ALEC TOZER (MOVIETONE)

To be the Merchant navy's first and only accredited newsreel correspondent was a great honour and my first assignment with them ... the invasion.

My ship, a 12,000 ton troop carrier, was lying out and it was a pleasant after-noon's trip by launch in order to board tier. We steamed back to the docks to pick tip some 3,000 troops. On the way I got 'invasion take-off' pictures of every type of landing craft, troop-carriers and their escorts. The whole sea appeared to be jammed tight with ships. Assault barges crammed with troops were already pushing off for the assembly point. These pictures with the embarkation scenes were useful for the first invasion issue of the newsreel as they were dispatched from the ship before she left the dock. The embarkation took place within full view of hundreds of people. They must have guessed that D-Day was approaching.

At dawn on D-Day we crept around the coast for the English Channel. As we entered the narrow Straits of Dover our escort began belching dense columns of black smoke screens. Slow-flying aircraft skimmed the water also leaving a wall of smoke behind them. Our balloons were pulled down to the mast head so that they would not be seen above the screen. Enemy coastal batteries were firing into the smoke screen but their shells were falling so far from us that they did not even make good pictures. We altered course somewhat when shells began bursting ahead of our convoy. With such a large ship as ours we were not due at the beach-head until D+2, and I wondered what we were doing in the Channel so near the enemy coast on D-Day: perhaps we were acting as a kind of decoy? Our convoy got through safely. I was told we were the first convoy through the Straits since Dunkirk.

At anchor that night and all the following day; I thought the waiting was the most nerve racking part of the whole trip.

On the night of D+1 we pushed our way across the Channel, through the mine-swept lane as enemy aircraft dropped flares around us searching for this invasion highway. One ship far to the end of our convoy was ablaze – an E boat was respon-sible for this.

At first light of dawn, instead of the expected enemy air attacks we saw nothing but swarms of our own air cover fighters, and above them the white vapour streaks of our bombers going to and from the enemy coast.

And then my first view of the French coast since May, 1940. Never have I seen so many ships, and so many different types of ship.

Enemy shells from some miles inland were bursting on the beaches whilst terrific broadsides from naval ships nearby were being thrown back at them. A landing craft hit a mine and was blown to pieces just behind me. Our troops, in good spirits, climbed down a rope netting to landing craft below to take them through the shallow water to the beach less than a mile away.

That night we had a grand firework display with all the ships flinging up everything they had against the enemy aircraft which hardly dared to show themselves in daylight. They were searching for us again the following night on the way back across the Channel and the droning of their engines did not leave us until the first glimmer of daylight.

An impressive trip but in my case not nearly so full of action as I had imagined it would be.

JACK RAMSDEN (MOVIETONE)

I was assigned to a destroyer, and the arrival of a 'khaki type' with loads of camera gear soon created a buzz on the lower deck. Our job was to protect the minesweepers going in ahead to sweep a channel for the invasion craft. If we were hit we were to beach and continue firing.

From my all-night station on the bridge I could see only dim shapes, but the coming of the dawn was like the raising of a curtain on the mightiest amphibious operation the world has ever seen. It didn't seem real until our sister ship, only a few hundred yards away blew up with startling reality. In spite of being busy filming I shall never forget the tenseness of that moment. Everybody was just watching – grimly – blowing up his lifebelt as fast as he could. A Petty Officer nearby grinned and said it reminded him of one of his pals – an old sweat – who was off Crete in the early days of the war when a similar thing happened. He was blowing away when a youngster who was on his first trip, said 'Ya, Windy!' 'Listen, my boy', said the old sweat, still blowing, 'If you take my advice' – blow, blow – 'you'll do the same – it's the only air support you'll get around here!'

We were now close in to the French coast and the fun had started. There was no doubt about our air support this time. Overhead the Allies were in complete mastery of the skies. Below them, as far as the eye could see, assault craft after assault craft was going in. Every ship in the British Navy seemed to be firing. Fifteen and sixteen-inch bricks from the big battle-wagons behind us and the smaller six- and eight-inchers from the cruisers went screaming over our bridge like machine-gun bullets. 2,000 tons of naval shells hit those beaches in ten minutes. The noise was incredible. Our own guns were also going full blast and only the footage indicator on my camera told me it was still running. It was quite impossible to hear it.

During the bombardment our forward observation officer on the beach was killed. For a time we had no target, much to the annoyance of our captain who was pacing the bridge like a caged lion. He made frantic signals to nearby ships who were still firing, such as 'Do you require any help?' – all to no purpose. It did seem a bit galling, as we could see the enemy tanks moving about but couldn't be sure how near they were to ours. Although we were but a small cog in the enormous machine he seemed annoyed that it should continue to function very well without us! Suddenly we found ourselves being shelled by a coastal battery and soon had plenty to do dealing with it. Thus our captain was appeased, and a good time was had by all, although I must say that the naval idea of a good time does not always conform with mine.

I was very satisfied with the pictures I got on this trip, those especially of the Airborne Division doing over in the late evening, which I think are some of the finest I have ever had the good fortune to make. However, a cameraman must always have his moan, and it was heartbreaking to have so much material censored, particularly some of my later stuff taken in Cherbourg. Otherwise the general arrangements for coverage functioned perfectly and I have nothing but praise for Commander Dillon Robinson, RN, and his staff, who provided us with such excellent facilities. I only wish they could arrange things so that we could have a 48-hour week on these jobs and maybe we could then get a little sleep instead of being on watch 24 hours a day!

JOHN TURNER (GAUMONT-BRITISH)

When daylight revealed our floating Army on June 6th, I found it hard to realise that this was D-Day. So thoroughly had the press and film arrangements been thought out (I echo the praise of Jock Gemmell for Commander Dillon Robinson and staff) that I was tempted to think that they had arranged this zero-hour to give the picture boys a chance!

I found the scene unreal because we'd expected something different. I was in a very old destroyer – it seemed unreal to all of us in that ship – we had been keyed up to expect blood and thunder, and instead, when we reached the Assault Area, it might have been any day in a very crowded harbour. Here we were, well within sight of the enemy coastline in daylight – the centre section of the invading forces. No wonder the scene seemed unreal – for where were the diving enemy planes, where the flashes of a hundred guns ashore, the splashes of their shells, where the shattered ships and the cries for help? 'I don't believe it,' said the Captain … 'it can't be Normandy!' But it was! 'It'll be worse this afternoon', said some-one – but it wasn't! 'They'll take two to three days to bring up subs and planes and other evils' a prophet suggested – but they didn't! They weren't allowed to.

We were lucky no doubt. There were incidents of course. There was a ship ahead of us which hit a mine shortly before zero-hour. But she only shivered, drooped her head a little, recovered and turned for England … a runner gone lame who has to walk back to the start. And there was the little tug which hit a mine too – for just a moment it lingered, then it sighed a long, long sigh of pure-white steam … and went, with all its men. There were incidents like that – pathetic, horrible – but they were rare and the general scene was one of busy little boats fussing about running errands to the beaches, taking messages to other ships – a quiet, efficient and splendid achievement. So much to film, and yet so little! That was D-Day from our ship, and I would not have had it otherwise for all the spectacular pictures in the world. A naval cameraman's best pictures in action are nearly always when he is at the wrong end of the gun … so when I thought of that I wasn't disappointed at the quietness of the scene. The picture is what the cameramen wants – and the enemy were getting plenty.

Like all the newsreel boys on this operation I've been to sea a lot since the war started. We've all had thrills – D-Day will take a lot of beating!

JIMMY GEMMELL (PARAMOUNT)

I was sitting in the wardroom of the ship that I had been allocated to when the news came to me that the big day had arrived. As my ship stole silently out of the harbour, we passed the ship I knew my brother Jock was in and I wondered if he would be there to see us go out. Yes, he was. The only khaki-clad man in the ship. We waved to one another and the thought came to me: 'I wonder if this is the finish or shall we see one another again?' But as I'd experienced other invasion attempts these morbid thoughts soon disappeared and I set about putting my house in order. The chief thing was a good position in the ship for my cameras. It is not very easy nowadays to find a good position as every camera position is a gun position, and what with the extra armament in the ship, one has to be careful, otherwise you are bumped off by your guns or blasted off your feet. Anyway, I got a good position on the flag deck. There I sat all that day and night waiting. At last dawn broke, and at Zero hour came one of our planes flying very low spreading smoke on our left flank to cover us going in on the Normandy beaches. Ships of all sizes seemed to come up out of the sea all making for the coast.

Then Hell was just let loose from the ship's guns and I understand that both the RAF and the Americans had been over the target area just prior to our arrival and had given the Huns 8,000 tons of bombs. The whole thing was fantastic. Big and small landing barges were going straight for the beaches defying opposition from the shore batteries, mines, and those horrible things called Spiders – twisted lumps of metal, semi-submerged in the sand that can rip out the bottom of those little landing craft.

A wonderful sight was a bunch of landing craft with guns in the bows shooting their way right in to the beaches. Heavy fighting continued all day, shells were flung at Jerry and they replied from dug-in positions in the alleged impregnable concrete Atlantic Wall.

Night-time came at last, only to be interrupted by Hun dive-bombers. One came so near to our ship that he almost took the mast off. I think this one was dropping acoustic mines as two went off a few hours later which stirred my circulation up a bit!

The morning after D-Day I was requested by Admiral Vine to go ashore with him. I guess he wanted to see how much damage his ships had done. That was pretty plenty! We had to transfer into a Duck to go ashore as the beaches are so shallow. Here the scene was unbelievable. Just a flag stuck in the sand denoted some H.Q. Hundreds of men were working incessantly unloading the various landing craft. There was no shouting of orders – every man seemed to know exactly what he had to do and principally to do it quick. Bulldozers were pushing out of the fairway landing barges which had been damaged. There were tired-eyed lads busy digging fox-holes in the dunes, and others filling in the graves of their fallen comrades. While all this was going on our ships were firing over our heads just up the hill, on the retreating Huns.

With all the tragedy and heartbreak that war brings, you will always find some little bit of humour among the troops. It was in the afternoon of the first day that I went ashore, prisoners were being brought in, and I came across about 200 of them being marched along with just a Cockney Sergeant in charge. I asked the Sergeant to stop them and when he saw that I was an official cameraman, he said 'Very good, sir. That's fine! I have walked these blinking baskets about three miles so I will just sit down on the sand while you muck them about a bit'. But, of course, 'muck' wasn't quite the word he used!

As I was going back to my ship with Admiral Vine and other staff officers, we had to transfer from the Duck to an American cutter. When it came to my turn to jump from one to the other, the boats had got adrift from one another about three yards. As I am rather a big man, it was impossible for me to jump this, but Vine's voice boomed out 'Come on, Gemmell, jump the bloody thing, otherwise we will go without you'. I said 'I am sorry, sir, I can't jump that', and he said 'Well bloody well try'. And as I didn't want to be left floating about all night in a Duck, I jumped! I landed on top of a most dignified staff officer who was already standing in the cutter. When I had finished taking his boot out of my ear, he stood up, brushed himself down and said 'Please don't do that again!' Everybody laughed like Hell as they expected me to land in the ditch!

There are plenty of things that could be told about this marvellous achievement but I will finish by saying that I was there thirteen days and I thought that to stay thirteen days might be unlucky, but it proves I was very lucky as the day I left the ship it was raked by rocket shells and shortly after it was struck by a mine but successfully towed to harbour. I came back holding on to the iron door of an MTB on one of the roughest seas I think I have experienced, for five hours, drenched to the skin.

May I conclude by saying 'May not the blood of these men be lost in vain'.

The Cine-Technician, September-October 1944.

Horror in Our Time: Images of the Concentration Camps in The British Media, 1945 [extract]

Hannah Caven

Hannah Caven's essay on the images of the concentration camps in the British media was published by the Historical Journal of Film, Radio and Television, where it won the Carfax-IAMHIST prize, 2001, for the best article by a younger author. The full essay covers the work of the Army Film and Photographic Unit (AFPU), the particular experiences of its members working in Belsen, and the impact of these images on British audiences in the newspapers and the newsreels. The extracts below cover the newsreels and the public's reactions to concentration camp images in the newsreels only.

THE STORY REACHES BRITAIN

Before these images reached the public they had to pass the scrutiny of editors and censors, challenging their perceptions of what should and should not reach the front pages of Britain's newspapers and what should and should not be shown on film at cinemas across the country. This was a very pertinent dilemma which seriously concerned the people responsible for making these decisions. The main issue was that throughout the war the British public had been deliberately sheltered, images of horror and particularly images of death had been conspicuous by their absence from newspapers and newsreels. As a result there was an understandable fear as to how the public would react when presented with the graphic images of the camps. The key concern was that the public would be so shocked that they would simply turn away in horror and refuse to look again, or that they would simply disbelieve what they were seeing and dismiss it as propaganda. Ultimately, if these images were to be shown to the British public they had to be utterly convincing and they had to be presented in a way which ensured that people looked and looked again, rather than turning away in disgust.

Two completely separate incidents reveal the depth of the concern that was felt and the attitudes that had to be overcome in order to actually publish the reports and footage of the camps. The first occurred when Richard Dimbleby sent his first report from Belsen, his editors at the BBC were anxious about its authenticity and repeatedly called Dimbleby to check its veracity. Dimbleby himself recalled:

... when they heard it some people wondered if Dimbleby had gone off his head or something. I think it was only the fact that I'd been fairly reliable up to then that made them believe the story.[1]

Even so, the BBC refused to broadcast the report until it had been verified by newspaper reports. In response Dimbleby said he would resign from his job if the report was not broadcast immediately. The result was an immediate, if abbreviated report, which was broadcast on 19 April 1945.[2]

The second incident occurred when the officials of the different newsreel companies met to discuss the footage of the camps that had emerged. An official from the Ministry of Information reported:

> I took the opportunity ... of seeing this film (of the camps) with the principals of the five newsreel companies ... Mr Cummins immediately expressed the intention of using the material ... Sir Gordon Craig and Mr Sanger took the view that, pictorially, it was not entirely convincing and that, to show such pictures unless they were convincing, might have a boomerang effect since the public might query the authenticity ... Movietone therefore, do not propose to use the material. So far as I can judge, the other three companies could not make up their minds one way or the other.[3]

In the end *British Movietone News* did issue a newsreel film along with the other newsreel companies, presumably having been convinced that the public would believe the authenticity of the footage, but the reticence which preceded their publication and the similar qualms of the BBC, provide a striking example of the concerns which existed about presenting the British public with reports that would have a dramatic impact.

THE NEWSREELS

The newsreel companies faced a major problem in dealing with the footage of the camps. Newsreels were shown, for about ten minutes, at the beginning of the main cinema programme. As a result people went to the cinema to see an entertaining film and not specifically the newsreels themselves.[4] However, a story as horrific as that of the liberation of the camps, was not something that the newsreels had had to deal with before and there was an inherent problem about how to handle people who had gone to see a popular film at the cinema and were then confronted with shocking scenes from the camps. There was the added consideration that they might be accompanied by their children and if there was no warning, then the shock of the revelations would be enormous and out of place. This raises the whole spectre of placing the holocaust within an entertainment setting. If people watched the newsreel story, would they then want to stay and enjoy the light-hearted programme that followed? If they did so, was it not nullifying all that the story of the camps represented? However, if the newsreels did not carry the story then they were not fulfilling their role of providing a wide audience with accurate news.

The newsreels provided an accessible format for news, so although newspapers had a much larger audience the newsreels had the potential to reach those who might not read the newspapers closely. In the specific context of the camps, the newsreel footage was particularly graphic. The images depicted the emaciated state of the inmates, the blank staring eyes, the charred remains of corpses at Gardelegen, the obvious distress of visitors to the camps and the corpses which littered the ground of the camps. They were powerful, shocking and moving images, which could not be ignored when presented on the cinema screen.

At this time there were five major newsreel companies, Movietone News, Gaumont-British, British Paramount News, Universal and Pathe. All became involved with the screening of the story of the camps and the initial reactions of their principals were varied.[5] The newsreel company principals met regularly in order to discuss sensitive topics and thereby avoid controversy. Paul Smith argued that this:

> … accounts for much of the banality of so much newsreel footage, for the very structure of the newsreel industry committed that medium to emphasise consensus rather than conflict.[6]

However, the companies did not settle for banality with the story of the camps. In contrast, the companies took the unusual decision to alter the standard practice of running two separate news stories per week, instead the story of the camps was reissued in the same week and therefore received double the exposure. An article in the *Daily Herald* also revealed that:

> The Ministry of Information has responded to the appeals of producers by giving them an increased allowance of film. The newsreels this week will be appreciably longer than usual.[7]

The Movietone commentaries also carried the further justification that these were:

> Grim pictures, but it's about time to dispel once and for all, any lingering doubt in anyone's mind about the truth of the things Germany has done. Only if all of us know the facts, can we hope to prevent their repetition in the future.[8]

The newsreel companies used a collective pool of footage from the camps and the sites of other atrocities. However their coverage remained individual in respect of how they used this material and particularly in the commentaries that accompanied the pictures. For example, Gaumont-British used an extract from a speech by

Photo courtesy of the Imperial War Museum, London

Josef Krämer, Belsen camp commandant, manacled and under guard.

Churchill which highlighted the fact that the same could have happened in Britain if a German invasion had been successful.[9] *British Movietone News* on the other hand used a speech by the American congresswoman Clare Booth-Luce to emphasise the authenticity of the camps and the footage that was being shown.[10] *British Paramount News* decided to let the pictures speak for themselves and added no speeches from other dignitaries, but lingered on close ups of Krämer and the corpses in Belsen.[11] Despite these variations in style, certain images still appeared regularly in all the newsreels, further reflecting some of the themes which had been evident throughout the earlier coverage of the AFPU and the newspapers.

The question of authenticity had already been raised as an issue by the principals of the newsreel companies and to some extent this explains why the images were largely focused on the delegation of MPs visiting the camps. The newsreels showed the MPs talking to a group of prisoners in Buchenwald, who have been rehoused in a room with windows and given blankets. The prisoners still sit or lie on the floor and the space is very crowded. Their faces are gaunt which make their eyes appear much larger and although they are clearly talking with the MPs they stare blankly when the camera focuses on them. The films also showed a cart-load of bodies in the yard at Buchenwald and a wooden club which was used to beat prisoners. While viewing these sights the camera focuses on Mavis Tate, whose face clearly expresses her distress. She holds smelling salts to her nose as she passes the camera, looks up briefly and then passes on. These images clearly establish the MPs in the camp, they clearly show them talking to emaciated figures, and looking at innumerable corpses scattered throughout the camp. They also demonstrate their reaction to such sights.

Having established this proof, the newsreels then tended to move on to show images of Belsen which did not include pictures of visiting officials. One of the most common images is that of a woman who walks past the camera, while in the foreground corpses lie on the edge of the path. The woman does not even glance at the bodies, giving a clear expression of how inured inmates were to the close proximity of death. An image which was used by both Paramount and Gaumont-British was that of two young boys who shared a bowl of soup while glancing at the camera. They are clearly emaciated and huddle round the bowl as if to protect it from the cameraman. The single image graphically illustrates the fact that there were children within the camps and emphasizes to the audience the innocence and youth of some of the victims.[12] Both films also ended with a general view of Belsen which shows '… piles of dead bodies strewn over field'.[13] The same image is used to close the Gaumont-British film while 'O God Our Help in Ages Past' is sung over this and repeats of further images of Belsen.

One image, which inevitably featured in all the newsreel footage of Belsen was the face of Josef Krämer, the Belsen comandant. The pictures which accompanied the commentary showed Krämer under the guard of British soldiers. The camera dwells on his face for a few seconds before moving to the corpses which lie nearby. The Paramount, Gaumont and Movietone footage also included pictures of the SS guards, both men and women, lined up under the guard of British troops. Little comment is made about them, but they make an immediate and striking contrast with the inmates. The guards are clearly well-fed, healthy and well dressed. They walk out of their barracks purposefully and briskly, unlike the tottering, wandering gait which the inmates use. The guards regard the camera openly and defiantly instead of gazing at it blankly. When these images are juxtaposed with those of the inmates they require no further comment.

There is one particular Belsen inmate who appears in all the newsreel footage. He is pictured amid a pile of rags and corpses, half naked while he searches the shirt that he holds for lice. He looks up at the camera but hardly seems to register that it is there, let alone what it is. Movietone describes him as a 'Prisoner – just a skeleton sits down handling garment'.[14] Paramount points him out as a '… living skeleton among dead bodies'.[15] Gaumont commented that he was indistinguishable from the corpses which surrounded him.[16] This one powerful image of a man closer to life than death, who probably did not survive for long after these pictures were taken, encapsulates the tragedy of liberation for many of these inmates for whom it came too late.

The newsreels did not simply restrict themselves to Buchenwald and Belsen. They also showed the effects of an atrocity at Stalag Tekla, close to Leipzig, where once again the Germans tricked their prisoners and destroyed them with fire. The twisted, charred remains, almost unrecognisable as human corpses, are dwelt on by the camera for several seconds, demonstrating how those that tried to escape perished on the electric fences. It is a graphic exposure and it is interesting that the story then shifts to Gardelegen, infamous for a similar massacre. This time however, there is evidence of Allied justice in action, as a huge party of male civilians are marched out carrying shovels with which to disinter and bury the dead properly. Paramount and Gaumont also showed a scene where former prisoners are seen attacking one of their former guards and smashing the windows of a building. The image provides a clear sense of retribution, but it is strangely detached from the pictures of inmates still in the camps who seem incapable of doing anything so physically demanding.

Gaumont's HORROR IN OUR TIME was the only film to show the formal burial of a Russian soldier. His fellow soldiers are followed as they gravely carry his plain, rough, wooden, open coffin to be solemnly buried. The commentary records that this is the first proper burial for a Russian prisoner of war. On a happier note however, both Gaumont and Paramount showed the link up of the Russian and American armies. Both these companies were keen to place the discovery of the camps within the context of the advance through Europe, as if to emphasise that such things could no longer persist or happen again. HORROR IN OUR TIME contains footage from the Battle of Britain which follows the speech by Churchill, forcefully reminding the public that if the battle had been lost then Britain would also have been exposed to such a fate.

Gaumont and Paramount also included the battle for Leipzig in their films. It shows happy citizens cheering the incoming troops, before switching to tanks and soldiers firing in the streets against an unseen enemy. The citizens are then contrasted to the Mayor of Leipzig, his wife and daughter, who committed suicide with cyanide at the approach of the Allies. However, a sad postscript accompanies the Gaumont footage; their cameraman was killed shortly after taking the pictures. This once again serves to underline the point that the camps were situated close to the front line. This is further illustrated in the Paramount story which shows a hospital truck at Belsen which has bullet holes in its side after being strafed by German aircraft.

The individual newsreels inevitably contained their own idiosyncrasies. There were images that appeared in one but not others, while some images appeared in all of them, but there were also identifiable themes that ran through all of the different productions. The question of establishing authenticity was primary and the parliamentary delegation served this purpose well. The use of children to emphasise the innocent nature of the victims was a clear way of exposing the extent of the cruelty.

This was emphasised further by showing the furnaces which were clearly intended to dispose of human bodies. The nature of the men and women who inflicted this suffering, and the role the Allied army played in forcing German civilians to witness and atone for this suffering are both prominent themes. In addition all the newsreels showed former inmates venting some of their anger at former guards. The newsreels then placed the camps within the context of ongoing war. To end the horrific revelations, the films lingered on graphic images of the horror, either the scattered piles of corpses in Belsen, or the emaciated inmate on the point of death turning over rags in his hands. The overall impact was undoubtedly shocking and left the audience in little doubt as to what the camps were all about and the extent to which it was possible for the human race to sink into barbarity.

The commentaries to the newsreels obviously had a great influence on the tone and message of the newsreel presentations as a whole. All the commentaries began to raise the issue of responsibility and again the question of the guilt of the German nation as a whole was raised in the national press. Movietone used the American Congresswoman, Clare Booth-Luce to make precisely this point;

> I have seen at Buchenwald how men were tortured, gassed, burned and slowly starved to death … The responsibility for those terrible crimes … falls squarely on the German people that have long born their responsibility in the eyes of God. They must be made now to bear it in the eyes of their fellow men.[17]

A British news supplement, made by Movietone, for occupied territories used the British MP, Mavis Tate, who had already been photographed in the camps, as a commentator. She began by saying that no words could exaggerate the reality of the camps, a voice-over then continued;

> Germany's crimes are no longer hidden from sight. At last the eyes of the world are opened. We believe it our duty to screen these pictures as a warning to future generations.[18]

It is interesting to note that this commentary implies that the outside world had known nothing of these events before now. The same thing is suggested in the commentary for HORROR IN OUR TIME, which claims that the atrocities have been hidden behind barbed wire for the last five years, but now they have been exposed. There is no indication that the British government or public, might have had an inkling of the truth. In contrast, the Movietone commentary states clearly;

> None of these atrocities are new; all this has been going on for years; what is new is the stark evidence; widely and openly presented in this country … now we see the incontestable truth – and truth has to be faced.[19]

This seems to imply that there had been some knowledge previously, and it is now the scale of the atrocities, rather than their existence which is so shocking.

This comment, however, also begins to shift the emphasis to the British public itself. It is now their responsibility to accept and learn from these pictures. A telling comment from Mavis Tate, which accompanied a picture of British soldiers entering a camp, said;

> It is these men who so strongly advocate the publication of these pictures, which show only in small part what they see in reality.[20]

The message was clear that the public had an obligation to remember the lesson of the camps. However, Movietone added;

> Can anyone, any longer, doubt the truth of German atrocities? And yet shall we remember these things in 10, 15, 20 years time?[21]

Another aspect which stands out in Mavis Tate's commentary is the fact that she specifically says the inmates are; 'as you and I'. In the same way as Monson in the

Dr Fritz Klein, SS doctor at Belsen, speaking into the newsreel microphone, a mass grave behind him.

Photograph courtesy of the Imperial War Museum, London

Evening Standard had illustrated the humanity of the people who appeared barely recognisable as humans, Mavis Tate now attempted to do the same. She mentioned that the inmates were of many different nationalities, but then added that many of them were intellectual and highly gifted men and women. She identified them as engineers and doctors, responsible, intelligent, citizens; 'as you and I'.[22] It is a powerful reminder to the audience of how fragile the trappings of civilisation really are when challenged. It also confirms, in a different way, Churchill's assertion that the same persecution really could have taken place in Britain.

The newsreel companies also put together footage which was sponsored by the British government. These features were known as *War Pictorial News*, and were produced in Cairo before being distributed abroad as a compilation of the main stories that had been shown in Britain. Within these programmes the camps tended to be featured as a prominent story, but unlike the newsreels that were shown in Britain, no additional space was cleared and the story of the camps was simply included within all the other stories that had been current during that week. As a result the story of the camps became obscured by images of Ethiopian troops celebrating victory in East Africa, or the return of Greek refugees to their homes. However the footage that is contained within these films is just as graphic as that shown to the British public, and the commentaries dwelt on many of the same themes.

The same footage was also used in programmes which were compiled for distribution throughout Germany. Inevitably the commentaries for these films focused on presenting the German population with irrefutable evidence of the atrocities that had been committed in their name. As a result the footage shown in Germany tended to be much more graphic than the images shown in Britain, similarly the commentaries for these films tended to be more hard hitting, allowing for no ambiguity.

The newsreels had continued the process of telling the story of the camps, using many of the images that had been collected by the AFPU in the first few days of liberation. But the results of all this work and commitment ultimately rested with the British public. How would they respond to the horrific images which now confronted them in places they had previously viewed as being for entertainment?

PUBLIC RESPONSE TO THE NEWSREELS

Newsreels were open to everyone who wished to see them, including children. As a result there was considerable debate about how the screening of footage from the camp should be handled. Several letters in the newspapers indicate that many people were of the opinion that warnings should be given that these images were not suitable for children. A letter in the *Manchester Guardian* expressed the concern felt;

The desirability of adults seeing these pictures may be argued … My concern, however, is with the children who suddenly see flashed on the screen pictures of unmitigated horror … if it is not possible under the law to prevent children from being admitted to performances … surely the local authorities should insist that notices should be clearly displayed stating that these films are not fit for children. My own judgement is that children should be excluded entirely.[23]

This fear about the impact that these images would have on children who saw them inadvertently was not unfounded. Bernard Crick, fifty years later, remembered that as a fifteen year old;

… we saw the film, just spliced in without warning to a routine newsreel, of the opening up of Belsen. We wept in the alley outside.[24]

It was exactly this kind of unsupervised viewing by children that public opinion was keen to guard against. However an article in the *News Chronicle* highlighted one of the problems;

… children could not be excluded from these showings, for newsreels made by private concerns had no certificates. News shots made officially, however, might be given a 'horror' certificate should their effect on children be considered too over-powering.[25]

Judging by the reaction of Bernard Crick it has to be assumed that these images were indeed over-powering, especially for children. A further *News Chronicle* headline read; 'Atrocity Film may Warp Children'. This article examined the danger that children could be encouraged by the images to become sadistic themselves.[26] In response to these concerns most cinemas used notices to warn people of the horrific nature of the material, others used attendants to warn people as they queued to see them. An article in *The Daily Herald* carried the headline; 'Don't let children see film'. It continues;

Cinema attendants walked along the queues outside West End news theatres yesterday warning people with children not to let them see the Buchenwald and Belsen atrocities film. Children who came alone were in most cases turned away … We cannot stop parents bringing their children. But we have instructed our staff to warn them of the film's terrible nature.

The audience were however unanimous in their opinion;

Show it everywhere. Let every person over the age of sixteen see for them-selves what Buchenwald means.[27]

There is a very clear distinction between what people considered children should see and what they as adults should see. Almost everyone who expressed an opinion believed that although children should be protected, adults had a duty and responsibility to see and absorb these films.

This is further reflected in an article in the *Evening Standard* which highlights the fact that the public regarded newsreels which contained footage of the camps should be viewed as being inherently different to other newsreel programmes. People went to the cinema specifically to see these newsreels, rather then viewing them as an incidental feature at the beginning of the cinema programme.

> ... there was a big crowd as soon as the theatre opened at 10.30. Four out of five people went specifically to see the film. Two out of five went away and came back until the film was showing. Three out of five left when the film was over without waiting for the rest of the programme. No one left in the middle of ... there was none of the usual chatter from the crowds going out.

The article also indicates that some people felt their children should see the films as well;

> Three women came to see if the film was suitable for their children; all told me that if possible they want their children to see it. Only one woman brought her daughter of nine and son of sixteen ... She left with her daughter before the atrocity film began; her son remained specially behind to see it.[28]

The *Daily Telegraph* recorded that; 'All box office records at London news theatres showing these films have been broken'. In view of people's determination to see the films it is easy to see why this was the case. The same article detailed the visit of the Lord Chancellor, Lord Simon;

> He was accompanied by Lady Simon and Mrs Mavis Tate ... At the cinema visited by the Lord Chancellor, queues, including children, elderly women, service men and clergymen, stretched from Charing Cross road into Trafalgar Square. They were still there late at night. Lord Simon who had made special reservations for the film ... As he left immediately after the film, he expressed his horror at what he had seen.[29]

It is obvious from these extracts that people were inordinately interested in seeing these films, and for whatever reasons they were determined enough to queue for extremely long periods.

It is a fitting tribute to the work done by the AFPU that the British public did respond in this positive way, to the footage that they had painstakingly gathered. This is further underlined by an *Evening Standard* article which reviewed the newsreel films and carried the headline; 'Steel Yourself to See This Film';

> It is your duty not to spare your feelings, but to see them … Nothing that our skilled reporters have told us, or the 'stills' that have been sent to us has revealed the terrible truth so fully and convincingly. For the cameramen who had to do their duty, and move among the mounds of dead, and the slowly writhing clusters of living dead, this must have been the most ghastly assignment of the war. They have done their work unflinchingly sparing neither themselves nor us. Those who still doubt the truth should now be silenced, and those who still hanker after Fascism be shamed.[30]

A similar attitude was expressed in *Time and Tide* in a review of HORROR IN OUR TIME;

> Ultimately 'Horror In Our Time' is too horrible to write about, but before I give up trying I should like to praise the moral courage of the cameramen who steeled themselves to make it and the decent reticence of its commentary. My mind was too assailed by grief to function critically but I think I am right in saying that some of the worst moments were silent … and I thought the silence right and sensitive. Yes, cinema has done its most hateful job honourably and decently and has provided a record for posterity that nothing can expunge.[31]

One has to think that if the films drew responses like this from reviewers, then the AFPU and the newsreel companies had indeed achieved their aim. They had set out to present the public with images that would be seen as irrefutable proof of unimaginable and horrific scenes. The reaction of the public seems to suggest that they had indeed achieved this primary aim of convincing a sceptical audience.

The newsreels did undoubtedly have a unique role in exposing in graphic images exactly what the camps were all about. As one review ended;

> These films should be shown throughout the world and nowhere more than in Germany. The printed word can glance off an inattentive mind, but the moving picture bites deep into the imagination.[32]

CONCLUSION

The work of the AFPU is unique among the history of the reporting of the concentration camps. The images that so shocked the British public in 1945, have gone on to shock subsequent generations and have provided an indelible record for the education of future generations. Their power rests in their simple evocation of the shocking reality that was the concentration camps, a lasting testament to the horror that existed in their time.

Historical Journal of Film Radio and Television, vol. 21 no. 3, August 2001.

NOTES

1. L. Mial (ed.) *Richard Dimbleby Broadcaster* (London: BBC Publications, 1966), p. 47.
2. Jonathan Dimbleby, *Richard Dimbleby: A Biography* (London, 1976), p.194.
3. Public Record Office INF 1/636, Letter from Mr Adams, 11 April 1945. Mr Cummins was the editor of *British Paramount News* while Sir Gordon Craig and Mr Sanger represented *British Movietone News*.
4. Jerry Kuehl, *Film as Evidence – A Review*: History Workshop No. 2 (Autumn 1976), pp. 135–139.
5. I have viewed the material produced by Movietone, Gaumont and Paramount. However, the Universal newsreels of the camps are part of the sequence that was not transferred to archives. I have not seen the Pathe footage, but there is no reason to suspect that it differs greatly from the material produced by the other companies, because it all came from a common pool of footage.
6. Paul Smith, *The Historian and Film* (Cambridge, 1976), p. 60.
7. *Daily Herald*, 28 April 1945.
8. Movietone Film Library: ATROCITIES – THE EVIDENCE, Index card and commentary.
9. Reuters Television Library/ITN Archive: *Gaumont-British News*: HORROR IN OUR TIME, Issue No. 1181; released 30 April 1945.
10. British Film Institute: *British Movietone News*: ATROCITIES – THE EVIDENCE, Issue No. 830 and 830a, released 30 April 1945.
11. Reuters Television Library/ITN Archive: *British Paramount News* : PROOF POSITIVE, Issue No. 1478, released 30 April 1945.
12. *British Paramount News*: PROOF POSITIVE, indicated on card number 2.
13. *British Paramount News*: PROOF POSITIVE, indicated on card number 3.
14. Movietone Film Library: ATROCITIES – THE EVIDENCE, Index card commentary.
15. Reuters Television Library/ITN Archive: PROOF POSITIVE, Index card commentary.
16. Reuters Television Library/ITN Archive: *Gaumont-British News*: HORROR IN OUR TIME.
17. Movietone Film Library: ATROCITIES – THE EVIDENCE, Index card commentary.
18. British Film Institute: *British News – Supplement for the Occupied Territories.*
19. Movietone Film Library: ATROCITIES – THE EVIDENCE, Index card commentary.
20. British Film Institute: *British News – Supplement for the Occupied Territories.*
21. Movietone Film Library: ATROCITIES – THE EVIDENCE, Index card commentary.
22. British Film Institute: *British News – Supplement for the Occupied Territories.*
23. *Manchester Guardian,* 4 May 1945, p. 4.
24. *The Independent,* 15 April 1995, p. 15.
25. *News Chronicle*, 26 April 1945.

26. *News Chronicle,* 3 May 1945.
27. *Daily Herald,* 30 April 1945.
28. *Evening Standard,* 30 April 1945, p. 5.
29. *Daily Telegraph,* 1 May 1945, p. 3.
30. *Evening Standard,* 28 April 1945, p. 6.
31. *Time and Tide,* 5 May 1945.
32. *The Times,* 1 May 1945, p. 8.

Belsen

Paul Wyand

Paul Wyand was one of the best-known British newsreel cameramen, a large, jovial figure who worked for British Movietone News for nearly forty years. His memoirs provide a lively, humorous account of the rough-and-tumble world of the newsreels, but Wyand was also one of those who filmed the liberation of the concentration camps. This extract from the memoirs relates how Wyand went about filming the unimaginable. The Martin to whom he refers is his sound recordist Martin Gray.

Belsen Concentration Camp, some fifteen miles north of Celle, lay hidden behind a perimeter of thickly planted trees and the barracks of a panzer grenadiers' training centre. The camp's concealment was so effective that from the main highway we saw absolutely no sign of it. But as we drove along a road that branched through the trees the sweet scents of spring were gradually replaced by another odour. Subtle and indefinable at first, it grew stronger and stronger as we went along.

At the barracks we were stopped by British M.P.'s. They asked us to leave the car and enter a building which we found to be occupied by members of the Royal Army Medical Corps. We were told to strip, and, after being inoculated against typhus, we had de-lousing powder poured over us. When we dressed again more powder was sprinkled on our uniforms. Then we drove beyond the barracks and parade ground to a barbed-wire fence. A gate creaked open, and we entered Belsen. The stench now completely dominated and polluted the air: a composite of rotten-ness and putrefaction that choked the lungs and made it almost impossible to breathe.

It is difficult to recall the exact order in which the sights of the concentration camp unfolded before us. Even now, fourteen years later, Belsen still has the unreal quality of a grotesque and terrifying nightmare.

Men, women, and children – barely human beings, but skeletal caricatures – shuffled, staggered, and stumbled towards us, their tattered pyjama-like uniforms flapping loosely against emaciated limbs and starved bodies. Some dropped even as they walked – not to fall to the ground, but to collapse into the ankle-deep human excrement with which the camp was carpeted. There was no awareness of sex, nor did any sense of decency remain: if breasts or genitals were exposed, neither men nor women made any attempt to cover themselves. Eighty per cent of the inmates were suffering from dysentery, and they emptied their bowels and their bladders inside their clothes as they walked along. I blinked away tears as these creatures tottered up to me, incredulity in their eyes, and raised skinny hands to pinch the fat on my jowls. As they did so I could see and feel the lice crawl from their fingers to my face. A number of people crumpled up and died as they stood there.

40,000 people were still alive in Belsen (the camp, measuring about a mile by 600 yards, was suitable for only 8,000), and 10,000 unburied bodies, twisted by death into grotesque postures, lay rotting in the sun. These are not my figures; they are from the official records. Of the 40,000 there were 200 children and 25,000 women Jewesses and partisans from all over Europe. The men were either Jews or political prisoners. This latter category included people convicted of the crime of secretly listening to the B.B.C.

There were 800 cases of typhus in the camp, and a further 13,000 people died of various ailments during the next month. Six weeks later there were still 11,000 people in hospital. Of the males in the camp when we arrived more than 2,000 were seriously ill, another 7,000 needed some sort of medical treatment, and there

BUFVC

Paul Wyand.

were sixty new cases of sickness every day. Of the women 2,000 were very ill, 18,600 were in need of less urgent treatment, and 125 new cases of sickness occurred daily.

Lieutenant-Colonel Taylor of the 63rd Anti-tank Regiment was the Camp Commandant, and the Tommies under his command, outraged by the horror of Belsen, were filled with hatred for the S.S. guards who had been kept on at the camp to bury the dead and clean the place. The Germans were put on much the same rations as their victims had received and were treated with little ceremony by the incensed soldiery. The women guards were put to the same sort of tasks as the men: cleaning out huts, loading corpses into lorries, and unloading them into the mass graves which had been bulldozed from the filth-covered earth.

We made our way round the camp, photographing scenes which, it seemed, could not possibly be the responsibility of civilized man. On three or four occasions Martin and I had to break off work in order to vomit.

There were sixty huts in the camp. Fifteen of them had been occupied by the sixty or seventy S.S. guards. The prisoners had lived in the others: 600 to 1,000 in a hut suitable for eighty. The prisoners' only water supply had been a concrete pond. In it floated rubbish, effluvia, and corpses. It came as no surprise to be told that the average life of a man in Belsen was twelve days. I was told that Irma Grese, the blonde woman guard who was later hanged, used to enter the huts of the prisoners, accompanied by an Alsatian dog, and empty a full revolver into the massed prisoners there. I saw bullet-holes in the woodwork which testified to the truth of the stories of this dreadful woman's sadistically lunatic idea of amusement.

I learned that before the British came the prisoners had been forced to drag the dead to communal graves which had been dug. They were so weak that four of them were needed to carry one emaciated body. 2,000 men, working for twelve hours, had toiled to clear away the dead – yet 10,000 still lay unburied. They had died of starvation, thirst, ill-treatment, and shooting. Some had been beaten to death; others were the victims of sickness. Their rations had consisted of one cup of ersatz coffee in the morning, and a noon meal of a little turnip soup, occasionally supplemented by a few ounces of bread. That was all – and many had received no food at all for five days before the arrival of the British. The forward patrols had distributed corned beef, chocolate, and biscuits to the prisoners, but their stomachs, unused to solid food for so long, could not accept it, and many died,

I have no desire to pile horror on horror – and God knows I have touched upon only the fringes of it – but when the men and women responsible for the running of Belsen were brought to trial the whole shocking, bestial story came out, and the factual evidence presented to the court is available for all to read. Referring to the films made at Belsen, Colonel T. M. Backhouse, M.B.E. T.D., who opened the case for the prosecution, said:

It is proposed to show a film which was taken when the British authorities went into the camp, and that will give you some idea of the conditions and the degradation to which the human mind can descend. You will see the thousands of corpses lying about and the condition of those bodies. You will also see the well-fed condition of the S.S. who were stationed there. You will see people fishing for water with tins in a small tank. What you will not see is that the water was foul and that there were bodies in it. That was all the water that was available to drink. You will see the dead, you will see the living, and you will actually see the dying. What the film cannot give you is the abominable smell, the filth, and squalor of the whole place, which stank to high heaven.

The army authorities worked as fast as conditions would allow. The camp's inmates were segregated into nationalities and put into makeshift quarters in the woods behind the huts. Medical supplies were rushed in, and the M.O'.s, under Brigadier Glyn Hughes, Chief Medical Officer of the British Second Army, performed minor miracles providing balanced diets from the limited stores at their disposal.

Catholic and Protestant priests and Jewish rabbis arrived at the camp, as did a British padre from Aberystwyth whom I knew only as 'Banger'. He worked like ten

Paul Wyand, top left, filming in Belsen concentration camp.

Photograph courtesy of Imperial War Museum, London

men, distributing clothing, helping to feed the sick, spreading, comfort, and holding services with his colleagues at the mass graves. I was with Banger when two prisoners approached him and tugged at his arm. They led him to two grave-like mounds, and the padre got a squad of men to uncover them. Two boxes, each measuring about ten feet by three, were unearthed. Buried there by the Germans, who hoped to return and remove them, the boxes were filled with rings and jewels and watches stolen from the prisoners. Banger gave Martin and I a lady's watch each. 'I am sure their owners would have wanted you to have them', he said. 'For the film you are taking here will prevent the Germans ever being able to act like this again. Ask your wives to think of Belsen whenever they wear them, and of their owners' tragic fates'.

Another man who dedicated himself to helping the people of Belsen was Michael Lewis, a Jewish cameraman with the Army Film Unit. Although his superiors considered two days to be the maximum time any photographer should stay in the camp; Lewis obtained permission to remain there until the concentration camp was finally destroyed by flame-throwers many months later.

After about nine hours at Belsen I felt exhausted and sick, both physically and mentally. We returned to the barracks, where we were deloused, and made some effort to clean our boots. We took the road to Oyle to put our material aboard an aeroplane. After Belsen it was the beautiful blossom-filled countryside that now had the air of unreality. I stopped at a farm about half a mile from the camp and sat for a while looking at a man and his wife busy in the fields, their children playing near by. It was a scene that could have been duplicated all over the world. I left the car, went over to the man, and asked him whether he was aware of what had been happening at the concentration camp. He said in broken English that he had known nothing.

'But you must have known', I insisted. 'You must have had an idea something was going on'.

He shrugged. 'It did not pay to think,' he replied. With that he turned and walked away.

Another view was given by the former Lord Chancellor, the Right Hon. Viscount Jowitt, who said: 'I myself find it quite impossible to believe that these events were not widely known throughout the German Reich; and it is to the eternal disgrace of the German peoples that they should have been, as they must have been, tolerated'.

En route to Oyle we stopped at Celle, where, in the military prison, I photographed Kramer, the aptly named 'Beast of Belsen', the camp's former commandant. Big and burly, his face set in a permanent idiot's grin, he seemed impassive and indifferent to his fate.

At Oyle I met Cecil Bernstein (brother of Granada's Sidney Bernstein), who was with the Ministry of Information. 'The Government want evidence', he said. 'The Ministry must have authentic pictures of the German guards against the Belsen background. Get each guard and you film to give the day and the date, then let him make any statement he likes. Do the same with the prisoners'.

After a fevered and sleepless night we returned to Belsen. Among those whom we interviewed was Dr Fritz Klein, the German doctor whose amusements had included injecting petrol into the bloodstreams of prisoners and watching as they died in the most frightful agonies. He was now at work unloading bodies. My interpreter was a Polish girl of eighteen who had been at the camp for only four days before its liberation and was therefore in a better mental and physical condition than the others.

I posed Klein on the edge of the pit into which he had been dumping corpses, and the background showed other bodies being disposed of in like manner. Two soldiers had been detailed to assist me, and one stood on each side of the doctor. Klein was trembling with fear and was half crazy after the work he had been doing for the past few days. The girl explained what was wanted, and as he started to talk I filmed him. He had spoken only a few words when the girl cried: 'Stop!' and explained that although Klein had told me his name and where he was, he had given the wrong year. On hearing this the Tommies clouted the German with their rifle butts, and the Polish girl screamed at him. Klein began again, and this time kept to the truth. When the interview was over he bared his chest and said: 'Shoot me'. He looked down into the grave, certain we would do so. I told him that shooting was far too good a death for him. He pleaded to be shot, but the Tommies dragged him away and put him back to work. Later he stood trial and was hanged.

I interviewed three guards, including a woman, and all their statements contained the words: 'We were forced to do what we did by the S.S. The others may have been wicked, but we were kind'. I also filmed interviews with those prisoners who were able to talk intelligently, and one amazed me by saying that he would have been even worse off at one of the other concentration camps.

I photographed the gas chambers at Belsen. The Germans had approached women prisoners and said: 'If you're nice to us we'll give you preferential treatment'. When a group of women had been won over in this way the guards would complain: 'It's no good us getting together while you are so dirty. What you need is a good wash. We have steam showers here, so why not come and have a decent bath?' But the showers ran gas, not water, and the guards considered it highly entertaining to watch the various ways in which their victims died under different poison gases. When the British arrived the Royal Engineers quickly improvised a water supply, and converted the showers back to their civilized purpose. They thought it only courteous to invite women and children to be the first to take showers – and they were nonplussed when the prisoners shrank away in horror. When the inmates had been convinced that it was safe to use the showers they formed long queues. They gambolled and chattered under the water like excited children, and it was the first rime I had seen any of them smile. By the end of that second day the improvement in the mental state of the prisoners was noticeable. The smell was still oppressive, but the huts had been cleaned, and much of the filth removed from the ground. The people had food inside them and clothes to wear, and were conscious of the fact that they were human being again. The first women to become aware of their femininity were the French. They had no cosmetics or pretty frills, but they tore up the rags of their old uniforms to make curlers and hair ribbons.

During my third day at Belsen all the burgomasters and councillors in the area, male and female, were rounded up and taken on a conducted tour of the camp. One grave was still being filled, and a loudspeaker van gave a non-stop commentary on the facts and figures of Belsen. The effect on these well-dressed, well-fed Germans made excellent coverage. Some shut their eyes and refused to look; some were sick; women fainted; others, unmoved, were as arrogant as ever. But the S.S. guards were now glassy-eyed, and many seemed on the verge of madness.

The interviews I filmed were not shown to the public, but were used in evidence during the Nuremberg trials. Copies of the rest of the film came back from England at the end of the week, and every German adult in certain selected areas was compelled to see it. M.P.'s stood outside the cinemas where it was shown, and those who came out smiling or arrogant were sent back to see it again. I am told that few came out either grinning or unaffected.

After the War I was in a London pub, listening to a loud-voiced woman telling the saloon-bar customers that the Belsen film was a complete fake. How did she know? Her boy friend helped to make it. I do not usually throw my weight about, but on this occasion I was sufficiently furious to tell her and her companions that she was talking arrant nonsense, because I was the cameraman who had shot the film. No one believed me. To-day, alas, the belief that the film was a fake is widespread both here and in Germany.

Neither Martin Gray nor myself have ever been quite the same after Belsen. In some subtle, imperceptible way my experiences there changed me. The taste and smell of the place were with me for a fortnight, and for years afterwards I suffered from nightmares.

Paul Wyand, *Useless if Delayed* (London: George G. Harrap, 1959).

Newsreels Must Find a New Policy

G. Clement Cave

Clement Cave became news editor of Pathe News in 1946, and its editor by 1947, but it was a problematic appointment because Cave felt that the newsreels could not be politically neutral. His belief that newsreels should begin to deal seriously with social and economic issues is expounded in this article, which calls for a more invigorated newsreel to counter the threat posed by television. Cave's article indicates the resistance to his ideas that was coming from exhibitors, and in June 1948 he was reduced to news editor once more, and left Pathe for Radio Luxemburg the following year.

> The main aim of the newsreel directorate is, therefore, to be as Complaisant as possible, to be inoffensive by rule, and when forced by exceptional circumstances to deal with social and political issues, to play safe.

That sentence sums up a chapter on the news film which appeared in the Arts Enquiry Survey, *The Factual Film*. It is, in my view, a fair assessment of newsreel policy as it exists in the, majority of the five British newsreels. Behind this not very vigorous mentality is the all-important truth that newsreels sell direct to exhibitors, and not, like newspapers, direct to the public. The cinema manager is anxious to please as many of his patrons as possible. In his view the audience pays for entertainment and not for thought-provoking news films on the social and political issues of the day.

This commercial caution is understandable. Should a newsreel select a topic which possesses certain highly controversial aspects from the public point of view, the reception such a subject will receive in a cinema must to a large extent be affected by the personal opinions of the audience. Thus, if the screen treatment is to be positive and not a series of compromises, some susceptibilities will be offended. And in terms of box office, the exhibitor who buys the newsreel will not regard it as good business. If he cannot please all the people all the time, he will at least do his utmost to ensure the minimum of irritation to his customers.

Unfortunately, the range of subjects within this category is considerable. I would say that something like 70 per cent of the news which fills the morning papers either comes into this class or is unsuitable for newsreels because it lacks picture value. And so the newsreel editor is left with the safe type of story that has become an annual event: the Boat Race, the Grand National, the Derby, the Cup Final and many others. All these are laced with Royal events, bathing beauty competitions and much triviality. The only bright spots are fires or death and disaster stories, and the strength of these depends on how quickly cameramen can reach the scene, with the very occasional pageantry, such as the Royal Wedding.

These subjects have a place in any survey of the news, but they do not merit the rating given them by the newsreels. All are a long way from the big issues which are nearest to the community and therefore make news.

My personal view is that both newsreel editors and exhibitors have played safe for too long. I believe there is far too much comfortable assumption on the part of the film industry about what the public does or does not want. I find very little evidence for some of the sweeping generalisations about public taste and entertainment and much that contradicts some of these almost traditional beliefs. From experience I know that one crank in an audience who, for example, complains to a cinema manager that the newsreel showing is just a vehicle for Government propaganda because it happens to carry a story involving an interview with Sir Stafford Cripps can be used, if the manager has a similar political outlook, to imply, that a whole audience was practically in revolt.

The war brought a great change in public outlook and taste; the tragedy is that many in the film industry have failed to recognise this fact. In some directions the trend has been seen and anticipated. Many British features which were decried because the theme was quite contrary to the conventional formula for box-office success have been astonishing successes with cinema-goers. Despite this lesson from the feature world, most news reels still hesitate to take a chance. Certainly the path of anyone who attempts to break away from the accepted style is hard.

A mild example was the Government's White Paper on Britain's economic situation and her requirements, published nearly a year ago. On news value I regarded this as important to the whole nation, and decided to build up a story. Cameramen were sent to factories, coal mines and industrial centres for material. There were brief interviews with national figures such as the miners' Will Lawther, industrialist Sir Miles Thomas, and Economic Chief Sir Stafford Cripps. The final story which occupied the greater part of a reel was designed to show some of the nation's resources and requirements. Emphasis was laid on the need for more production. Such public reaction as was available was favourable, but the trade considered it 'propaganda' and not entertainment.

On another occasion, following a report on the conditions in some institutions for old people, we got inside some of these homes and showed the conditions as they were. The commentary was based on the report and pointed out the public's responsibility in the matter. Throughout I was advised by Lord Amulree, who is

Robert Robinson, *Gaumont-British News* commentator, early 1950s.

associated with the Ministry of Health; and, who has given the problem considerable attention.

The topic was in the news, and it was one of public interest. From members of the public I received letters of congratulation; from the trade the opinion that it was far too controversial for the cinema. The list is endless.

My own newsreel is the only one to have attempted to face these issues, and while the trade has argued the merits or otherwise of such stories, adverse criticism from the public has not reached me. Very largely it has meant revising policy and taking the ditches one by one instead of two at a time. As a compromise I have developed the technique which gives the product a *March of Time* treatment. There is one main title and one story which form the theme and shape of the reel. Into that setting is packed the world news, supported by a commentary which reviews, explains, comments and is all of a piece. It is an editorial must that the commentary is positive. There must be no 'ifs' and 'buts', no sugary, old-world phrases. At least this gives the reel precision and character.

But there is still a long way to go. A great newsreel public was built up during the war, when the reels had great and vivid pictures to show and stories of great daring to tell. Through lack of imagination, much of this goodwill was destroyed. But audience interest will have to be captured again, and soon. For on the horizon is a new competitor – television. It may take a long time to develop and to command such an audience as is available to radio. But this possibility may come into being before the film industry has turned television to its own purpose. If newsreels wait until that challenge arrives, they will be, too late. The time for new ideas and a complete change of mentality is now.

By all this is meant a reorientation of thought. The assessment of news by the criterion of what exhibitors are supposed to want is venal and bad journalism. Neither do I believe it essential to be overawed by this bogy. The answer is to move forward slowly and to demonstrate that audiences have a wider interpretation of the word entertainment than is generally supposed. At home the nation is in a stage of transition and uncertainty. This stage brings problems and questions. In their hands newsreels hold an immensely powerful medium which can be used objectively to report, to inform and to explain. Any medium that can fulfil those aims may be said to meet the demands and requirements of the moment.

Abroad the peoples are caught up in international politics which must ultimately influence their lives. The news film can show the ordinary man in this country how his counterpart in other lands is meeting the problems of the day. By such interpretation the newsreel would be meeting the obligations it has. In a world where so much is confused and where explanation is so necessary there can be little room in a balanced news film for the nonsense of a Texas rodeo or a Miami beach parade. A new set of values must take over.

A new form of technique in presentation is required. The formal method of title and then story is as old and out of date as some of the news carried. It needs streamlining, and tricks used which give the reel a punch. News is always urgent and often vital. It should be handled that way. The most prosaic story in the world can be given life and meaning if the imagination is there when it is conceived.

There will be room for television and a bright future for the news film only if newsreels become invigorated. By this I mean the adoption of a real and understanding news sense, the imagination to think of something to say and the courage to say it, a relegation of much of the present trash which is at present given importance and a far deeper faith in themselves and in the part they should play in national and international affairs. It will take a long time to convince all exhibitors of the common sense of this new policy, but it is a move that will have to be made if the news film is to hold its place in the cinema.

Penguin Film Review no. 7, 1948.

If I Owned Newsreels ... What A Row There Would Be!

J.B. Priestley

The polemical novelist and broadcaster J.B. Priestley tells the readership of the Left-wing newspaper the Daily Herald, who it is owns the newsreels which are so influential upon public opinion: the Americans, and J. Arthur Rank. He points out that the emphasis on seemingly apolitical light entertainment items is political in itself, and calls for a complete change in the way newsreels are produced and distributed.

Several times a day, in thousands of our cinemas, the lights fade, there is heard a fanfare of trumpets, and the newsreels appear on the screen.

It may be said that for all their trumpets and fuss, those things are not taken very seriously by anybody, that we are all waiting to see Laurence Olivier or the Marx Brothers.

Nevertheless, we are probably far more under their influence than most of us imagine. And it is certain that vast numbers of adolescents, caught by the films at an impressionable age, are profoundly affected by the newsreel point of view. This, they feel, is how the great world lives.

Clearly the people who select and present all the items on those newsreels have a task of some responsibility. Every day, to vast audiences relaxed in the dark after the day's work, they are offering revealing glimpses of our world.

The men who control the newsreel companies can do much good or a great deal of mischief. They are among the most powerful educators of public opinion. Now let us see who is doing the job.

The following newsreels are produced in this country: *Gaumont-British News*; *Universal News*; *Movietone News*; *Paramount News*; and *Pathe News*. And two of them are controlled by one man, the other three by the Americans.

Gaumont-British News is produced and owned by the Gaumont-British Picture Corporation Ltd. It is distributed by General Film Distributors Ltd. Both these companies are controlled by Mr J. Arthur Rank. *Universal News* is produced, owned and distributed by General Film Distributors Ltd., controlled by Mr Rank. One man – two newsreels.

Movietone News is produced by British Movietonenews Ltd, and is distributed by 20th Century-Fox Pictures Ltd., a subsidiary of 20th Century Picture Corporation of America. *Paramount News* is produced and owned by British Paramount News Ltd, and distributed by Paramount Film Services Ltd. Both these companies are wholly-owned subsidiaries of the Paramount Picture Corporation of America.

Pathe News is produced, owned and distributed by Pathe Pictures, which belongs to the Associated British Picture Corporation. This company is controlled by Warner Bros, of America, who own 37 per cent of the ordinary shares and whose nominee (an American) is Managing Director of the company. Thus these three newsreel enterprises are, in fact, controlled by Americans.

WILL NOT DO

Now this simply will not do. There need not be any question of dishonesty, of deliberate misrepresentation and falsification of news. All the men and women concerned in the production of these newsreels are probably trying to do a decent, honest job. But the boss's point of view, the directives form the head office, have to be taken into account. Even the order, 'Give us more light entertaining items', can have serious political-social consequences.

We must not forget the comfortable Tory notion, from which I have suffered myself on various occasions, that only Left Wing politics are to be condemned as being 'political'. Thus if you are accused of 'dragging in politics' – into a broadcast, a play, a film – it is because you are on the Left and not the Right.

SUPPOSE ...

What a row they would be – what letters to the Press, what questions in the House – if it were discovered that out of our five newsreels, three were being controlled by the *Daily Herald* and the other two by J.B. Priestley!

And what a scream of rage would go up from the Americans if they found themselves in our position. If more than half of their newsreels were being distributed throughout the United States by the British!

We are making here a very difficult political and social experiment, of importance not only to ourselves but to all the rest of this bewildered and bruised world.

This experiment and everything of significance that happens inside or outside it should be adequately reported on our screens. It cannot be a matter of indifference how nearly thirty million of our people are offered the news in cinemas.

THEIR OWN

Obviously, action should be taken in two different ways. First, we should decide that no one group should own more than one newsreel, and that American companies should either combine to produce one newsreel, clearly labelled *American*, or cease to exercise their contol altogether. Secondly – and this is even more important – the whole production and distribution of newsreels should be more broadly and soundly based.

Responsible organisations – such as co-operative societies, trades unions and cultural associations – should be definitely encouraged to produce their own newsreels, and arrangements should be made to give such newsreels the widest possible distribution. This, to say the least of it, would add interest and variety to our film programmes.

Finally, such groups and organisations, learning the technique of film production through their newsreels, might find themselves encouraged to go forward to produce other types of film, various hinds of 'shorts', documentaries, and even dramatic feature films.

I am all for good entertainment – I have to earn my living by providing it – but I see no reason why, at this late date, we filmgoers should be regarded as being permanently half-witted. But let us first settle the newsreel problem.

Daily Herald, 11 June 1948.

Beware of the Newreels

Anon

An unnamed film technician writes in the socialist journal Tribune of the kinds of biases, editorial tricks and omissions which the pro-Tory newsreels could employ, and of which the general public were generally ignorant. He also reveals the practice of staging news stories, especially 'vox pop' interviews, which were becoming more common in the newsreels at this time.

Socialists fighting the next general election will not only have to contend with the opposition of most of the national press, but with an even more powerful weapon – the film. While there is a healthy distrust of what is read in the newspapers, a myth still exists that the camera cannot lie. But – if all goes according to plan – the camera will lie throughout the entire Odeon, Gaumont and American-owned ABC cinema circuits, which cater for some nine million people weekly.

Mr J. Arthur Rank and his associates together with Sir Philip Warter, chairman of Associated British Cinemas, and the directors of ABC, are conscious or semi-conscious parties to a conspiracy on the part of the film trade to get rid of the present Government. Of the independent cinema exhibitors, Sydney Bernstein, who controls Granada Theatres, Mr Walter Eckart, managing director, of Star Cinemas with headquarters in Yorkshire, and Mr J. Wilson of Accrington, are refusing to enter into the Plot.

How then will the film industry go about job? The answer is simple. They will work through the newsreels. In the current issue of the film magazine *Impact*, Paul Sheridan, the Editor, continues to expose their methods.

For many months the newsreels have shown their political bias, but in the past it was confined to veiled innuendoes, pointed omissions and a glamorisation of Churchill and prominent Tories. It may have been noticed how often Churchill is presented in close-up on the screen with cheering crowds and flattering comments. Anthony Eden's tour abroad was covered in great detail. In the filming of state occasions, if the Prime Minister is present he is usually seen in long shot while Mr Churchill is given greater screen footage in close-up. These tactics were too ineffective worth mentioning, though for some time they have irritated Socialist film technicians.

Now the newsreels have got down to their business in earnest. They are making

Ted Candy of *Gaumont-British News*, filming an FA Cup Final at Wembley.

plans for the general election – plans which should be made public as quickly as possible. To get some idea of the impact of the newsreels on the general public, it is not sufficient to see merely one. It is necessary to do what the majority of voters do – to see one or two a week. Recently, many prominent critics of the Government have won film fame, the latest being Lord Ammon. But it was in the travesty which the newsreel cameramen, or rather the newsreel editor, made of the Labour Party Blackpool Conference that the really dangerous aspect of film technique was revealed.

It is an old journalistic trick to quote only one sentence from a speech which, taken from its context, conveys a meaning never intended. The film editor not only does this, but in addition, while the Minister is speaking, cuts to a different shot of another Minister who is apparently very annoyed at what is being said, although this shot, in fact, was taken on quite a different occasion. Then the editor cuts back to the Minister who was speaking, but shows him looking round bewildered as though he has dried up and does not know what to say next. This shot may have been taken when he was about to go off for lunch.

The three shots cut together in quick succession create the lie, a horribly convincing lie which can only be detected by film technicians and those who were

235

present on the occasion. It is a dangerous lie, because even Labour supporters may be unable to see through it. That was the manner in which the Blackpool Conference was filmed, and we come away with the impression that Labour Ministers did not know what they were talking about, but were united in being worried about nationalisation. In filming the Blackpool Conference there was foul play. It is nothing compared with what the Socialists are in for.

As film technicians we claim that with judicious cutting and an adroit use of camera angles, it is simple to make a fool of anybody. We can distort the emphasis and meaning of Ministers' speeches not only by cutting out statements but by the simple use of long shot, medium shot and close-up. For any statement said in close-up is given greater significance on the screen than one said in long shot. There is no end to the tricks we can play with this simple device. By combining the unsympathetic shooting of Labour Ministers with glamorised shooting of Tories, accompanied by appropriate background music, the cinemas are already working sufficiently on the emotion of their audiences to create the intended mood. This has, been clearly evident in the cinemas lately. When there is not sufficient film footage available to employ these tricks, the commentary attempts to make up for it.

Nor is it generally realised that it is not necessary for film cameramen to film news. As Paul Sheridan rightly points out, they can concoct it. They are doing so regularly. An office charwoman was recently filmed by one newsreel unit in an office rigged as a typical housewife's parlour where she was paid to whine about Strachey and food problems. A very old sandwichman was recently seen in London being paid by a newsreel cameraman to pick up a cigarette-end from the gutter. This was carefully filmed. A group of factory workers standing together talking in a street can be called strikers whether they are on strike or not. There were plenty of concoctions over the filming of the dock strike. They are always of an anti-Government nature.

The newsreel companies are supposed to be suffering from a shortage of film stock. In fact, they have accumulated over a long period a tremendous library of anti-Government shots ready for the general election. In addition they have just completed a film on behalf of the Tory Central Office at Brighton studios, a film which is supposed to be news. There will he no mention of the sponsor on the screen.

What sort of shots can we expect to see in the future? If Mr Aneurin Bevan is seen opening a block of flats, do not be surprised if there is only a small section of the flats in the background and a view of bomb damage and a depressing row of derelict-looking houses, houses built incidentally under the Tories. There were certainly several angles from which the shot could have been taken, one of them including a proper view of the flats. Anyone can be filmed sympathetically or unsympathetically, from the right angle or the wrong one. There is plenty of filming of prominent Tories and Socialists going on, to the deliberate disadvantage of the Socialists.

The general election newsreels are to provide the final bombshell. There is surmise only as to the precise form they will take. But the type of editing tricks we can expect is a quick succession of shots of strikes giving a depressing picture of labour unrest in Britain today, with no mention of the fact they have been carefully accumulated over a period of years. We can expect shots of overcrowding, mal-administration, lack of houses and great personal hardship. Many of the shots will have been rigged, many of the people presented on the screen will seem like typical British citizens with a just grievance and truly representative of thousands like them. In fact, they may be merely playing a part because they have been paid to do so. But it will all seem thoroughly convincing because the newsreel technique is convincing and the public have not yet got wise to it. Often the presentation will hardly seem like propaganda, merely a disinterested desire for justice on the part of the cinema. It will have an emotional appeal which is all the stronger for its novelty. The combination of words, music and a powerful visual impact is far more moving that any journalistic or poster campaign. For these reasons it is most urgent that the public should be widely informed of the newsreels cinematic tricks.

If any further proof were needed of the political bias of the newsreels, it may be sought in the fact that one of them is partly owned by Lord Rothermere. And this one company is joined with the others in an effective newsreel monopoly. Presumably Lord Rothermere has woken up to the political ineffectiveness of the *Daily Mail* and is turning his attention more seriously to the film industry. For the rest the newsreel companies are partly financed by American film companies and the American film industry has a grievance against the Government over the working of the Quota Act.

Sydney Bernstein and Paul Sheridan excuse one company – Pathe newsreel – in their criticism of political bias. If Pathe are less blatant they are no less diligent in filming Churchill. Churchill's statement of Tory policy was covered by every newsreel, while the Prime Minister's speech on the same day at the much bigger Durham miners' gala was not covered at all. Nor have any of the miners' galas been screened though if is difficult to imagine anything more spectacular from the film point of view, and the miners must provide of the most substantial sources of revenue for the film trade. Any worthwhile cameraman would be overjoyed at the opportunity of filming the miners' galas.

The fact that J. Arthur Rank and Sir Philip Warter are happy to show these films is a clear indication of where the Labour Government stands with these men. Mr Rank is entitled to his view, and some might argue that no one should interfere with his right of free expression, a principle he does not apply to British film directors. But that the American film trade should seek to influence British people politically is sheer impertinence. It is further proof of the danger of American domination of the British film industry, a danger which the film technicians union – the Association of Cine Technicians – continually stresses.

For a long time past the film technicians, backed by such papers as *Tribune*, have been advocating the establishment of a fourth circuit of cinemas owned by the Government or the Municipalities, so that the monopolistic tendency within the industry might be effectively challenged. The case for such action is strong on this general ground. But the case becomes stronger still with the accumulating evidence that the film monopolists are now planning to use their monopoly power for direct political propaganda through the newsreels.

Tribune, 5 August 1949.

The B.B.C. Television Newsreel

P.H. Dorté

Before the Second World War, the BBC television service showed Gaumont-British and British Movietone newsreels to its few thousand viewers. After the war, the BBC developed its own newsreel, Television Newsreel (first broadcast, 5 January 1948), which became the precursor of the BBC television news programmes of today. In form, however, it was exactly like a cinema newsreel, and was originally shown only twice a week, in common with the newsreels. The article, written by the BBC's Head of Television Outside Broadcasts and Films and founder of Television Newsreel, gives a good account of how Television Newsreel was produced, and gives a clear indication of the perceived limitations of the cinema newsreels and how television news would soon supplant them.

When the B.B.C. started its television service again on June 7, 1946, the programme-planners were not able to include the film newsreels which had been a regular feature before the war; this was because post-war policy in Wardour Street prevented the Corporation from renting for television purposes nearly all commercial films produced for the cinema – including newsreels. In the case of newsreels, however, this prohibition proved, curiously enough, to be a blessing in disguise because it led ultimately to the B.B.C. Television Film Unit itself going into production with a newsreel carefully designed to meet the special requirements of viewers. The B.B.C. *Television Newsreel* which thus came into being in January 1948 is different in content, tempo, and length from the commercial cinema newsreel which, although presumably satisfactory for the cinema, is definitely not best suited to television consumption (even though it had proved to be acceptable enough before the war).

Because of the ban imposed by the film industry, the B.B.C. Film Unit had made, between the reopening of the television service in 1946 and the beginning of 1948, a not inconsiderable number of news films – each film dealing with one news-event only. In most cases the news-events selected were those happening beyond the range of the outside broadcast units – events ranging from the blowing-up of the fortress of Heligoland to the 1947 royal tour of South Africa. In other cases the event was one which had been made the subject of an outside broadcast at a time when the majority of television viewers were at work and thus unable to see it; examples of these were the victory parade in June 1946 and the wedding of Their Royal Highnesses the Princess Elizabeth and the Duke of Edinburgh in November 1947. The average length of these films was ten to fifteen minutes, as compared with the average of one to two minutes usually allocated to a story in the eight and-a-half minute commercial newsreel. Possibly because the television viewer in the home is more relaxed both physically and mentally than is the occupant of the cinema stall, this longer treatment proved to be more than welcome on the television screen. And so of course did the technical treatment of each film, with long 'takes', more close-ups, and the careful selection of camera positions so that the viewer would not be whisked from, say, one side of a football field to the other, as he is so often in the commercial newsreel. The placing of the cameras was the result of experience gained with the live outside broadcast cameras, where it had been proved beyond question even before the war that it tired the viewer if, over a long period, he has to keep reorientating himself as the producer cuts backwards and forwards from camera to camera – particularly if the cameras are far apart in the horizontal plane.

With the experience thus gained in the production of these news films, fairly simple reasoning provided the formula for the compilation of a regular television newsreel – that is, a news film containing more than one story: a total running time of about fifteen minutes and with not less than two or more than seven minutes devoted to one item – the antithesis of commercial newsreel procedure which rarely devotes more than two minutes in all to one subject.

Three important factors had to be taken into consideration when it was decided to put a television newsreel into production:

1. What would be the effort required to organise such a reel on first a one-reel-per-week basis, then a bi-weekly reel basis, and so on until a target of seven reels a week could be met?
2. What would be the amount of equipment and the number and classification of technicians required at each stage?
3. Could the reel be truly a *News*reel within the B.B.C. interpretation of the word 'news' or would it, *faute de mieux*, have to contain only a small proportion of news stories and a large proportion of documentary, magazine, or interest stories?

I should like to deal with the third point first, because it is clearly debatable how long a filmed news-event remains 'news', and the B.B.C. is very jealous of its reputation where news is concerned. The B.B.C. prides itself on the fact that its news reports are as up-to-the-minute as they are strictly accurate, whether they take the form of the straight Home, Light or Overseas Programme news bulletins, or the Light and Overseas Programme 'Radio Newsreel'.

Accurate, television newsreel certainly could be, and it could equally be devoid of the brand of humour which is the stock-in-trade of the cinema newsreel commentary-writer and which, although acceptable to a cinema audience numbering many hundreds, is inclined to be embarrassing when listened to by a mere handful of television viewers in a sitting-room at home. But, bearing in mind the dictionary definition of news as 'fresh information', what would be the maximum permissible delay in transmitting it? The advent of sound broadcasting some twenty-five years ago made it possible to convey a given news story to a rural home many hours before the long established newspaper could get it there, and the news columns of the newspaper thus acquired a new role in many households – that of merely amplifying, and/or commenting on, news that was already known. But with the later perfection of facsimile picture-transmission, the newspaper could do much better than broadcasting in that it could illustrate an important piece of news with a photograph, even if the news concerned an event which had only just occurred on the other side of the world. And by reproducing more and better-printed photographs, weekly news magazines could still carry a story which had been made known to the world by wireless and the daily newspapers long before the magazine would appear on the bookstalls. On this score, of course, moving photographs could still be justifiably issued under a 'Newsreel' title concurrently with the weekly news

Television Newsreel producer Philip Dorté in the mixer room.

magazine version; and even if the newsreel would not get on to the screen of a small country cinema until several weeks after the west end of London had seen it, it would still be bringing to the patrons of that cinema the first moving pictures of that news story that they would see and thus convey 'fresh information' to the district.

This does not logically apply to a *televised* newsreel however. The B.B.C. television service is no more and no less than a visual-broadcasting service, and if it is to transmit a newsreel, it has to do so just as quickly as it is technically possible and practically feasible to get the reel ready for televising – this so as to ensure that the 'fresh information' which it supplies really is fresh to the television viewer who, if the televised reel were delayed, might already have seen similar pictures in his cinema.

The compiling and transmission from any given television station of as many newsreels as a sound broadcasting station would transmit news bulletins will never, in my opinion, be justified. But the target of any serious television broadcasting system could and should be one completely new reel daily, and on some of the American networks it is now actually up to five reels per week. This brings me back to the first two points which I raised earlier – those concerned with the effort required and the amount of equipment and the number of technicians necessary for the production of a given number of reels per week. And in order that this can be readily understood, I must relate briefly how a newsreel is produced.

The producer of a newsreel can rarely plan the complete make-up of a given issue far ahead. He knows that certain events will be happening during the relevant period before the reel is made up, but he cannot guess what unexpected ones will occur, either at home or abroad. Further, he can never be sure that even a planned story will, when shot, justify the length which he has provisionally allocated to it, and equally he must always bear in mind that a minor item may prove to be so interesting that it will deserve more time. And if the pictorial value of a given news story is greatly inferior to that of another which has less news value, the producer must be able to lengthen the latter at the expense of the former. Again, where an overseas story is planned for inclusion in a particular reel, it is always possible that the film will be delayed in transit and will not reach him in time; and he must be in a position to relegate straight to his library some or all overseas stories intended for a specific issue if he is suddenly faced with a plethora of home stories of greater interest to the home audience. Thus the newsreel producer must always plan more footage than he will really require so that he can select and reject in order to make a balanced reel of maximum interest, although, clearly, the greater the number of issues which he is producing, the less will be wasted, as a story rejected from one issue may well find a place in the next.

A story may be shot silent, or with sound, and the usual practice is not to send out a bulky combined sound-and-picture camera unless a dialogue or musical scene will form an integral part of the story or unless it will call for a specialised sound effect – say the whine of a new type of jet engine which is not available either on film or disc in the library. A 'silent story' can often be covered by one cameraman using a small mechanically-operated hand-camera costing only a few hundred pounds. A 'sound story' will require a sound recordist in addition to the camera crew, and a combined sound-and-picture camera which, with all its sound recording equipment, costs several thousand pounds. The silent camera and crew of one can be transported to and from the scene of action in a small car; the bulky sound camera with its bigger crew and its batteries, amplifiers, and cables will require a large car and, as silent cut-away shots will also be required, a silent camera and cameraman will have to accompany the sound outfit – probably in a second car. Thus a sound camera should only be used when a story really calls for it.

But the shooting of a story is only the beginning of its inclusion in a newsreel. After development and printing, the print has to be edited, shots selected and cut to the right lengths, sometimes additional library material added, sound effects and music tracks cut and synchronised so that, say, the noise of a siren will coincide exactly with the steam seen issuing from it, and so that the music will start at the beginning of a story and, by cross-fading at low level behind dialogue, conclude at the end of it. The commentary has to be written, based on the 'dope sheets' brought back by the cameramen, but supplemented often by information obtained from the reference library. A title or caption has to be painted and photographed and the story-picture and sound tracks, which by now may well amount to four (viz. synchronised dialogue, effects, and two music tracks) – has to be cut in the agreed place into the whole reel. The picture negative then has to be cut to tally exactly with the edited picture positive. And then and then only is the reel ready for the re-recording session, in which the commentator is carefully cued to speak his script while the 'natural sound', music and effects tracks are, together with more effects from discs, mixed behind his voice to produce a new sound negative. Finally this new soundtrack is developed, and then printed, with the picture negative, to provide a 'married' print. To handle two fifteen-minute reels per week the minimum editorial staff required for cutting and synchronisation is four, backed by a film librarian; the re-recording session calls for the presence of one or more commentators, producer, supervising editor, a sound crew of two, a gramophone operator, and three projectionists – the last-named to handle the picture projector and the film-phonographs which play the music and effects tracks.

It can be argued that with television this last phase – re-recording – be eliminated by mixing the outputs of the film-phonographs and disc reproducers behind a live commentator who speaks his script as the picture is actually transmitted; in fact it is the practice at some American television stations to do this, although such stations use gramophone records entirely instead of film sound tracks. There are, however, two-fold objections to such a scheme. First, one loses the ability to cut if the commentator is mis-cued, if a sound track breaks, if an effect is brought in early or late or too loudly o too softly, and so on; in other words it does not enable one to obtain the polish which is possible through the use of intermediate film. Secondly, not only have the commentator, the editor who cues him, and all the film-phonograph and/or gramophone operators to be present for each rehearsal and transmission, but studio time has to be allocated, whereas a complete sound film can be transmitted at any time without rehearsal, fuss or bother.

The full drill described above (including re-recording) is at present carried out by the newsreel component of the B.B.C. Film Unit twice a week, and requires a staff of twenty technicians. Their output is a minimum of thirty minutes of new screen-time each week plus repeats (at present, in so far as evening programmes are concerned, there is one repeat per issue). The present combined sound-and-picture cameras employed are two in number and in some ways obsolete in design; they are being replaced by three really modern equipments which will be in addition to the several silent cameras now in daily use. We now have to re-record at a remote dubbing theatre, but our own re-recording equipment is on order and will be working at the television headquarters at Alexandra Palace by the spring. These improvements will not immediately make it possible to increase the weekly output of *Television Newsreel*, but should ensure a better reel, and ease the burden on the camera, sound, and editorial staffs.

The next step I envisage is to have three editions a week, the Monday reel to be repeated Tuesday, the Wednesday reel Thursday, and the Friday reel Saturday. I personally see little point in going from three to four editions a week, and I suspect that the logical step at some time in the future will be to go straight from three to six or even seven. This will, unquestionably, mean doubling nearly all the facilities needed for three reels and obtaining more material from overseas. At present we purchase overseas stories from agents and freelance cameramen throughout the world – the United States of America excepted – and we obtain a small selection of 'handout' stories from various home, dominion, colonial, and foreign government offices. In so far as the United States is concerned, we have an exchange arrangement with one of the big American networks whereby each has free access to everything shot by the other's own staff cameramen. And I suspect that more and more similar exchanges will come into force as and when more countries install television broadcasting systems and concurrently build up their own television film units, and/or produce film transcriptions of their topical television outside broadcasts.

If, therefore, I may presume to end this article in prophetic vein, I would record that I foresee each major national television system having an eventual daily international television newsreel shot, in the main, by television film-cameramen and edited and commented on specifically for the home television audiences even though, in some countries, it may be relayed on big-screen in the cinemas because, on account of the 'urge' in television, it will invariably be more frequent and thus more up-to-date than the commercial cinema reel. At present the B.B.C. *Television Newsreel* is one of the very few of its kind. Soon it will have, I believe, many counterparts, each similar in structure and differing only in the language in which the commentary will be recorded on the sound-track.

BBC Quarterly, no. 4, January 1949.

Television and the Land of Morning Calm

Ronnie Noble

Ronnie Noble, one of the few newsreel cameramen to publish his memoirs, worked for Universal News before joining the BBC's Children's Newsreel in 1950, graduating to its Television Newsreel in 1952. Noble filmed with distinction for Television Newsreel during the Korean War. In the chapters on the war in his memoirs, Noble turns from a previously cheery anecdotal style to a anxious questioning of what his camera could actually record, faced with human anguish.

I borrowed a jeep and drove down the strange roads to find the pontoon bridge across the Han river. All other bridges into the capital were destroyed. With every retreat they were blown, and now they were completely useless. I watched the British convoys approach the pontoons, then slowly clatter their way across the river. I wondered at the strength of the American bridge that it could take heavy tanks without collapsing. I made shots of the vehicles approaching. I felt an inward thrill: this was the first story in Korea; this opening shot showing the American military policeman in the foreground and the olive-green vehicles carrying the British contingent of troops was the beginning of a new phase of war-reporting for me. Films I had shot to-day would be seen inside the British homes in a few days' time. I made shots of the troops, but through the view-finder I found myself trying to catch a glimpse of their faces. This had never happened before. Faces in the view-finder are usually nothing but pieces of continuity. But on this first day I wanted to see their eyes, their expressions. This was a new war; I'd jumped into the middle of it. Were the men that fought it any different to those in the Second World War? I need not have wondered. There was the same casual efficiency of the too-young-looking subaltern. There was the British soldier's face, ordinary when seen in the mass, yet so individual and different on closer inspection. These were the same British soldiers – only the place and time were different. I had a warm feeling of security as I watched them. If you've got to be in a war, then these are the best men in the world to be with.

The town of ruins was silent. It was as London might have been in 1940 if as a result of Nazi bombing it had been evacuated. A capital city with no inhabitants! I'd imagined a township of grass huts, and here at my feet were tramlines.

Then I remembered reading that before the Korean war, and before the Iron Curtains were drawn across the world, it had been possible to board a train here in Seoul and travel right through to the Channel ports of France! A journey I'd love to film.

I let my jeep drive me. It seemed to know where to go. It had an instinct of its own. It steered me into a narrow street, then the engine cut out. I looked around, feeling very scared. I was being watched! I'm not psychic, and am too insensitive to have leanings towards spirits, ghosts, and the like. But I knew I was being watched. Quickly I looked around, turning my head suddenly in this direction and then in that, hoping to catch sight of movement. There was none. Above the silence I heard the roar of an engine as it revved up, and then its sound died away. All was quiet again. I wound the camera and made a shot of the silence. I was getting feeling for the story now. It was taking shape in my mind. This was no time to film the armies. We knew all about them. But what of Korea and the Korean people? Surely they are the story of Korea?

Why should somebody watch me so intently that I could feel their eyes, yet not speak? Where were the people of this city? How were they living? Had they too as with our men, been pumped full of drugs, suppressives, and preventive medicines? Or were we, the 'saviours of the country', the only ones wealthy enough to fight disease as well as Communism? My mind was jumbled full of intangible ideas as I wound the camera springs, but already I was making the decision to film the Koreans, their problems and their way of life, as well as the activities of the United Nations troops. It's one thing to save a country from aggression, but we should not forget the suffering of the saved. Suddenly I saw a movement behind a wooden shutter. I dropped the camera and ran towards the spot, pulled the shutter outward, and looked into a yellow wrinkled face. Its owner must have been very old – perhaps ninety. His straggly greywhite beard, thin and sparse, hung miserably down to his thin chest. Not by a blink or movement did he acknowledge my presence. He sat perfectly still, looking, it seemed, straight through me. I saw immediately he was blind. I spoke to him in English. He did not reply. I looked into his eyes – they were grey; not brown, as they should have been for an Asiatic. These eyes were wet – small tears formed a continual stream flowing on his mahogany face. I spoke again. Still he remained motionless. I went to the jeep and found some tinned rations, and placed them beside him. Then instinctively I closed the shutter. It was like closing the door of life on a living idol. Who was he? Why had he been left behind? Had he preferred death and starvation in his own home to the dangers of evacuation? Had he sat in that window for minutes, hours, days, or weeks?

A thin white cat streaked from a doorway and shot across the rough earth road, looked around once with crazy, hungry eyes, then hopped over a window-sill and vanished amid the ruins of another house. I made close-ups of doors, streets, pots, ruins, empty streets, window-frames. By a series of completely static shots I began to build up the atmosphere of deserted Seoul.

A huge stone carving stood in a stonemason's yard. It was a Korean king. I made a shot of the opaque eyes staring at the camera, then climbed up beside him and made a shot from such an angle to see the god's-eye view! He looked down at a broken Japanese doll which lay in the gutter – dropped by a child as she left her home on the road south? I wondered if I could put this loneliness into pictures. Could people sitting in the comfort of their English homes feel any of this when they saw it on their twelve-inch screens? Never had silence and stillness affected me so. Suddenly I panicked. I wanted to hear an English voice – any voice, for that matter.

I jumped into the jeep and pressed the starter. Thank God, it started, and I drove off as fast as possible, the scream of the jeep's engine racking through my head. It seemed crazy to be lost, but lost I was. I drove through fifty streets trying to find a place I recognized, and they were all deserted. I tried to find my blind man, but he was lost to me. The feeling of unreality bothered me. Five days ago I was in Richmond, Surrey, and now I was lost in a town inhabited by a blind Korean. I was driving too fast, forcing myself on like an ant near to exhaustion, when suddenly I rounded a bend and saw a woman and child sitting in the middle of the road.

The pair were hauling up water from an open sewer. I expected them to run as I approached with the camera, but the little girl smiled, her grimy face splitting into a radiant grin, and suddenly all my fear was gone. I gave her some biscuits, and sat with her for a while before making shots of her and her bomb-happy mother, whose eyes had the same shell-shocked look of the blind man. A few minutes later I found the way back to the correspondents' billet. I'd only been away two hours, yet I felt as though I'd just returned from a lifetime dream. Korea was a little unreal from the very start, and, somehow, it never changed.

From *Shoot First! Assignments of a newsreel cameraman* (London: Harrap, 1955).

The Truth About Newsreels

This strident British Paramount News publicity brochure, aimed at cinema exhibitors, defends the newsreel's place in the cinema programme, and the ways in which it is superior to television news. Although it demonstrates that the newsreels were now fighting a losing battle, it is revealing of the newsreels' priorities and their particular sense of news values.

IT'S A PARAMOUNT FACT THAT:

A good show consists of more than a good feature (or even two). It is a complete, balanced programme of entertainment – a programme consisting of feature, shorts, AND NEWSREEL!

IT'S A PARAMOUNT FACT THAT:

Over the years, film fans have been conditioned to expect a newsreel at every show. This is true to the extent that a recent survey revealed that 83% of the cinema-going public prefers to attend the cinema that shows newsreels. To these people a show is simply not complete without the newsreel, and the exhibitor who does not give this service is not saving money; he is losing money by losing patrons to the exhibitor who does give it to them. To send his patrons home with the feeling that they have been given their money's worth, the astute business man-exhibitor gives full value, and full value includes a newsreel.

IT'S A PARAMOUNT FACT THAT:

The British public is the best-informed public in the world and a great deal of this is due to newsreels. Some exhibitors do not realize the part that the newsreel plays in the cinema-going life of his patrons. No other place but in the cinema – and the smart exhibitor makes it his cinema – can the public be kept visually abreast of the times with the kind and quality of news coverage that he gets in the cinema.

For a time TV was advanced by some exhibitors as an argument against the usefulness of cinema newsreels, but careful analysis and thorough, public surveys exposed this for the fallacy it was.

IT'S A PARAMOUNT FACT THAT:

Only cinema newsreels have the advantage of expert editing, the finish and polish that results in patrons getting the important highlights of events that interest them, rather than having to sit through endless, dull footage before getting to the heart of the matter. And only cinema newsreels present this news smoothly and professionally, without annoying interruptions.

IT'S A PARAMOUNT FACT THAT:

The far-flung staff of cinema newsreels, stationed all over the world, gives newsreel cameramen the advantage of being at the scene of action at a moment's notice. This speed of filming and editing, matched by a speed of delivery that is a phenomenon of motion picture accomplishment, has the finished newsreels on the nations screens almost immediately after the events have occurred.

IT'S A PARAMOUNT FACT THAT:

Britain is probably the most sports-minded country in the world and because of that, newsreels devote considerable footage to important sports events. Cinema newsreels offer coverage of football games that positively cannot be obtained anywhere else, and are not limited in any way, consequently the visual coverage given to sports in cinema newsreels is unsurpassed by any medium.

ITS A PARAMOUNT FACT THAT:

There are millions of homes without television, which means that many millions of people look to cinemas for a visual presentation of the news. By giving them this service you give them something they cannot get anywhere else – and every good business man knows that when he gives his customers something they cannot get anywhere else, he is creating goodwill for himself and his business; he is creating satisfied customers – and satisfied customers always come back for more.

AND IT'S A PARAMOUNT FACT ...

All these facts add up to the all-important one that:

Every well-run cinema ... every successfully-run cinema ... gives itself the advantage of the 'added attraction' that is the newsreel ... and this fact, too, is paramount:

Among newsreels ... and the record proves it ... there is none better than ... *British Paramount News*

LET'S LOOK AT THE RECORD

WORLD NEWS:

The excellence of Paramount's world-wide staff is apparent in every issue. Paramount not only gives all the important news, but our method of presentation is one in which we take great pride. Expert editing assures audiences of the finest visual aspects of the news. Expert analyses via commentator's remarks, bring out angles that might otherwise be overlooked, making the news presentation not only more exciting but more informative.

FASHION NEWS:

In the newsreel survey recently conducted, it was found that fashion news was second in popularity to world news to the majority of people polled. Every woman is interested in this part of the newsreel and they are especially well-serviced by Paramount's complete seasonal coverage of fashion trends that high-light the work of leading designers at home and abroad.

DOMESTIC NEWS:

Right here at home there are many different phases of the news recorded by newsreel cameras, and just as many different ways of covering them.

SPORTS NEWS:

With the long lens treatment afforded by *Paramount News*, audiences are given sensational close-ups of the high spots of Britain's top games. Our sports experts edit the footage so that the most exciting moments become part of the newsreel. The professional analysis of every play that accompanies the finished newsreel is that something extra that makes Paramount's newsreel commentators the best in the business.

PEOPLE IN THE NEWS:

Another special feature of *Paramount News* is the interesting presentation of personalities currently in the public eye. This service introduces to audiences people they have been reading about and hearing about, and our expert commentators analyse the importance of their activities in relation to the world.

From among these various features included in *Paramount News*, every issue has at least one particular item of special interest to your audiences.

Therefore BOOK *British Paramount News* (TWICE A WEEK) together with Paramount Features and Shorts ... and you'll be getting – and giving – *the best complete show in town!*

IF IT'S BRITISH PARAMOUNT NEWS IT'S THE BEST NEWS IN TOWN

British Paramount News publicity leaflet, c.1953.

The Cinema Newsreel and the Impact of Television

G. Thomas Cummins

Tommy Cummins was the Editor and Executive Producer of Pathe News. This article presents a robust defence of newsreels in the face of the increasing competition they were experiencing from television news – it was published only seven months after British Paramount News had closed – and envisages a clear future for the industry. Pathe, a part of Associated British Picture Corporation, was linked through its parent company, to the Independent Television company ABC-TV, which had the contract to supply weekend ITV services to the Midlands. The final paragraphs look to future developments and even envisage a future for the newsreels on tape rather than film.

Since the BBC introduced its daily television newsreel two years ago, millions of people have become accustomed to expect pictures of the day's events on their television screens at home that same night. The pictures are not perfect – often they are little better than stills – but they are pictures nonetheless.

What has been the impact of these daily newsreels on the much older established cinema newsreel? The view was expressed at the outset that the television newsreel would be to the cinema newsreel as the guided missile is to the bow and arrow. Yet in the big majority of cinemas, the newsreel is still showing. Where lies the reason for this survival?

In the first place, the BBC discovered that it was not possible to produce a newsreel of reasonably good quality every night – not, at least, without entering fields of reporting distasteful to Broadcasting House. (A similar reserve in this respect is apparent in independent television.) After a time, therefore, the BBC gave up trying and compromised with a news bulletin consisting of the announcer accompanied by a few picture shots of the events described. That formula has one merit, in that it deals with events of the day.

INITIAL ADVANTAGE

It is obviously difficult for cinema newsreels to come out every day. Even if they could afford the production cost, the exhibitors would not thank them for the additional labour and expense involved in collecting seven reels a week.

Reluctantly, but of necessity, the cinema newsreels concede the initial advantage to television.

But, this advantage has not, turned out to be by any means an overwhelming one. What is true in the newspaper world applies no less faithfully to the screen – interesting news bears seeing more than once, indeed often gains by a second viewing. The daily Press prints Saturday's news on Monday quite happily, just as if Sunday papers did not exist. This practice is not resented by readers.

Most people would probably agree that in general presentation and quality of both picture and sound, cinema newsreels are superior to those shown on television. The cinema's production is professional, whereas time and technical factors inevitably impose a certain degree of amateurishness on the television newsreel producers. In their case, the newspaper law of the deadline equally holds good.

Then, too, most of the pictures in television newsreels are taken on 16 mm cameras, in contrast to the cinema's 35 mm equipment. As the emulsion of film is of granular composition, the proportion of visible grain on 16 mm pictures is more than double that of 35 mm, which explains why television news pictures often appear badly defined and in soft focus. As for sound on the television newsreels, this is usually of a quality which could only be tolerated within the home.

EVEN EXPOSURE

Another weakness of the television newsreel derives, strangely enough, from what is technically an advantage – namely, that it is able to transmit a positive picture from a negative film without having to wait for a print. Television 'electronically reverses' the negative image. But that process demands an evenly exposed film, an impossible ideal under newsreel conditions, where the light often varies too quickly for the cameramen to adjust their apertures. The negatives of cinema newsreels, on the other hand, are carefully graded to ensure an evenly exposed print, pleasing to the eye.

For all this, while every exhibitor is prepared to admit that cinema newsreels are technically far better than television's, he has been tempted to discard them, in order mainly to reduce his costs. Obliged to pay a percentage of the gross takings (less entertainment tax) for his main film (the first feature), he wants to get the rest of his programme as cheaply as possible. If he can dispense with the newsreel, he is considerably in pocket.

Several exhibitors have tried this experiment. Most of them have subsequently abandoned it. Television or no television, people expect a newsreel when they go to the cinema, and many complain if it is missing.

The newsreel undeniably makes the cinema programme more attractive, and, therefore, over a period brings the cinema a substantial profit. If that were not so,

Ted Candy of *Gaumont-British News*, filming in Cannes in the 1950s.

and so recognised (if not always admitted in exhibition circles), the newsreels would not nowadays be showing anywhere outside the circuit houses. For, as a body the independent exhibitors are the most hard-headed and astute people in the business.

All the same, cinema newsreel salesmen seeking renewals of contracts are nowadays inured to the exhibitor's opening gambit: 'I saw all this on television last week'. This is an exaggeration, but a useful argument in the early stages of bargaining. Beyond question, television has the cinema – and for that matter, the newspapers – beaten on the score of topical news.

For that reason newsreels try to avoid covering events that go stale in 24 hours. Such stories are the lifeblood of television, but are not missed in the cinema. Often, before the war, a newsreel contained one or two topical subjects which lost their interest after the first day but had to remain in the programme. Dispensing nowadays with stories of this kind, the newsreels still have a vast field to exploit.

My own newsreel often uses interpretative stories, rather on the lines of the *March of Time*, though necessarily shorter. The response, from both exhibitors and audience, has been good and the policy will be continued. In this field the scope is immense, for as a people the British love anything which they can talk about for days afterwards.

I believe this policy will much increase audience interest in cinema newsreels. Most pleasing is the fact that additional interest comes through television itself. The daily showing of news items on both channels has made millions of people far more news-conscious than they were a few years ago. Both the BBC and ITA have made everybody accustomed to having news regularly mixed with entertainment programmes. Their listeners' and viewers' research organisations tell us that their newsreels are very high in the popularity poll. Neither Corporation would dream of abandoning news, and it is surely inconceivable that the cinema will not continue to follow the accepted pattern. After all, the cinema began it.

PROPAGANDA

Again, if the cinema newsreel were to disappear Britain would lose heavily in the field of propaganda. There are eighty-eight countries to which British cinema newsreels are exported. By nothing else is the foreigner more vividly acquainted with the British way of life.

There is one other way the newsreels can help the exhibitor, if the Government will co-operate. That is by strenuously demanding that their production shall in future rank as British quota. The Board of Trade and some sections of the film industry have hitherto resisted that demand, and the newsreels have not hitherto been insistent enough to carry their point.

If they could rank as 80 per cent supporting films quota, in return for using 80 per cent of British filmed items in the newsreels, they would lessen the exhibitors' difficulty in obtaining quota films of this category. The demand for newsreels would then be increased. In this age of rising costs such an expansion of output is important. For whereas television newsreels do not have to make a profit and have very large budgets (enormous by comparison with ours) the cinema newsreels must make money or go out of business.

STIMULUS WELCOME

We welcome the stimulus of television competition; we are grateful for the growing audience of news-conscious people and we are extremely interested in another advantage likely to accrue indirectly from the same source – picture on tape.

Already television programmes in New York are recorded on tape, transmitted to the West Coast and re-televised there. Sound recording on magnetic tape was perfected by the Germans during the war. Pictures can now be recorded on the same medium, and much sooner than was estimated tape may supersede photographic film throughout the industry.

Mass production of magnetic tape would make it considerably cheaper than film. But that would be its least advantage; for tape needs neither developing nor printing. It would save the producer all his processing charges, which are one of his major costs. Moreover, when the magnetic 'prints' had exhausted the market and were withdrawn from circulation they would be magnetically 'wiped clean' ready for fresh use. In fact tape can be used several hundred times.

Highly advantageous as this would be to all film producers, the newsreels would benefit most. A newsreel with, say, 500 first-run customers must make 500 prints – ten times the number required by the most popular feature films. If, therefore, the backroom boys of television have brought the tape revolution measurably nearer we can't thank them too warmly.

Financial Times, 23 September 1957.

The Newsreel Association of Great Britain and Ireland

Jeff Hulbert

The Newsreel Association represented the interests of the British news-reels between 1937 and 1960. This newly-commissioned guide to its minute books reveals the rich amount of information about the way the newsreels operated, argued, collaborated and defended themselves that the books contain. It is a guide, therefore, to the British newsreels as an industry.

This article is about the British newsreels' trade body the Newsreel Association of Great Britain and Ireland (NRA). It is not a definitive study, but rather seeks to provide a taste of the treasures that are contained within the Association's bound minute books, now held in the British Film Institute's Special Collections department. The minutes are the best record that is left to posterity by an organisation now long gone. It was active as an industry watchdog, protector, promoter and occasional referee for over twenty years and there is much to be learned about the newsreels and the people who played an active role in the business of bringing newsfilm to the cinema screen. At some time between its creation and dissolution all of the correspondence files – that would probably have included many gems as well as the routine stuff of business – disappeared, probably consigned to the dustbin. There were plenty of opportunities for this, as the Minutes record several changes of address for the NRA secretariat. The minute books thus provide a record of the way the *industry* operated – rather than how the companies themselves functioned. An important point to bear in mind is that the minutes themselves only show the business items that reached the NRA council for decision. Other issues would have been decided without reference to it. In this respect the NRA was no different to any other business.

This study is not a review of historical events, but rather is about issues as the NRA minutes recorded them. It is, therefore, a one-sided account that deliberately does not seek elaborate confirmation of details from outside sources. What it does do, however, is indicate what sorts of issue concerned the NRA and how it worked. The Minutes were written by the Association's five successive Secretaries and, as expected, demonstrate different approaches to recording decisions that range from the nearly bland to the almost detailed. The Minutes are numbered sequentially with Minute 1 dating from the first meeting (held on 1 November 1937) and Minute

5490 dating from the extraordinary meeting held on 15 June 1960, at which the NRA was wound up.

CREATION OF THE NRA

The News Reel Association of Great Britain and Ireland Limited was set up as the industry's trade association – a sort of employers' trade union. It provided the member companies with a forum in which to get together to resolve industry-wide problems and to promote and protect their collective interests. It was also established as a regulator, an arbitrator, and an information source and supplier. It was thus cast in the classic mould of the trade association and bears more that a passing resemblance to its present day counterparts.

Four of the five newsreel companies established the NRA on 21 October 1937, the date on which the organisation's Memorandum and Articles of Association were signed by Sir Gordon Craig (General Manager of *British Movietone News*), Jeffrey Bernerd (a director of *Gaumont-British News*). W.J. Gell (Managing Director of *Pathe Gazette*) and S.F. Ditcham (*Universal News*).

The NRA's principle objective (and one offering a stab at a legal definition of a newsreel) was set out in paragraph 1 of its memorandum of incorporation:

> To promote the interests, financial welfare and success of the trade or business of manufacturing, producing and distribution of cinematic films of current events known as newsreels, and to devise means to promote co-operation amongst those engaged in the said trade or business ...

The Memorandum comprises a further 24 paragraphs which added flesh to the bones of paragraph 1. The Organisation's Articles of Association, dated the same day, comprised 68 paragraphs of operational matters. Chairmen, initially, appointed at the start of each meeting, were from July 1940, generally appointed for a three-month tour of duty on a rotational basis, although variations did occur as the need arose. Thus the responsibility was shared: no one company dominated, but at the same time a measure of consistency was attained.

The NRA was a seriously thought through organisation that had a clear role and, over the next twenty-two years or so it exercised the powers with varying degrees of success. One thing that is remarkable is the fact that it was able to operate at all. An industry body that managed to function in spite of being led by diverse buccaneering free spirits as Castleton Knight (Gaumont-British), Tommy Cummins (British Paramount and, from 1947, Pathe) and the duo from Movietone (Sir Gordon Craig and Gerald Sanger) was clearly one that all sides knew they needed.

By the time that the NRA was wound up on 15 June 1960 the age of the cinema newsreels had passed. By then three of the five companies had ceased production

BUFVC

Letterhead of the Newsreel Association of Great Britain and Ireland.

and the impact of television in the field of topical news presentation was over-whelming and undeniable.

THE NRA'S BUSINESS

What did the NRA do in the intervening period? What issues occupied its meetings? The first year – up to the end of 1938 – can be regarded as a settling-in period, a testing of the muscles and systems. An early issue of interest was making representations to the government on the Films Bill, in particular helping with the construction of a legal definition of a newsreel. Another topic considered was the need to establish mechanisms for resolving differences between member companies. This included the agreement 'that all members should refrain from including in their issues anything in the nature of a "fake" or "hoax"'. Two other matters of particular interest were discussed during this period. First it was considered 'desirable' to abolish the practice of issuing 'Flash' copies, other than in the West End of London. This revolved around film of the 1938 Derby. It was agreed that no film of the race should be issued until 2 June, although 'West End-only' copies could be released to cinemas on the day the race had been run (1 June). The decision was subsequently rescinded when it was agreed that it should be left to the companies themselves to decide. This was an early demonstration of the limits of the organisation's power. The second matter concerned 'official and political party films'. There had been an exchange of letters between Sir Joseph Ball, an associate of the arch political fixer of the period, Sir Horace Wilson, and Pathe about a speech by Prime Minister Neville Chamberlain. Ball had filmed the meeting and was distributing it. Pathe felt films such as Ball's should have been made by a newsreel company. While not all companies were completely sympathetic with this view, their 'readiness to assist Government and Public Departments on all suitable occasions' was conveyed to government, as was their declared motive: it was a question of prestige, not financial profit. This resulted in a sympathetic response from government, but with the rider that ministers' hands could not be bound. The only other major event of 1938, as told by the NRA minutes, was the protracted process of trying to persuade *British Paramount News* to join. While it remained the sole non-aligned newsreel it could upset plenty of apple carts without suffering the consequences. The process of persuasion took several months, the membership application only being received in October.

1939 began relatively quietly for the organisation, although three council meetings were held in January. A matter to which it returned several times concerned the supply of regular news films to the British exhibition at the New York World's Fair. During the course of the year the darkening shadows that were creeping across Europe also affected the NRA. For instance, it discussed whether key newsreel staff could be exempted from national service, tried to obtain facilities to film the Royal Navy, and had an informal meeting with Sir Samuel Hoare about the work of the new Ministry of Information (MOI). The passing from peace into war is not recorded, although the meeting held on 13 September 1939 did discuss working arrangements during the hostilities. This recorded the five companies agreeing, initially until the end of the year (possibly it was expected to be all over by Christmas?), to suspend normal commercial sales competition in the national interest. Thus they stopped poaching one another's customers; provided the NRA with customer rental lists showing those that were due to mature on or after 18 September 1939; agreed to pay a fine for any transgression; and agreed to provide details of any renters cancelling their contracts. The arrangement does not appear to have been formally renewed, but seems nevertheless to have survived until the end of 1945. One surprising point of interest, given the primeval jungle from which they had recently emerged, is that they agreed (and later reaffirmed) that, should one company fall on hard times as a result of enemy action, the others would help them out. This proved to be no idle promise, for exactly this happened when Universal's premises were bombed in 1944.

The war years demonstrated that the NRA had a definite role to play. For the first three years there was an enormous number of special meetings, after which it was resolved that the council should meet fortnightly. On occasion meetings were held weekly or even twice-weekly. The range of issues covered was wide. There were many instances where the NRA was establishing (or enforcing) accepted scales of charges for the supply of newsfilm to feature film production companies. There are numerous references to the MOI about the supply of film to the MOI, its contractors, and the armed services. Some details emerge of its participation in the MOI Films Committee and, latterly, the News Film Sub Committee. There are a number of references to meetings with, and correspondence from, the likes of Jack Beddington, Director of the MOI's Films Division, Sir Kenneth Clark, Duff Cooper and Sir Edward Villiers. Brendan Bracken, the Minister of Information from 1941, also makes a number of guest appearances as reports of meetings with him are given to the assembled council members. There were also discussions about the despatch of war correspondents, the payment of danger money for cameramen flying over or otherwise engaged in battle zones, insurance policies for both war correspondents and their equipment, the need for additional camera equipment, plans for the dispersal of film processing laboratories, censorship of commentaries, and film stock shortages – the 1943 Film Stock Order. Throughout the war years, and stretching into the late 1940s, the NRA supervised the system of liaison with government departments. Each newsreel company was allotted one or more Ministries with which they acted as the contact point, on behalf of all member companies. These duties were rotated every six months. The list of departments covered is revealing because it gives a glimpse of the newsreels' news priorities. They were parcelled up as follows: (a) Home Office/Ministry of Supply/Ministry of Works and Planning/Ministry of Town and Country Planning; (b) War Office; (c) Ministry of Labour/Ministry of Aircraft Production/Scotland Yard and Police; (d) Air Ministry; (e) Admiralty. Interestingly, the Treasury was not covered. There are also several examples of parsimony and small-mindedness. As might be expected there were a few minor squabbles. However, one major theme pervading the minutes from this period is the rota system. This was the pooling of cameramen and other resources on the basis of mutually shared costs. Under this system one cameraman at a location shot his film for all five companies. It enabled expenditure to be conserved and scarce resources to be spread across all of the major war theatres and fronts. The NRA officers (the chairman and the secretary) were the principal regulators, but all of the companies acted responsibly. Collective decisions were taken about the location of rota cameramen, their insurance, sending sound units to cover the war, and meeting the cost of lost equipment.

One final thing about the Second World War also relates to the immediate post-war period. It concerns two stories that were controversial – both from 1945. The first was discussed only once and the second at several separate meetings, but they reveal a curious contradiction. The first story was about showing film of the concentration camps. Government had made noises about the importance of the film and of the need for it to be given a wide showing. Under the item title, 'Atrocity Stories', the NRA asked the Chairman (at the time, Clifford Jeapes of *Universal News*) to suggest to the MOI that film of the 'irreverent' handling of corpses should not be shown. This presumably concerned images of bulldozers being used by British troops at Belsen to speed up the burial. The other comes a few months later and concerns the Belsen War Crimes trial. This topic was discussed on several occasions. The NRA was initially intent on securing equal treatment with the US and other newsreel camera teams to record the event. However, on 25 October 1945 it asked the chairman (by this time Castleton Knight of *Gaumont-British News*) to suggest to the MOI that the NRA should be given the opportunity to shoot film of the passing of the sentences at the Belsen trial and, 'if possible, the execution scenes'. The NRA's disappointment at not being granted these facilities was recorded at the following meeting.

The period after the end of the Second World War was one of change, for the country as well as for the newsreels. Normal competition was restored, although there was never a return to the bad old days of the newsreel war. Difficulties with the unions – principally the ACT – began to emerge, as did the threat of television, which was discussed on many occasions under various headings during the latter years of the 1940s. The Cold War did not really happen, at least according to the NRA minutes, since there are few references to the dangers confronting the post-war world. However, the 1948 Olympic Games and the wedding of Princess Elizabeth to Philip Mountbatten did; and these occupy a number of meetings. It was also at this time that the NRA welcomed a new member into the fold: Metro Goldwyn Mayer's *Metro News*. It was 'elected' on 23 January 1947 and by early 1948 it had stopped attending meetings. It is not known for sure when its membership lapsed because that is not recorded in the minutes. 1946–48 witnessed a dark cloud descending over the Secretary (E.L. Maddox) and he resigned. Details are only hinted at in a particularly oblique, but sinister minute. February 1947 witnessed the

John Cotter of *Universal News*.

recruitment of a typist, Mrs Burns-Shearer, who within months progressed to become the Association's Secretary, a post she was to hold until the organisation was dissolved.

The NRA opened the 1950s with preparations for the impending general election. It planned to film interviews with the three party leaders and to use standardised titles and make the film available worldwide. This, of course, was at the end of an era when the world hung on British politicians' every word. During this decade the NRA negotiated with the cinema industry unions, with government about coverage of the 1953 Coronation, film stock restrictions, the film levy and restrictive practices. The NRA was an established and credible force within the industry, although its limits continued to be recorded in the minutes, where individual member companies' interests often seemed to outweigh the need to act in unison. It was consulted – formally and informally – by government. It represented the employers in negotiations with the cinema unions, it negotiated with government about things such as the 1953 Coronation coverage, film stock orders, the film levy and, lastly but not least, restrictive practices.

The NRA had assumed responsibility for operating the Royal Rota from its creation. From June 1944 the system was formalised: a cameraman was seconded to the NRA from a member company who was then placed on permanent attachment to the royal household. The first cameraman used in this way was Graham Thompson of *British Movietone News*. He was appointed on 8 June 1944. After two or three years there seem to have been rumblings that all was not well. There are several minutes that refer to the NRA asking Buckingham Palace officials if they were content with the way the system was working. However a cat was allowed out of a bag in October 1948: it appeared that rather than Buckingham Palace being dissatisfied it was the newsreels. Howard Thomas, the general manager of Pathe expressed unhappiness with Thompson's coverage: he was suspected of metamorphosing from cameraman into Palace official and appears to have used medium shots in preference to close-ups. The King seemed to prefer this. In June 1950 it was announced that Thompson had 'left Buckingham Palace to join the BBC's television staff'. The Minutes of 7 June 1950 record that by the King's command 'cameraman Turner be accredited to the Palace' with the same facilities granted to Thompson. There then followed a protracted process where the employment arrangements – including pension – were settled. This took over two years, at the end of which John Turner was employed by the NRA as the Royal Rota cameraman through a subsidiary company, British Newsreel Association Services Ltd, so that no one NRA member could claim credit for his services.

In addition to the Royal Rota, the NRA operated a peacetime equivalent of the ordinary rota through its wholly-owned subsidiary company, Newsreel Technical Services Ltd. Under this banner it negotiated royalty payments with sports promoters for the big events – the FA Cup Final, the major horse races, test matches and athletic events. The NRA also set charges for the use of library film supplied to compilation and other filmmakers and, increasingly, to television. It also was the manager of the UK's contract with the Soviet Union for the supply of news film of Soviet events (supplied by Sovexportfilm), and supplied this to, among others, the BBC.

A glance at some of the issues with which the NRA grappled during the years of decline show the diverse and complex range of its business. *Picture Post* magazine was charged 1,000 guineas (£1,050) for rights to the film of the Royal world tour of 1953. The NRA became a member of the Television Technical Sub-Committee, which had been set up by four trade associations to prepare a report for the Television Advisory Committee. Movietone was permitted to accept business from the Central Office of Information (COI) to compile a film of the Coronation, providing 'the film is not shown in the British Commonwealth'. The Minutes record the shares of the bill paid to the Ministry of Works for the cost of services rendered at the Coronation, including lighting. The NRA was also concerned that it was being disadvantaged: it was exercised about the need to receive government news releases at the same time as the BBC's *Television Newsreel* received them, rather than some time later. This was one of those occasions when the newsreel companies could not agree amongst themselves and demonstrates quite neatly the limits of the NRA's authority. The NRA also considered longer-running business items. Among these was concern that the BBC had negotiated a six-day working deal with a Film laboratory. There was also detailed planning for the filming of the 1958 state opening of Parliament. This was different from the previous occasions as Black Rod's ceremony was to be filmed for the first time.

SPORTS

Several sporting issues were discussed during this period. The points of interest lay as much in the differences between fees paid for rota coverage as in the occasional differences of opinion resulting from company self interest. Here are a few examples. In 1953 the MCC was offered £100 by Movietone, on behalf of the NRA, for rights to the 1954 England v Pakistan cricket test series; in 1954 £75 was offered to Cambridge University Boat Club for a camera position in one of the launches to aid coverage of the Boat Race; in January 1957 the NRA agreed to pay the organisers of the Grand National £5,000 for the rights; and in 1958 the NRA was unceremoniously elbowed from the space that it had hitherto shared with the BBC at the White City Stadium.

In 1954 a row broke out because Paramount and Pathe had both purchased film of Roger Bannister's 4-minute mile from the BBC, as they had not filmed the event themselves and could not find an alternative picture source. In 1958 Movietone and Gaumont were discovered to be paying £10 per football match (instead of the NRA's stipulated facilities fee of £5). This prompted Pathe's Tommy Cummins to say that in future he would pay what he liked, thus further breaking down the consensus.

THE ROTA

The Rota was under some pressure in 1956. There was a discussion about some event organisers restricting the facilities offered for newsreel coverage due to insufficient space being available for more cameras and then being able to discover 'room for television cameras ...' Movietone got into hot water with the NRA in 1957 when it was discovered to have supplied rota lavenders (fine-grain prints for duplication) to its UPMT customers (without having told the NRA) and its penalty was to make an extra financial contribution toward the cost of the rota system. The rota provided the companies (and event organisers) with many benefits (including clarity and simplicity of operation) but was eventually to bring the NRA into dispute with the government. The issue revolved around restrictive practices.

RESTRICTIVE PRACTICES

Conservative governments of the mid-1950s had taken action against what they saw as some of the factors inhibiting the growth of British industry. One of these areas was that of restrictive trade practices. They established a Monopolies and Restrictive Practices Commission to identify and tackle the problem at source. Movietone's Sir Gordon Craig was responsible for drafting the NRA's case for submission to government. The NRA was vulnerable in three areas. First, the Library Material Agreement, which set a scale of charges for providing library footage to be applied by all member companies. This meant that purchasers could not negotiate rates with individual newsreel companies. Secondly, Newsreel Technical Services Ltd, which operated the Royal Rota and the rota for major sporting and other events, limited competition. Finally, the NRA was responsible for determining the eligibility for membership and negotiating with, among others, cinema owners on behalf of member companies. Thus the industry was able to operate as a closed shop. The Newsreel industry was also under pressure by the government's Film Levy and the Film Quota (one was a fiscal burden placed on the film industry and the other was a requirement to ensure that a certain proportion of films exhibited in cinemas were British). The NRA sought exemption from the Levy and inclusion in the definition of British film under the Quota.

TELEVISION AND TRADES UNIONS

Feathers continued to be ruffled by various requests for film, mainly from television. For instance, at the meeting on 21 November 1957 Movietone (possibly after some pressure from the chairman) owned up to the fact that it had supplied material to BBC and ITN for 'recognised rates'. There was a discussion about the television film MAN OF THE CENTURY – a celebration of Winston Churchill's life:

Gaumont's Castleton Knight (in the chair) alleged that Pathe and Movietone had supplied film for inclusion but, interestingly, only Movietone denied the charge. There is no evidence of any penalty having been imposed and it is likely that the discussion arose from the chairman's well-known mischievous disposition.

The NRA was responsible for negotiating rates with the industry's trades unions. There is evidence of the protracted nature of some of the negotiations. However, there is also an indication of pique. For instance, Howard Thomas of Pathe had reportedly spoken to Geoffrey Cox (the Editor of ITN) about the NRA's agreement with the ACTT union and suggested that he (Cox) should seek the NRA's advice before concluding an agreement. In the nature of things it is likely that this revolved around two related issues: not upsetting current arrangements and preventing the poaching of staff through the payment of higher wages.

THE END

The newsreel industry and the NRA were in decline, even though Tommy Cummins had made a robust statement about the newsreels' future in an article published in the *Financial Times* in September 1957. 1957 saw the departure of *British Paramount News*, the closure of which had been announced at the end of 1956. It resigned from the NRA on 9 February 1957. The usual homilies were recorded in the minutes to mark this event. However, old friends quickly fell out and, as with all such matters, the financial entrails outlived the corpse. By April the NRA had agreed to pay, pro rata, an amount due to Paramount for its work in connection with the COI's *British News*. By the end of May 1957 Paramount had sent a bill to the NRA about film shipments from Suez during the 1956 Anglo-French invasion (£233 9s 9d). Wrangles ensued during which the NRA told its accountant not to pay, since in its view Paramount had not 'adopted the normal procedure'. Further wrangles involved the date to which Paramount's share of the income from *British News* should be calculated. By October Paramount and the NRA were still arguing and, at one stage the NRA voted to retain £45 7s 3d and to give that sum to charity. There was also the matter of what rota material Paramount had retained. The Secretary was still checking Paramount's holding of Royal Rota material as late as March 1958.

The next shrinkage occurred at the end of 1958 when the Rank organisation announced that it would be closing down both the *Universal* and *Gaumont British* newsreels at the end of January 1959. Initially, the Rank Organisation wished to remain a member of the NRA and to pay two subscriptions. This was agreed on a trial basis. But matters soon began to get complicated. Again it was over money. The NRA was asked to consider distributing the income from *British News* to member companies on the basis of the amount of footage supplied, since British Movietone was by then supplying 54 percent of the total, rather than pro rata as had previously been the case. A decision was deferred, but the matter resurfaced at the meeting held in March, when it was argued that as the Rank Organisation had ceased to produce newsreels it should leave the NRA. Rank countered saying that it wished to remain in membership as it assembled newsreels for the COI. The Chairman (G. Grafton Green of Rank) said that all benefits accruing should be distributed to member companies pro rata. British Movietone said it was no longer prepared to supply such material to the Rank Organisation and Rank was asked to resign from the NRA. Rank finally announced its departure on 18 March. Then, paradoxically, it was asked to become an honorary member as the NRA had by then recognised that it needed the company. Among other things, Rank was asked to continue to make its preview theatre available for twice-weekly newsreel previews. The same meeting agreed that Pathe should store the Royal Rota equipment and that Pathe and Movietone should take Gaumont's sporting events. Pathe and Movietone also became jointly responsible for assembling the COI's *British News* in rotation. Rank was still demonstrating its commitment to the NRA in May 1959, when it sent two representatives to a meeting. That meeting heard that British Newsreel Association Services Ltd had been put into liquidation, but that the NRA would continue in operation. However, that is where the record of meetings comes to an end.

It is clear that the end was swift in coming, since the last minute in the bound volume dates from the final meeting held on 15 June 1960. That resolved to cease all operations. The last Annual General Meeting followed immediately on the same day and dealt with such matters as the sale of the curtains at the Association's Nascreno House offices, on which a loss of £120 0s 4d is recorded, and it was agreed to sell the remaining items of furniture to British Movietone for £25. It was a rather ignominious end for an organisation that had helped steer the newsreel companies into maturity and had proven so useful during the Second World War. In a flash – like so many of the newsreel review stories themselves – it was over. History does not record whether the organisation was sadly missed, but an inexplicable listing in the 1968 *British Film and Television Yearbook* records the organisation still operating, this time from offices at 71 Baker Street, London W1. Perhaps like old soldiers it just faded away ...

NOTE

A fuller version of this essay, with detailed annotations, is available online via the British Universities Newsreel Database (BUND), www.bufvc.ac.uk/databases/newsreels/resources/texts.html.

Everything that Constitutes Life: Pathe Cinemagazines 1918–1969

Jenny Hammerton

Cinemagazines were a regular feature of cinema programmes between 1918 and 1969, and were closely allied to the newsreels, often being produced by the same companies. Issued weekly or monthly, they were generally concerned with the light-hearted and the ephemeral, and as a consequence have enjoyed little critical attention. Jenny Hammerton is Senior Cataloguer at British Pathe, and in this specially-commissioned piece gives a history of the British cinemagazine, concentrating on those produced by Pathe, in which she argues for their re-evaluation.

Cinemagoers attending screenings of MONTY PYTHON'S LIFE OF BRIAN in 1979 were treated to an extra item squeezed between trailers, ads for ice cream and the main feature; a travel film called AWAY FROM IT ALL recommending Venice as a holiday destination. A laudatory voiceover praised the city's waterways, architecture and scenery. Some cinemagoers probably groaned at the prospect of what appeared to be a dull travelogue, but then gradually recognised the voice of John Cleese as his patter descended into a diatribe against the detestable gondolas.

The travelogue would have been a recognisable format to viewers of a certain age who remembered the *Pathe Pictorial*, a weekly cinemagazine shown in cinemas all over Britain until the late 1960s. Foreign destinations regularly made their way into the screen magazine along with films of popular entertainers, the latest fashions and crazy inventions. The cinema screen became a 'window on the world' for ten minutes or so, as a trip on 'Pathe's magic carpet' took us far and wide in search of the novel, amusing and strange. Although extinct by the time Monty Python parodied the format in the late seventies, these short informative films had been a part of the full supporting programme for over fifty years, since 1918.

The cinemagazine was a fun and frivolous entity combining entertainment and edification, with humour and an eye for the bizarre. Although the subject matter and narrative tone of the cinemagazine was very different to that of the newsreel, its format was very similar. It ran for around ten minutes with several separate items within each 'magazine'. These items were not linked by theme or story line but were self contained entities. The unwritten motto of the cinemagazine was 'variety is the spice of life', and items as diverse as fashion parades, animals performing tricks and demonstrations of household gadgets might be contained in the same issue.

The longevity of the form suggests that like the newsreel, the cinemagazine was enjoyed by audiences and valued by exhibitors. Many cinemagazines were available between the late 1910s and late 1960s including the *Ideal Cinemagazine* (1926–1938), the *Gaumont Mirror* (1927–1931), and *Look at Life* (1959–1969).[1] This article seeks to explore the success of the cinemagazine focusing on those made by Pathe, and to celebrate the form as a revealing insight into the daily life and preoccupations of the great British public between 1918 and 1969.

PATHE PICTORIAL 1918–1969 – 'BRITAIN'S FIRST CINEMAGAZINE'

Pathé's Weekly Pictorial, as was only to be expected, is being snapped up right and left. In every way does it meet the views and requirements of the keen and progressive exhibitor, and once it is released there will be few cinema theatres throughout the United Kingdom that will not be showing it to their patrons.[2]

So announced a publicity puff for Britain's first weekly cinemagazine. Although it was optimistic to expect that the reel would be shown in 'almost all' cinemas throughout the country, the *Pathe Pictorial* and other cinemagazines certainly became a staple ingredient of most cinema programmes for the next five decades.

When the reel was first released it seems that there was some confusion amongst cinema exhibitors as to what this strange new entity actually was. Pathe took great pains to differentiate the new product from their successful weekly newsreel and show that they were offering something new and exciting. An explanation was planted in the trade press:

'Pathe's Weekly Pictorial' … is a moving picture journal made up of interest and educational items which will include exquisite Pathécolor subjects, also cartoons, fashions, novelties, etc forming a delightful kaleidoscope of film subjects that will appeal to the senses and delight the eye … Think of the *Gazette* as a daily moving picture newspaper, and the *Pictorial* as a weekly illustrated. Both are unique and distinctive in their different ways, and the *Weekly Pictorial* ought soon to be able to reckon on as great a following as the *Gazette*.[3]

The concept of the *Pathe Pictorial* being a moving picture magazine was a useful *aide memoire* which persisted throughout the production's life. Names of newsreels and cinemagazines often echoed print counterparts, there were many magazines which used the name Pictorial, for example: the *Family Pictorial*, *Gentleman's Pictorial* and *Pictorial Mirror*. As precursors to the *Pathe Gazette*, *Warwick Bioscope*

Chronicle and *Gaumont Graphic* newsreels, early twentieth century newspapers included the *Westminster Gazette, Daily Graphic* and *Daily Chronicle*. In a 1926 article entitled, 'Hints to the Programme Builder' the relationship between these print and screen entertainments is expressed to the cinema exhibitor as follows:

> … a very large proportion of the population, however much they may enjoy a novel, like to be able to entertain themselves with magazines and newspapers. As a parallel, the same people, regular kinema goers though they may be, definitely demand and appreciate the shorter items.[4]

It took a while for the *Pathe Pictorial* cinemagazine to find its niche. From a contemporary report[5] the first issue seems to have featured an odd combination of subject matter. The reel comprised four items. IN THE GOOD OLD DAYS was a reused news item showing the King at Ascot five years earlier in 1913. This was followed by a story entitled HOW FRENCH FISHERMEN SUCCEED IN SPITE OF THE WAR featuring armed motorboats and hydroplanes protecting fishing boats from submarine attack. A Pathecolor[6] item showed the Haute Vienne region of France in FROM LIMOSIN TO QUERCY and the reel concluded with a cartoon entitled JOHN BULL. Although at first sight a bizarre combination of items, this

Pathe Pictorial title design.

British Pathe

pioneering issue set the pattern pretty well. The 'newsy' sounding French fishermen story seems a little out of place, but a look back to events of the past was a regular motif of cinemagazines to follow. The Pathecolor travelogue became a regular feature of Pathe's early cinemagazines as did cartoons.[7] The template had been cut.

The cinemagazine began its life as a miscellany of odds and ends and continued in the same vein for over fifty years. The phrase 'all human life is here' might have been invented to describe the form. The British branch of the company bought in or exchanged film with Pathe operations overseas, thus many of the films featured in the *Pathe Pictorial* show life in foreign countries. Other popular strands were films of sportsmen, explanations of various trades and occupations, and demonstrations of large industrial machines and modes of transport. That the reel was mostly directed at men is quite obvious from its general subject matter. For example: THE LOG ROUND UP (1926) shows the logging industry in Norway, A MAMMOTH OF THE AIR (c.1921) details facts and figures about the Caproni flying boat, DRYLAND SKIPPERS – A FASCINATING HOBBY (c.1921) shows model boats being demonstrated and THE SWINGER (c.1925) contains footage of a new swing bridge in operation. Of course, some women would have shared an interest in civil engineering and the timber trade, however I think it is fair to conclude that the *Pictorial* mostly featured traditionally male oriented subjects. Pathe may have realised before 1921 that some female cinemagoers had different tastes to their men friends but it took until then for the company to plug the gap with a cinemagazine specifically 'for women' (see section below on *Eve's Film Review*).

Pathe's claim in later years that the *Pictorial* was the first cinemagazine is untrue – the portmanteau style 'interest film' had been around for a while.[8] In the *Bioscope* of 7 March 1918 there is a review of a release called 'Screen-Magazine' produced by a company called Trans-Atlantic.[9] This predates the first issue of the *Pathe Pictorial* and a list of its contents shows that quirky and unrelated choice of subject matter was not unique to the Pathe production:

LIFE-SAVING PRACTICE WITH THE ROCKET APPARATUS
KEEPING BABY WELL
CHARACTER DOORKNOB
X-RAY PHOTOGRAPHY OF THE HUMAN SKELETON

However, it seems that Pathe's was the first British weekly cinemagazine and its success prompted Gaumont to follow suit in 1919 with a cinemagazine called *Around the Town* and later, the *Gaumont Mirror*.

The '*Pathe Weekly Pictorial*' had two mottoes. The first showed the intention of the filmmakers to present a global perspective: 'Pathe Pictorial Puts the World before You'. The second hinted at its edificatory impulse: 'To See Much is to Learn Much'. The idea that there was much to be learned from these short films was expressed by the reel's creator and editor Frederick Watts, when he stated the following:

> We realise our primary business is to entertain, amuse and interest our audiences – though, if at the same time anyone wishes to learn anything new from the pictures (and all of us are able to) he or she is very welcome.[10]

The promise that the reel was educational may well have been a selling technique; however, there does seem to be a real desire to show the wonders of the world around us through these short films. Audiences seeing films such as CURACAO – A CAMERA VISIT TO LITTLE HOLLAND IN THE LAZY CARIBBEAN (1929) and BORNEO AND THE PYGMY CANNIBALS (1929) were being given a glimpse into other cultures and lifestyles. HOW WE FLY (1931) is an attempt to explain theories of aviation, PYRAMIDS OF CORNWALL (1929) details processes involved in extracting China Clay from pits in the West Country and WALKING ON THE WATER (1930) explains how insects can balance on liquid thanks to the phenomenon of surface tension.

EVE'S FILM REVIEW 1921–1933 – 'THE WEEKLY FILM FOR WOMEN'

In 1921 Pathe decided to offer exhibitors a third product to accompany their *Gazette* and *Pictorial*: they could now supply a second cinemagazine entitled *Eve's Film Review*.[11] The *Pathe Gazette* newsreel was issued twice weekly in the 1920s and from 1921 the cinema manager could vary his cinemagazine programme by taking the *Pathe Pictorial* for half a week and *Eve's Film Review* for the other. Pathe differentiated their new product by featuring subject matter designed to please the female cinemagoer. *Eve's Film Review* focused on fashion, beauty, health, women's sports and home crafts – very much tying in with the subject matter of women's print magazines of the day. The launch of this exciting new entertainment was reported in the *Bioscope* as follows:

> The latest venture of the company is the production of a weekly film dealing in a novel and interesting manner with all matters of interest to women ... Everything that appeals to the innate Eve in women will be covered by this feature, which in view of the large percentage of ladies who consistently patronise cinemas should supply a long-felt want. Hints and advice on the domestic arts, such as cooking and dressmaking, will be shown. Peeps at famous stage stars in their dressing rooms, and women at work in novel and interesting occupations, are a few of the subjects which will be dealt with.[12]

British Pathe

From *Eve's Film Review.*

Pathe's rival Gaumont recognised the impact that a weekly film directed specifically at women might have on their sales. A full page advert in *The Cinema* proclaimed that *Around the Town* was: 'The original review of fashion, the Arts and the theatre' and claimed that although it had 'particular interest for women' it also held 'an additional interest for men'.

Every week for twelve years a new issue of *Eve's Film Review* was seen in cinemas and subject matter remained fairly constant. Mixed in with fashion and beauty items there were illustrations of unusual jobs for the fair sex, feminine sporting events and reports of the achievements of extraordinary women. As a kaleido-scopic reflection of the working lives, leisure pursuits and home life of women of the 1920s and early 1930s, *Eve's Film Review* is a truly inspirational and remarkable series. When the weekly film for women ceased production at the end of 1933 the *Pathe Sound Pictorial* seized the mantle and featured a regular spot called 'Feminine Pictorialities'. These items were announced as 'Something for The Ladies' and featured subjects familiar from *Eve's Film Review* including fashion, women's sports and home crafts. The items were usually only one or two minutes long in comparison to the full ten minutes audiences had come to expect from *Eve's Film Review*. This later strand seems rather an aside to the female spectator. There would never again be a weekly cinemagazine made specifically for the female audience.

PATHETONE WEEKLY 1930–1941 – 'VARIETY AND THE WORLD BEFORE YOU'

The press announcement in the *Bioscope* of 26 March 1930 which heralded the forthcoming release of Pathe's third cinemagazine seems to suggest that the reel would be a cross-breed; part newsreel, part cinemagazine:

> Harry Sanders and Fred Watts are working night and day upon subjects of great novelty interest in order that each edition of this new publication may contain, in addition to striking reproductions of the latest news, many features which will shed light upon matter quaint, grave and gay.[13]

Boundaries separating suitable subject matter for news and cinemagazine stories had always been hazy so it is not so surprising that Pathe believed that they could combine the two in their newest offering. A review in the 12 March 1930 issue of the *Bioscope* illustrates how in the early 1930s the newsreel was featuring material traditionally the domain of the cinemagazine:

> *Pathe's Sound Gazette.* An extremely varied and interesting number includes singing by Hughes Macklin, the famous tenor; the unveiling at Nice of the memorial to Mistral, the poet of Provence; George Clarke and Company in the amusing whiskers song, from 'Darling, I Love You'; concluding with finely photographed pictures of the massive interior of St Bartholemew's Church, Smithfield ...[14]

The producers of the *Pathetone Weekly* cinemagazine may have had aspirations of making the reel more respectable through the inclusion of more topical 'news' items. The first issue featured only two items. The first was 'an exclusive sound picture' of the Grand National commentated by Geoffrey Gilbey, racing correspondent to the *Daily Express*. High profile horse races were traditional battle-grounds for the newsreel companies and Pathe had exclusive rights to film this particular event. The other story featured the legendary musical instrument, the theremin.[15]

Under the heading 'Pathetone Goes Nap' (a horse racing reference suggesting that Pathe are on to a winner) a review of the first issue of the new series shows that the reel had its fans:

> *Pathétone Weekly*, the latest sound news reel, launched this week by First National Pathé, has scored top honours everywhere it has been shown. At the

Regal, it was warmly received by patrons, who were highly entertained by the thrills and spills of the Grand National. When the news reel opened on Monday it was so popular that Captain Simpson, the manager had to put it on again at the end of the performance, in response to numerous requests from all sections of the house.[16]

Despite its early dabblings with 'news', *Pathetone Weekly* soon settled down to the less topical material generally associated with the form. It also settled down to the format of four or five short items per reel rather than two long items. Most issues included a musical performance or comedy 'turn' and it is these acts for which the reel is best known today. Pathe were picking up on the early sound cinema's penchant for musical entertainers and variety style film presentations. Pathe wired up its Wardour Street studio for sound and thanks to Pathetone, performances by Leslie Sarony, Gertrude Lawrence, Robb Wilton and Gus Elen amongst many others have been preserved for posterity.[17] The reel also featured subject matter familiar to earlier cinemagazines such as fashion reports, travelogues and animal stories.

In an article called 'World's Best Variety Talent in Pathe Pictorial' which appeared in 1935, *Pathetone Weekly* and *Pathe Pictorial* are given high praise. That most of the article sounds like a press release is probably not a coincidence. Much of it seems to be a rehash of a plug for the *Pathe Pictorial* and *Eve's Film Review* written by Frederick Watts in 1928.[18] The piece begins:

> Eighteen years ago the 'Pathe Pictorial' the recognised first screen magazine, first saw the light of day. At a later date the 'Pathetone Weekly' made its appearance. The history of the development of the magazine 'short' is interwoven in these two films seen weekly by millions all over the British Isles. Every camera development and novelty may be said at one time or other to have originated in various forms through the medium of these weeklies. The cartoon vogue, slow motion, stop motion, colour sections, reversal photography, multiple exposure novelties, sporting series, fashion, and all forms of industrial and scientific progress have all been featured.[19]

Although using the hyperbole of the publicity puff (the claims that all these things originated within the cinemagazine are somewhat overblown) there is truth in the fact that trick and novelty effects continued to find a space in the cinemagazine when they had all but disappeared from the feature films they accompanied. The cinemagazine was a film format that gave filmmakers immense scope. If something seemed interesting, it could be filmed. As Andrew Buchanan, producer of the *Ideal Cinemagazine* writing in 1932, observed:

The fact that the interest reel is non-fictional is its greatest advantage over the dramatic feature. It can bring to the screen places near and far, industries, sports, clothes, everything which constitutes Life, without straining to find a reason for doing so.[20]

SOUND AND COLOUR IN THE PATHE PICTORIAL

With the coming of sound, the *Pathe Pictorial* began to feature variety acts, musicians, comedians and novelty performers. Apart from these additions, the subject matter of the *Pictorial* remained pretty consistent. The tone of the reel changed somewhat with the coming of war in 1939. The cinemagazine became a place for patriotic statements and rousing singalongs such as 'We're Gonna Hang Out the Washing on the Siegfried Line' and a song encouraging cinema patrons to give scrap to help win the war. Syd Walker sings the chorus holding up the words so the audience can sing with him. Scenic shots of picturesque British villages and photogenic landscapes were often used to illustrate songs such as 'This Is Worth Fighting For'.

In 1955 the motto of the *Pathe Pictorial* became 'Picturing this Colourful World' when the reel burst into colour. It is obvious that Pathe sought out stories that would maximise the potential of Technicolor. Fashion items came to the fore with unusual crafts and hobbies also being popular colourful subjects. In the mid 1960s Pathe picked up on the Swinging Sixties phenomenon and began filming bands performing their latest ditties, harking back to the glory days of the Pathetones. These films are precursors to the 'pop video' and bands caught on celluloid include the Unit Four Plus Two, the Bonzo Dog Doo Dah Band and Pink Floyd. Always having a soft spot for glamour girls, the Pathe cameramen managed to capture 'The Windmill Girls' getting up to all sorts of antics in their vibrant costumes.

Other favourite subjects include outrageous artist Roland Emett and the fabulously photogenic crimper Teasy-Weasy who not only shows us the latest fashions in hairstyles but hair colour too – including green! Just as in the *Pictorial*'s earlier incarnations the bizarre, weird and quirky were presented to cinemagoers as aperitifs to the main feature.

The travelogue aspect – always a staple of the cinemagazine – increased greatly in the colour *Pathe Pictorial* with whole editions of the reel being given over to explorations of such destinations as Las Vegas, Niagara Falls and the Canary Islands. As the reel began to run out of steam in the late 1960s, the travelogue seemed to become a fall back position – it is no surprise that Monty Python chose this element of the cinemagazine to parody. The life seemed to have been knocked out of the cinemagazine with bland, humourless commentaries and stock-shot style footage of foreign destinations. Perhaps cinemagoers no longer needed the cinemagazine to show them the wonders of the world around them now that they had television in their homes. Alas, the *Pathe Pictorial* finally left our screens in 1969 after over 50 years of entertaining and informative slices of life on film.

SEEKING THE ODD AND CURIOUS AND ACHIEVING NOTHING?

Although the British documentary movement is popularly believed to have begun in the late 1920s with the John Grierson school, it is worth remembering that the cinemagazine had been a forum for short, informative films of everyday life since the late 1910s. The cinemagazine reached far wider audiences than any of the documentaries made by Grierson and his colleagues and for some was an ideal format for social education. However, those making the cinemagazine had a duty to entertain their audiences without being overly serious and some saw this prioritising of entertainment over education as a failing in the form.

D.F. Taylor launched an attack on what he saw as the lack of depth to cinemagazine stories in an article in *Cinema Quarterly*. He begins:

> It is impossible to define Public Opinion or know 'what the public wants' though we do know to-day that there is a growing audience who want to know, an audience who demand more in their relaxation than just entertainment. Financial crises and world economic collapses beset us, and affect us individually. Far from seeking an opiate, there is a large body of people who want to know more about this crazy, chaotic world.

Cinema Quarterly was a magazine with close links to the Documentary Movement and it is clear that Taylor believed that the cinemagazine should be more serious in its edificatory purpose. He writes:

> Through the screen magazine, the thin end of the wedge of knowledge could be given to the waiting audiences, To-day it is the lowest type of film produced. In form it owes much to 'Tit-Bits' and 'Answers', a speedy collection of odds and ends from here and there, designed to pass ten minutes and then to be forgotten. Its constant seeking after the odd and the curious satisfies the unintelligent lust for curiosity, but achieves nothing.[21]

Taylor's argument is essentially the view of the highbrow. He believes that the captive audience should be given something meaty to mull over. He suggests that the cinemagazine should have closer links with the newsreel and believed it should reconstruct the motivation of political events seen in the newsreel, cover social problems such as unemployment, developments of industry, new theories of education and innovations in social services. But audiences often resisted blatant attempts to 'educate'. *The March of Time* was a weekly presentation which attempted to look in some depth at the kind of issues critics such as D.F. Taylor might have considered worthy. Leslie Halliwell's mention of the reel in *Seats in All Parts* suggests how, in his experience audiences reacted to this attempt to educate as well as to entertain:

> *The March of Time* came in with a flourish of critical acclaim, but at twenty minutes it seemed dry and overlong to us, telling us things we did not want to know about countries of which we had scarcely heard. What we did enjoy about it, for we then knew that the endurance test was over, was the spontaneous chorus which rose from stalls and circle alike to echo the commentator's last portentous 'Time Marches On'.[22]

ENJOYMENT OF THE CINEMAGAZINE

That the format had lasted so long has to be proof that cinemagazines were valued by exhibitors and enjoyed by many cinemagoers. For the exhibitor of course it could have just been a handy 'filler', something to plump up his programme to show he was offering value for money. For audiences it may have been a chance to grab some popcorn or chat with their friends before settling down to the main feature.

Contemporary audience reaction to the cinemagazine has been hard to find. Most discussion in fan magazines and the trade press relates to feature films rather than the peripheral parts of the programme. However, as part of an oral history project investigating cinemagoing in the 1930s, Denis Houlston recounted his memories of the 'full supporting programme'. The transcripts of these spoken memories are written in a style to suggest local dialects.

> … looking back at the programmes, there again … you got such a load of little bits, you got a big film but then there were all the little bits and I estimate, lookin back, you used to get about seven different shawrt films to, to boost the programme. So [pause] if you didn't liike any of them you didn't suffer very long because they wouldn't be on for very long!

Mr Houlston goes on to state that cinemagazines, as well as newsreels, were definitely enjoyed by cinemagoers:

> Ah mean this is your only way of seeing things happening, the Launching of a Thing, or a crash, or Aa think the Hindenburg went up in flames in those days, Aa might be wrong, and you got the newsreel and that it was really something to see but em nowadays you see it all on television you're blasé so. But Pathe, Pathe News also used to run short films about quarter of an hour or something like that of music-hall acts, a bit of entertainment. You might get a couple in that time and we liked those because you got clowns and eh unicyclists and jugglers which we enjoyed.[23]

As a filmic entity which existed outside the conventions and boundaries of the narrative form, the cinemagazine is a rich and fertile source of enlightenment as well as entertainment. A surprising number of these films still exist: there are over 13,500 in the British Pathe collection alone. The cinemagazine offers a fascinating insight into 'real life' through its documentary style. We can learn a great deal about how life was lived in the past and can discern much about the way non-narrative films were constructed before what became known as the British Documentary Movement came into being. Far from being an 'opiate for the people' the cinemagazine is a complex and fascinating format worthy of a great deal of further investigation.

NOTES

1. See the Appendices to this Reader for a chronological listing of the main British cinemagazines alongside the British newsreels.
2. Anon, 'Trade Topics,' *The Film-Renter*, 2 March 1918, p. 13.
3. Anon, 'Trade Topics,' *The Film-Renter*, 9 March 1918, p. 12.
4. Anon, 'Hints to the Programme Builder,' Newsreel and Shorts Supplement, *Kinematograph Weekly*, 28 March 1926, p. 3.
5. The first issue of *Pathe Pictorial* is not known to survive. British Pathe's collection of cinemagazine material is rather patchy until the early 1920s.
6. 'Pathecolor' was the trade name for a stencil colour process devised by the French branch of the Pathe company. Many of Pathe's cinemagazines featured one Pathecolor item; these were almost exclusively travelogue-style pieces or fashion reports.
7. The *Pathe Pictorial* featured animated series with such characters as 'Sammy and Sausage', 'Jerry the Troublesome Tyke' and 'Bobby Bumps'. The Pathe cinemagazine *Eve's Film Review* launched the hugely popular 'Felix the Cat' cartoons in Britain.
8. The short weekly films under discussion here were variously known as 'screen magazines' and 'cinemagazines', although they were occasionally also referred to under the wider banner of 'interest films'. For the purposes of this article they are referred to as 'cinemagazines' unless given another name by contemporary sources.
9. *Bioscope*, 7 March 1918, p. 34.
10. Quotation from a press release entitled 'Just "Pic and Eve" by Editor Watts' in the *Pathe Pictorial* and *Eve's Film Review* correspondence file, British Pathe. This press release is a fascinating insight into the aims of the creator of these cinemagazines; it was written in response to a memo dated 24 October 1928 from a Mr Judge of First National Pathe Limited asking Mr Watts to write an article on the production policy of the two cinemagazines. Some of the material is this press release was used in a much later article, 'World's Best Variety Talent in Pathe Periodicals,' *Kinematograph Weekly*, 14 November 1935, p. 25.
11. An in-depth study of the weekly film for women can be found in Jenny Hammerton, *For Ladies Only? Eve's Film Review: Pathe Cinemagazine 1921–1933* (Hastings: The Projection Box, 2001).
12. *Bioscope*, 28 April 1921, p. 48.
13. Anon, 'Pathetone on March – New F.N.P. Reel,' *Bioscope*, 26 March 1930, p. 37.

14. Anon, 'Short Features,' *Bioscope*, 12 March 1930, p. 40.

15. Unfortunately, the first *Pathetone* issue does not exist in the British Pathe vaults.

16. Anon, 'Pathetone Goes Nap,' *To-Day's Cinema News and Property Gazette*, 3 April 1930, p. 8.

17. See Denis Gifford, *Entertainers in British Films: A Century of Showbiz in the Cinema* (Trowbridge: Flicks Books, 1998), which lists most of the performers in Pathe cinemagazines. Howard Thomas, Producer-in-Chief at Pathe stated that the performers were paid ten guineas a time to record their acts. He writes, 'Antique cameras and sound apparatus held together by string, recorded performances which, in spire of primitive film quality, have become little classics and a regular source of income for the Pathe library from compilers of nostalgic television programmes'. Howard Thomas, *With an Independent Air: Encounters During a Lifetime of Broadcasting* (London: Weidenfeld and Nicolson, 1977), p. 123.

18. The original press release is held amonst original Pathe paperwork. It is transcribed in full as Appendix 1 in Hammerton, *For Ladies Only?*

19. 'World's Best Variety Talent in Pathe Periodicals', op. cit.

20. Andrew Buchanan, *Films, The Way of the Cinema* (London: Pitman, 1932), p. 187.

21. D.F. Taylor, 'Screen Magazines,' *Cinema Quarterly*, Winter 1933–4, p. 93.

22. Leslie Halliwell, *Seats in All Parts: Half a Lifetime at the Movies* (London: Granada Publishing, 1985).

23. Extracts from transcript T95–18, quoted in Annette Kuhn, 'Memories of cinema-going in the 1930s,' *Journal of Popular British Cinema*, issue 2, 1999, p. 102.

A Game Women Cannot Play ...?
Women and British Newsreels

Sarah Easen

The aim of this specially-commissioned article is twofold. Firstly, it examines the way women were portrayed in the general newsreels, as opposed to the specific cinemagazines produced for women, concentrating on the peak years of the 1920s, 1930s and 1940s. Secondly, and perhaps more importantly it provides a brief survey of the women who worked in the industry as commentators, members of the editorial staff and in post-production.

Newsreels in Britain ran for almost seventy years, outlasting the might of the Empire that nurtured them as well as providing much of the material for their twice-weekly screenings. The abiding impression of the personnel involved in putting the newsreels together is of intrepid, adventurous, hard-living men's men; a world in which men were men and women were most definitely the weaker and gentler sex. This was reflected in the employment of women in the less glamorous and lower profile jobs of administration and post-production; stereotypical duties for women in the film industry since the film business had begun. Consequently, there is very little to be found in published histories of the five major newsreel companies: British Movietone, British Paramount, Gaumont-British, Pathe and Universal, about the role women played in bringing the news to the screen. Nor are many newsreel women mentioned in the film-trade weeklies, which frequently documented the tricks of newsreel editors to get a 'scoop' and the exploits of their cameramen to get a story. My access to the newsreel company archives has been limited so this survey of women involved in the newsreel industry is by no means comprehensive. These research limitations coupled with the lack of credit information on the newsreels themselves means that this article may be a little sketchy in places, but it will begin to document the otherwise neglected roles of women in this sector of the media.

WOMEN'S PORTRAYAL IN BRITISH NEWSREELS
While it is not within the remit of this article to examine comprehensively the changing portrayal of women in the newsreels from 1910–1979, the 1920s and 1930s should be singled out as especially interesting. Not only was this the peak time for

the reception of the newsreel, it was also a time when more women than men attended the cinema. In order to understand the representation of women in newsreels it is important to acknowledge this gender breakdown of the cinema audience and their reaction to the newsreels. By the end of the 1910s, it was an acknowledged fact that women comprised the majority of the cinema audience, making up more than fifty percent of the weekly audience by 1917.[1] Indirect evidence suggests that this trend was maintained throughout the 1920s.[2] While fan magazines regularly polled their readers about film stars and their pictures, there is very little about the reception of the early newsreels by either gender. However, a survey conducted by Sidney Bernstein in 1927 divulged that over eighty-two percent of men and more than eighty-seven percent of women liked 'News' pictures.[3] According to Nick Hiley, the trend of more women cinemagoers than men continued in to the 1930s and 1940s:

> In 1929 it was estimated that, in an average audience, 'roughly sixty percent are women'. *The Social Survey of Merseyside* in 1934 demonstrated that married women visited the cinema more frequently than their husbands, and when B. Seebohm Rowntree surveyed cinema audiences in York in 1939 he estimated that 'of the adults about 75 per cent are women'. The disproportionate attraction of the cinema for women persisted into wartime, and a survey of civilian cinema attendance in 1943 revealed them to be making 2.3 visits a month by comparison with 1.9 visits made by men; as a result, they still accounted for 60% of the adult audience.[4]

However, by the 1930s, specialist news theatres with thirty-minute programmes of news and cinemagazines were springing up around London. Contemporary observations noted that the news theatres attracted more men than women with the majority of the programmes devoted to more 'masculine' interests such as sport and military manoeuvres; thirty percent of the programme alone was devoted to sport. The question was also raised of whether the surfeit of men in the news-theatres was responsible for the amount of sport shown or whether the amount of sport shown put women off using the news-theatres.[5] The 'Better Newsreels Campaign' run by a fan magazine in the early 1930s asked its readers what was wrong with newsreel content. The campaign editor, John Gammie, was amazed that over half his responses came from women, adding that 'their comments and criticisms have shown that they take a lively and intelligent interest in the newsreel as in the rest of a cinema programme'.[6] Three things stood out as objectionable to women viewers: machinery demonstrations, sport and accidents/fatalities. Popular items included anything to do with royalty and interviews with famous female flyers. Interestingly, by the end of the decade, it looked as though the newsreel companies had become aware of their programming flaws; an analysis of a news-theatre's programme content indicated that sport had lost its position as the most covered item and over the period of a year it accounted for only five percent of the programme.[7]

Although women made up the majority of the audience, very few newsreels catered specifically for women. Only one company, Pathe, recognised a gap in the market and in 1921 released *Eve's Film Review* which ran until 1933. It consisted primarily of fashion and beauty items, camera interviews with female celebrities including artists and authors, domestic tips, handicrafts, new dance steps and even some sporting items. A survey of all general newsreel stories produced between 1920 and 1929 from the British Universities Newsreel Database (BUND) reveals that over half the stories featuring women were sporting items, particularly women's hockey, golf, football, athletics and motor speed records. Following a long way behind with fifteen percent were beauty contests and fashion items. Interestingly the next most common category was stories about female members of parliament, councillors, mayors and demonstrators. However, this apparent celebration of women's liberation was not all it seemed. *Topical Budget* seemed especially irritated by the sporting female with titles such as A GAME WOMEN CANNOT PLAY (issue 787–2, 27 September 1926) referring to the fact that women were not strong enough to lift the heavy wooden balls in lawn billiards; EVE AGAIN INTRUDES! (issue 877–1, 14/6/1928) showing dirt track racing at Crystal Palace with women motorcyclists and EVE ON ADAM'S TRACK (issue 878–2, 25 June 1928) featuring two women motor racing drivers at Brooklands: Miss Maconochie and Mrs Victor Bruce competing against Malcolm Campbell. Not all newsreels were quite so damning. Unusually, the relatively reactionary *Universal News* championed equal pay for women in a bizarre item about pole squatting. The commentator says, 'For the longest squatters there's a prize. The man gets – £10, and the girl £5. Puzzle why does a girl get less than a man?' (issue 165, 8 February 1932), and a *British Paramount News* item titled TOO OLD AT THIRTY suggests that such a statement is absurd, commenting, 'To the unmarried woman of thirty work has ceased to become a stop-gap and has become a career: consequently she is more interested in her job than is the youngster. In occupations where con-scientious work is called for, the wise firm employs the woman over thirty' (issue 529, 23 March 1936).

In 1925, the first items on women aviators appeared and by 1929 accounted for seven percent of all newsreel stories of the 1920s. This continued throughout the 1930s with reports on the flying records broken by both male and female aviation pioneers. Movietone, Paramount and Universal all featured stories throughout the decade on Amelia Earhart, Amy Johnson, Jean Batten, Joan Meakin, Beryl Markham, Peggy Salaman and the Duchess of Bedford. There were also several stories in the early 1930s on the feats of female parachutists. These aviation story titles lean towards the patronising with their puns on women's acts of bravery and endurance in the air: a *Universal News* story dated May 1931 is called THE (F)AIR

SEX and a *British Paramount News* story dated November 1932 is called A SLIP OF A GIRL while the intertitle reads 'Powder and 'chute. Cool young lady takes no risk with complexion on daring 5,000 feet parachute drop'.

As the Second World War drew closer, the newsreels began to promote the idea of women working for the war effort and throughout 1939–45 there were many stories about the good work they were doing. However this did not mean that the women were regarded as equal to men. They were still patronised as is evidenced by a *Pathe Gazette* story about women roof spotting for enemy aircraft on the East Coast. The commentary puns that, 'These good lookers fit themselves out in warm hooded coats for protection against approaching storms' (issue 40/78, 27 September, 1940). *British Paramount News* also seemed surprised that 'girls' could be trained to do a man's job; in a story on the training of draughtswomen the commentary says, 'At first it was thought they could only be taught unskilled work. Soon they were tackling better jobs, thereby releasing men for the fighting services' (issue 1032, 20 June 1941). *British Paramount News* also seemed surprised that women drivers were not harming the war effort with a story on women supplying ATS convoys to the army in which the commentator notes that the women can 'tackle anything up to 30-hundred-weight trucks, and they're so good that accidents are almost unheard of' (issue 1037, 5 February 1941).

Once the war ended the newsreels tended to return to their staple stories for women: beauty contests (although I'm sure the men in the audience didn't mind either!), domestic items, fashion, women politicians, sportswomen and celebrities. As television began to take their audience, the newsreels became less forums for news and more magazine like in their make up. With the liberated 1960s and 1970s, stories became more light-hearted as can be seen by a story released by *British Movietone News* in 1969 called BEAUTIFUL BOYS. The intertitle reads 'While women have been busily assuming equal rights and opportunities with men, the latter have been acquiring a whole lot of feminine vanities. We visit a Men's Beauty Clinic in Paris where facials and massage are part of the plan to make Dad more beautiful to live with' (issue 2115A, 18 December 1969). The item goes on to show women parachuting and taming lions before showing men exercising, having manicures, pedicures, facials, massages and trying on wigs. Equality in newsreel terms at last! Ten years later the last newsreel company in Britain, British Movietone, screened its last issue.

WOMEN WORKING IN BRITISH NEWSREELS

The position of women in British society changed dramatically from the early days of the newsreels in 1910. By the close of the newsreels at the end of the 1970s women had relatively more freedom, both in the home and the work place, than they had sixty years previously. Although working class women had been part of the work force for many years, as the twentieth century progressed more women had the choice of actually having a professional career. By the end of the 1910s, a woman MP had a seat in the House of Commons; the first woman barrister was admitted to the Bar in the early 1920s and by the end of the decade women had finally achieved suffrage in Britain. However, within the film industry women were not making as much headway. A handful of women filmmakers were writing, directing and producing feature films in the UK, USA and Europe but not to the same extent as men. There were also a number of women shooting actuality footage; although they tended to be wealthy, as in the case of Jessica Borthwick, a general's daughter who took film of the 1913 Balkan War which she later screened during lecture tours.[8] It is also alleged that Will Barker (owner of the Warwick Trading Company) hired women camera operators to shoot topicals requiring large camera teams in the early teens, for fifteen shillings a week – half what a male camera operator would get![9]

Women were also involved in the non-fiction sector of the film industry: camera-man Joe Rosenthal's sister, Alice, who was sales manager and ran the office at the Warwick Trading Company (before Will Barker's time), later set up her own company, A.R. Films. Abby Meehan produced and edited the *Kinemacolor Fashion Gazette* for the Scala Theatre in 1913 as well as filming a fashion revue in association with the *Evening News*.[10] Actuality footage was also shot by women travelling abroad, but they tended to be wealthy and the films did not necessarily receive wide distribution. The first woman to make any impact in the non-fiction arena was Mary Field who was involved in the making of documentary and educational films in the 1920s and 1930s. The 1930s also provided a fertile breeding ground for many women technicians who were given their start in the business by the growing documentary movement in Britain. Many of these women continued making public information films during the war years which also introduced a whole new generation of women to higher profile roles such as directing and producing. The 1950s were not so kind to women filmmakers although many continued to work, directing sponsored films until the 1960s.

By contrast, the majority of the women in the newsreel business worked quietly behind the scenes in post-production and administration. Unlike their technical counterparts, the cameramen, with their clearly defined media personalities, these women are relatively unknown. By the 1920s, many women were employed in the British film industry as laboratory workers. This was not unusual; Pathé in Paris had employed women for the delicate jobs of hand colouring their films in the early years of the century. Laboratory work involved such jobs as negative and positive developing, grading, stock joining, negative cleaning, positive examining, and negative and positive cutting. In October 1924 a fire broke out in the Wardour Street premises of *Topical Budget*'s laboratories cutting off a number of women laboratory staff on the first floor. Many of them jumped, suffering minor injuries. However Julia Ginsberg was not so lucky and died in hospital a month after the fire.[11] The 1920s were the beginning of the golden era of the newsreel and as mentioned in the first part of this article, included at least one cinemagazine made specifically for women, *Eve's Film Review*. One would think that women would have had some input into this but even *Eve's Film Review* was made by men. In her research on the cinemagazine Jenny Hammerton found reference to only four women, but they were mentioned on the 'Late Sheets' implying that they held menial positions within the company.[12] However one woman does stand out in post-production and that is Helen or 'Nellie' Wiggins, the daughter of Jack Wiggins who worked at Film Laboratories and later became chief cutter at British Movietone. Nellie Wiggins entered the film industry in 1920 working in the cutting rooms and laboratories specialising in newsreel. She was Chief Film Editor on *Universal Talking News* and the cinemagazine that presented pro and con arguments on issues of the day, *Point of View*. After a brief sojourn at a colour newsreel managed by her father, *National News*, she became Chief Film Editor at Pathe from 1946–48. She then set up her own company, Helen Wiggins Films Limited making advertising and television films until the early 1970s. There was at least one other woman working as a cutter in the 1950s and that was Margaret Caley at Pathe, who was featured in a film made in 1953 called PATHE NEWSREEL STAFF AT WORK.

Kay Mander directing a news item on an exhibition for the rebuilding of Bermondsey, for *Worker and Warfront*, September 1944.

Photograph courtesy of the Imperial War Museum, London

During the war, Paul Rotha Productions released the news cinemagazine *Worker and Warfront*. Rotha employed many women as directors, producers and editors and there is evidence that at least one woman shot film for *Worker and Warfront*. Kay Mander, a documentary filmmaker during and after the war, shot at least four stories for the news magazine during 1943 and 1944 so one could assume that other women filmmakers were also receiving *Worker and Warfront* assignments.

At this point in my research I have only found evidence of one woman working in the editorial department of a newsreel company in the peak years of the 1920s–1940s, and that is Sophie Mardon who was editorial assistant at Pathe from 1910–33. There were also several female commentators working in the newsreels during the 1930s. Often they would only commentate on a single newsreel which required a 'woman's touch' such as fashion items. Shelia Borrett and Dorothy Hope commentated for *British Movietone News* fashion stories in 1935, as did Beryl de Querton, an actress, who also worked on 'feminine' stories as well as society and royal items and stayed at Movietone until 1938. Jasmine Bligh commentated for *British Movietone News* in 1938 before her career in television. Vera Clive Smith worked on the commentaries for *War Pictorial News* from 1940–46.

Otherwise women worked primarily as secretaries, finance assistants, clerks or in the film libraries. Pam Turner worked for Paramount, and then became Chief Librarian at Visnews and Reuters, Millie Dobson worked in the British Movietone library in 1950 and her colleague, Patricia Holder remained at British Movietone from 1951–70 becoming Chief Librarian. Peggy Noble was Office Manager at British Movietone from 1938–49 and Jackie McCarten worked as Ted Candy's secretary when he moved to British Movietone as production head in the 1960s. In his BECTU Oral History interview he remembers her with great fondness for her hard work and ability to 'make a cotton reel do the work of a tank'.[13] He added that if there was a subject he knew nothing about she would research it, have the information to him the following day and that he could always rely on her.

It was not until the later period of the newsreels, the 1950s through to the 1970s, that women began to reach higher positions. Winifred Cooper was news editor for *Pathe News* from 1946–47, but little more than that is known about her. Grace Field was a production manager and then news editor for *Pathe News* from the early 1950s to 1962. One of her colleagues thought her pleasant, almost apologetic but not very bright. He also thought that she was lacking in the technical expertise that he thought important when making a contact for a story.[14] When the editor, Tommy Cummins retired, Field was moved sideways and eventually took early retirement. Jane Baldwin was originally a secretary for the cameraman, Paul Wyand at *British Movietone News*. She also commentated on three stories in a 1968 issue of the newsreel: EUROPEAN CUP – UNITED TRIUMPH (Manchester United's 4–0 victory over Benfica in the European Cup), TOP GEAR FOR GETAWAY MALES (men's fashions) and 1968'S FANTASTIC DERBY (the Epsom Derby). She eventually made it to the heady heights of assistant news editor in the mid-1970s. In over fifty years of the newsreels, only two women reached executive positions. Miss D.M. Vaughan was the General Secretary of the Association of News and Specialised Theatres in the 1940s. Unfortunately I have not been able to trace her subsequent career trajectory. Perhaps of greater importance is Doris N. Burns-Shearer who started as typist at the Newsreel Association and became its Acting Secretary from 1947–48. In 1949 she was promoted to Secretary becoming part of the decision-making process involving newsreel production and finances until 1959.

The observations made in this article are embryonic and are by no means exhaustive. As is the case with much of the work done by women in the film industry, their jobs were often at the bottom of the film business hierarchy. Records are scarce or difficult to locate due to the short-term nature of some of the work. Consequently, very little research has been done on the role and representation of women in the cinema newsreel with the notable exception of Jenny Hammerton's work on the Pathe-produced *Eve's Film Review*. There were women working on the documentaries and magazine reels such as *Pathe Pictorial* in the 1950s and 1960s as the newsreel companies attempted to wrest their audiences back from television. These women have not been included in this piece because they did not work on the general newsreels nor did they work on cinemagazines specifically produced for a female audience. However, as with the editors and technicians of the 1950s and 1960s, those women who have been acknowledged in this piece need further research to establish whether they are only the beginning.

NOTES

1. Nicholas Hiley, 'The British Cinema Auditorium', *Film and the First World War*, Karel Dibbets and Bert Hogenkamp (eds.), (Amsterdam: University of Amsterdam Press: 1995), p. 162.
2. Some areas of popular British film culture were undoubtedly dominated by women. For example, the 'great majority' of readers of the film fan magazine *Picturegoer* in 1925 were said to be female – see *Picturegoer* Popularity Poll dated April 1925.
3. 'Illuminating Response to Bernstein Questionnaire: Betty Balfour Again Tops the Poll', *The Bioscope*, 4 August 1927, p. 20.
4. Nicholas Hiley, 'Let's Go to the Pictures', *Journal of Popular British Cinema*, no. 2, 1999, p. 47.
5. David Ritchie, 'That News-Reel Villainy', *Sight and Sound*, Autumn 1934, pp. 113–114.
6. John Gammie, 'Women *Are* Interested in Newsreels', *Film Weekly*, 18 November 1932, p. 10.
7. Miss D.M. Vaughan, 'The News Theatres and Specialised Cinemas', *Documentary News Letter*, May 1940, pp. 10–11.

8. Luke McKernan, *Topical Budget; The Great British News Film*, (London: BFI, 1992), p. 149.
9. Ken Gordon, 'Forty Years with a Newsreel Camera', *The Cine-Technician*, Mar-Apr 1951, pp. 44–50.
10. Information from Luke McKernan.
11. McKernan, *Topical Budget*, p. 138.
12. Jenny Hammerton, *For Ladies Only? Eve's Film Review: Pathe Cinemagazine 1921–33*, (Hastings: The Projection Box: 2001), p. 9.
13. Ted Candy interviewed by Roy Fowler, transcript to BECTU Oral History interview number 26, 26 October 1987, p. 38. Available on the British Universities Newsreel Database, www.bufvc.ac.uk/newsreels.
14. John Turner, *Filming History: The Memoirs of John Turner, Newsreel Cameraman*, (London: British Universities Film & Video Council, 2001), p. 220.

The Nature of the Evidence

Penelope Houston

The newsreels exist for most people today as the raw materials out of which so many historical television programmes are made. Reacting to the emergence of the television history series with substantial 'archive' content, notably the BBC's THE GREAT WAR (1964), Penelope Houston considers the problems of considering film footage as document, while championing its unique subjective qualities. If film is 'untrustworthy, superficial, vulnerable to every kind of distortion', yet at the same time it is 'irreplaceable, necessary, a source material that no twentieth century historian ought to disregard'. As such historical documentaries were beginning to be compiled, so the newsreels themselves were fading away. In 1970, three years after this article was written, Pathe News came to an end. British Movietone News, the last of the British newsreels, finished in 1979. But their film libraries live on.

Exhibit A is a piece of film: two sequences, to be exact, from Frédéric Rossif's compilation MOURIR À MADRID. The first is a famous scrap of news film: the overhead shot looking down on the streets of Madrid as people scatter for shelter in an air-raid. A fragment which has turned up in one compilation after another, because of the way it seems to sum up the onset of panic, the first realisation of air power directed against civilians. The second sequence comes later in the film: a description of the raid on Guernica. This opens on quiet shots of the town, with Irene Worth, voice at full organ-throb, driving the commentary hard at the descriptive hurdle ahead. Then comes the raid itself: bombers, destruction, shots of victims lying in the rubble of the streets. It's discreet, hasty, not very moving or persuasive. And the reason, one suspects, is that in this case the footage is not genuine – or certainly not all of it. It's an assembly of authentic air-raid film, of course, but is it Guernica? Or is some of it? And does it matter anyway?

Within the context of the film, it certainly matters: there's too much work for the commentary, not enough conviction on the screen, and the emotional impact wavers. But it also matters, it seems to me, from the point of view of simple accuracy. Here, as so often in compilation films, one is made aware of something not quite right. A cameraman would hardly find himself in a position to take at least one of these shots. Therefore, did a cameraman at Guernica get any of them? One is not charging the film-makers with any duplicity. Their job was to communicate the mood of a war, and to that end they were entitled to employ whatever film they could find. They didn't guarantee the precise accuracy or the provenance of every shot, and probably couldn't do so in any case. If anything, it's the film itself that betrays them, as it does when for an instant in a battle sequence they slip into the trap of using what looks like fiction footage,[1] when again one realises that the camera has got itself into a position where no news reporter would be.

It may seem pedantic to stress a point which is unlikely to trouble most audiences of most compilation films. On the whole, this has been a propagandist medium, and all's fair in propaganda. Even MOURIR À MADRID, for all its apparent dispassion, is more concerned with the atmosphere than the facts of the Spanish war. There's fighting on the screen. Men are rushing a hill; tanks track through snow; suddenly there are ragged troops dashing by on bicycles. But what hill, whose tanks, why bicycles? Don't look to the film to give the answers. In the present state of the cinema's presentation of history, I doubt whether one could do so anyhow. But films are documents, and documents which peculiarly invite falsification. If historians are to be persuaded into using and trusting them, there's a good deal of past debris to be cleared away.

From the outset the audience has had to take the camera's evidence on trust. Unless a shot positively declares itself in its content, it's the commentary which does the job of identification. Jay Leyda, in his book *Films Beget Films,* quotes one enchanting case of primitive faking. In 1898, Francis Doublier was touting the Lumière programme around Jewish areas of Southern Russia where there was particular interest in the Dreyfus case. Doublier put together 'a scene of a French army parade led by a captain, one of their street scenes in Paris showing a large building, a shot of a Finnish tug going out to meet a barge, and a scene of the delta of the Nile'. In other words: 'Dreyfus before his arrest, the Palais de Justice Dreyfus being taken to the battleship, and Devil's Island where he was imprisoned'. A masterly case, as Leyda notes, of 'commercial necessity sharpening the inventive spirit,' or how to make the most of one tug and a palm tree.

Elementary faking wasn't it seems all that uncommon: Boer War skirmishes shot on Hampstead Heath or Wimbledon Common; the Boxer Rebellion with the cameraman's friends dressed up as Chinese insurgents. Méliès' CORONATION OF EDWARD VII (which was not filmed as a fake) was apparently spliced by some exhibitors on to the real newsreel, because it looked so much better. And I've read somewhere of a cutter, having to work fast to get out his newsreel of Edward VII's funeral, putting in a few shots from Queen Victoria's funeral to make things easier for himself. If by any chance the just dead Edward was actually to be seen in his version, in attendance on his mother's coffin, then presumably no one was likely to notice the indiscretion.

Such endearing deceits belong to the cinema's childhood. One would assume that if anyone more recently has been faking newsfilm (is there, in any case, enough profit in this to make it worth the trouble?), they have done it less detectably. Though it would never surprise one to see a masterly bit of acknowledged faking, such as Kevin Brownlow's Christmas truce newsreel in IT HAPPENED HERE, turning up in a compilation as the real thing. It becomes trickier when the shot itself is genuine, and only the attribution false. The National Film Archive has among its silent newsreels a bit of film which purports to show the launching of the *Titanic*. It rested there with that identification until an expert pointed out that this is a record of something that was never filmed – the shot is of a sister ship of the *Titanic,* which has been sailing under false colours ever since someone, more than fifty years ago, wanted to patch up a non-existent news item. More up to date, here's another case of false attribution: I'm told by Dr Frankland, Director of the Imperial War Museum, that in the week or so after D-Day German cinemas were able to show film of the Allies being driven back from the beaches. They did this very simply – Dieppe Raid footage, with a new commentary.

Once started on this track, it becomes fascinating – if extremely unprofitable – to wonder how many news shots may have gone round the world, and taken their place in compilation annals, with either a deliberately or an unconsciously misleading identification. Take for instance, the acres of Nazi propaganda film: shots of ecstatic welcomes to the advancing stormtroopers (the crowds too big for faking, but just where were they taken?); shots from the films made deliberately to terrorise, like BAPTISM OF FIRE, where the line between raw actuality and controlled documentary becomes blurred.

Closer home, it's worth looking into the origins of the Western Front footage used in the BBC's GREAT WAR series. Tony Essex, producer of this and of the later series THE LOST PEACE, acknowledges that in both authenticity had to some extent to be a matter of mood as well as facts. And one action which the BBC took in the cause of mood, or at least of making the action more intelligible, was to reverse film where necessary, so that the advancing Germans would always be seen moving from right to left across the screen, and the Allies left to right. They went to some trouble over this, blacking out the name on a bit of German equipment so that no one would spot it reading backwards. Scathingly, the Imperial War Museum, which supplied a good deal of the film, asks whether it was necessary at all.

First War footage, in any case, seems to be something of a jumble. On the British side, there is little actual front line material shot in action: cameramen moved up with the second line troops, partly because generals felt they were a nuisance on a battlefield and liable to get themselves shot. After this, there are various stages of reconstruction: film shot a few days after an action, with the troops who had taken part; film shot later in the war; documentary reconstruction; fictional reconstruction. On the air war, there is authentic film of training and stunting, but anything that purports to be combat footage points to one of two things: recutting of training film, or recourse to the ubiquitous, invaluable stock shots from HELL'S ANGELS. And on top of this, there's film whose identification has been lost, film which military experts must place, or try to place, on the evidence of terrain or uniforms.

Most people would probably consider that the BBC did a masterly job: inaccuracies in detail, no doubt, emphases to be argued over, criticism of the use of music to plaster over the cracks – but still a historical compilation, rather than a propagandist one, which in its overall effect stands up to a good deal of scrutiny. In a paper published by the Journal of the Society of Archivists, however, Christopher Roads of the Imperial War Museum takes a sterner view:

> 'Continuity' was a constant threat. It led to the utterly anachronistic use of film material solely for linking purposes and, in that some material was more suitable than other, to tedious repetition. But continuity was not so demanding as drama, for dramatic effect almost everything was sometimes sacrificed.

Dr Roads claims that the amount of reconstructed material in the programmes averaged out at about 9 per cent.

> We understood the difficulties that the BBC faced in trying to avoid its use, and agreed that if certain programmes were not to break down completely its use had to be accepted. Where, however, there was a relative abundance of original material but reconstructed sequences were preferred to heighten dramatic effect, we felt that the commercial element was victorious over the historical.

There's a revealing clash here, in which it's hard for the neutral observer not to feel that there can be sense on both sides. Tony Essex argues a more scrupulous use of the material by the BBC than the Imperial War Museum seems ready to concede. In any case, 91 per cent genuine footage sounds a fair average. But even assuming that reconstruction was preferred on occasion to reality, only a film man could effectively arbitrate, setting one bit of film against another, and both against the context of a programme which wouldn't be doing its job if it failed to be popular. The compilation filmmaker has by tradition allowed himself some licence, partly because his material so extravagantly encourages it. I would suspect that the BBC were more scrupulous than most.

On the other hand, there's the question of the integrity of the film document – the argument of the historian and the archivist. In so far as films are a primary source material, they ought to be protected by the same disciplines as written documents. Reconstruction should be identified, not allowed to masquerade as the real thing. Doubtful attributions might be acknowledged; distinctions might be drawn between first-hand material which can be exactly identified, and material which has already been put through one propagandist mincer or another, and reaches the compiler as a secondary rather than a primary source. Because film is so vulnerable, so misleading, can lead the spectator up so many garden paths, it should be used more, not less, scrupulously.

All of which might seem to suggest that the ideal compilation should be accompanied by a battery of footnotes; or, as Dr Roads actually suggests, that there should be colour tinting (impracticable, of course, on television) of reconstructed sequences. It's an intriguing suggestion, which one can't for an instant imagine anyone with a commercial stake being willing to accept. At any reasonable level of scholarship, the reading public will expect footnotes, identification of quotations all the apparatus that protects textual authenticity. But what about films? Jay Leyda's book quotes an identification by Paul Rotha of just the first 23 shots in his THE WORLD IS RICH. Seven were specially taken; for the other 16 Rotha drew on five separate sources, including Flaherty's THE LAND. A point intriguingly raised by Leyda is whether a concealed quotation from a filmmaker like Flaherty is itself morally justifiable. Or did Flaherty in any case get the material from somewhere else …?

In any case, it is perhaps unreasonable for historians to criticise film men for not doing their own job for them. 'Historians show a total indifference, even an acute aversion to such (compilation) resurrections', Pierre Billard has written. Historians have so far been remarkably distrustful of film, perhaps because there are such clear limits set to its value and such mistrust of its objectivity. But an answer would seem to be for historians to make their own specialised use of film; and this, it seems, some of them are increasingly ready to do.

Professor Grenville of Leeds University, one of several historians thinking along these lines, talks of the value of the film record not only for teaching but for research. 'Historians have paid a good deal of attention to the role of newspapers in influencing public opinion. What about the role of films? For instance in the late Thirties there is great emphasis in newsreels on the horrors of aerial bombardment, combined with displays of Britain's might in the air and on the seas. The newsreels must have confirmed public opinion that war was to be avoided at all costs, that Britain was safe and could argue from a position of strength. All the arguments of Chamberlain's appeasement policy are heavily reinforced by the way in which the films were put together …'

When I suggested doubts about the possible value to historians of the newsreel record, other than at the obvious level of showing what people looked like, or making history a palatable subject for the easily distracted, Professor Grenville sturdily defended a much more fundamental level of concern. Which is encouraging, as well as bringing up some tantalising questions of the oddities of the film record, the way it looks and the way it works, as against the record in print.

The actual impact of the past, as refracted through film, is often unexpected, sometimes melancholy, usually comic. There is an impartiality about the written record which films can't begin to capture. Read, for instance, a political speech of thirty years ago, cold print long divorced from the speaker, and one can analyse its arguments, its relevance, what effect it may or may not have had. Watch the man making the speech, in the cinema's perpetual present tense and a new relationship, a tension, is set up between spectator and subject. There are all the immediate factors that would have struck anyone at the time: Hitler's obsessive drive, for instance, his two-handed, downward chopping gesture, like a man slicing through wood; or Chamberlain's wan, dejected oratory, like a man being slowly choked by his own collar. And there are the quite other and fundamentally distracting elements which can't be edited out of reactions to a film: the fact that already it's 'period', that a style of speech-making, as of clothes, belongs to a decade. Inescapably, old newsreels are played in costume. So they become involving, in a way that the objective written record can't manage, and at the same time more remote.

These are dilettante reactions, but they are hard to avoid. The Soviet compilation ECHO OF THE JACKBOOT, for instance, includes an irresistible little passage in which Hindenburg, in full presidential panoply, loses his way in a parade, then is seen fumbling for change in a neat little leather purse. A gift to any compilation film-maker; a scene which sets up an instant reaction; therefore a scene; to be mistrusted. At this moment, the style of approximately forty years ago looks profoundly ridiculous: the sea of silk-hats the walrus moustaches, the slightly grubby, dishevelled look of the French politicians, the German generals tottering under the weight of their spiked helmets, Lloyd George skipping in and out of cars with his air of theatrical shagginess. How soon, how misleadingly, does a visual impression colour opinion?

Such stray impressions can be positive and useful. One thing emerged for me very strongly from the BBC's LOST PEACE series, and that was a sense of Hitler as, whatever else, a modern politician. Briand, Ramsay MacDonald, Hindenburg look like men on the other side of a great gulf, men whose transport would be a Daimler or the Blue Train, and who would approach a microphone with the utmost wariness. Hitler brings with him on to the screen an atmosphere of loudhailers and tape recorders, the open landrover and the light aircraft all the apparatus of the communications world.

All the same, film tends to violate the old journalistic edict that facts are sacred and comment is free. Fact, on film, carries its own built-in comment with it; and a comment that will change as the audience changes, so that the constant – the piece of evidence on celluloid – is not in itself something fixed and certain,

Pathe News team lined up for the coronation of Queen Elizabeth II in 1953.

but something that must look a little different at different times and to different people.

I've suggested that, at this moment in time, it's hard to take entirely seriously a speech by a man in a silk-hat and a walrus moustache. The awful comicality of the past has caught up with this particular uniform. In a few more years, it will have entered the protected zone of 'history' as opposed to 'period', as the parade shuffles along a few paces and something else takes its place in the line. And what about the protected figures, the idealised statesmen, the heroes of the newsreels? Jay Leyda quotes one instance of protection: the fact that audiences were never allowed to remember that Roosevelt was a cripple. 'Not only did newsreels never show – *they never even photographed* FDR being lifted up to the speaker's stand'. Newsreels are a heavily edited form of source material they speak with the authority not of impartiality but of national public relations.

Depending on which side of the Iron Curtain you happen to be standing, a scene of royalty carrying out a military inspection can be edited to look like an inane piece of pageantry or a reassuring demonstration of order and stability. Mikhail Romm, whose ECHO OF THE JACKBOOT collects its own joker's pack of 1930's kings and queens is also able to suggest, with no distortion other than in the commentary, that Mosley was receiving special police protection during an East End riot against the outraged anger of the honest London workman. Look at enough news film, in fact, and one begins to feel that the most constant image of the 1930s is of a mounted police charge into an unarmed street crowd. But I realise, as I write this, how little real idea I have of the facts. How often was this scene actually enacted, in London, or Paris or Madrid, or Berlin? How far is it an impression gained from well deployed screen use of a few unfailingly dramatic shots?

Film carries still more elusive, more tenuous associations, further hazards to that impossible, ideal objectivity before the fact which should represent the researcher's frame of mind. Jay Leyda's book contains an appealing quotation from one of the subtlest of compilation filmmakers, Nicole Vedrès, on her approach to her material:

> This bearded gentleman – a politician – though very smiling and briskly walking, seems sinister. Or rather, he does not, but the picture does. Why? Maybe only because he walks from right to left. And this landscape – why does it seem agreeable, even quite soothing, although the trees have no leaves, and the road is completely empty? Maybe it is only the proportion of visible sky, or the allure of the clouds …
>
> So you take two or three metres of the bearded gentleman, with appropriate music (or silence) and place him just at the moment (1913) when rumours of war have been first indicated. And the soothing landscape can be used just as the word 'hope' is spoken …

However the compiler manipulates shots, one is still left with Nicole Vedrès' question. Why is film so rarely completely neutral, why is the bearded politician sinister, the empty landscape reassuring? It's a matter of the direction of movement and perspective, the 'proportion of visible sky', the way the light falls: a reminder that even record film is, first and last, *film*. The makers of THE LOST PEACE might have been following Nicole Vedrès' exact precept when they inserted, into the context of some very ordinary newsreel of the 1919 Peace Conference, a few shots of Paris streets, bleak, empty, the camera gazing away down a long wintry perspective. The shots, Tony Essex said, happened to come from a film made in 1919; but it wouldn't really have mattered. This dateless, anonymous, and in any orthodox sense quite meaningless scrap of film brought awareness into a thoroughly conventional sequence of politicians submitting to their dutiful parade before the cameras.

To make sense out of news film, the compilers need the hindsight of history. For another comment one might make on historical record film, in general, is that it's the record made by and for the man in the street. In peace, the news cameraman has been kept on the doorstep, or allowed in for the few carefully posed, unrevealing shots. In war, he has been with the troops rather than the generals. He hasn't seen the processes of secret diplomacy, the forming of strategy, the details of economic policy. Cameramen have provided us with a kind of shorthand visual imagery for this century: a British political crisis means a crowd in the rain outside Number Ten; the Depression means cloth-capped men on street corners; the General Strike a shot of idle machinery or empty railway lines; the Battle of Britain, that shot from FIRES WERE STARTED of fire-hoses snaking away down a London street after a raid. But look behind the shots, and the film image can't help you. What political crisis? How many men out of work? Which air-raid, and which street? Even when the camera records an assassination, it answers no questions. We saw the shooting of Kennedy, and of Lee Harvey Oswald, and the circumstances of the killings still defy belief.

These are a filmgoer's rather than a historian's stray reflections on the nature of film as evidence: untrustworthy, superficial, vulnerable to every kind of distortion: and at the same time irreplaceable, necessary, a source material that no twentieth century historian ought to disregard, though many still seem prepared to. But one thing, it seems to me, that historians are going to have to reckon with is the unfixed nature of the image, and its partisanship. With time, words take on neutrality; film never seems to – or at least it hasn't done so yet.

Because film is not, in the phrase of the McLuhan school, a 'cool' medium, but a distinctly hot one. It is strewn with booby traps. Film which has been shot one way, assembled one way, and for a purpose, can't easily be dismantled. In fact, the dead passages in compilations are not only those where inert film is having to bear the weight of commentary, but where shots may have been wrenched out of sequence, in an attempt to create a neutrality that isn't there. It will be a long while before TRIUMPH OF THE WILL, for instance, can be regarded as entirely defused. There it is, a thirty year old bomb, rusty but still alive.

As historical film, TRIUMPH OF THE WILL is in a rather special category: an actual event and therefore primary source material, but an event controlled, staged and manipulated for the cameras. Back in the field of news film, I asked Tony Essex what areas of twentieth century history seemed to offer the richest source of unexploited film. He suggested the Cold War, given access to Soviet records and the history of China, particularly China in the Thirties. This was still the age of the newsreel scoop, and it was distant wars, uninvolving wars in which the major powers were neutral, that attracted the cameramen. But to carry on after the end of the LOST PEACE series into the later Thirties didn't seem to him feasible: the grand design could no longer be held – self-evidently, the second series was already far more resistant to control than the Great War film. The nearer one approaches a subject in time, the more sheerly overwhelming the material.

It may not, however, remain like this. Everyone's general feeling must be that although film newsreels have surrendered so much of their responsibility to look out for the news, television coverage ensures that there are more cameras recording more happenings than ever before. It is what happens to the record afterwards that is less encouraging. TV news treatment is ruthlessly professional in shaping material, inserting stock shot, if necessary to clarify a point, cutting film to commentary. Mr Essex suggests that future compilation historians may find it harder than they expect to track down basic film material which hasn't been severely processed, or chopped about for day to day journalistic purposes. It's even possible that more screen news could mean less screen history. At least, it seems something that the archivists ought to consider.

Sight and Sound, Spring 1967.

NOTE

1. Is the disputed shot in MOURIR À MADRID from ALL QUIET ON THE WESTERN FRONT? Jay Leyda suggests (Films Beget Films, p. 130) that Russian compilers make such extensive use of ALL QUIET footage that I'm inclined to suspect its identification has been lost and that Soviet film-cutters think that its shots are documents'. Esther Schub's SPAIN and another Spanish war film, apparently both use the same ALL QUIET shot. Has it, via one of these sources, turned up again in Rossif's film?

APPENDICES

1. CHRONOLOGICAL LISTING OF BRITISH NEWSREELS AND CINEMAGAZINES

Listed here are the main British newsreels and cinemagazines, arranged chronologically by first release date. Each record notes the main name of the reel, its years of production, description, and at the end of each entry the archive(s) with the principal holdings of that reel (ITN = ITN Archive/Reuters Television; IWM = Imperial Museum; NFTVA = National Film and Television Archive). All newsreels before 1929 were silent, but over the period 1929–1932 most reels operated both a silent and a sound service, as the process of cinemas converting to sound was gradual.

PATHE GAZETTE/PATHE NEWS (1910–1970)
Newsreel. *Pathe's Animated Gazette* began in June 1910. By 1918 it was known simply as *Pathe Gazette*. In January 1926, the reel was supplemented by a longer version called *Pathe Super Gazette*. In June 1930, Pathe launched *Pathe Super Sound Gazette*, which it ran alongside the silent *Pathe Gazette* and *Pathe Super Gazette*. The silent reels were eventually discontinued, but the sound version, renamed *Pathe Gazette*, continued until December 1945. In January 1946 the name was changed to *Pathe News*, used until the closure of the reel in February 1970. **British Pathe/NFTVA**

WARWICK BIOSCOPE CHRONICLE (1910–1915)
Newsreel. The second newsreel to be produced in Britain, first issued in July 1910. Produced by the Warwick Trading Company, which also made the concurrent *The Whirlpool of War*. **NFTVA** (few copies survive)

GAUMONT GRAPHIC (1910–1932)
Newsreel. *Gaumont Graphic* was issued from 25 October 1910 to 29 December 1932. In November 1929, Gaumont launched a new sound newsreel, *Gaumont Sound News*, and for the next three years the *Graphic* functioned as its silent counterpart for smaller cinemas which did not possess sound. **ITN/IWM/NFTVA**

TOPICAL BUDGET (1911–1931)
Newsreel. Produced by the Topical Film Company, first issued in September 1911. During the First World War, the British Government took control, which led to a variety of names, including *War Office Official Topical Budget* from May 1917, and the *Pictorial News (Official)* from February 1918. In May 1919, the reel reverted to private ownership and the name *Topical Budget*. From September 1922 to August 1923, it was called the *Daily Sketch Topical Budget*. The reel never converted to sound, and ceased production in March 1931. **IWM/NFTVA**

ECLAIR ANIMATED JOURNAL (1913–1917)
Newsreel. *Eclair Journal* was launched in March 1913, but failed during the First World War, probably in 1917. It was the British off-shoot of the French parent company Éclair. **NFTVA**

WILLIAMSON'S ANIMATED NEWS (1913–1914)
Newsreel. Produced by the Williamson Kinematograph Company. **NFTVA** (few copies survive)

KINEMACOLOR FASHION GAZETTE (1913)
Cinemagazine. Produced and edited by Abby Meehan in the early colour film system Kinemacolor for the Natural Color Kinematograph Company. It ran September-December 1913. **No longer extant?**

THE WHIRLPOOL OF WAR (1914–1915)
Cinemagazine. *The Whirlpool of War* was a First World War weekly news cinemagazine produced by Cherry Kearton and the Warwick Trading Company in tandem with the newsreel *Warwick Bioscope Chronicle*. The first issue was released in August 1914, and by October the issues had individual titles. The series ended in February 1915 with issue no. 33. **NFTVA**

PATHE PICTORIAL (1918–1969)
Cinemagazine. First released in March 1918. The introduction of sound saw a brief change of name, with *Pathe Sound Pictorial* appearing on issue sheets from no. 704 of October 1931. In September 1944, colour was introduced to the reel, and for a short time the reel appeared as *New Pathe Pictorial*, with renumbering from no. 1. *Pathe Pictorial* continued in production until March 1969. **British Pathe**

SCOTTISH MOVING PICTURE NEWS (1918–1922?)
Newsreel. Produced by Green's Film Service and shown primarily in Scotland. For a short period around 1919 it changed its name to *British Moving Picture News*. **Scottish Screen Archive**

AROUND THE TOWN (1919–1923)
Cinemagazine. Weekly entertainment cinemagazine produced by Gaumont, specializing in scenes from current London shows. **NFTVA**

DAILY CINEMA NEWS (1919–1920)
Newsreel. Rare example of a daily newsreel, produced by Bertram V. May. Ran from October 1919 to January 1920. **No longer extant?**

FOX NEWS (1920–?)
Newsreel. Anglo-American bi-weekly, first issued April 1920, produced by Fox. It is uncertain how long it lasted, but there is some evidence of it being issued in 1928. **NFTVA** (few copies survive)

EVE'S FILM REVIEW (1921–1933)
Cinemagazine. Produced by Pathe primarily for women audiences, though in the late 1920s it was known as *Eve and Everybody's Film Review*. **British Pathe/NFTVA**

EMPIRE NEWS BULLETIN (1926–1930)

Newsreel. *Empire News Bulletin* was launched in May 1926 by British Pictorial Productions; it appeared bi-weekly until July 1930, when it was superseded by a synchronised-sound newsreel called *Universal Talking News* issued by the same company. *Empire News Bulletin* afterwards survived only as the silent edition of *Universal Talking News*, for cinemas which had not yet converted to sound. **ITN/NFTVA**

GAUMONT MIRROR (1926–1931?)

Cinemagazine. Produced by Gaumont. A sound edition was also produced, probably from 1930. **NFTVA** (few copies survive)

IDEAL CINEMAGAZINE (1926–1933)

Cinemagazine. Produced by Andrew Buchanan for Ideal Films to 1933, when it changed into *Gaumont-British Magazine.* **NFTVA** (few copies survive)

BRITISH SCREEN NEWS (1928–1932?)

Newsreel. Produced by British Screen Productions. Had added a concurrent sound service by 1931. **NFTVA**

BRITISH SCREEN TATLER (1928–1931?)

Cinemagazine. Produced by Screen Productions to accompany its newsreel, *British Screen News.* **NFTVA** (few copies survive)

BRITISH MOVIETONE NEWS (1929–1979)

Newsreel. *British Movietone News* was launched on 9 June 1929 by an offshoot of the US company Fox Movietone. It was the first sound newsreel to be distributed in Britain, and ran until 27 May 1979. In the 1970s it changed its name to *Movietonews.* **British Movietonews/NFTVA**

GAUMONT SOUND NEWS (1929–1933)

Newsreel. Produced by Gaumont to run concurrently with its silent newsreel, *Gaumont Graphic.* Began in November 1929, though an experimental sound release had been produced in June 1929. There was also an extended version called *Gaumont Super Sound News.* **ITN/NFTVA**

BRITISH MOVIETONE GAZETTE (1930–1935)

Cinemagazine. *British Movietone Gazette* ran from 3 February 1930 to 18 July 1935. The *Gazette* was a shorter version of the *British Movietone News* newsreel, but occasionally carried different stories; it was designed as a cheaper alternative to the main Movietone newsreel, and came under the same editorial control as *British Movietone News.* **British Movietonews**

PATHETONE WEEKLY (1930–1941)

Cinemagazine. This sound cinemagazine was first released weekly in March 1930. **British Pathe**

WORKERS' TOPICAL NEWS (1930–1931)

Newsreel. Three issues of this silent newsreel were released by the Federation of Workers' Film Societies, but only *Workers' Topical News* no. 1 of March 1930 and no. 2 of May 1930 are known to have survived. *Workers' Topical News* no. 3 was first shown in March 1931, but no copies exist. **NFTVA**

UNIVERSAL NEWS (1930–1956)
Newsreel. *Universal News* was produced by British Pictorial Productions and was the sound newsreel successor to *Empire News Bulletin*. It ran from 14 July 1930 to 31 December 1956. There is evidence, however, that it continued as a business entity until 1959. From January 1952 a separate reel called the *Universal Irish News* was also released, consisting of the general reel with items of specifically British interest removed and items of local Irish interest substituted. From 1949 it was absorbed by Rank into *Gaumont-British News*, though it continued to be released under the Universal name. **ITN/IWM/NFTVA**

BRITISH PARAMOUNT NEWS (1931–1957)
Newsreel. *British Paramount News* began on 2 March 1931, as a subsidiary of the US Paramount company, and ran until 31 January 1957. **ITN/IWM/NFTVA**

GAUMONT BRITISH NEWS (1934–1959)
Newsreel. Produced by the Gaumont-British Picture Corporation, which in 1941 became part of the Rank Organisation. *Gaumont British News* was first released in January 1934, as a replacement for *Gaumont Graphic* and *Gaumont Sound News*, and ran until January 1959. A special edition of the reel was also regularly released in Ireland. It effectively absorbed *Universal News* in 1949. Upon its closure in 1959, Rank replaced it with *Look at Life*, using much of the same production team. **ITN/IWM/NFTVA**

GAUMONT BRITISH MAGAZINE (1934–?)
Cinemagazine. Produced by Andrew Buchanan for Gaumont-British as the successor to *Ideal Cinemagazine*. **No longer extant?**

THE MARCH OF TIME (1935–1951)
Cinemagazine. American monthly news and documentary cinemagazine produced by Louis de Rochemont for Time Inc. The British run had a different numbering system to the American and substituted some original stories shot in Britain, as well as dropping some items considered unsuitable. **NFTVA**

ACE CINEMAGAZINE (1937–1938)
Cinemagazine. Produced by Ace Films. **NFTVA** (one copy only)

SHELL CINEMAGAZINE (1938–1952)
Cinemagazine. General interest cinemagazine produced by the Shell Film Unit. **NFTVA**

POINT OF VIEW (1939)
Cinemagazine. Current affairs film magazine offering pro and con arguments on issues of the day, produced by Spectator Short Films. **NFTVA** (one copy only)

BRITISH NEWS (1940–1967)
Newsreel. Compilation from each of the major British newsreels, produced by the Newsreel Association for the British Council for overseas use. After 1948 production was continued by *British Movietone News* and *Pathe News*. In September 1966 it was retitled *News of the Week*, and in May 1967 it became *News Pictorial*. **NFTVA**

WAR PICTORIAL NEWS/WORLD PICTORIAL NEWS (1940–1946)

Newsreel. *War Pictorial News* ran from September 1940 until October 1945, when its name was changed to the *World Pictorial News*. *War Pictorial News* was released by the Cairo office of the Ministry of Information, and distributed to all Allied troops stationed in the Middle East. It carried many stories from the domestic British newsreels, but was released with a special commentary in either English, French or Arabic. Under the title *World Pictorial News* it continued to be distributed in occupied territories until August 1946. **IWM**

WARWORK NEWS (1942–1945)

Newsreel. *Warwork News* was produced by Paramount for the Ministry of Supply. It was intended for war workers and was released from the spring of 1942 to the end of 1945. **IWM**

WORKER AND WARFRONT (1942–1946)

Newsreel. *Worker and Warfront* was an official newsreel produced between May 1942 and January 1946. The last issue was *Worker and Warfront* no. 18, after which the reel was renamed *Britain Can Make It*. **IWM/NFTVA**

ALLIED NEWS MAGAZINE (1943)

Newsreel. Compilation war newsreel comprising surplus news stories from the main British newsreels, produced by the Inter-Allied Information Committee. **NFTVA**

THE GEN (1943–1945)

Newsreel. *The Gen* was intended for RAF personnel in bases all around the world, and released between April 1943 and mid-1945. Eighteen issues were produced. **IWM**

THE AIRFRONT GEN OPERATIONAL SUPPLEMENT (1944–1945)

Newsreel. A Royal Air Force newsreel produced from the middle of 1944 to the middle of 1945. The series consisted of a pilot release entitled *Airfront RAF Operational Film Record No. 1*, and seven further issues under the title *Airfront Gen Operational Supplement*. **IWM**

OUR CLUB MAGAZINE/OUR MAGAZINE (1945–1956)

Cinemagazine. Rank Organisation cinemagazine for children, produced by Wallace Productions for Gaumont-British Instructional. Supplementary reels *Our Club Scrapbook* and *Our World Magazine* were produced, and in 1952 it was succeeded by *Our Magazine*. **NFTVA**

WELT IM FILM (1945–1952)

Newsreel. German-language newsreel produced by the British and American elements of the Allied Military Government and shown in the British and American zones of post-war Germany. An Austrian edition was also produced. **IWM/NFTVA**

BRITAIN CAN MAKE IT (1946–1947)

Cinemagazine. Produced by Films of Fact for the Central Office of Information (COI), a cinemagazine emphasizing British industrial achievement. Successor to *Worker and Warfront*. **NFTVA** (few copies survive)

THIS IS BRITAIN (1946–1951)

Cinemagazine. Produced by Merlin Films for the COI on behalf of the Board of Trade. **NFTVA**

THIS MODERN AGE (1946–1950)
Cinemagazine. Rank Organisation news magazine, the British 'answer' to the *March of Time*. **NFTVA**

CINE GAZETTE (1947–1957)
Cinemagazine. Produced by British Transport Films, with transport-related stories. **NFTVA**

MINING REVIEW (1947–1982)
Cinemagazine. Coal industry news magazine produced for the National Coal Board initially by the Crown Film Unit, then Data Film Productions, finally by the National Coal Board Film Unit. Changed its name to *Review* in 1972. **NFTVA**

CONSERVATIVE AND UNIONIST NEWS REVIEW (1948–1952)
Cinemagazine. Produced by British Movietone for the Conservative and Unionist Film Association. Changed its name in 1950 to *Conservative News Review*. **NFTVA**

TELEVISION NEWSREEL (1948–1954)
Newsreel. The BBC's first self-produced newsfilm series for television was in a newsreel format. It was first televised bi-weekly from January 1948, increasing to three editions a week in December 1950, and five editions a week from June 1952. It was replaced by *News and Newsreel* in July 1954, which was a combination of the traditional (faceless) spoken news bulletin and the filmed news reports. Newsreaders were introduced in September 1955. **BBC/NFTVA**

WEALTH OF THE WORLD (1948–1951)
Cinemagazine. Occasional cinemagazine made by the Pathe Documentary Film Unit. **NFTVA**

INGOT PICTORIAL (1949–1958)
Cinemagazine. Steel industry magazine produced by Technical & Scientific Films (and others) for Richard Thomas & Baldwins Company. **NFTVA**

ASTRA GAZETTE (1950–1951)
Cinemagazine. *Astra Gazette* was produced by Pathe on behalf of the Royal Air Force during 1950 and 1951. Twelve issues were released, with many items copied from *Pathe Pictorial*, but others specially produced. **No longer extant?** (but footage used exists at British Pathe)

CHILDREN'S NEWSREEL (1950–1961)
Cinemagazine. Children's 15-minute 'newsreel' produced by the BBC. **BBC/NFTVA** (very little survives)

INTERNATIONAL REVIEW (1950–1952)
Newsreel. American newsreel produced by Telenews Productions and shown in Britain with some items replaced by British stories (produced by National Screen Services). The reel became progressively more British in tone. Midway through the run its name was changed to *International News*. **NFTVA**

LOOK AT LIFE (1959–1969)
Cinemagazine. Rank Organisation colour magazine, the successor to *Gaumont-British News*, covering general topics, one per issue. **British Movietone/NFTVA**

2. CURRENT BRITISH NEWSREEL COLLECTIONS

British newsreels are held in the main by three commercial companies and two national film archives. It is important to note that the commercial newsreel companies cannot normally handle academic research requests, and such researchers should normally approach the National Film and Television Archive and the Imperial War Museum Film & Video Archive. These both have extensive newsreel collections that often overlap the commercial collections, and which are designed for academic research. Researchers are particularly encouraged to contact the British Universities Newsreel Database at newsreels@bufvc.ac.uk, telephone 020 7393 1500 as a first port of call regarding any access to newsreel collections.

NATIONAL FILM ARCHIVES

NATIONAL FILM AND TELEVISION ARCHIVE
British Film Institute
21 Stephen Street
London W1T 1LN
Tel: 020 7255 1444
Fax: 020 7580 7503
E-mail: footage.films@bfi.org.uk
Website: www.bfi.org.uk/collections

Holds selected material for the newsreels *British Movietone News, British News, British Paramount News, Eclair Journal, Empire News Bulletin, Gaumont-British News, Gaumont Graphic, Gaumont Sound News, Pathe Gazette/Pathe News, Topical Budget, Universal News, Welt im Film, The Whirlpool of War*, and many cinemagazines, minor newsreels and industrial and sponsored reels.

IMPERIAL WAR MUSEUM FILM & VIDEO ARCHIVE
Lambeth Road
London SE1 6HZ
Tel: 020 7416 5291/2
Fax: 020 7416 5379
E-mail: film@iwm.org.uk
Website: www.iwm.org.uk/collections/film.htm

Holds newsreels and cinemagazines for the First and Second World Wars: *Airfront Gen Operational Supplement, The Gen, Topical Budget, War Pictorial News, Warwork News, Welt im Film, Worker and Warfront*, and war-time issues of *British Paramount News, Gaumont-British News* and *Universal News*.

COMMERCIAL ARCHIVES

BRITISH PATHE
New Pathe House
57 Jamestown Road
London NW1 7DB
Tel: 020 7323 0407
Fax: 020 7436 3232
E-mail: info@britishpathe.com
Websites: www.britishpathe.com

Holds the newsreels *Pathe Gazette* and *Pathe News*, and the cinemagazines *Pathe Pictorial*, *Pathetone Weekly* and *Eve's Film Review*. British Pathe has received Lottery funding from the New Opportunities Fund to make its film holdings available online.

BRITISH MOVIETONEWS LIBRARY
North Orbital Road
Denham UB9 5HQ
Tel: 01895 833 071
Fax: 01895 834 893
E-mail: library@mtone.co.uk
Website: www.movietone.com

Holds the newsreel *British Movietone News*.

ITN ARCHIVE
200 Gray's Inn Road
London WC1X 8XZ
Tel: 7430 4480
Fax: 7430 4453
E-mail: archive.sales@itn.co.uk
Website: www.itnarchive.com

Holds the newsreels *Empire News Bulletin*, *Gaumont-British News*, *Gaumont Graphic*, *Gaumont Sound News*, *British Paramount News* and *Universal News*, managed on behalf of Reuters Television.

3. BRITISH UNIVERSITIES NEWSREEL DATABASE

This book has been published as part of the British Universities Film & Video Council's (BUFVC) on-going commitment to the British cinema newsreels and their importance to historical study and film research. Since 1974 the BUFVC has held a major collection of documents relating to news and historical film, the Slade Film History Register, which now forms the basis of its British Universities Newsreel Database (BUND).

The BUND is available online at www.bufvc.ac.uk/newsreels, and it contains:
- A database of 160,000 British newsreel and cinemagazine stories, 1910–1979
- 80,000 digitised newsreel production documents, including commentary scripts, cameramen's dope sheets and shot lists
- A biographical database of over 700 British newsreel staff, with detailed biographies of cameramen, editors, commentators etc.
- A database of over 700 abstracts of newsreel literature, originally published in the *Researcher's Guide to British Newsreels* and now brought up to date
- Streamed audio interviews with newsreel veterans, with accompanying simultaneous transcripts
- Original and republished articles, including texts from this Reader, some in extended form, among them a complete set of Mass-Observation file reports on British newsreels in wartime
- A guide to resources for the study of newsreels, including archives, video sources, databases, bibliographies, research centres and CD-ROMs

- Case studies on the use of newsreel resources in academic study, in particular the digitised newsreel production documents available through the BUND
- A history of the British newsreels, and accounts of the individual newsreels and cinemagazines represented on the BUND

The BUFVC also holds books and articles on British newsreels, an extensive collection of newsreel issue sheets, and a unique collection of newsreel production documents. It also has special collections relating to the newsreels, including the personal papers of cameraman David Samuelson and the photographic collection and diaries of cameraman Norman Fisher.

For further information, visit the website, or contact the British Universities Newsreel Database, BUFVC, 77 Wells Street, London W1T 3QJ, Tel: 020 7393 1500 Fax: 020 7393 1555 E-mail: newsreels@bufvc.ac.uk.

4. BIBLIOGRAPHY

This is a general bibliography of the British newsreel, taken from that given on the British Universities Newsreel Database (BUND). It lists the main book publications wholly or partly about British newsreels and cinemagazines. For articles on the newsreels, researchers should consult the database of abstracts to newsreel literature on the BUND, at www.bufvc.ac.uk/ databases/newsreels/resources/abstracts.html.

Aldgate, Anthony, *Cinema and History: British Newsreels and the Spanish Civil War* (London: Scolar Press, 1979)
Detailed account of the workings of the British newsreels in the 1930s, in particular covering the Spanish Civil War, asking questions about objectivity, bias and the forming of public opinion.

Baechlin, Peter and Maurice Muller-Strauss, *Newsreels Across the World* (Paris: Unesco, 1952)
A worldwide study of the structural and financial aspects of the newsreels, including analyses of British newsreels and cinemagazines.

Ballantyne, James (ed.), *Researcher's Guide to British Newsreels* (London: British Universities Film & Video Council, 1983)
A guide to resources on British newsreels, with abstracts of articles and books, and lists of newsreel staff, libraries and organisations.

Ballantyne, James (ed.), *Researcher's Guide to British Newsreels Volume II* (London: British Universities Film & Video Council, 1988)
A further guide to British newsreel sources, with updated information from the first volume, comments on newsreel staff records, more abstracts, and further information on newsreel information sources.

Ballantyne, James (ed.), *Researcher's Guide to British Newsreels Vol III* (London: British Universities Film & Video Council, 1993)
Third volume in series, with more abstracts, articles by Ray Densham, Nicholas Hiley, Luke McKernan and John Turner, further comments on newsreel staff and other supplementary information.

Fielding, Raymond, *The American Newsreel 1911–1971* (Norman: University of Oklahoma Press, 1972)
The standard history of the American newsreel, with some useful points about newsreels in general, including a general account of British newsreel production.

Fielding, Raymond, *The March of Time, 1935–1951* (New York: Oxford University Press, 1978)
A history of the American news cinemagazine The March of Time, which ran a British edition. Includes details of general newsreel production as well.

Hammerton, Jenny, *For Ladies Only? Eve's Film Review: Pathe Cinemagazine 1921–1933* (Hastings: The Projection Box, 1921)
A lively, thoughtful history and analysis of the cinemagazine for women, Eve's Film Review, produced by Pathe.

Jeavons, Clyde, Jane Mercer and Daniela Kirchner (eds.), *"The Story of the Century!": An International Newsfilm Conference* (London: British Universities Film & Video Council, 1998)
The proceedings of a wide-ranging conference on newsreels and newsfilm, their history, significance, present use and archiving, held at the National Film Theatre in London in 1996.

Low, Rachael, *Films of Comment and Persuasion of the 1930s* (London: George Allen & Unwin, 1979)
Contains a detailed and informative (if somewhat negative) chapter on newsreel ownership, production and style during the 1930s.

McKernan, Luke, *Topical Budget: The Great British News Film* (London: British Film Institute, 1992)
A history of the 1911–1931 British newsreel Topical Budget, which was controlled by the War Office during the First World War.

Mitchell, Leslie, *Leslie Mitchell Reporting...* (London: Hutchinson, 1981)
Autobiography of the BBC television and radio announcer and commentator for British Movietone News.

Noble, Ronnie, *Shoot First! Assignments of a Newsreel Cameraman* (London: George G. Harrap, 1955)
Thoughtful autobiography from Universal News and Television Newsreel cameraman Ronnie Noble, including his filming of World War II and the Korean War.

Pronay, Nicholas and D.W. Spring (eds.), *Propaganda, Politics and Film, 1918–1945* (London: Macmillan, 1982)
Collection of essays predominantly on British political and propagandist films 1918–1945, with numerous references to the newsreels.

Reeves, Nicholas, *Official British Film Propaganda During the First World War* (London: Croom Helm, 1986)

Includes an account of the War Office Official Topical Budget, the British propaganda newsreel operated by the War Office and the Ministry of Information 1917–1918.

Richards, Jeffrey and Dorothy Sheridan (eds.), *Mass-Observation at the Movies* (London: Routledge & Kegan Paul, 1987)

Includes a section on the Mass-Observation reports on newsreels and their reception in Britain during the Second World War, with a selection of texts from the original documents and an interview with cameraman Ken Gordon.

Short, K.R.M. and Stephan Dolezel (eds.), *Hitler's Fall: The Newsreel Witness* (London: Croom Helm, 1988)

Comparative study of the newsreel record of the final days of the Third Reich, from British, German, Soviet, American, Polish and Swiss perspectives.

Smith, Paul (ed.), *The Historian and Film* (Cambridge: Cambridge University Press, 1976)

A collection of essays considering different aspects of the use of film as historical evidence, with numerous references to newsreels, including Nicholas Pronay's essay, 'The newsreels: the illusion of actuality'.

Smither, Roger and Wolfgang Klaue (eds.), *Newsreels in Film Archives: A Survey Based on the FIAF Newsreel Symposium* (Trowbridge: Flicks Books, 1996)

Proceedings of a symposium on the history and preservation of newsreels held by the International Federation of Film Archives.

Turner, John, *Filming History: The Memoirs of John Turner, Newsreel Cameraman* (London: British Universities Film & Video Council, 2001)

Detailed memoirs of John Turner, who was a Gaumont-British News cameraman in the 1930s–1950s, served as the royal rota cameraman, then became news editor for Pathe News in the 1960s.

Wyand, Paul, *Useless if Delayed* (London: George G. Harrap, 1959)

Entertaining and informative autobiography by British Movietone News cameraman Paul Wyand.

Contributors

The contributors past and present to this Reader are described in brief below. For some writers from the earlier years it has not been possible to trace any biographical details.

ANTHONY ALDGATE is Reader in Film History at the Open University. He is the author of several books on modern history and film, including *Cinema and History: British Newsreels and the Spanish Civil War* (1979).

EDGAR ANSTEY was a leading documentary filmmaker, who worked with John Grierson at the Empire Marketing Board, formed the Shell Film Unit in 1934, directed British productions of *The March of Time* in the 1930s, and formed British Transport Films in 1949. He was film critic of *The Spectator* 1941–1946.

ALEC BRAID was editor of the *Gaumont Graphic* newsreel 1913–1915.

'BENN' was film critic of the Independent Labour Party's weekly journal *The New Leader*. His identity is uncertain, but he is thought to have been the Left-wing intellectual Gary Allighan.

RICHARD BUTLER was a cameraman with *Pathe Gazette* and *Pathe Pictorial* 1935–1938, during which time he filmed in Spain during the Civil War.

G. CLEMENT CAVE was the editor of *Pathe News* 1947–1948, during which time he became controversial for his concentration on political issues. He left the newsreel to join Radio Luxembourg in an executive capacity.

HANNAH CAVEN is a producer for Two Four Productions, an independent television company. Her article is based on a thesis submitted for an MPhil in Historical Studies at Cambridge University.

BOB COLWYN-WOOD was a cameraman with *Universal News* throughout the Second World War.

G. THOMAS CUMMINS was a cameraman before becoming editor of *British Paramount News* 1931–1947, and then editor and executive producer of *Pathe News*.

CECIL DAY-LEWIS, one of a group of young Left wing poets that included W.H. Auden, was politically active throughout the 1930s, joining the Communist Party in 1936. He became Professor of Poetry at Oxford 1951–1956 and Poet Laureate 1968–1972.

PHILIP H. DORTÉ worked for BBC television on outside broadcasts in the 1930s, and after the war became the BBC's Head of Television Outside Broadcasts and Films. He created the BBC's *Television Newsreel* in 1948.

SARAH EASEN works for the BUFVC on the British Universities Newsreel Database. Her research interests include British women non-fiction filmmakers.

LEN ENGLAND joined the social survey organisation Mass-Observation in 1939 straight from school. He carried out its film observation work throughout the Second World War.

JIMMY GEMMELL was cameraman with *British Screen News*, then from 1934 to 1957 with *British Paramount News*. He was the younger brother of Jock Gemmell.

JOCK GEMMELL was a newsreel cameraman for over fifty years, working chiefly at Pathe.

GRAHAM GREENE, known best as a novelist, also reviewed films between 1935 and 1940 for *The Spectator* and *Night and Day*.

JENNY HAMMERTON is Senior Cataloguer at British Pathe. She is the author of *For Ladies Only? Eve's Film Review: Pathe Cinemagazine 1921–1933* (2001).

ROBERT HERRING was a poet, film critic on the *London Mercury* 1925–1927, wrote for the pioneering film theory journal *Close Up* from 1927, and in the 1930s edited *Life and Letters To-day*.

PENELOPE HOUSTON was editor of the British Film Institute's *Sight and Sound* magazine 1956–1990 and is the author of *Keepers of the Frame: The Film Archives* (1994).

JEFF HULBERT researched newsreels as a postgraduate, where his thesis was on post-war newsreels and 'military' subjects. He currently works for the BUFVC on the British Universities Newsreel Database.

ROBERT HUMFREY was a cameraman active in the pre-First World War period.

CHERRY KEARTON was a pioneering wildlife photographer and cinematographer, the author of numerous books on wildlife subjects. He ran the *Warwick Bioscope Chronicle* newsreel 1913–1915 and its partner reel *The Whirlpool of War* (1914–1915).

CAROLINE LEJEUNE was film critic for *The Manchester Guardian* (1922–1928) and *The Observer* (1928–1960), renowned for her literary, witty style.

LUKE MCKERNAN is Head of Information at the BUFVC. He is the author of *Topical Budget: The Great British News Film* (1992) and manages the British Universities Newsreel Database.

CHARLES MARTIN was a *Pathe Gazette* cameraman, celebrated for being the only person to film the British withdrawal at Dunkirk.

ERIC MAYELL was editor of *Pathe's Animated Gazette* 1913–1916. He moved to America in 1916, working for *Pathe Weekly* before becoming a cameraman. He served on a freelance basis with Movietone in the United States for many years.

E.H. MONTAGU was a sales representative in Britain for the American film company Selig's in the pre-First World War period.

RONNIE NOBLE was a cameramen with *Universal News* 1939–1950, before joining the BBC for its *Children's Newsreel* and then in 1952 joined its *Television Newsreel*. He wrote an autobiography, *Shoot First! Assignment of a newsreel cameraman* (1955).

PHILIP NORMAN is a novelist, biographer and journalist, whose books include *The Skater's Waltz* (1979), *Shout! The True Story of the Beatles* (1981) and *The Age of Parody: Dispatches from the Eighties* (1990). He is the grandson of newsreel cameraman Frank Bassill.

ARTHUR PEREIRA wrote on technical issues for the film trade journal *Kinematograph Weekly* in the 1920s.

J.B. PRIESTLEY was a novelist, playwright, journalist, broadcaster, social historian and critic.

NICHOLAS PRONAY is Emeritus Professor at the Institute of Communications Studies, University of Leeds. His publications include *British Official Films in the Second World War* (1980) (with Frances Thorpe) and *Propaganda, Politics and Film, 1918–1945* (1982) (with D.W. Spring).

JACK RAMSDEN was a cameraman with *British Movietone News*, graduating to production manager in 1948.

GERALD SANGER was the first editor of *British Movietone News* in 1929 and remained in editorial control until 1954, when he joined Associated Newspapers as administrative director, and later worked in television. He was Honorary Production Adviser to the Conservative and Unionist Films Association from 1948 to 1959.

VALENTIA STEER became the first editor of Britain's first newsreel, *Pathe's Animated Gazette* in 1910. In 1913 he became editor of *Eclair Animated Journal*, and after war service was editor of *Fox News*. He wrote the *Romance of the Cinema* (1913) and *The Secrets of the Cinema* (1920).

FREDERICK A. TALBOT was the author of several popular science and education works, including *Moving Pictures: How They are Made and Worked* (1912) and *Practical Cinematography and its Applications* (1913).

JAMES TAYLOR is the Archivist at the Media Archive for Central England, the regional moving image archive for the English Midlands.

ALEC TOZER was a cameraman war correspondent with *British Movietone News* throughout the Second World War, and served with them up to the coronation in 1953.

JOHN TURNER was cameraman for *Gaumont-British News* 1937–1952, royal rota cameraman for the Newsreel Association 1952–1962, and production manager and news editor for *Pathe News* 1962–1970. In 2001 the BUFVC published his *Filming History: The Memoirs of John Turner, Newsreel Cameraman*.

PAUL WYAND was a motor mechanic at Brooklands before joining Pathe as a cameraman in 1927. He joined *British Movietone News* in 1929 and remained with them until his death in 1968. He published his memoirs under the title *Useless if Delayed* (1959), the message stamped on all Movietone newsreel cans.

Index